Advances in
Therapies for Children

Charles E. Schaefer
Howard L. Millman
Steven M. Sichel
Jane Riegelhaupt Zwilling

Advances in
Therapies for Children

 Jossey-Bass Publishers

San Francisco • London • 1987

ADVANCES IN THERAPIES FOR CHILDREN
by Charles E. Schaefer, Howard L. Millman, Steven M. Sichel, and
Jane Riegelhaupt Zwilling

Copyright © 1986 by: Jossey-Bass Inc., Publishers
433 California Street
San Francisco, California 94104
&
Jossey-Bass Limited
28 Banner Street
London EC1Y 8QE

Library of Congress Cataloging-in-Publication Data

Advances in therapies for children.

(The Jossey-Bass social and behavioral science
series) (Guidebooks for therapeutic practice)
Contains edited articles reprinted from various
sources.
Companion v. to: Therapies for children / [compiled
by] Charles E. Schaefer, Howard L. Millman. 1977.
Includes bibliographies and indexes.
1. Child psychotherapy. 2. Behavior disorders in
children—Treatment. I. Schaefer, Charles E. II. Therapies for children. III. Series. IV. Series: Guidebooks
for therapeutic practice. [DNLM: 1. Child Behavior
Disorders—therapy—collected works. 2. Psychotherapy—
trends—collected works. WS 350 A244]
RJ504.A35   1986   618.92′89   86-45625
ISBN 1-55542-010-9 (alk. paper)

Manufactured in the United States of America

The paper in this book meets the guidelines for
permanence and durability of the Committee on
Production Guidelines for Book Longevity of the
Council on Library Resources.

JACKET DESIGN BY WILLI BAUM

FIRST EDITION

First printing: December 1986
Second printing: October 1987

Code 8628

The Jossey-Bass
Social and Behavioral Science Series

GUIDEBOOKS FOR THERAPEUTIC PRACTICE
Charles E. Schaefer and Howard L. Millman
Consulting Editors

*Therapies for Children: A Handbook of Effective
Treatments for Problem Behaviors*
Charles E. Schaefer and Howard L. Millman
1977

Therapies for Psychosomatic Disorders in Children
Charles E. Schaefer, Howard L. Millman,
and Gary F. Levine
1979

Therapies for School Behavior Problems
Howard L. Millman, Charles E. Schaefer,
and Jeffrey J. Cohen
1980

*Therapies for Adolescents: Current Treatments
for Problem Behaviors*
Michael D. Stein and J. Kent Davis
1982

Group Therapies for Children and Youth
Charles E. Schaefer, Lynnette Johnson,
and Jeffrey N. Wherry
1982

Therapies for Adults
Howard L. Millman, Jack T. Huber,
and Dean R. Diggins
1982

*Family Therapy Techniques for Problem Behaviors
of Children and Teenagers*
Charles E. Schaefer, James M. Briesmeister,
and Maureen E. Fitton
1984

*Therapeutic Practice in Behavioral Medicine:
A Selective Guide to Assessment, Treatment,
Clinical Issues, and Therapies for Specific Disorders*
David I. Mostofsky and Ralph L. Piedmont
1985

Advances in Therapies for Children
Charles E. Schaefer, Howard L. Millman, Steven M. Sichel,
and Jane Riegelhaupt Zwilling
1986

Contents

Response Prevention, Extinction, and Systematic
Desensitization to Reduce Nightmares—
R. N. Roberts and S. B. Gordon

Contents

Preface

In the helping professions, we are witnessing an information explosion that requires innovative systems of data storage and retrieval. Most child therapists have an eclectic orientation that requires them to keep abreast of the latest developments in a wide variety of therapy systems—a Herculean task. By facilitating a review of available practices, *Advances in Therapies for Children* will be an effective problem-solving tool for therapists in the field. It is designed to help them find creative adaptations of and new approaches to methods of helping clients.

This book is the ninth volume in the series Guidebooks for Therapeutic Practice. The first volume in this series, *Therapies for Children,* was published in 1977. It was enthusiastically received because it met the need of busy practitioners for practical information presented in a concise format. The goal of this companion volume, which surveys the literature from 1977 to 1985, is to present innovations in child therapy that have appeared since *Therapies for Children* was published.

The innovative feature of all the books in this series is the digest format—a clear, easy-to-assimilate presentation of highlights of specific therapeutic practices described in original articles that have appeared in a wide array of professional publications. By eliminating technical research data and lengthy theoretical discussions, the digest format offers the reader more clinically relevant information than would a traditionally structured collection of full-length readings. This book contains succinct condensations of more than 130 professional articles, none of which are included in any other volume in this series.

In writing the digests, our goal was to give a brief but clear description of techniques by summarizing the clinical methods described in the original articles. In the commentaries at the ends of the digests, we have highlighted indications and contraindications for using the techniques. To supplement the digests, we have provided lists of additional readings at the ends of most sections on behavior disorders. We hope these will help readers broaden their knowledge of the therapeutic approaches that others have found successful.

The selections in this handbook have been drawn from a wide number of journals and books, as well as from papers recently presented at scientific and professional meetings. For this reason, very few of our intended readers will have easy access to more than a small sample of these works. By bringing together this widely dispersed material, we hope to enable the reader to quickly identify an appropriate method for treating a particular childhood problem. Once a promising approach has been located, the therapist should read the original article in order to obtain a complete description of the technique and its application and thus realistically judge its efficacy and suitability. Not to read the original article is to rely on incomplete material taken out of context, which may result in inefficient or harmful clinical practice. The digests are intended to help readers locate useful journal articles, not to substitute for them.

A word of caution about the techniques described in this volume: Some of the procedures are based on extensive empirical validation while others appear promising but were successful with only a limited number of cases. Some of the methods have been rigorously developed from well-established theories while others have little or no theoretical basis. Consequently, a number of the techniques described in this book should be viewed with full recognition of the need for more extensive independent replications.

The complexities of psychotherapy outcome research ensure that definitive findings will be extremely long in coming and will probably always be somewhat inconclusive. Even well-controlled research investigations generally measure the characteristics of whole populations and generate results that cannot be applied to any given individual without consideration of that person's uniqueness. Nevertheless, informed clinical decisions are undoubtedly better than blind chance in selecting treatment methods.

For ease of reference, the content areas of this book are almost identical to those in *Therapies for Children*. We have, however, deleted a few sections where the current literature was sparse—for example, destructiveness—and added a section on the treatment of sexual problems in childhood. We find the observations and conclusions in the introduction to *Therapies for Children* to be as true today as when they were first written about a decade ago, and, for this reason, we are substantially reprinting the introduction to the earlier volume.

We are grateful to the authors of the articles for permitting us to include digests of their works in this book.

We believe that this handbook will be useful to practitioners and students in many different disciplines, including the fields of psychology, social work, counseling, child care, psychiatry, and pediatrics.

October 1986   Charles E. Schaefer
                                              Hackensack, New Jersey

                                              Howard L. Millman
                                              Scarsdale, New York

                                              Steven M. Sichel
                                              Stamford, Connecticut

                                              Jane Riegelhaupt Zwilling
                                              Melville, New York

The Authors

Charles E. Schaefer is director of training for the Division of Psychological Services at Fairleigh Dickinson University in New Jersey. He was formerly director of staff development and psychological services at the Children's Village, a residential treatment center in Dobbs Ferry, New York. He also maintains a private practice for children, adolescents, and their families. In 1967 he received his Ph.D. degree in clinical psychology from Fordham University, where he remained for another three years conducting research with Anne Anastasi on the identification and development of creative thinking in children and youth.

In addition to numerous psychological tests and more than sixty articles in professional journals, Schaefer is the author, coauthor, or editor of fourteen other books relating to children, including *Game Play* (with S. Reid, 1986), *How to Talk to Children About Really Important Things* (1984), *Family Therapies for Children and Youth* (with J. Briesmeister and M. Fitton, 1984), *Group Therapies for Children and Youth* (with L. Johnson and J. Werry, 1983), *Handbook of Play Therapy* (with K. O'Connor, 1983), *How to Influence Children: A Handbook of Practical Parenting Skills* (2nd ed., 1982), *How to Help Children with Common Problems* (with H. L. Millman, 1981), and *Therapies for School Behavior Problems* (with H. L. Millman and J. J. Cohen, 1980).

Apart from clinical practice, his current professional interests include the identification of effective ways for parents and teachers to influence children—that is, better ways for adults to promote the personal and social development of children. His affiliations include the American Psychological Association, the American Orthopsychiatric Association (fellow), and the Association for Play Therapy (co-founder).

Schaefer resides in Yonkers, New York, with his wife, Anne, and their children, Karine and Eric. His avocational interests include tennis, swimming, jogging, and reading.

Howard L. Millman is the director of Psychological and Educational Services of Westchester, which provides help for psychological, behavioral, and learning problems. He practices individual, marital, and family psychotherapy in Scarsdale and supervises, consults, and lectures on the practice of psychotherapy. For many years he was the director of psychology and research at the Children's Village, a residential treatment center in Dobbs Ferry, New York. Millman received his Ph.D. degree in clinical psychology from Adelphi University in 1964 and completed an internship in clinical psychology at the Neuropsychiatric Institute at the University of California at Los Angeles. For several years, he was the chief psychologist at the Middlesex County Mental Health Clinic in New Jersey. He has taught psychotherapy and supervised doctoral students in psychology at the City College of New York and at Rutgers—the State University of New Jersey. For several years he taught group psychodynamics to graduate students at Manhattanville College.

Millman has published many articles in professional journals concerning psychotherapy, treatment outcome, and psychological and behavioral problems related to learning disabilities. He is the coauthor of *Therapies for Adults* (with J. T. Huber and D. R. Diggins, 1982), *How to Help Children with Common Problems* (with C. E. Schaefer, 1981), *Therapies for School Behavior Problems* (with C. E. Schaefer and J. J. Cohen, 1980), *Therapies for Psychosomatic Disorders in Children* (with C. E. Schaefer and G. F. Levine, 1979), *Therapies for Children* (with C. E. Schaefer, 1977), and coeditor (with J. T. Huber, 1972) of *Goals and Behavior in Psychotherapy and Counseling.* Television appearances include "A.M. America" (ABC), "Creativity in Crisis" (NBC), "Midday" (NEW), "Sonya" (DIV), and "Sixty Minutes" (CBS). Millman is currently a member of the Division of Psychotherapy of the American Psychological Association and the New York State Psychological Association. He is a past president of the Westchester County Psychological Association.

Millman lives in Bedford, New York, where he indulges in long-distance walking, tennis, listening to Baroque music, playing the drums, and writing. He has two sons: one is in high school, the other attends Harvard University.

Steven M. Sichel is a licensed psychologist and director of the Center for School Psychological Services in Stamford, Connecticut. He also serves as school psychologist for the Van Cleve Program of the New York Institute for Special Education, which serves children and adolescents who are emotionally disturbed and learning disabled. He is also a member of the adjunct graduate faculty at Manhattanville College in Purchase, New York. He has taught at Queens College and Queensboro Community College of the City University of New York and at Southern Connecticut State University, and he formerly served as a school psychologist in Greenwich, Connecticut. He received his Ph.D. degree in school psychology from New York University in 1984, after completing an internship at Queens Children's Psychiatric Center and fieldwork in New York City at the Roosevelt Hospital and at the Robert Louis Stevenson School, a therapeutic high school serving gifted underachievers.

In addition to his applied service and teaching roles, he

has served as a consultant to numerous school districts and regional cooperative educational agencies concerning educational program improvement and enhanced interdisciplinary team functioning. He also serves on an intercommunity task force on teenage suicide prevention. He has developed and hosted cable television programs directed at parents and adolescents. He is a member of the American Psychological Association and its Divisions of School Psychology, Psychologists in Independent Practice, Law and Psychology, and Psychologists Interested in Religious Issues. Other professional affiliations include the National Association of School Psychologists, the New York Association of School Psychologists, and the Connecticut Association of School Psychologists, where he served as president and co-chair of the Professional Ethics Committee.

Sichel lives in Stamford, Connecticut, with his wife, Ronnie, a speech and language pathologist, and their children, Rena and Daniel.

Jane Riegelhaupt Zwilling is a psychologist in the Half Hollow Hills Union Free School District in Dix Hills, New York, and also maintains a private practice for children and their families in Woodbury, New York. She received her Psy.D. degree in school and clinical psychology in 1983 from Pace University upon completion of her clinical internship at the Children's Village, a residential treatment center for emotionally disturbed boys in Dobbs Ferry, New York.

Zwilling has worked in a variety of settings, including schools and a children's rehabilitation hospital. Her professional interests include early identification of and intervention in child and family difficulties. She is a member of the American Psychological Association, the Nassau County Psychological Association, and the Suffolk County Psychological Association. She served one year as the editor of the newsletter for the Association of Play Therapy.

Zwilling lives in Plainview, New York, with her husband, Howard, an executive for a major retail company. Her interests include aerobics, swimming, spending time with friends, and home decorating. She also enjoys jogging with her dog, Annie.

Advances in
Therapies for Children

Introduction

The approach of this book reflects several current trends in child therapy. First, there is a growing emphasis on the prescriptive approach to therapy; that is, given a specific behavior disorder of the child, what specific remedy or therapeutic technique can best be applied? The long-term goal of this approach is to refine therapeutic methods so that one can eventually say what technique is best, given certain child, therapist, and situational variables. Physicians operate in this manner when they write an individualized prescription for a physically sick child. Rather than attempting to force a child into one "all-purpose" therapeutic mold, then, therapists are now trying to individualize, to fit the remedies or techniques to the needs of the individual child. Ideally, the prescriptive approach will result in maximum therapeutic effectiveness in the briefest possible time period.

1

Another name for this prescriptive approach is differential therapeutics.[1] This approach involves selecting a treatment based on the latest research about the effectiveness of various therapies for the particular problem, one's clinical experience, and the desires of the client. An empirical orientation is the foundation for this approach; that is, research studies are needed to document the specific effects of different treatments for each childhood disorder.

The thrust toward selectively applying different methods reflects the research evidence that no one therapeutic approach is equally effective with all types of problems and all types of people. Psychodynamic approaches seem most effective with bright, verbal, highly motivated adults exhibiting neurotic problems, whereas behavioral techniques have proven particularly successful with habit disorders and simple phobias. A combination of stimulant medication and cognitive-behavioral interventions has been successful with hyperactive children. Therapists are increasingly combining therapies to augment the therapeutic impact and reduce the length of treatment.

The prescriptive approach has led to a greater interest in the specifics of therapeutic practice, that is, in the concrete application of general principles. Professionals working directly with children want to offer more than a general diagnosis, global approach, or analytical explanation of etiology; they seek to offer a practical approach for alleviating a child's problems. For example, they want to suggest concrete actions to take when the child has his next temper tantrum. The state of the art in child therapy has advanced in recent years to the stage at which behavior modifiers, nondirective counselors, and others can now give specific "how to's" rather than teaching only process or general goals and principles. Of course, we are far from being an exact science. Clinical judgment and skills based on extensive training and experience are still needed to effectively select and apply the available therapeutic tools and to avoid using them in a standardized or mechanical fashion.

[1] A. Francis, J. Clarkin, and S. Perry. *Differential Therapeutics in Psychiatry* (New York: Brunner/Mazel, 1984).

The skillful application of the prescriptive approach involves the development of expertise in a wide variety of therapeutic methods, such as behavioral, cognitive, and dynamic approaches. This means adopting an "eclectic," "pluralistic," or "generalist" position rather than relying on one or two approaches. Concomitant with an increased interest in developing a broad spectrum of clinical skills has been a decreased interest in fostering specialty fields, such as counseling, clinical, and school psychology. Professionals are showing more and more interest in developing clinical skills that cut across disciplines, theories, and specialty fields.[2] Consequently, there seem to be fewer distinctions and more cooperative interplay between the various professional and therapeutic camps.

An eclectic approach to child therapy means using clinical judgment to decide whether to focus on alleviating overt behavior problems; developing cognitive skills; resolving unconscious self-reported or family conflicts; treating organic difficulties; promoting more adaptive, self-enhancing behaviors; or some combination of these objectives. In the past, theoretical biases have led therapists to pursue one of these objectives, although, in actuality, other goals may have been equally, or more, important. Clearly, it is important for clinicians to work together and pool their knowledge and skills, because no one discipline has proved sufficient to resolve the complex and diverse behavior disorders exhibited by children.

Freed from the constraints of orthodox adherence to a particular theoretical scheme, clinicians are now flexibly applying the methods of diverse approaches. Often the methods that seemed so appealing in theory and proved so successful in laboratory studies turn out to be complete disasters when first applied by the clinician. In the real world, there are simply many more uncontrolled and uncontrollable factors. Thus, the child therapist discovers that the bell-and-pad apparatus does not work because the child either sleeps through the alarm or removes the plug every night before he goes to sleep. Only after

[2]J. I. Bardon, "The State of the Art (and Science) of School Psychology," *American Psychologist*, 1976, *31*, 785-798.

more extensive preparations or adaptations does the procedure prove successful in such cases. To be successful in practice, then, clinicians are discovering they need to develop creative problem-solving skills—to become keen observers, flexible thinkers, creative adaptors of methods, and effective collaborators with others and to become self-confident and persistent in the pursuit of more effective practices.

Recognizing the complex and interrelated nature of human functioning, therapists frequently combine theories and techniques to effect changes in several dimensions, such as in thoughts, images, and motivation. There seem to be fewer radical behavior therapists or Freudian analysts practicing in an orthodox manner today. Rather, therapists are attempting to integrate methods from such currently popular approaches as social learning theory, general systems theory, and nondirective counseling. Combining methods often increases the therapeutic impact by tapping the child's capacity to participate in the experience in a more intense, holistic manner.

In this connection, the psychologist Arnold Lazarus has developed a therapeutic approach—multimodal therapy[3]—that assumes that lasting therapeutic change can only result if the therapist assesses and, where appropriate, alters the following modalities—the behavioral, affective, sensate, imagery, and cognitive modalities in the context of interpersonal relationships, and sometimes, in conjunction with medical professionals, in administering drugs and other medical procedures. Rather than stressing a single panacea, core construct, or critical mode of functioning, the multimodal approach asserts that people experience a multitude of specific problems across the various modalities that can best be treated by a variety of specific techniques. The multimodal approach supplies a framework and rationale for applying technical eclecticism.[4] Rather than gener-

[3]A. Lazarus, *Multimodal Behavior Therapy* (New York: Springer, 1976).
[4]Technical eclecticism is discussed in detail by R. L. Woolfolk in his chapter, "The Multimodal Model as a Framework for Decision Making in Psychotherapy," in A. Lazarus, *Multimodal Behavior Therapy* (New York: Springer, 1976).

ating theory from laboratory knowledge, the multimodal approach organizes inquiry around the problems themselves as experienced in clinical practice. In an inductive, empirical fashion, problems are observed, treatment performed, and judgments made concerning what additional approaches and modalities are needed to be effective.

A common finding of psychotherapy research is that little or no generalization of therapeutic success occurs across settings. Thus the progress a child exhibits in the therapist's office frequently dissolves when the child returns to the natural environment. As a result, another emerging trend is for therapists to train significant adults from a child's natural environment to apply therapeutic principles and techniques. Parents, teachers, college students, and others have all been helped to effectively modify children's deviant behaviors that had previously been considered the domain of highly skilled professionals. Typically, these nonprofessionals have little background in psychology and receive relatively little training, so that considerable supervision is required. This trend has important implications for the reduction of treatment costs and the multiplication of therapeutic effectiveness. In a real sense, then, clinicians seem to be actively attempting to "give psychology away" to the general public now in a variety of ways.[5] It is noteworthy that an evaluative study[6] found that a training program in which parents were taught to implement a behavioral approach was more effective than conventional treatment strategies employed by a child guidance clinic. The children involved showed less problem behavior after treatment and maintained more of these gains over a two-year follow-up period.

In regard to working with parents, there is a greater ten-

[5] B. G. Guerney, Jr. (ed.), *Psychotherapeutic Agents: New Roles for Nonprofessionals, Parents, and Teachers* (New York: Holt, Rinehart & Winston, 1969). Also, G. Goodman, *Companionship Therapy* (San Francisco: Jossey-Bass, 1972).

[6] J. D. Barnard and others. "The Family Training Program: Short- and Long-Term Evaluation." Paper presented at the 84th Annual Convention of the American Convention of the American Psychological Association, Washington, D.C., Sept. 1976.

dency now for child therapists to see the father's role as particularly important in the socialization of a child. A survey[7] of child psychiatrists and psychologists, for example, revealed that half of these therapists reported that they routinely see both parents in therapy when a child has a problem. An additional 43 percent of the therapists reported that they generally arrange for some participation by the child's father in the therapeutic process. Both society and child therapists are showing increasing recognition of the impact of both parents on a child's psychosocial development.

Another trend is toward preventative and educational models of practice. Rather than waiting until people come seeking help for serious, deeply entrenched problems, child therapists are now reaching out more into the community to teach ways of heading off or minimizing psychological conflicts. Thus therapists are actively teaching courses on parent effectiveness training, building marital relationships, coping with developmental crises, sex and drug education, assertiveness training, and effective study habits. Psychological growth and inoculation against predictable crises and problems of living are the goals of these efforts. Therapists are broadening their roles and scope and are becoming as well versed in ways to promote psychological health and adjustment as in ways to remediate maladjustment. This trend reflects the current emphasis on "outreach" or "community mental health" programs, which seem to comprise at least three basic elements: (1) broadening the client population for whom services are available, (2) providing services in facilities more accessible to clients, and (3) moving away from remedial treatment toward prevention of psychological disorders.[8]

In conclusion, the selection of appropriate treatment techniques is very likely the most crucial of all decisions made

[7] G. P. Koocher and B. M. Pedulla, "Current Practices in Child Psychotherapy." Paper presented at the 84th Annual Convention of the American Psychological Association, Washington, D.C., Sept. 1976.

[8] I. Iscoe and C. D. Spielberger (eds.), *Community Psychology: Perspectives in Training and Research* (New York: Appleton-Century-Crofts, 1970).

by the therapist. We hope that this volume will aid such decisions by encouraging therapists to break down general complaints into specific components that can be more readily attacked and by helping therapists quickly locate the most effective technique or combination of techniques for relieving a specific behavior disorder. Consistent with an orientation of technical eclecticism, this book stresses the development and refinement of specific, replicable procedures based on clinical practice, rather than emphasizing the role of clinical theory.

Many of the aforementioned trends in child therapy are apparent in this book, particularly the prescriptive approach, the emphasis on practical techniques, and eclecticism.

Within the past few decades, a specialized field of child therapy has emerged that contains a significant body of clinical knowledge. Although a number of excellent books are available pertaining to the theoretical and research aspects of psychotherapy, the practice component of child treatment—that is, specific application of clinical knowledge in real-life situations—has received less emphasis. The task of converting theory into practice is both an art and a science, and it is just as important as theoretical formulations and empirical investigations. Because of the large number of variables underlying human behavior, effective clinical practice requires extensive knowledge and development of clinical skills, careful observation and analysis of a problem, creative and flexible application of techniques, and expert clinical judgment based on considerable training and experience.

This book contains a variety of specific practices for dealing with the common behavior problems of children. The focus is on the clinical application of therapeutic principles and techniques to real-life situations. The need for this handbook became most apparent from our experiences in supervising beginning child therapists. While these therapists were generally well versed in the theories of psychotherapy, they tended to be uncertain when it came to the concrete application of these general theories to the troublesome behavior of children. Our experiences in private practice also convinced us of the need for comprehensive reference books on child therapy that were oriented more to practice ("how to do it") rather than to theory or research.

Most books on child therapy begin with a broad theoretical orientation and then attempt to relate this theory to specific childhood problems. In contrast, we constructed this book by starting with a list of the common behavior problems of children and then locating specific therapeutic techniques that others have found useful or successful in resolving them. Instead of presenting only one therapeutic technique for a problem, we sought to reflect the current eclectic trend by presenting the reader with at least two or three different approaches to problems. The question we tried to answer was this: What do therapists from different orientations actually do and say when working with a child who has a specific problem? By comparing different approaches to a particular disturbance, therapists will be encouraged to become more flexible in their own approaches. The importance of providing alternate approaches is underscored by the growing realization that the field of psychotherapy encompasses a variety of useful treatment practices. It is now apparent that not all approaches or techniques are equally successful in helping children who exhibit a certain type of difficulty.

The number of alternate techniques that this volume offers for particular problems varies considerably, depending on the variety of specific practices reported in the literature. Because some childhood behavior problems have been extensively researched (for example, bedwetting and school phobia), we are able to present a wide variety of alternate approaches for these problems. Because of space limitations, we have listed some of these alternate techniques in the annotated bibliographies at the end of each chapter. In general, the practices presented in the bibliographies were judged to be less specific than, or somewhat similar to, the techniques presented in the chapter digests.

The main criteria for selecting practices for this book were *quality* and *specificity*. First, we sought high-quality techniques that are based on sound theoretical and/or research foundations. Thus, we tried to exclude esoteric or highly controversial practices. Second, we looked for specificity—both of technique and of application to a particular disorder. The goal of this approach is to help the practicing clinician locate detailed treatment plans for each of the common childhood disorders. In other words, we want the book to be prescriptive in nature; that is, given a specific problem, what exactly can one do about it? Since a key feature of *learning theory* is its specificity, approaches that systematically apply learning theory principles in an attempt to change maladaptive behavior are overrepresented in this book. Included under the learning theory approach are counterconditioning techniques (systematic desensitization, reciprocal inhibition, and other variations of the classical conditioning theme), modeling strategies (use of models who display adaptive behavior to the disturbed child), and operant conditioning (application of positive and/or negative consequences following a child's behavior).

Notwithstanding the larger number of learning theory articles, we sought to provide an eclectic orientation in the book. Accordingly, the reader will find a number of articles based on other major orientations, such as *psychodynamic* and *psychopharmacological* approaches. The aim of psychodynamic therapy is to treat the underlying psychic cause of a problem rather than the overt behavior manifested. The principal forms of dynamic therapy are (1) the child-therapist relationship, (2) working with the family, (3) spontaneous play with conversation, (4) release and acceptance of fantasy and feelings, and (5) interpretation. Examples of dynamic orientations to child therapy are psychoanalytic, Gestalt, family systems, and nondirective play therapy. Psychopharmacological approaches use drugs either to remedy underlying physiological causes of maladaptive behavior or to alter the psychological state of a child in order to facilitate the use of other therapeutic approaches. A basic assumption of this book is that the reader is familiar with both the theoretical and research foundations of the major therapeutic approaches.

The therapeutic practices presented in this book are organized around the common behavior problems exhibited by children, primarily during the middle childhood years. Thus, each chapter is devoted to techniques for treating one of the six

broad types of disturbances typical of this period, namely, neurotic disorders, habit disorders, antisocial behaviors, hyperkinetic behaviors, disturbed relationships with other children, and
disturbed relationships with parents. A continuing problem for
child therapists is the lack of a reliable and valid classification
system for childhood disorders. The particular classification system used in this book is based on the factor-analytic research of
Alderton.[9] This research was selected for several reasons. First,
it is one of the more comprehensive and behaviorally specific
classification systems currently available, including over thirty
specific categories of maladaptive behavior, such as fire setting
and encopresis. These concrete behaviors are clustered into the
six broad categories previously mentioned. Apart from its specificity and comprehensiveness, another feature of this system is
the fact that it gives as much weight to disturbed social interactions (such as maladaptive peer, sibling, and parental relationships) as it does to personality problems (such as neurotic behaviors). Other advantages are that it is expressly designed for
children and emphasizes concrete target symptoms rather than
the general diagnoses found in DSM III.

The focus of this particular classification system is on
parent-reported behavior problems that are of moderate rather
than severe intensity. Beyond the scope of this book are behavior problems related to autism, childhood psychosis, mental retardation, psychosomatic disorders, speech (such as stuttering),
and overt organic problems, such as focal brain lesions and epi-
lepsy. However, some of the digests and additional readings
used pertain to children with these disorders or to somewhat
younger or older children than our target population. These
articles were included because the techniques employed were
deemed applicable to the behavior disorders covered in this
book.

To maximize the usability of this handbook, we have in-

[9]H. R. Alderton and B. A. Hoddinott, "The Children's Pathology
Index," *Canadian Psychiatric Association Journal*, 1968, *13*, 353–361;
H. R. Alderton, "*The Children's Pathology Index* as a Predictor of Follow-
up Adjustment," *Canadian Psychiatric Association Journal*, 1970, *15*,
289-294.

cluded two indexes at the end of the book: author and subject. The Author Index lists authors of the original articles as well as authors of all other references cited. In the Subject Index we have attempted to provide a comprehensive cross-referencing system to both problems and treatment modes.

1

Neurotic Behaviors

Neurotic behaviors are patterns resulting from attempts to handle anxiety. Covered in this chapter are nightmares, obsessive-compulsive behavior, hysterical behavior, depression, shy and withdrawn behavior, school phobia, fears, and reactions to trauma. Nightmares, school phobia, fears, and reactions to trauma are clear examples of overtly anxious reactions to fearful stimuli. Obsessive-compulsive, hysterical, and shy and withdrawn behaviors are mechanisms to *avoid* anxiety. A compulsive, electively mute, hysterically paralyzed, or withdrawn child does not experience overt anxiety; depression can be a way of withdrawing, giving up, and avoiding the stress associated with everyday living. (As will be seen in the rest of this book, the reader does not have to agree with the rationale for categorizing

behaviors into chapters to find the book useful. As explained in
the introduction, we used factor-analytic research to find the
clusters of behaviors that make up our chapters. The tailoring of
approaches to specific problems, such as nightmares, is the
theme of all the books in this series—Guidebooks for Therapeutic Practice.)

Anxiety is a normal experience in a child's development:
Learning about and avoiding danger has important survival
value. Harsh or inconsistent parental behavior and frequent
negative criticism are early sources of anxiety. Serious difficulties with siblings or peers also can cause anxiety. Children often
develop "neurotic" patterns of coping, which then have to be
unlearned. Thus, whenever possible, we believe that changing
the cause of anxiety should be a goal. If a child's nightmares are
caused by fear of bullies, then one might deal with the situation
by openly discussing the fear with the child, teaching him or her
verbal or physical self-defense, or having adults intervene and
get the bullies to leave the child alone. Similarly, if a school
phobia is caused by a child's fear of peers in school or fear of
meeting academic demands, then those causes must be addressed.

This discussion is meant as a caution to therapists who
tend to use one or several treatment methods without spending
the time to find possible causes of particular behaviors. However, we have great respect for direct therapeutic methods that
reduce anxiety, such as relaxation, desensitization, and cognitive behavior modification. Since the publication of *Therapies
for Children* in 1977, we have seen increasing reports of effectively combining various therapeutic approaches. Successfully
treating any of the neurotic behaviors may well involve some
combination of environmental manipulation, family therapy,
parent counseling, insight therapy, modifying cognitions and behavior using some form of reward, social skills training, and
some relaxation technique. There have been many reports,
which our experience confirms, of effective brief therapy in
contrast to previously reported long-term therapy of neuroses.
Recently, there has been a rapidly growing trend for therapists
to integrate eclectic psychotherapeutic methods. We have long

advocated this type of eclecticism, and the reader may find the following books useful: Beutler, L. E., *Eclectic Psychotherapy: A Systematic Approach* (Elmsford, N.Y.: Pergamon Press, 1983); Driscoll, R., *Pragmatic Psychotherapy* (New York: Van Nostrand Reinhold, 1984); Hart, J., *Modern Eclectic Therapy: A Functional Orientation to Counseling and Psychotherapy* (New York: Plenum, 1983); and Lazarus, A. A., *The Practice of Multimodal Therapy* (New York: McGraw-Hill, 1981).

Nightmares

A nightmare is a fear reaction occurring during sleep. A frightening dream with feelings of helplessness, suffocation, or oppression usually awakens the child. Peak incidence is between four and six years and is particularly prevalent in five- and six-year-old girls (Schaefer, C. E., and Millman, H. L. How to Help Children with Common Problems. *New York: New American Library, 1982). Approximately one-quarter of children ages six to twelve have nightmares. Up to age four, children often dream of being chased by wild animals. From ages four to twelve, nightmares concern being threatened by evil strangers or center around personal difficulties. Avoiding stress, scolding, or threats before bedtime reduces the likelihood of nightmares. A night terror* (pavor nocturnus) *is an extreme form of nightmare that usually involves frantic motor activity, sleeptalking, extreme anxiety, and difficulty reorienting to reality. Usually the child sits up, screams, breathes heavily, often perspires, and is in great distress. She often stares at an imaginary object and appears to be hallucinating. The child is disoriented, not fully awake; she does not recognize people but does answer questions and respond to reassurance. After awakening, she has no memory of the frightening experience. Night terrors are most common in preschoolers, who are often overly sensitive and active and who go to sleep tense and exhausted. A medical examination is essential to rule out thyroid, electroencephalogram, or other physiological problems. Medication has been used successfully to prevent night terrors from occurring. (Also see section on* Sleep Disturbance.)

Response Prevention, Extinction, and Systematic Desensitization to Reduce Nightmares

AUTHORS: Richard N. Roberts and Steven B. Gordon

PRECIS: Case report describing behavioral assessment and treatment of a five-year-old girl's nightmares and night terrors following an accident in which she was severely burned.

INTRODUCTION: The occurrence of childhood nightmares often signals that anxiety is present. While the origin of the child's anxiety might be readily determined, as in the present case, sometimes decisions about treatment methods to be used need to be made for practical as well as theoretical reasons. Here, the potential physical danger to the child from her thrashing about in bed during her nightmares led Roberts and Gordon to use treatment methods that combined elements of effectiveness and safety.

CASE STUDY: Debbie was a well-adjusted girl prior to suffering extensive burns on her chest, arms, neck, and ears when her nightgown caught fire as she and her younger brother played with matches one night. A six-week hospitalization followed, during which two skin graft operations were performed. Her nightmares began immediately after the accident. They occurred from eight to fifteen times per night while she was in the hospital and ten to twenty times almost every night after she returned home. Debbie was not able to recall the content of her dreams, but her behavior during the nightmares suggested the likelihood that she was dreaming of the traumatic fire. Frequently, the nightmares began with Debbie clutching her nightgown and moving her hands toward the region where she suffered the most severe burns. Then she screamed and flailed about in her bed until she was awakened and comforted. Her wild thrashing about caused her parents to fear that Debbie would injure herself. Treatment began eight weeks after the accident occurred.

TREATMENT: The therapists conducted intake interviews with Debbie's parents, at which they reported the pre- and post-trauma history of their daughter's behavior and answered questions about the quality of their own relationship. The parents provided a detailed description of the frequency and course of Debbie's nightmares and their reactions in response to them. Because of the risk of injury associated with the child's kicking and flailing during the nightmares, Roberts and Gordon decided to make use of a response prevention procedure to interrupt the nightmare at the earliest sign of Debbie's clutching her nightgown. Observations had shown that the girl's panic reactions during sleep invariably followed this initial cue.

Response Prevention. Debbie's mother was told to return to the girl's room ten to fifteen minutes after Debbie fell asleep. She was instructed to awaken Debbie but not talk to her when she noticed her daughter beginning to clutch her nightgown. She was to allow Debbie to fall asleep again immediately. Debbie was to remain in her own room the entire night.

Extinction. During this treatment phase, Debbie's parents were instructed to totally ignore the girl's nightmares and to allow Debbie to spend the entire night alone in her bedroom.

After one week of the response prevention intervention, Debbie's nightmares occurred just once each night at most. When the extinction plan was instituted for a period of four weeks, this trend continued. Her nightmares resumed when Debbie was rehospitalized for another skin graft operation. After the hospital visit, two nightmares per night were recorded. Additionally, Debbie exhibited generalized fear of fire, including the gas stove in the kitchen, lit cigarettes, and fires depicted on television. To combat this generalization phenomenon, the authors implemented systematic desensitization.

Systematic Desensitization. The therapists chose a series of ten magazine pictures to represent a desensitization hierarchy. The pictures depicted fires in a wide variety of settings and uses. Debbie's mother showed these to her daughter and had her rate each picture on a "scariness" scale ranging from 1 (not scary at all) to 5 (very scary). After she was exposed to a picture, Debbie played with her favorite toys for a few minutes.

The exposure trials lengthened gradually from fifteen seconds to sixty seconds. Daily presentations of the hierarchy continued for three weeks until Debbie reached the picture that was scariest for her and she was able to rate it as "1."

Debbie's nightmares ceased during the desensitization phase, and she displayed no fearful reactions to fire-related stimuli. Her nightmares did not recur for six months of follow-up, during which Debbie had to return to the hospital once more for an additional skin graft operation.

COMMENTARY: Roberts and Gordon demonstrate that effective therapy must mesh with pressing needs, such as concern for a child's safety, as well as other considerations, such as a child's developmental level. Their choice of pictorial rather than imaginal stimuli for Debbie's desensitization hierarchy reflected their understanding that the girl's young age required more of a concrete intervention approach than is commonly used with older individuals. Also, their case study is an excellent example of how professionals can train and supervise parents acting as data gatherers and therapists for their own children. Such a triadic approach to therapy is especially useful when children present symptoms that are not evident in the therapist's office.

SOURCE: Roberts, R. N., and Gordon, S. B. "Reducing Childhood Nightmares Subsequent to a Burn Trauma." *Child Behavior Therapy*, 1979, *1* (4), 373–381.

Play, Reinforcement, and Extinction in the Treatment of a Young Child's Night Terrors

AUTHOR: Jonathan Kellerman

PRECIS: Case illustration of the use of behavioral analysis and treatment to eliminate persistent night terror syndrome in a three-year-old with concomitant medical problems.

INTRODUCTION: The incidence of *pavor nocturnus,* or night terror syndrome, is not known, but the syndrome appears most often among preschoolers. The disorder is manifested by the sleeping child awakening, sitting up, screaming, and moving about. He or she is not responsive to efforts to provide comfort. The child returns to sleep and afterward has little to no recall of the incident. It has been speculated that night terrors relate to previous psychological trauma. Drug treatments have produced symptom remission. In this article, Kellerman describes a behavioral treatment approach in a three-year-old girl receiving medical treatment for leukemia.

CASE STUDY: T's cancer, which had been diagnosed about half a year earlier, was in remission. Her night terrors appeared to be related to the trauma of the multiple medical procedures she had endured, her separation from her mother, and reinforcement of inappropriate sleep patterns. T had undergone chemotherapy treatments, venipunctures, lumbar punctures, surgery for a submandibular abscess, and bone marrow aspirations (BMAs). The latter were especially painful, and T's mother reported that she left the treatment room during her daughter's BMAs because she became extremely anxious as they were being performed. Before therapy, T's parents had brought her into their bed when the nightmares began. At the time therapy began, T had experienced one to six nightmares each night for the past month. Her mother reported that T's sleep tended to be more disturbed on nights after the child had undergone BMAs.

Kellerman's treatment entailed these components: (1) *Written Records.* T's parents noted the occurrence of the girl's night terrors, their antecedents, and what happened afterward. (2) *Parent Training.* The therapist instructed the parents about young children's separation anxiety, and he taught the mother to use progressive muscle relaxation to enable her to remain with T during the BMA procedure. (3) *Play and In Vivo Desensitization.* During twice-weekly therapy sessions, Kellerman engaged T in play activities with dolls, syringes, swabs, and other medical apparatus so that she could simulate various medical procedures. While this was going on, T's mother spent progressively less time in the treatment room in order to build T's tolerance for being apart from her mother. (4) *Positive Reinforcement.* Each time T's sleep was nightmare-free, she received a special treat the next morning. (5) *Extinction.* T's parents left her in her own bed when she did have a nightmare. They said little to her at such times (for example, "Mommy's here").

The treatment completely eliminated T's nightmares after four months. Follow-up three months later indicated that there was no recurrence of the child's night terrors. T showed concurrent gains in her ability to play without her parents' presence for extended periods.

COMMENTARY: Kellerman presents an effective behavioral analysis and treatment to help a young child whose nightmares were remarkably persistent and recurrent. The therapist's basic approach entailed reducing the youngster's anxiety both indirectly by decreasing her mother's level of anxiety and directly through desensitizing play activities and exposing her to progressively longer separations from her mother. Positive reinforcement of each night of peaceful sleep counteracted the inappropriate rewards that previously had followed episodes of night terror.

SOURCE: Kellerman, J. "Single Case Study: Behavioral Treatment of Night Terrors in a Child with Acute Leukemia." *Journal of Nervous and Mental Disease,* 1979, *167* (3), 182–185.

Rapid Elimination of Nightmares
by Incompatible Response Training

AUTHOR: Jonathan Kellerman

PRECIS: Analyzing behavior, teaching children alternatives to anxious behaviors, plus parent counseling with children who exhibited fearful responsiveness at night.

INTRODUCTION: Using a combination of behavioral approaches, Kellerman developed a program to modify night fears and sleeplessness of three children who ranged in age from five to thirteen years. The case of D was reported in detail.

CASE STUDY: A five-year-old boy, D, had displayed nightmares, sudden waking, motility, and screaming for seven months since he had witnessed a horror film on television. The frequency of these incidents ranged from two to seven times per week. After an episode of deviant nocturnal behavior, D was unable to remember the event. His anxiety generalized such that he was fearful of going to his grandmother's house because that was where he had seen the Dracula movie that triggered his nightmares.

TREATMENT: The therapist performed a behavioral analysis, which determined that D's parents, by allowing him to sleep in their bed and comforting him whenever he expressed fear, had inadvertently reinforced the child's inappropriate sleep behavior. Further, their refusal to allow him to view any television program they felt would evoke an anxious reaction was considered to have an opposite effect—that is, confirming in his mind that television and film characters were to be feared. The therapist developed a four-phase plan of treatment to reverse the problem behavior:

   1. The therapist told D that he could feel better if he became angry at Dracula and that it was impossible to feel angry and afraid simultaneously. The therapist modeled, and D imitated, angry verbal responses. Also, D drew pictures of Dracula,

voiced his rage at the drawn figures, ripped them up, and threw them away.

2. The therapist told D's parents to refrain from censoring his television viewing. They were instructed to say, "You can handle it," and to advise D to get mad at Dracula whenever the boy said he was scared of Dracula.

3. D was notified that he could not sleep with his parents anymore and that he would receive five cents the next morning each time he recorded a full night of sleeping in the proper place (anywhere in the house except his parents' bedroom for the first week; then in his own room). D and the therapist generated a list of counter-anxious behaviors besides anger which D could use when he felt scared. The list included turning on a night light, going to the refrigerator, turning on the bedside radio, and leafing through a book he enjoyed. The therapist instructed the youngster to begin one of these activities instantly when he felt frightened.

4. The therapist provided D's parents with examples of assertive behaviors that the boy might exhibit that were incompatible with fearful responsiveness. Each time he exhibited these, they were to provide verbal praise.

D's total treatment occurred over three one-hour sessions. On the first night after his initial treatment session, D's parents ignored his attempt to enter their room. They ignored his tantrum, and this extinguished the inappropriate behavior as he fell asleep outside the door to their room. Within two weeks, D's nightmares were eliminated and he was sleeping the entire night in his own room. Monetary reinforcement was phased out after four weeks. Therapeutic gains were maintained at follow-up eighteen and twenty-four months later, with the boy able to play Dracula and talk about the monster without any ill effects. D's mother observed a general increase in her son's assertiveness, as well.

COMMENTARY: This case illustrates that parents' protectiveness may act to exacerbate a child's anxiety by restricting his or her opportunity to engage in counter-anxious behavior. Also, the parents' reinforcement of fearful behavior can perpetuate its occurrence. Effective therapy for the child, then, must often entail defining and facing the problem as a family problem, with therapeutic intervention including reeducation and redirecting the behaviors of members of the child's family. Most children respond better to role playing when the therapist or parent promotes a fun, game-like atmosphere.

SOURCE: Kellerman, J. "Rapid Treatment of Nocturnal Anxiety in Children." *Journal of Behavior Therapy and Experimental Psychiatry*, 1980, *44*, 9-11.

Hypnosis for Treating Night Terrors

AUTHOR: Erwin L. Taboada

PRECIS: Describes the use of hypnosis during a single session of psychotherapy, resulting in elimination of a boy's fearful nighttime behaviors.

INTRODUCTION: Taboada notes that night terrors may persist for years or even decades. Treatment methods reported in the literature have included psychoanalysis and the use of medication, such as Diazepam. While this drug has successfully suppressed night terrors after being administered for one to two weeks, treatment effects have not always endured. In this article, Paul, age seven, exhibited nightly terror episodes over a two-week period during which he sweated profusely, screamed and tossed, and sat up and mumbled incoherently. These episodes started one to one and one-half hours after Paul went to sleep, lasted several minutes, and were forgotten by the boy the next morning. Before seeing the boy, the therapist met with the boy's mother and learned that Paul told her about a traumatic experience that had occurred at camp—the capsizing of a boat carrying the boy, some of his friends, and a counselor.

TREATMENT: The therapist induced a hypnotic trance by asking Paul to imagine that his fingers were ten children and then having him rest several fingers of each hand on the desk "like children asleep." Then Paul imagined that his remaining fingers were "getting tired" as well, and he was instructed to "put them asleep" with the others. After this, the therapist told Paul to place his head on the desk, close his eyes, and go to sleep with the ten "children."

While the boy was in the trance state, he and the therapist talked about the boy's account of the boating accident to his mother. The therapist had Paul summon up an image of himself, as an older and stronger child who was more proficient at swimming, enjoying a boating outing.

For at least eighteen months after the therapy session, Paul experienced no further episodes of *pavor nocturnus*. Interestingly, about one month after Taboada saw the boy, he admitted to his mother that the capsizing incident had never actually occurred but that he had imagined it after becoming very frightened by huge waves.

COMMENTARY: This case illustrates that children's disturbed sleep can sometimes be treated successfully with short-term therapeutic intervention. Many therapists use a similar approach without hypnosis. Here, Paul's fear of death brought on his night terrors. An *imagined* event triggered the boy's anxieties. Real-life experiences with death and exposures to it on television—such as witnessing the fatal explosion of the *Challenger* space shuttle—can precipitate children's fearful reactions, as well. The longer such symptoms continue, the greater is the likelihood that a child's anxieties will become internalized and form a major psychological disorder.

SOURCE: Taboada, E. L. "Night Terrors in a Child Treated with Hypnosis." *Journal of Clinical Hypnosis,* 1975, *17,* 270–271.

Additional Readings

Alford, G. S., Zegiob, L., and Bristow, A. R. "Use of Instructions and Apparatus-Enhanced Suggestion in Treating a
Case of Headaches, Nightmares and Nocturnal Enuresis."
Psychotherapy: Theory, Research and Practice, 1982, *19,*
110–115.

The authors describe how the target symptoms of a ten-
year-old girl responded rapidly and disappeared after four
thirty-minute placebo treatment sessions conducted over a five-
week period. Verbal instructions played a central role in treatment. The therapists told the girl that all her "bad thoughts and
dreams" were going to be removed and that a machine would
eliminate her pain and bed wetting. Additionally, they used an
elaborate placebo ritual and apparatus consisting of a polygraph, relay rack, and oscilloscope in treatment. The polygraph
inkwriter was turned on, along with the oscilloscope and relay
rack lights. Surface electrodes were attached to the girl's fore-
head at the focal point of the headaches. In fact, the electrodes
were plugged into a disconnected relay box, and deflections on
the oscilloscope and inkwriter were produced by a calibration
signal generator. Treatment gains were maintained at a follow-
up after two years. The authors feel that cognitive process variables, such as expectancy and attribution, were responsible for
the success of the intervention.

Blau, S. B. "A Guide to the Use of Psychotropic Medication in
Children and Adolescents." *The Journal of Clinical Psychiatry,* 1978, *39,* 766–772.

In this article, Blau discusses general considerations pertaining to administering medication to children, and then he
proceeds to outline the most common medications used for
childhood psychiatric problems. The discussion is arranged according to clinical entities. In treating night terrors, Blau feels
that the child's screaming, crying, and possible running in his
sleep may be so frightening for the family and potentially dangerous as to warrant the use of medication. Diazepam (Valium)
administered in dosages of 1 to 15 mg. before bedtime has been
found to be effective in 80 percent of cases. Because the child
sleeps while the drug is acting, side effects are uncommon.

Hunyady, H. "A Report on a Drawing Therapy for Children's Nightmares." *Journal of Evolutionary Psychology,* 1984, *5,* 129-130.

Hunyady describes a technique using children's drawings to help them overcome their fears. The method is outlined with reference to children who experience night fright. Unlike other interpretive systems for graphomotor productions, the drawing therapy discussed by the author does not rest on a Freudian framework.

Kales, J. D., Kales, A., Soldatos, C. R., Chamberlin, K., and Martin, E. D. "Sleepwalking and Night Terrors Related to Febrile Illness." *American Journal of Psychiatry,* 1979, *136,* 1214-1215.

The authors present three case reports of children ranging in age from nine to twelve years whose sleepwalking or night terrors were associated with high fevers. In none of these cases was there any apparent psychopathology. The authors observe that sometimes the onset of the sleepwalking or night terrors occurs during the active course of febrile illness; in such instances, antibiotic treatment may be sufficient to eliminate the problem as the fever subsides. When the symptom emerges during the recovery period, parental caution is needed to avoid overreacting while taking necessary safety measures and returning the child to bed.

Richman, N. "A Double-Blind Drug Trial of Treatment in Young Children with Waking Problems." *Journal of Child Psychology and Psychiatry,* 1985, *26,* 591-598.

In this study, the author reports the use of trimeprazine tartrate (Vallergan Forte) in a double-blind investigation with twenty-two children, one to two years old, whose sleeping patterns were severely disturbed (waking three or more times each night or once for more than twenty minutes). The treatment dosage of the drug, 30 mg. given at bedtime, was doubled after three nights if the parents discerned no improvement. During the two-week trial and for two additional weeks, the parents kept diaries on their children's sleep. The results of the investigation were somewhat ambiguous. According to parental reports, the drug produced significant improvements; however, the diary data indicated that the extent of improvement was limited and that many wakeful nights still occurred. Persistence of sleep problems was found in most of the children at follow-up six months later. Richman suggests that behavioral methods of treatment be explored to help parents of wakeful children.

Richman, R., Douglas, J., Hunt, H., Landsdown, R., and Levere, R. "Behavioral Methods in the Treatment of Sleep Disorders—a Pilot Study." *Journal of Child Psychology and Psychiatry,* 1985, *26,* 581–590.

In this study, the authors treated for severe sleep disorders thirty-five children between one and five years old; each child received up to six sessions of treatment over a six-month period. The techniques employed were withdrawal of parental attention to the wakeful child, social and token reinforcement for the desired behavior, shaping (for example, by making a gradually earlier bedtime), and cueing (by distinguishing clearly between daytime and nighttime and developing a bedtime ritual). The therapists rated 77 percent of the children as markedly or completely improved as a result of the behavioral treatment.

Obsessive-Compulsive Behavior

To obsess is to be intensely preoccupied with an unreasonable idea or feeling. Obsessive doubting or thinking are common, and the thoughts often serve to undo "bad" thoughts that could lead to guilty feelings. Omnipresent disagreeable thoughts can be very bothersome. Being compulsive means feeling compelled to repeat certain stereotypical or irrational acts. Examples of compulsive behavior include washing one's hands very frequently, lining up objects, opening and closing or locking and unlocking doors, and walking up and down steps. Some children are compulsively perfectionistic: They become very upset if things are not done in a perfect manner. When compulsive behavior is not performed, their anxiety becomes high. Repetitious or symmetrical (to balance some behavior) acts are common. Compulsive behavior often pertains to cleanliness, safety, or superstition. Compulsive children are usually fussy, punctual, overly conscientious, and orderly. Compulsiveness is most common between eight and ten years of age. From two to seven years, many children perform rituals, say things, and play games in a repetitive, rigid manner. By age twelve, children are expected to be more flexible and adaptive and understand that rules are not absolutes but standards that are agreed upon. Reasons for developing compulsivity include a need to feel safe and good, relieving tension and reducing fear, coping with guilt, reacting to strict parental expectations, and avoiding confronting real problems. Parents who promote tolerance, competency, open expression of feelings, and avoidance of superstition and ritual reduce the likelihood of their children developing compulsivity (Schaefer, C. E., and Millman, H. L. How to Help Children with Common Problems. *New York: New American Library, 1982). When guilt causes compulsivity, a resolution of the cause is appropriate. If anxiety leads to compulsiveness, some form of desensitization is effective.*

Using a Functional Analysis Approach
to Treat Obsessive-Compulsive Problems

AUTHORS: Luis Otavio de Seixas Queiroz, Maria Aparecida Motta, Maria Beatriz Barbosa Pinho Madi, Dirceu Luis Sossai, and John J. Boren

PRECIS: Treating obsessions and compulsions by finding the factors that instigate and maintain the problem behaviors and counteracting them.

INTRODUCTION: In the authors' method, treatment of obsessive-compulsive (o-c) behavior focuses on extracting the environmental conditions that maintain each problem behavior and treating these through appropriate therapeutic techniques. Procedures may vary across cases according to this approach, which emphasizes the maintaining variables and the behavior, not the "o-c personality" or the "o-c disease." The therapeutic principles presented by the authors apply to treatment of cases of child as well as adult obsessive-compulsiveness.

PROCEDURES: The following nine principles guide the functional analysis approach:

　　　1. *Describe the o-c behavior.* This involves detailed specification of the identified obsessive characteristics and compulsive responses accomplished through interviews.
　　　2. *Determine how the behavior is maintained.* Ways to do this may include taking a history concerning the child's early development, observing directly in the child's home, or interviewing the family members.
　　　3. *Formulate behavioral alternatives for the o-c responses.* This usually entails discussions with the parents and/or with the child directly.
　　　4. *Identify important positive reinforcements for the child.*
　　　5. *Make a hierarchy of adequate behavior for which positive reinforcement can be given.*

6. *Work on decreasing the social variables that maintain the o-c responses.*

7. *Collaborate with people who can reward alternative behavior.*

8. *Teach assertiveness.*

9. *Apply fear reduction techniques.*

CASE STUDY: A nine-year-old boy was referred because of compulsive behavior and phobic responses.

Description of the O-C Behavior. The boy's unusual obsessions and behaviors included: (1) feeling compelled to and actually picking up large amounts of trash, including scattered papers, food wrappers, cigarette butts, fragments of wood, and other items, which he stored in his pockets or inside his shirt; (2) remaining in front of the television for the duration of any program he was watching, regardless of what else he had to do; (3) feeling compelled to cross the street or to travel from one side of a sidewalk to the other before he passed anyone; (4) refusing to leave his house unless he was with one of his parents or his brother; (5) sipping water from a garden faucet every time he prepared to leave the house; (6) constantly fearing that his father was about to punish him and frequently begging his mother in a tearful fashion to refrain from telling his father when he did something wrong; (7) allowing others to take advantage of him—for example, loaning money to relatives without arranging for repayment; (8) acting very dependent on others —not choosing his own clothes or dressing himself, not serving his own plate at meals, and so on; (9) displaying frequent tantrums; (10) exhibiting varied, excessive fears—of the dark, of being alone, of stormy weather, of thieves, and so forth.

Maintenance of the O-C Behavior. Interviews determined that the boy's mother manifested numerous ritualistic behaviors of her own and harbored assorted extreme fears similar to her son's. She perpetuated the boy's obsessions and compulsions in various ways: giving excessive attention to his unusual behaviors, bowing to his angry demands, dissuading him from playing away from the house, spanking his older brother in the boy's presence for leaving home without permission while showering

the younger boy with praise for not following his brother's example, threatening the boy with punishment from his father,
telling him to disobey his father when she and her husband were
fighting in the boy's presence, infantilizing the youngster by in-
sisting that she bathe him, choose his clothes, and so on. The
authors observed that the boy's o-c behavior appeared only in
his mother's presence.

Alternative Behavior. The therapists targeted behavioral
goals for the boy: playing with his brother and with friends inside and outside the home, going shopping, attending parties,
selecting his own wardrobe and dressing himself, serving himself at meals, leaving the house after dark, asserting his rights.

Important Reinforcers. The therapists devised a token
system in which the boy won or lost points according to the behaviors he exhibited. These were posted on a wall chart. When
the boy earned 100 points, he traded in his points for money,
which he could spend freely. Simultaneously, his parents praised
him for appropriate behavior.

*Hierarchy of Behavior to Produce Positive Reinforce-
ment.* For the leaving goal, places were listed in sequence according to their distance from the boy's home. For the goal of
traveling alone by bus, the boy's father was instructed to establish a seven-step procedure for fading out support. The steps
were: (1) accompanying the boy to the bus stop, flagging down
the bus, and placing the boy on the bus; (2) taking the boy to
the bus stop and showing him which bus to take; (3) going with
his son to the bus stop and waiting as the boy did the rest;
(4) going to the stop and then returning home while the boy
flagged down the bus and got on; (5) going halfway to the bus
stop with his son; (6) going only as far as the edge of the yard
with him; (7) having the boy perform all approach and boarding behaviors by himself.

Sources Maintaining O-C Behavior. Through weekly counseling sessions with both parents, the counselors helped the parents realize how their behaviors helped maintain their son's o-c
behavior. Also, the counselors advised the parents to ignore
their son's tantrums, obsessive behavior, and other inadequate
performances while recognizing and praising instances of behavior that was adequate and appropriate.

Social Agencies to Reinforce Alternate Behavior. In this case, the parents' involvement and the token system previously described fulfilled this procedural step.

Assertiveness Training. With this boy, assertiveness training in the clinic did not occur. In other instances, such training is done in the office or in the child's natural environment.

Reduction of Fear Response. The parents were told to tolerate without undue alarm the boy's talking about his fears. Additionally, the authors accomplished *in vivo* desensitization of some of the boy's fears by gradually exposing him to the fear stimulus plus awarding him tokens and praise for progressively greater tolerance of the fear source. As an example, the therapists handled the child's fear of being alone by exposing him to this situation for incremental five-minute segments and applying positive reinforcement as he mastered each successive extension.

The functional analysis procedures used with the boy were effective in eliminating many of his o-c behaviors and reducing others. Simultaneously, improvement was seen in his assertiveness, his social participation, and his academic work. Then, after three virtually problem-free months, the boy had a relapse in many areas as his mother was preparing to enter the hospital for surgery. Renewed parental counseling led to reinstatement of the original procedures and to the reemergence of adequate behavior on the boy's part, which was maintained over a period of at least fifteen months.

COMMENTARY: The authors show how a functional analysis approach can be applied to obsessive-compulsive behavior. They combine therapeutic procedures used directly with the child with indirect methods to modify the environmental factors that serve to establish or maintain the problem behavior. Their work highlights the importance of discovering and addressing what parents and other key individuals are doing to reinforce the troublesome behavior. It is a striking contrast to approaches that focus only on the child's psychodynamics and miss the importance of changing environmental responses.

SOURCE: Queiroz, L. O. de S., Motta, M. A., Madi, M.B.B.P.,

Sossai, D. L., and Boren, J. J. "A Functional Analysis of Obsessive-Compulsive Problems with Related Therapeutic Procedures." *Behavioral Research and Therapy*, 1981, *19*, 377–
388.

Behavioral Treatment of a
Boy's Chronic Lip Biting

AUTHOR: Lionel Sasson Lyon

PRECIS: Rapid cure of compulsive lip biting and face scarring
in a twelve-year-old boy by combining several behavioral methods.

INTRODUCTION: In this case, chronic and compulsive lip biting was eliminated by means of behavioral techniques involving
self-monitoring, self-control, and aversive response substitution
in the context of a collaboration between the therapist and the
youngster.

CASE STUDY: A sixth grader, M, had disfigured his face by repeatedly biting his lips and wiping excess saliva from his cheeks.
At the time treatment began, his lips were raw and sore, and he
had a three-inch red line with open sores along his left cheek
that extended diagonally alongside the edge of his mouth. M
was highly motivated to work on ways to stop his compulsive
behavior, which had been happening since he was in kindergarten.

TREATMENT: The treatment took place over a period of five
weeks. Lyon first counted the frequency of M's lip biting in the
boy's classroom over three observation periods, and he obtained
a baseline rate of about one incident per minute. Then he gave
M a knitting counter and instructed him to (1) record each time

he felt the lip-biting impulse and (2) dab Vaseline on his lips instead of biting them at these times.

M's lip biting was reduced from more than 1,500 episodes during the first week of treatment to a single episode during the fourth week the treatment procedure was in effect. However, he persisted in wiping his sleeve across his lips to remove excess Vaseline. This caused his facial irritation to remain unhealed. At this point, Lyon introduced an aversive response substitution method to help M control sleeve wiping. A three-inch by eight-inch swatch of sandpaper was attached to the boy's left wrist, coarse side up, with two rubber bands. Masking tape at the edges of the stiff sandpaper kept it from causing discomfort to the boy's wrist. The presence of the sandpaper ended M's sleeve-wiping behavior within one day. Then Lyon taught the boy to substitute relaxation for sleeve wiping, by following Wolpe's procedure (see Wolpe, J. *The Practice of Behavior Therapy.* [3rd ed.] Elmsford, N.Y.: Pergamon Press, 1982). Whenever the boy raised his hand, he was to recognize that action as a signal for relaxing instead of the beginning of the compulsive face-wiping ritual.

The treatment eliminated all occurrences of lip biting and all traces of M's facial sores by the fifth week. The youngster reported no more urge to bite his lips, and he said that he often used the relaxation response. Through observation two-and-a-half months later and telephone follow-up seven months after treatment, Lyon concluded that all gains were fully maintained.

COMMENTARY: Lyon demonstrates the effectiveness of a behavioral treatment for compulsive lip biting. The success of the intervention reported here may be attributed in part to the boy's high level of motivation to be rid of the annoying and disfiguring compulsive behavior. Where such incentive is not initially present, therapists might do well to invest time at the beginning of treatment in establishing incentive to change. This may involve emphasizing the relationship-building aspects of therapy at first and sometimes working with others in the child's environment (parents, teachers, and so on) to arrange response contingencies in reaction to the youngster's observed patterns of behavior. When quick, effective treatment methods for compulsive behaviors are available, we believe that therapists are obligated to use them regardless of their theoretical beliefs.

SOURCE: Lyon, L. S. "A Behavioral Treatment of Compulsive Lip-Biting." *Journal of Behavior Therapy and Experimental Psychiatry*, 1983, *14* (3), 275-276.

Rapid Elimination of Obsessional Symptoms via Response Prevention and Desensitization

AUTHOR: Lynn Stanley

PRECIS: Quickly extinguishing the compulsive rituals of an eight-year-old girl by involving her entire family as therapists to restrict expression of the compulsive behaviors.

INTRODUCTION: On the basis of a survey of research relating to obsessional symptoms, Stanley concludes that symptom control is least likely to be accomplished via systematic desensitization and most probable when the treatment chosen is response prevention. This treatment method involves restricting the expression of the ritualistic behavior. Since ritualistic behavior patterns often involve members of a patient's family, as was the case with the girl in Stanley's report, it makes sense to follow a treatment strategy that aims to manage the compulsions in the home.

CASE STUDY: Amanda's "fussiness"—her excessive checking behavior while dressing and undressing and regarding toys and ornaments—worried her parents. Because of the girl's ritualistic actions, for example, insistently dressing herself three times, she needed more than twenty minutes each morning to get dressed, where previously she could get dressed in five minutes.

The rituals had been observed for a half year before therapy began. They first became evident after Amanda's family relocated to a new area for the second time over a three-year period.

Amanda admitted being saddened by the way her "fussiness" restricted her relationships with her friends. Because she feared the ornaments, toys, and so on in her bedroom tampered with, she no longer invited playmates to her home. A once-happy child, Amanda now appeared cranky and tearful a majority of the time.

TREATMENT: Stanley enlisted the entire family as Amanda's therapists, under the professional therapist's supervision and with her guidance. The first step of the treatment program entailed the family members writing down everything they did to keep Amanda from becoming upset. The therapist discussed with the family members how they might have been inadvertently contributing to maintaining Amanda's rituals, and the family members modified such behaviors. For example, Amanda's mother stopped spending several minutes daily checking that the fringes of the bedcover in her daughter's room fell equally on all sides of the bed, because this was a part of Amanda's checking ritual at bedtime each night.

Stanley learned from Amanda that she was upset the most by feeling compelled to repeat such actions as dressing several times. The therapist forged an agreement with the girl whereby her parents were permitted to stop her from performing any dressing action more than once. Stanley explained to Amanda and her parents that by preventing a ritual from being carried out in this way, Amanda would lose the compulsive urge and thus would observe the ritual progressively less.

After an initially high level of anxiety that lasted for two days, Amanda began to relax, and the number of symptoms decreased sizably. After a week, Stanley had Amanda's parents introduce a desensitization hierarchy. They presented her with situations of progressively greater "upset" value. These were chosen because formerly they would have set off ritualistic behavior by the youngster. Such triggering situations included getting dressed and undressed, making her bed, toileting, and putting her toys away after she finished playing with them. Amanda's parents observed her as these situations were introduced, and they prevented her from carrying out any rituals by talking to her about the unwanted behavior whenever it emerged.

The response prevention and desensitization program led to the disappearance of all symptoms within two weeks. No symptoms were substituted for those that were extinguished. The girl felt increasingly at ease, and she resumed her active regimen with friends. After six months, and at twelve-month follow-up, treatment gains were fully maintained.

COMMENTARY: Stanley believes that treatment of compulsions at home is most beneficial. This case offers a good example of a therapist coalescing the resources and motivation of an entire family to eliminate one family member's ritualistic behaviors. Stanley's approach appears particularly promising where other family members desire to be of help to the compulsive member. Also, in cases such as Amanda's, in which the symptomatology has been of short duration and where the child very much wants to be rid of the rituals, the method of intervention described in this article appears to hold great promise.

SOURCE: Stanley, L. "Treatment of Ritualistic Behaviour in an Eight-Year-Old Girl by Response Prevention: A Case Report." *Journal of Child Psychology and Psychiatry*, 1980, *21*, 85-90.

Treating Obsessive-Compulsive Youngsters Who Are Angry

AUTHORS: Derek Bolton and Trevor Turner

PRECIS: Containing distress and fury, providing warm support plus behavior therapy to help children with obsessive-compulsive neurosis and impulse control problems.

INTRODUCTION: Most obsessive-compulsive children tend to be over-controlled and compliant. Treatment is complicated when obsessive-compulsive problems coexist with conduct disorders. Bolton and Turner address the requirements of a treatment program for such youngsters, whose treatment needs to take into account their impulse control problems.

METHODS: Bolton and Turner believe that the management of obsessive-compulsives who exhibit conduct disorders needs to involve a number of professional disciplines (for example, psychology, psychiatry, nursing) and a combination of therapeutic modalities (individual therapy, group and family therapy, medication), varying in combination and duration according to the circumstances of each case. In their view, essential requirements of treatment for such youngsters are: (1) a safe, private inpatient treatment facility, where wards and areas within them can be locked, (2) a veteran staff of psychiatric nurses working together with psychological and medical professionals, (3) consensus about the objectives and procedures used for assessment and treatment, with a comprehensive, clear program of treatment, (4) explicit agreement granted in writing by the patient and his or her parents allowing the therapists to set limits on tantrums (as by locking wards) and to continue treatment even though the patient may be resisting, (5) determination to persist in treating the youngster when he or she shows acting out and threatening behavior.

CASE STUDY: Fourteen-year-old Colin was tyrannical in his home. Also, for the past year, he had had a phobia about dirt and germs, which caused him to engage in washing rituals and to avoid objects he believed were "contaminated." Two years earlier, he had threatened to kill himself. At the time residential treatment began, Colin appeared depressed and anxious, and he expressed guilt about "wronging his family."

Colin's hospital treatment did not progress for several months until Colin agreed to try a program entailing progressive exposure to feared situations with response prevention. While good progress was made relative to the boy's compulsive behavior, he exhibited self-injuriousness, expressed a wish to die, vandalized the ward, set a fire, and triggered fire alarms. Over six weeks of treatment totaling 100 hours, Colin was closely supervised and contained. Most of the time, two nurses observed him. Tranquilizing and antidepressant medications were administered during this period.

A year after the behavioral program ended, Colin was doing well. He attended a regular boarding school, and he showed no disturbed behavior there or at home. His obsessive-compulsive behaviors were not at all evident.

COMMENTARY: Children often display a combination of problematic behaviors. Treatment of certain symptoms requires strong structure when the child poses a danger to himself, others, or property. Bolton and Turner provide a good example of a situation in which strict external behavioral controls needed to be established and adhered to in order for a child's obsessive-compulsive symptoms to be treated. Throughout, he needed reassurance and support—to allow the behavioral program to begin and continue and particularly when he became flooded by anxiety and self-destructive ideas. The authors aptly remind the reader that the timing and pace of interventions is, in the end, a matter of clinical judgment.

SOURCE: Bolton, D., and Turner, T. "Obsessive-Compulsive Neurosis With Conduct Disorder in Adolescence: A Report of Two Cases." *Journal of Child Psychology and Psychiatry*, 1984, *25*, 133-139.

Additional Readings

Allyon, T., Garber, S. W., and Allison, M. G. "Behavioral Treatment of Childhood Neurosis." *Psychiatry*, 1977, *40*, 315-322.

The authors successfully treated a five-year-old boy for obsessive-compulsive fascination with electrical devices, ritualistic sleeping with his parents, and negativistic refusal to follow his parents' instructions. Treatment was conceptualized and carried out within a behavioral framework. The therapists introduced a motivational system that consisted of a token economy for rewarding desired behavior together with time-out from reinforcement and a response-cost procedure to respond to the boy's inappropriate ritualistic behaviors and disobedience. The behavioral procedures eliminated all the boy's symptoms within four weeks. At follow-up two years later, he remained symptom-free.

Bolton, D., Collins, S. and Steinberg, D. "The Treatment of Obsessive-Compulsive Disorder in Adolescence: A Report of Fifteen Cases." *British Journal of Psychiatry*, 1983, *142*, 456-464.

Fifteen youngsters, ages twelve to eighteen, with a primary diagnosis of chronic obsessive-compulsive disorder, received response-prevention treatment and family therapy. They also received milieu therapy, counseling support, and/or medication concurrently. Treatment duration ranged from one month to two years. Thirteen of the patients improved; of these, seven had their symptoms eliminated. In most cases, treatment gains were maintained.

Clark, D. A., Sugrim, I., and Bolton, D. "Primary Obsessional Slowness: A Nursing Treatment Programme With a 13-Year-Old Male Adolescent." *Behaviour Research and Therapy*, 1982, *20*, 289-292.

Primary obsessional slowness, as opposed to slowness that is a by-product of other compulsive rituals, is characterized by debilitating slowness with self-care activities in the absence of intrusive and unacceptable thoughts, anxiety, or resistance to the slow, meticulous behavior. A prepubertal thirteen-year-old with a five-year history of this disorder was treated by means of a nursing intervention program that consisted of prompting, pacing and shaping, and participant modeling of four types of self-care behavior. Treatment resulted in improvement within two weeks. However, the boy suffered a relapse. The authors suggest as possible reasons for the decay the long-standing and probably severe nature of the boy's disorder and the insufficiency of the behavior change that resulted from treatment.

Kellerman, J. "Hypnosis as an Adjunct to Thought-Stopping and Covert Reinforcement in the Treatment of Homicidal Obsessions in a 12-Year-Old Boy." *International Journal of Clinical and Experimental Hypnosis*, 1981, *29*, 128-135.

Kellerman reports that an integration of hypnosis and behavior therapy techniques produced quick and durable reduction in a boy's matricidal obsessions. The author helped the boy redefine the symptoms so that he came to view them not as strange "feelings" that had a hold over him but, rather, as fairly common thoughts amenable to cognitive control. Hypnotic training facilitated relaxation in the boy and increased the vividness of the images he created before the cognitive restructuring procedures of thought stopping, covert reinforcement, and paradoxical instruction were used. The boy practiced the behavior therapy techniques at home, and his parents helped by refraining from discussing his obsessions within the family and expressing confidence in his ability to help himself.

Phillips, D., and Wolpe, S. "Multiple Behavioral Techniques in Severe Separation Anxiety of a Twelve-Year-Old." *Journal of Behaviour Therapy and Experimental Psychiatry*, 1981, *12*, 329-330.

A twelve-year-old boy's obsessive-compulsive disorder and severe separation anxiety failed to respond to psychoanalytic treatment. Subsequently, two years (eighty-eight sessions) of behavior therapy proved effective in diminishing his symptoms. Procedures included relaxation; systematic desensitization; *in vivo* desensitization at the clinic, at home, and in school; and graduated reduction of ritual behaviors. The authors note that the severity of the boy's problems and extreme family stress necessitated the unusually lengthy treatment in this case.

Hysterical Behavior

Hysterical behavior is some loss or alteration of physical functioning that is not due to any physical disorder. It usually involves sensory or motor systems. Many terms are used to describe this problem, such as hysteria, hysterical neurosis, conversion hysteria, *and, more recently,* conversion disorder *(see* American Psychiatric Association. Diagnostic and Statistical Manual of Mental Disorders. *[3rd ed.] Washington, D.C.: American Psychiatric Association, 1980). Symptoms can resemble those of many diseases, and physical disorders (especially neurological) must be carefully ruled out. Conscious malingering where secondary gains are prominent must also be considered. Recent evidence suggests that underlying depression must be evaluated and treated if present.*

At one time, hysterical behavior was thought to be rare, but more and more cases have been reported recently. Much of the literature has been based on a psychoanalytic or psychodynamic point of view. Thus, symptoms are viewed as expressions of repressed or emotional conflicts, and treatment focuses on resolving these conflicts. An alternative approach is based on learning theory. Here symptoms are viewed as learned maladaptive behaviors, and behavioral methods are used to eliminate the symptoms and promote adaptive functioning. We believe that effective treatment often involves a direct behavioral method to eliminate symptoms and treatment of family or personal problems if they exist.

A Behavioral Treatment Package in Treating Elective Mutism

AUTHORS: Johnny L. Matson, Karen Esveldt-Dawson, and Daniel O'Donnell

PRECIS: Restoring speech in a nine-year-old boy through the use of overcorrection, modeling, and reinforcement.

INTRODUCTION: Todd spoke normally until he was six years old, then he ceased speaking altogether. He tapped, pointed, and nodded his head to communicate. A fourth grader in school, Todd had acquired academic skills at grade-appropriate levels, but he was starting to fall behind his classmates' level of achievement on reading and memory tasks. Todd had no neurological or physical problems. Prior to treatment, the boy had undergone thirty-seven speech therapy sessions, which proved ineffective.

TREATMENT: A treatment package involving various positive and aversive methods, such as modeling, performance feedback, and overcorrection, was applied in one-to-one sessions by staff members of an inpatient hospital for emotionally disturbed children, in which Todd resided. They held two sessions daily (morning and afternoon), which lasted ten to twenty minutes each. Each session was recorded on audiotape. The therapist presented Todd with ten four-inch by four-inch white stimulus cards in random sequence. Each of these portrayed one animal or familiar object or body part in silhouette. The boy's task was to name the picture he was shown after the therapist modeled it. When ten seconds of exposure elicited no response, the therapist repeated the query. After another ten seconds, if Todd did not respond, the therapist moved on to the next stimulus (baseline phase) or used overcorrection (training phase). Then ten stimulus cards showing one noun each were presented to the boy. The therapist pronounced a word and then Todd had to say it. After this, the therapist asked Todd to imitate "yes" and "no." Finally, the boy was required to respond appropriately to "yes" and "no" questions.

The treatment contingencies were applied in the following manner:

Positive Reinforcement. When Todd gave an appropriate response, he received one cent plus verbal praise. Also, he received a two-inch by two-inch slip of white paper on which was written the number 1. Todd could exchange this for one minute of free time with any adult he chose. Backup reinforcers could be purchased with various sums of the money Todd accumulated.

Overcorrection. When he responded inappropriately, Todd had to write the stimulus word ten times.

A ten-inch by ten-inch chart posted in Todd's room showed how many minutes of exclusive attention and how many pennies Todd earned during each session. Target behaviors for which Todd earned reinforcement progressed over time, as follows: imitates lip movements, imitates sounds, imitates "yes" and "no" words, imitates nouns, answers "yes" and "no" questions.

The treatment procedure succeeded in reestablishing all the speech behaviors targeted. Imitating "yes" and "no" was trained at a slower rate than the target behaviors that preceded it, but still only a few treatment sessions were needed. Generalization was slow, as Todd at first resisted speaking in the presence of adults other than the trainer. However, some verbalization, including saying words that had not been trained, was observed on the ward during the latter part of the two-month treatment. Two months after treatment was concluded, Todd maintained the gains that he had achieved.

COMMENTARY: The authors successfully used learning theory principles in the treatment of elective mutism. The combination of positive and aversive methods is probably better suited to cases such as this one, in which reinstating speech is the objective, than it is to instances in which the teaching of speech is the issue. The importance of training for generalization cannot be overemphasized. Opportunities for practice of newly acquired or reacquired skills in different places with different people should be built into the training regimen in order to ensure that therapy establishes skills that can be transferred across sit-

uations and settings. Therapists should be encouraged to use
these procedures in the natural environments of home and
school. Positive results may be obtained when reinforcement is
used in a less formal manner. Parents and teachers can use the
methods presented as adapted to their settings by the therapist.

SOURCE: Matson, J. L., Esveldt-Dawson, K., and O'Donnell, D.
"Overcorrection, Modeling, and Reinforcement Procedures
for Reinstating Speech in a Mute Boy." *Child Behavior Therapy,* 1979, *1* (4), 363–371.

Treating Conversion Disorders by Helping Children Understand Their Learning Disabilities

AUTHOR: Larry B. Silver

PRECIS: Eliminating pseudoseizures by identifying unrecognized and untreated learning disabilities as major sources of children's stress and building the children's coping repertoires.

INTRODUCTION: Learning disabilities that presumably derive
from central nervous system dysfunction are increasingly recognized as a major mental health problem, as well as an educational challenge. Silver observes that many learning disabled
children and adolescents develop emotional problems secondary
to their learning disorder because of their chronic frustrations
with the demands of school. In the case studies Silver presents,
two adolescents whose learning disabilities had not been diagnosed or treated developed a conversion disorder with pseudoseizures as a way to cope with the stresses they experienced.
Conversion disorders, formerly called *hysteria,* are characterized
by loss of or alteration in physical functioning that suggests
physical disorder but that instead apparently is an expression of

a psychological conflict or need. Conversion disorders are involuntary and inexplicable by any physical disorder or known pathogenic factor. One of the two cases Silver describes is that of John.

CASE STUDY: John always did poorly in school. When he was in third grade, John's teacher told his parents that he was lazy. In fifth grade, the school reported that he "might not be as bright as you would like." Every year he received mediocre and near-failing grades, but no formal evaluations were ever conducted. John's two younger siblings received mostly A's. Over time, John developed an image of himself as stupid, and he doubted that he would ever complete high school. When he was younger, John fought a lot with other children. This was the result of the enormous frustrations he felt ("I took it out on other kids"). Later, he held in the anger he continued to feel toward his teachers, but his peer relationships failed to improve, and he spent much time by himself. During his senior year of high school, John evidenced three to four "seizures" weekly. These appeared as convulsive movements and wild thrashing about while he made gurgling sounds. Just prior to the onset of each seizure episode, John felt as if he were going to panic and scream. Afterward, he could not recall the episodes. Comprehensive medical and neurological evaluations found no apparent cause for John's seizures. A trial of phenytoin sodium (Dilantin) and phenobarbital yielded no improvement.

TREATMENT: Silver saw John alone, with his parents, and with his entire family. He learned that John felt extremely dependent on his parents and that he was afraid of leaving home to go to college. Another central theme brought out was John's sense of himself as "damaged" and as one devoid of much intelligence. The author helped John understand that a major source of tension for him was the community, school, and family value system that placed a premium on attending college immediately following graduation from high school.

The therapist shared his impressions, derived from interviews and psychological and educational testing, first with John and then with his parents and siblings. Silver felt that John was very intelligent but that he manifested tremendous unevenness in his mental abilities, with his visuo-perceptual skills being much weaker than his verbal comprehension capabilities. His short-term memory, sequencing, and perceptual-motor problems were explained to the boy and his family. The insights that he gained served to relieve John of the burden of thinking of himself as retarded and altered his self-image ("You mean there's a reason for my problems . . . I'm not dumb or lazy?"). His parents' anger at the school for the years John suffered misdirected education at first reassured the boy; later, he voiced his anger at his parents for not "doing something about it."

As individual and family psychotherapy continued, along with private special education therapy, a post–high school plan was developed for John. This entailed getting a job, living at home, and continuing educational therapy while deferring any decisions about college. One month after his initial appointment, John's seizure activity was evident once a week, where it had been three times more frequent before Silver began seeing the youngster; from the date of the meeting at which the therapist reviewed the full evaluation results, John was entirely "seizure-free." Over the next several months, psychotherapy helped John better understand how his past behavior problems related to his frustrations in learning. He became more self-confident, insightful, and able to talk about his feelings with his family and friends. A year after graduating from high school, John was working successfully at a sales job, living with friends, and maintaining good relations with members of his family.

COMMENTARY: This article illustrates how stresses that originate in school can bring about a generalized poor self-image, lack of confidence, noncoping state, and conversion disorder. It highlights the enormous therapeutic value of identifying and clarifying the source of stress and building the patient's repertoire of coping skills. Therapists must make sure that learning disabilities are specifically identified. Many children and adolescents today experience extreme pressures to achieve in school. These pressures start in the early grades and continue unabated, accelerating as the youngsters progress through the secondary grade levels. Young people with learning disorders are particularly vulnerable to developing psychosomatic symptoms in such circumstances. Mental health professionals can play a vital role in early detection and secondary prevention efforts with the youths and members of their family. In addition, they can help in primary prevention efforts, through the in-service training of teachers and sensitization of nonhandicapped youngsters about their peers who are learning disabled, as well as consultatively— by advising school administrators as to suitable accommodations and classroom approaches for educating handicapped students alongside their nonhandicapped peers.

SOURCE: Silver, L. B. "Conversion Disorder with Pseudoseizures in Adolescence: A Stress Reaction to Unrecognized and Untreated Learning Disabilities." *Journal of the American Academy of Child Psychiatry*, 1982, *21*, 508-512.

Integrative Psychotherapy for Treating Psychogenic Pain and Cough

AUTHORS: Saul Lindenbaum and Deborah Clark

PRECIS: Two cases illustrating a multilevel approach to treatment of psychosomatic illness in children.

INTRODUCTION: Lindenbaum and Clark observe that psychogenic abdominal pain is found among 10 percent of six- to fifteen-year-old children and that psychogenic cough is a common phenomenon. The authors describe the use of an integrated approach to psychotherapy with children suffering these and other disorders. Their approach entails investigating three levels of the presenting problem and its antecedents and consequences: the *biological, interpersonal,* and *intrapsychic* levels of explanation. Among the cases the authors present to illustrate how the approach can contribute to matching techniques to problems and integrating diverse psychotherapies are the two cases described below.

CASE STUDY 1: Beth, age nine, coughed in a bark-like fashion so frequently that conversation with her was difficult. Within her family, Beth was the youngest of three children, and she habitually played the role of peacemaker. She did very well in school, and she had no history of behavior problems. Tests (*biological* level) found no medical basis for her coughing problem. At the *interpersonal* level of analysis, the authors hypothesized that Beth was deriving many secondary gains from her family members (such as attention), which contributed to maintaining her symptom. Also, they surmised that her brother's history of croup provided Beth with a role model for choosing this particular symptom. *Intrapsychically,* the authors felt that Beth's cough masked angry feelings. Also, death anxiety triggered by the death of the girl's great-uncle was thought to play a role.

On the basis of this analysis of Beth's problem, the authors selected family therapy as the initial treatment modality. They carried out behavioral change with extinction procedures because her cough was so bothersome to others. This entailed teaching behavior modification methods to Beth's parents. The therapists utilized reframing to modify the parents' thinking toward Beth. For example, "noise" was substituted for "cough" in discussing the symptom; "Beth's difficulty waiting her turn" replaced talk of her feeling left out and not getting enough attention.

After the cough abated, the therapists instituted other interventions to address how the family thought and behaved regarding the expression of anger. Beth participated in play therapy and role plays, and she observed role models. Reframing allowed her parents to appreciate their daughter's new "assertiveness" instead of complaining of her "rudeness." Treatment proceeded for nine months, until terminated by the family. Follow-up after one and two years showed that Beth was doing nicely, with no symptom recurrence.

CASE STUDY 2: Twelve-year-old Seth suffered severe and chronic lower abdominal pain, which caused him to remain home all but four days during the first four months of school. He remained awake very late at night and then slept much of the subsequent day. Seth was the only child in his family, and his parents were in their forties when he was born. Theirs was a marriage devoid of much shared time or interests. Seth's history included mild hyperactivity and learning disabilities.

It was unclear, at the *biological* level, whether any actual lesion caused Seth pain. At the *interpersonal* level, the boy's stomach pains were viewed as useful in channeling his mother's energies toward him so as to ward off overt marital problems and depression. They also allowed him to remove himself from his stressful school setting. *Intrapsychically,* then, Seth was able to protect his self-esteem, but this was at the cost of relinquishing his striving for independence and his sense of physical well-being.

Ten therapy sessions were held over a period of six months. The authors selected the following treatment modalities on the basis of the integrative evaluation of Seth's problem: (1) Family therapy. This was chosen to modify the familial interaction pattern that created and maintained the boy's symptoms; (2) Self-monitoring (creating a diary). The authors hoped to gain more understanding of the pain's onset and its course; (3) Paradoxical request. Seth was asked to produce the pain at a prearranged time daily, as a way to help him gain control over it; (4) Anxiety arousal. This entailed sharing "horror stories" about families that were prosecuted for not sending their child to school in order to arouse the family's fear level about allowing Seth to remain at home; (5) Application of logical consequences. If Seth did not go to school, he had to wake up at schooltime nonetheless and do house- and yardwork during school hours. At night, he was required to go to bed at a normal time.

The combination of methods led to the disappearance of Seth's pain and his return to school within two weeks. At follow-up eighteen months after treatment ended, Seth was still attending school, and he was free of abdominal discomfort.

COMMENTARY: The advantage of Lindenbaum and Clark's integrative approach is its comprehensiveness. By considering biological, interpersonal, and intrapsychic bases for symptoms and interactions of antecedents and consequences across all three of these domains, therapists may effect individualized matches between techniques and problems. Also, they can construct a framework for integrating diverse psychotherapeutic modalities. The eclectic approach used fits directly with the purpose of this book: specific, effective treatment methods for identified problems.

SOURCE: Lindenbaum, S., and Clark, D. "Toward an Integrative Approach to Psychotherapy with Children." *American Journal of Orthopsychiatry*, 1983, *53* (3), 449–459.

Operant Methods in the Treatment of Hysterical Paralysis

AUTHORS: Alan M. Delamater, Neil Rosenbloom, C. Keith Conners, and Linda Hertweck

PRECIS: Describes the use of behavioral techniques, including withdrawal of reinforcement for hysterical behavior and the use of successive approximations of walking behavior, with a ten-and-a-half-year-old boy exhibiting hysterical paralysis of both legs.

INTRODUCTION: The authors observe that most literature on child conversion reactions assumes a psychoanalytic orientation, with sensory, motor, or psychic symptoms viewed as manifesting a repressed conflict. Their work represents an alternative point of view based on learning theory and behavioral methods. The authors see symptoms as learned maladaptive behaviors to be modified through the application of learning principles. This article represents one of the few published accounts of treating children's conversion disorders with operant techniques.

CASE STUDY: The boy studied was a patient hospitalized in an intensive psychiatric program for children. In the four months before he entered the hospital, he took ill, displaying multiple somatic symptoms, including congestion, vomiting, abdominal pain, and severe weight loss. He entered the hospital, but testing at that time revealed no medical basis for these problems. They persisted, however, and a couple of months later the boy developed a leg paralysis, which led to another hospitalization. When, again, no medical problems could be detected, the boy was transferred to a psychiatric inpatient unit.

Significant features of the youngster's history included transgenerational psychosomatic reactivity on both sides of the family. The boy's school record revealed a school phobic diagnosis made in third grade, at which time he was absent forty-five days. The patient's symptoms began two days after his father had returned home from a six weeks' stay in a vocational rehabilitation center, where he had gone after experiencing functional illnesses due to anxiety. Simultaneously, the youngster's mother left home to visit relatives. At the time he was seen initially, the boy was completely immobile, ate little, looked lethargic and dejected, isolated himself from other children on the ward, and remained inactive. He spoke little, except for stating physical complaints, moaning, and crying out for help.

TREATMENT: The treatment goal was for the boy to walk by himself. The authors decided to work toward gradual realization of this goal. Accordingly, the boy was rewarded with a star posted on a chart in his room every time he completed a step of a twelve-part program, each of which successively approximated walking. The twelve steps ranged from maintaining a kneeling position on his hands and knees without collapsing for five seconds to walking six feet without support. Social reinforcers were administered as payoffs when the child achieved specified behavioral objectives within the twelve-step sequence. These payoffs included an activity with a staff member, play time with a toy he chose, or an activity with other children. The boy could choose to spend forty-five minutes so engaged, or he could save up the reinforcers he earned in order to accrue more time for later use. To make the reinforcers more salient, the authors arranged that the boy remained confined to his room, which was devoid of entertainment (books, toys, radio, cards, and so on) or of opportunities to engage with other children, during times other than those he earned as reinforcers. Prior to beginning the treatment program, the boy signed an agreement that spelled out the terms of the behavior contingency system.

The behavioral program was administered simultaneously with twice-weekly supportive individual therapy, weekly family therapy, and milieu therapy on the ward, which included nine other severely disturbed children. Staff nurses who were trained in a naturalistic observation system recorded the boy's behaviors on dimensions of gross motor movement, inactivity, vocalizations, and isolation over three sampling periods weekly. These occurred during school instruction periods, at lunch, and while the boy had a free play period.

Over a ten-week period, the behavioral program achieved a dramatic increase in the boy's gross motor behavior, defined as trunk movement through space. Also, his periods of complete inactivity were drastically reduced, the number of spoken words he addressed to others increased over fourfold, and his isolation from others was lessened considerably. Also, over this time, the staff reported a marked decrease in his deviant behaviors. This was confirmed by the boy's parents, who observed dramatic reductions in his deviant symptoms, with the most pronounced improvements occurring in the areas of physical symptoms, affect and interpersonal behavior, and speech and thought. These were sustained over a six-month period following the boy's discharge from the hospital.

COMMENTARY: The authors demonstrate the effectiveness of behavioral treatment techniques for children who develop conversion symptoms. Their results attest to the fact that behavior modification techniques are particularly effective when, as was the case here, therapy is directed toward making the symptoms unrewarding while shaping incompatible desired behaviors. The use of social reinforcers in this case indicates that such behavioral treatment programs can be carried out relatively economically. Also illustrated here is the role resident professional staff members can play in conducting a program of behavior modification. Perhaps paraprofessionals can be trained to fulfill some of the data-gathering and reward-administering functions of such a program, in order to safeguard valuable professional time and result in even greater cost savings. It would be wise whenever behavioral methods are being introduced within an institutional setting to attend carefully to staff training, including giving consideration to any negative attitudes staff may initially have toward behavior modification.

In the present case, clearly, the child's symptoms appeared in the context of long-standing family psychopathology. Consequently, the concurrent use of other therapeutic modalities, including family therapy, had to be carefully carried out. The chances of recurrence of the main symptom in the future are diminished as the behavioral program is backed up by therapy that brings about structural changes in the family process; this in turn allows the child's continued development to occur.

SOURCE: Delamater, A. M., Rosenbloom, N., Conners, C. K., and Hertweck, L. "The Behavioral Treatment of Hysterical Paralysis in a Ten-Year-Old Boy: A Case Study." *Journal of the American Academy of Child Psychiatry,* 1983, 22, 73-79.

Using Psychotropic Drugs to Eliminate Conversion Symptoms

AUTHORS: Elizabeth B. Weller and Ronald A. Weller

PRECIS: Removing a prominent conversion symptom that masked major depression by treating a ten-year-old boy with amobarbital.

CASE STUDY: John presented with acute pain in his right ear that did not respond to antibiotics and other medication. After two months, he became worse; John could no longer move his neck because of the intense pain. Hospitalized, the boy showed negative CAT scan and EEG records. When his pain subsided somewhat, he returned home. The next day, upon returning to school, John's right foot became numb. The numbness departed when the boy's shoe was removed, but it returned the next day. John said to his mother, "My foot is dead." Admitted once again to a hospital, John soon reported that his trunk, upper extremities, and left leg were paralyzed. The boy became quadriplegic. Tests found no neurological or physiological basis for this condition, and John was transferred to a child psychiatry unit. There he looked sad, averted his eyes from others, and called himself "stupid" and "a fool," but he denied that he was bothered by any problems.

TREATMENT: Amobarbital (250 mg.) was administered intravenously, and John was interviewed. During the amobarbital interview he cried and told of being awakened at night by voices telling him to kill his parents and himself. He reported that two months prior to the onset of his ear and facial pain, he had set a fire to kill his entire family "because the voices told me I was no good and did not have any reason to live." Following the amobarbital interview, John was able to walk without pain, but depressive symptoms surfaced, with ideas about suicide and auditory hallucinations. Imipramine treatment was begun for the youth's obvious depression. Within three weeks, noticeable improvement was evident in the youngster's schoolwork, his amount of verbalization, and his appetite and sleep behavior. The homicidal and suicidal ideation disappeared, and John no longer experienced hallucinations.

COMMENTARY: This brief case presentation reported a conversion reaction that was prominent in the context of and that obscured a major depressive episode with psychotic features. After John's conversion symptom was recognized as functional, it was removed with an amobarbital interview, enabling his depressive symptoms to become more obvious. The depression was then treated with imipramine. Weller and Weller state that the possibility of a major depressive episode should be considered whenever children's conversion reactions are being evaluated. Once the conversion symptom has been removed, individual and family treatment procedures for the child's depression can proceed. Although the authors report the successful use of medication, psychotherapeutic approaches have been effective without drugs.

SOURCE: Weller, E. B., and Weller, R. A. "Case Report of Conversion Symptom Associated with Major Depressive Disorder in a Child." *American Journal of Psychiatry,* 1983, *140* (8), 1079-1080.

Additional Readings

Goodyer, I. "Hysterical Conversion Reactions in Childhood." *Journal of Child Psychology and Psychiatry,* 1981, *22,* 179-188.

Goodyer reviews the literature on childhood hysteria and perform a retrospective analysis of fifteen cases. He states that compared to adult hysterical conversion reactions, far less has been written about children with this disorder. Also, there is lack of clarity about the definition and incidence of conversion reactions. It appears that boys and girls are about equally likely to suffer conversion symptoms and that presentation before five years of age is extremely rare. Family-oriented assessment and treatment merit consideration, Goodyer believes, when children manifest hysterical conversion reactions.

Hendrix, E. M., Thompson, L. M., and Rau, B. W. "Behavioral Treatment of an 'Hysterically' Clenched Fist." *Behaviour Therapy and Experimental Psychiatry,* 1978, *9,* 273-276.

The authors implemented a behavioral program to relieve a fourteen-year-old hospitalized girl of a hysterical conversion reaction. Prior to treatment, the girl's right fist had been clenched for three months. The girl was taught to use progressive muscle relaxation procedures, for which she received rewards in the form of praise from the therapist and congratulations from the ward staff and other patients. Her discharge from the hospital was made contingent on symptom remission. Simultaneously, the girl's parents ceased reinforcing her complaints and requests to leave. Monthly follow-up for nine months revealed that the fist clenching did not reappear. However, other somatic ailments surfaced and were apparently reinforced. The authors feel that family members play a vital role in preventing and diminishing sick role enactment. They conclude by suggesting ways that intervention might have been more successful.

Lazarus, P. J., Gavilo, H. M., and Moore, J. W. "The Treatment of Elective Mutism in Children Within the School Setting: Two Case Studies." *School Psychology Review*. 1983, *12*, 467–472.

The authors present two case studies in which behavior therapy techniques were used to treat electively mute children in school. With the first child, a six-year-old girl, the classroom teacher and speech pathologist applied contingency management treatment techniques (shaping and successive approximations) over four months to produce spontaneous conversation. The authors used a combination of family and behavior therapies to help the other child, a seven-year-old girl. In three family sessions (one per week for an hour apiece), the therapist defined and clarified each member's role within the family and discouraged their overinvolvement, control, and dependency relative to the others. The therapist then used shaping and reinforcement of successive approximations of normal speech in three-per-week behavior therapy sessions for six weeks. Toys, food, and social activities were used as reinforcers. One-to-one therapy sessions employed a tape recorder and practice and rehearsal techniques Subsequently, first one other child, then several children, then the teacher, and finally the girl's reading group participated as the therapy site was moved from an isolated room to the back of the classroom. As therapy progressed, responsibility for promoting speech was transferred gradually from the school psychologist to the classroom teacher. The authors report that these interventions produced change in the amount the girl talked with the teacher and with classmates.

Lipton, H. "Rapid Reinstatement of Speech Using Stimulus Fading with a Selectively Mute Child." *Journal of Behaviour Therapy and Experimental Psychiatry,* 1980, *11,* 147–149.

A combined stimulus-fading and contingent management program was used to help a six-year-old girl who did not speak at all at school or at home with her friends. Speech was reinforced initially in one-to-one structured game-playing and activity sessions with the therapist. Beads for a necklace served as reinforcements. The girl earned these, at first, for whispering loudly enough to move a piece of string held approximately five inches from her mouth. Later, the string was removed and the girl earned beads first for louder volumes and then for conversational speech with the therapist. Subsequent sessions were conducted in the library and in the classroom, where conversational interaction with peers was rewarded. Over four weeks, a total of ten therapy sessions established a consistent pattern of speech, which was maintained both at school and at home.

Mizes, J. S. "The Use of Contingent Reinforcement in the Treatment of a Conversion Disorder: A Multiple Baseline Study." *Journal of Behavior Therapy and Experimental Psychiatry,* 1985, *16,* 341–345.

A thirteen-year-old girl complained of low-back pain and an inability to bend at the waist or move her torso. These symptoms appeared in the absence of organic pathology. Mizes treated her by means of a contingent social reinforcement program wherein she earned telephone privileges and parental visiting time whenever she tensed her stomach muscles hard enough to match or exceed a goal displayed on a biofeedback oscilloscope and performed these contractions a prescribed number of times. In similar fashion, Mizes subsequently administered social reinforcement for leg raising, walking unassisted, back bending, and wheelchair use. Marked improvement resulted from the behavioral treatment; although the girl had a relapse about a month later when she was hospitalized for an organic illness, the gains were reestablished with additional behavioral treatment.

Sanok, R. L., and Ascione, F. R. "Behavioral Interventions for Childhood Elective Mutism: An Evaluative Review." *Child Behavior Therapy*, 1979, *1*, 49–67.

Sanok and Ascione present a detailed discussion of clinical and theoretical information on elective mutism in children. They review alternative treatment approaches and consider their efficacy. The authors state that available evidence indicates that the stimulus-fading technique and approaches that combine treatment procedures are the most efficacious.

Scott, E. "A Desensitization Programme for the Treatment of Mutism in a Seven-Year-Old Girl: A Case Report." *Journal of Child Psychology and Psychiatry*, 1977, *18*, 263–270.

Scott presents a case history of the treatment of a seven-year-old girl's elective mutism by a combination of desensitization and operant procedures. The girl read into a cassette audiotape recorder while the therapist moved gradually from outside the room with the door closed to a face-to-face position relative to the girl. Physical contact with the therapist and candies served as reinforcers. The girl's verbal responses to the written word were transferred to simple responses to questions she was asked by the therapist and then to more elaborate verbalizations. In the final stage of treatment, the therapist programmed generalization of the girl's verbal behavior toward other people and in her daily activity schedule. The entire program required forty-five-minute sessions daily (five days per week) for one month.

Williamson, D. A., Sanders, S. H., Sewell, W. R., Haney, J. N., and White, D. "The Behavioral Treatment of Elective Mutism: Two Case Studies." *Journal of Behaviour Therapy and Experimental Psychiatry*, 1977, *8*, 143–149.

This article presents case descriptions of two electively mute children's successful treatment entailing the sequential application of behavior modification procedures. The authors observe that multiple techniques often must be used because it is difficult to determine which method will elicit the initial verbal response. They describe a working strategy for the behavioral treatment of elective mutism.

Depression

Depression in children usually involves feelings of sadness, grief, loss, helplessness, guilt, and low self-image. Depression may underlie many problems, such as psychosomatic complaints, acting out, and poor grades. Commonly, a child suffering depression has difficulty in thinking and concentrating and appears lethargic and pessimistic. The American Psychiatric Association's Diagnostic and Statistical Manual of Mental Disorders *(3rd ed.) (Washington, D. C.: American Psychiatric Association, 1980) lists the following common symptoms of a depressive neurosis (also called dysthymic disorder): insomnia or hypersomnia; low energy and chronic tiredness; feelings of inadequacy and lowered self-esteem; decreased productivity at school or home; decreased attention, concentration, and thinking ability; social withdrawal; nonenjoyment of pleasurable activities; irritability or excessive anger at adults; not positively responding to praise or rewards; lessened activity or talkativeness; pessimism and brooding; tearfulness or crying; thoughts of death or of suicide.*

Schaefer and Millman, in How to Help Children with Common Problems *(New York: New American Library, 1982), discuss the estimate that one out of five children has some form of depression and over half the parents of depressed children are depressed. Among such children, self-injurious behavior and suicide are frequent and increasing; among older adolescents, suicide is the second leading cause of death. Parents can prevent depression by encouraging their children to maintain open communication and to express their feelings. They must encourage their children's feelings of adequacy and effectiveness and be sure the child has many sources of self-esteem. Parents should model optimism and flexibility. When children are depressed, parents should be urged to openly discuss sadness and possible thoughts of hurting oneself. Children need to experience the setting and achieving of goals and the planning and doing of enjoyable activities. Therapists and parents have effectively taught children positive self-talk as an antidote to depression and negative self-statements.*

Multimodality Treatment for Depression

AUTHORS: Theodore A. Petti, Mitchell Bornstein, Alan M. Delamater, and C. Keith Conners

PRECIS: Combining intensive milieu interventions, dynamically oriented psychotherapy, antidepressant medication, and behavior therapy to help chronically depressed children.

INTRODUCTION: The techniques described in this article are intended for children whose depression is so severe as to require psychiatric hospitalization and a total milieu approach. The therapeutic program is comprehensive and practical. Interventions take place at the internal physiological level and in the child's surroundings and are directed toward helping the child better understand his or her feelings and develop an improved self-image.

TREATMENT: The authors describe a case that illustrates the combination of therapeutic interventions. The ten-and-a-half-year-old girl, Gertie, presented multiple problems, including depression, anxiety, educational difficulties, anger and aggression, poor self-image, suicidal ideation, and runaway behavior. The following techniques were used to help Gertie.

Psychotherapy. Individual psychotherapy sessions with an empathic, nonthreatening therapist were carried out. The primary goal of psychotherapy was to assist Gertie in developing an understanding of her inner conflicts and to deal with the girl's ambivalent feelings toward her natural parents and her foster parents. A secondary goal of therapy was to boost Gertie's self-esteem.

Prescriptive Teaching. Daily individualized instruction addressed Gertie's areas of perceptual deficit and her cognitive skills weaknesses. She participated in both independent learning activities and group instruction sessions. Academic achievement and the development of appropriate school behaviors were both emphasized.

Creative Dramatics. Gertie participated in a creative dramatics group in which she interacted with her peers in a rela-

tively unstructured way. The group experience allowed the girl
to express her feelings and to experiment with alternative ways
of behaving. It also provided a medium for her to receive both
positive and corrective feedback concerning her behaviors.

Family Therapy. The focus of family therapy with Gertie's foster parents and later with her biological mother was to
support and train the key adults in Gertie's home environment
to be more approving of Gertie. The adults were advised to recognize and respond to the girl's positive behaviors, and they
were taught ways to deal with her inappropriate behaviors and
to manage her relationship with a sibling.

Medication. During Gertie's fifth week of hospitalization,
tricyclic antidepressant (imipramine) administration was initiated at a dosage level of 100 mg. daily. The medication lessened her moody and oppositional behavior and made more accessible the girl's inner feelings. The imipramine was continued
through the rest of Gertie's fourteen-week hospitalization, and
it was withdrawn gradually within one year.

Social Skills Training. The primary goal of the social skills
training intervention was to improve Gertie's peer relationships.
Specifically, the training incorporated the following elements:
(1) instruction in appropriate ways to interact with others; (2)
modeling how the therapist demonstrated these behaviors; (3)
behavior rehearsal; and (4) performance feedback. The therapist
observed Gertie via a one-way mirror while the youngster and
two prompters, one of each sex, sat in a playroom. Training
scenes were selected that required Gertie to make use of various social skills. For example, the therapist-narrator announced,
"Imagine you got a new sweater for your birthday. You like it
a lot. Your friend says . . ." Prompt: "Hey, that's a neat sweater!" Based on an analysis of Gertie's behavior across several
such scenes, which were videotaped, four social skills were selected for training: making eye contact, smiling, answering
appropriately in response to being complimented, and making
assertive requests for new behavior when unreasonable demands
were made of her. Nine social skills training sessions of fifteen
minutes' duration apiece were held over a three-week period.

The combined therapeutic interventions enabled Gertie
to make marked progress in all areas, with the exception of

learning math. These gains endured long after her discharge from the hospital. Progress was sustained by Gertie's subsequent participation first in individual therapy and then in activity group therapy.

COMMENTARY: The authors illustrate quite well how very depressed children can be assisted by a comprehensive blending and progression of therapeutic modalities. They provide a good example of a treatment plan that considers interpersonal as well as intrapersonal factors, recognizing that therapeutic success is multiply determined. Therapists cannot afford to neglect the child's ability to cope adequately with the demands of school and with social situations. We agree with the authors' multifaceted and pragmatic approach to treating depressed children, and we see the comprehensive point of view they advance both as a worthwhile perspective for dealing with a host of disorders and in terms of preventive work. Although more difficult, this eclectic approach can be used without hospitalization.

SOURCE: Petti, T. A., Bornstein, M., Delamater, A. M., and Conners, C. K. "Evaluation and Multimodality Treatment of a Depressed Prepubertal Girl." *Journal of the American Academy of Child Psychiatry*, 1980, *19*, 690–702.

Alleviating Depression in Children with Cancer

AUTHORS: Betty Pfefferbaum-Levine, Karen Kumor, Ayten Cangir, Mary Choroszy, and Elizabeth A. Roseberry

PRECIS: Relieving depressive symptoms in cancer patients through the use of tricyclic antidepressant medications.

INTRODUCTION: The tricyclic antidepressants have been widely used in the treatment of adult depressive disorders. Also, they appear to be the only pharmacological treatments with proven effectiveness in prepubertal major depressive disorder. In this article, the authors report the treatment of eight depressed children with cancer, who range in age from four to sixteen years. The four girls and four boys in this study showed various depressive symptoms, including sleep disturbance, anorexia, separation anxiety, sadness, withdrawal, and regressed behavior.

TREATMENT: The drugs imipramine and amitriptyline were selected because of the physicians' familiarity with their use in a variety of childhood disorders. Four children were treated with each drug. The youngsters' specific symptoms did not influence the choice of medication. Low doses of imipramine or amitriptyline (less than 1 mg./kg. per day) were administered at bedtime. Then, if the drug was tolerated, the dosage was increased to two divided doses two or three times daily. Final doses ranged from 0.7 mg./kg. per day to 1.9 mg./kg. per day.

The authors report that all eight depressed children with cancer showed a rapid clinical response to the low doses of the drugs. The most notable improvement was seen with respect to symptoms of anxiety and sleep disturbance. All the patients showed improved mood. The side effects that were observed— dry mouth, lightheadedness, and constipation—were not serious.

Pfefferbaum-Levine and her associates report the case of one of the patients, an eleven-year-old girl, Marie. After the amputation of her femur because of osteogenic sarcoma, Marie experienced panic attacks. During these, the girl screamed, regressed to the fetal position, and sucked her thumb. In addition, she refused food. Initial improvement was seen when she was treated with chlorpromazine, and she returned home. Later, Marie's panic recurred at the times when she had to return to the hospital for cancer chemotherapy. She refused chlorpromazine because she did not want to be sedated. She expressed her fear that this drug was being administered so that procedures could be carried out without her knowledge. With imipramine, Marie showed improved sleep and appetite within two days. After three days, the girl participated without protest or regressive behavior in her cancer chemotherapy. Continuation of the imipramine treatment allowed Marie to be discharged from the hospital so that she could begin school.

COMMENTARY: Since this study was neither double-blind nor controlled, it is not possible for the authors to definitely conclude that imipramine and amitriptyline produced the beneficial response. Should future, methodologically rigorous investigations lend support to the encouraging findings reported in this article, it is still vitally important that the enormous impact of other variables on depressed hospitalized children be realized. Such factors as the attention of the hospital staff and family supports are very important. In many situations, family therapy can be most beneficial when a child in the family is seriously ill.

SOURCE: Pfefferbaum-Levine, B., Kumor, K., Cangir, A., Choroszy, M., and Roseberry, E. A. "Tricyclic Antidepressants for Children with Cancer." *American Journal of Psychiatry,* 1983, *140* (8), 1074–1076.

Social Skills Training with a Depressed Boy

AUTHORS: Cynthia Frame, Johnny L. Matson, William A. Sonis, M. Jerome Fialkov, and Alan E. Kazdin

PRECIS: A case report of a severely depressed ten-year-old boy trained to improve bodily posture, eye contact, speech quality, and bland affect.

INTRODUCTION: Ten-year-old Dale, a boy of borderline intelligence, was hospitalized because he had attempted suicide. His recent history included violent temper outbursts and poor school performance. In a variety of measures, he placed well within the clinically depressed range. Hospital staff reported that Dale was often uncommunicative, made poor eye contact, spoke inaudibly or gave one-word answers, exhibited bland facial expression, and often assumed inappropriate body positions—turning away from the speaker or covering his face with his hands.

TREATMENT: Treatment focused on establishing competent behaviors in the following four target domains:

Body Position. The authors defined an appropriate body position as one that indicated interest or participation in the conversation during a response to a question. Thus, Dale had to refrain from turning his head away, covering his face with his hands, bending forward or away from the interviewer, or turning his back to the interviewer.

Eye Contact. The aim was for Dale to maintain eye contact with the person to whom he was responding.

Speech Quality. The criteria for good quality included speaking all words loudly and clearly enough to be heard, trying to answer all questions and developing responses of three or more words, and responding to a question less than three seconds after it was asked.

Affect. The authors defined appropriate affect as incorporating emotional tone and voice inflection and demonstration of facial, hand, or arm gestures while speaking.

Twenty sessions of twenty minutes each took place on consecutive weekdays. Each session followed the identical sequence: the therapist gave the boy instructions concerning the target skills; the therapist modeled appropriate social behavior; the therapist and the boy role played social situations; and the therapist gave Dale feedback on his performance. Training concentrated on body position and eye contact simultaneously for six sessions. Then it focused on speech quality for five sessions. Appropriate expression of affect was taught in the final nine treatment sessions. At the end of each daily session, Dale was given a reward (candy or chewing gum) for cooperating that day, regardless of the quality of his responses. The social skills training package produced improvement in all four target behaviors, and these gains were maintained up to a twelve-week follow-up assessment.

COMMENTARY: The authors illustrate that a social skills training package can be efficacious in treating depressed children.
They provide a useful reminder to set *specific* goals. The authors caution that the package treatment's impact in reducing
the depressive disorder is unclear, as is the generalization of the
treatment gains to the child's daily life situations. However, the
study represents an encouraging first step in treating symptoms
of childhood depression through behavioral methods. Perhaps
through involving significant adults in a child's life, generalization from the therapy session can be maximized.

SOURCE: Frame, C., Matson, J. L., Sonis, W. A., Fialkov, M. J.,
and Kazdin, A. E. "Behavioral Treatment of Depression in a
Prepubertal Child." *Journal of Behavior Therapy and Experimental Psychiatry,* 1982, *13* (3), 239-243.

Brief Psychotherapy After a Loss

AUTHOR: Stanley Turecki

PRECIS: Treating children who have suffered a loss by brief intervention based on psychoanalytic principles.

INTRODUCTION: Brief therapy with children has included
such interventions as short-term group and family approaches,
crisis intervention, behavior modification, reeducative techniques, and psychotropic drugs. To date, no single concept of
brief psychotherapy with children unifies the various forms of
shortened treatment. Turecki describes a technique based on
psychoanalytic theory to help children deal with loss.

PROCEDURES: Turecki addresses various technical and theoretical considerations relative to the treatment method. The
therapy is primarily recommended for children who have suf-

fered a loss. Through the initial evaluation process, the therapist selects a central dynamic treatment issue or determines one from what the child has said. Next, the therapist enlists the parents' support for focusing the child's treatment on the psychodynamically determined central issue. Then, the child is asked to agree to stick to the mutually defined focus in the therapy sessions. The therapy's termination date, perhaps after ten to twelve sessions, is fixed before therapy starts.

During brief psychotherapy, the therapist attends to keeping treatment focused. This involves making repeated choices about addressing and avoiding particular issues. Establishing and maintaining a warm, trusting relationship is vital, as the child must view the therapist positively if the latter's selected interpretations and clarifications are to truly affect him or her. The therapist's personal style is particularly important in brief therapy, according to Turecki; he or she needs to use active and occasionally directive approaches. Since termination is scheduled before psychotherapy begins, handling the termination issue is inevitably a matter that the therapist must deal with all along. Turecki advises that, as treatment approaches the end date, the therapist "persistently explore" how the child feels about saying good-bye to him or her.

CASE STUDY: A nearly eleven-year-old boy was referred after he cut his wrist following an argument with his mother. Several months previously, the mother had been hospitalized for psychotic depression. The boy emerged feeling that he had somehow caused his mother's illness.

The therapist scheduled eight sessions of brief psychotherapy, of which the boy attended seven. The central issue focused on in treatment was the boy's wrong ideas about his mother's illness. The boy showed significant improvement following clarification and correction of these distortions, and he maintained this improvement for at least two-and-a-half years, according to multiple evaluative criteria that were utilized.

COMMENTARY: In contrast to those who view brief treatments as mere Band-Aids, Turecki asserts that substantive and enduring psychodynamic changes can ensue from elective brief psychotherapy. Setting a termination date in advance communicates that success is expected within a specific time frame. In some of the cases reported in this article, parents are seen concurrently by another therapist during the time that their child participates in time-limited therapy. Such a strategy may enable the parents to provide vital, ongoing home support during and after the time the child contends with his or her loss.

SOURCE: Turecki, S. "Elective Brief Psychotherapy with Children." *American Journal of Psychotherapy,* 1982, *36* (4), 479–488.

Additional Readings

Butler, L., Miezitis, S., Friedman, R., and Cole, E. "The Effects of Two School-Based Intervention Programs on Depressive Symptoms in Preadolescents." *American Educational Research Journal,* 1980, *17,* 114–119.

Fifty-six fifth- and sixth-grade children were treated for depression. The children were divided into four groups (of fourteen children apiece) for a period of ten weeks; each group received one of the following interventions: (1) Role plays: these were conducted for one hour per week and focused on problems relevant to the depressive child; (2) Cognitive restructuring exercises: these also were conducted for an hour weekly, based on rational-emotive therapy and Beck's cognitive therapy; (3) Attention placebo: children were taught for one hour each week to solve problems operatively by sharing research and pooling information; (4) Classroom controls: these children remained unidentified to their teachers, and they stayed in their classrooms over the course of the study. The authors found the most notable gains for the children in the role play condition, which also proved to be the most popular with the children. They also observed gains in the cognitive restructuring condition, although they were of lesser magnitude and the approach lacked the appeal of the role plays.

Clarizio, H. F. "Cognitive-Behavioral Treatment of Childhood Depression." *Psychology in the Schools,* 1985, *22,* 308–322.

Clarizio reviews the literature on childhood depression and outlines explanations and treatment approaches of two types: Behavioral and social skills approaches focus on behaviors to alter. Cognitive approaches emphasize the role of distorted thinking in depression; in therapy, depressed children are taught to identify and correct distortions in their thinking and beliefs that contribute to their being depressed. The author observes that these models for treating childhood depression arise largely from treatment models of adult depression, since many authorities now view childhood depression as being similar in nature to adult depression.

Kashani, J. H., Shekim, W. O., and Reid, J. C. "Amitriptyline in Children with Major Depressive Disorder: A Double-Blind Crossover Pilot Study." *Journal of the American Academy of Child Psychiatry, 23,* 1984, 348–351.

The authors report the results of a study of the effects of amitriptyline and placebo in nine depressed prepubertal children. Six of the children, who ranged in age from nine to twelve years, showed a favorable response to the amitriptyline in that their dysphoric mood either disappeared or dramatically improved. The children received successive four-week trials of amitriptyline and the placebo according to a random assignment schedule. The dosage started at 1 mg./kg. per day in three divided doses and increased after three days to 1.5 mg./kg. per day, with this dosage maintained throughout the rest of the four weeks. In addition to mood elevation, the amitriptyline responders in this study also showed an increase in their level of interest—that is, more involvement with other children and in playful activities.

Lopez, T., and Kliman, G. W. "Memory, Reconstruction, and Mourning in the Analysis of a Four-Year-Old Girl." *Psychoanalytic Study of the Child,* 1979, *34,* 235-271.

Lopez and Kliman discuss the psychoanalysis of a four-year-old girl, whose unhappiness and fearfulness originated with her mother's suicide two-and-a-half years earlier and were worsening when the analysis began. In the authors' view, the child's mourning process was facilitated by the psychoanalysis. Initially, themes associated with death dominated the therapy sessions. Later, themes emerged that involved searching for her mother; these mingled with themes of sexuality and death. The authors considered the mourning accomplished in analysis to have been instrumental in enabling the girl to move to oedipal dominance. At the end of two years of analysis, the girl's sadness and fears had disappeared.

Pallmeyer, T. P., and Petti, T. A. "Effects of Imipramine on Aggression and Dejection in Depressed Children." *American Journal of Psychiatry,* 1979, *136,* 1472-1473.

Pallmeyer and Petti present two cases to demonstrate that depressed children treated with imipramine therapy become angrier and more hostile as their lethargy and dejection decline. The authors discuss two boys, ages twelve and six respectively. Their drug dosages and the duration of the medication trial varied. In each case, the aggressive behavior began to abate as the imipramine was decreased in dosage and eventually discontinued. The authors speculate that imipramine may in some way facilitate the outward projection of aggression.

Puig-Antich, J. "Major Depression and Conduct Disorder in Prepuberty." *Journal of the American Academy of Child Psychiatry,* 1982, *21,* 118-128.

The author describes a double-blind placebo-controlled study of imipramine treatment of twenty-six prepubertal children with major depressive disorder. All of the children had been unresponsive to two weeks of psychosocial intervention in an inpatient unit. For five weeks, the drug was administered in daily dosages beginning with 1.5 mg./kg. and raised gradually to 5 mg./kg. The therapist monitored blood pressure, EKG, and clinical side effects. While Puig-Antich found no differences between the placebo and the imipramine response rate (both averaged about 60 percent), the data analysis led the author to suggest that clinical response to the drug may be related to the drug's steady-state plasma level.

Shy, Withdrawn Behavior

Shy children avoid or participate minimally in social situations. They are usually timid, easily frightened, and reserved. Withdrawing removes the child from participation, thereby avoiding his or her anxiety that is aroused by anticipation of social failure or criticism. The problem is seen equally in males and females. Many young children think of themselves as shy, and 40 percent of college students say that they are shy people. Shy children usually do not cause problems for others, but shyness is serious because it interferes with good psychological adjustment and appropriate peer interaction. Therapists often work with parents to reduce shyness and encourage social interaction (Schaefer, C. E., and Millman, H. L. How to Help Children with Common Problems. *New York: New American Library, 1982). The most effective treatment methods have been teaching and rewarding social skills, behavioral rehearsal (including role playing and role reversal), positive self-talk, densitization, encouraging assertiveness, and enrolling children in supervised play or social skills training. (Also see section on* Social Isolation.*)*

75

Combining Filmed Self-Modeling and
Medication to Modify Social Withdrawal

AUTHOR: Peter W. Dowrick

PRECIS: Associating the use of a videotaped self-model and a psychotropic drug to alleviate extreme shyness in a five-year-old boy.

INTRODUCTION: Dowrick describes the use of a single dose of medication (Valium) and a videotape that was carefully edited to show Charles engaging in approach and verbal behaviors. Prior to treatment, Charles rarely spoke, nor did he play with peers in response to their overtures to join them.

VIDEOTAPING: Three videotapes were created. The first captured Charles as he moved in the direction of a group of peers. Photographically, his approach behaviors were enhanced by using a telescopic lens, and the film was edited so that his approach behavior sequences reappeared several times. The second self-model film portrayed edited scenes of Charles engaging in nonverbal interactions with others. The third film was made thirty minutes after 5 mg. of Valium (diazepam) had been administered to the boy orally. The drug had a disinhibiting effect such that the "talking film" of Charles conversing with a playmate in a sandbox required little editing.

TREATMENT: During twice-weekly half-hour sessions, Charles viewed a three-minute film segment in the presence of his mother and the therapist. Then he spent the next twenty minutes in a playroom with one peer and a nurse-therapist who was ignorant as to the film content. During this time, the children engaged in prearranged activities that required their frequent cooperation. For example, in one such activity they had to create a collage given just one pair of scissors, pictures, and a single container of paste.

The three self-modeling videotapes were introduced as follows: (1) The approach film was first shown to the boy before the fifth session of treatment. (2) The nonverbal interaction film was presented for the first time before session nine. (3) The verbal interaction film was introduced before the twelfth session of treatment. The therapist observed improved socialization on all measures: reduced time of approach to the other child in the playroom; nonverbal interactions, including eye contact, adding to the other child's play, reaching in front of the other child, offering something to or taking something from the other child; quantity of speech. Additional home measures of talkativeness by Charles's mother confirmed the boy's increased verbal behavior. Three-, six-, and twelve-month follow-ups revealed that these changes were enduring.

COMMENTARY: The self-modeling technique was employed effectively with this socially withdrawn young child. The one-time use of medication to help create a self-modeling film was a novel idea, and Dowrick's data suggested that neither the drug nor self-modeling alone would have produced the improved verbal behavior that the two in combination yielded. This combining of procedures may hold promise in other situations. Examples of possible applications meriting study include use with school phobic children and use in cases of performance anxiety centering around public speaking. It would be an exciting idea for a professional association to pool modeling tapes that could be shown to children with similar problems.

SOURCE: Dowrick, P. W. "Single-Dose Medication to Create a Self-Model Film." *Child Behavior Therapy,* 1979, *1* (2), 193–198.

Social Skills Training
to Combat Extreme Shyness

AUTHORS: Daniel P. Franco, Karen A. Christoff, Daniel B. Crimmins, and Jeffrey A. Kelly

PRECIS: Building conversational competence by combining several behavioral methods.

INTRODUCTION: A majority of seventh and eighth graders consider themselves excessively shy. Shy youngsters tend to experience greater loneliness, and they display more conversational skill deficits than others their age. Until this study by Franco and associates, social skills training had not been directed to the very common problem of extreme shyness in youngsters of this age group.

CASE STUDY: A fourteen-year-old boy was treated at the outpatient clinic because of his parents' concern about his chronic shyness and deficient peer relationships. Reportedly, he had no friends his age, and he spent considerable time alone in his room. His interactions with neighbors and relatives were characteristically brief. During these, the youth avoided eye contact, and he displayed little affect. School personnel confirmed that the boy had few friends and that he rarely talked to others. Mostly, his agemates referred to him, derisively, as a "dope," a "nerd," and so on. Teachers' records revealed that the problems of extreme shyness and friendlessness had been evident for at least three years.

TREATMENT: Building conversational skill became the primary task of treatment. The therapists targeted four different components of skillful conversation: (1) asking questions, (2) making reinforcing or acknowledging comments, (3) establishing eye contact, and (4) displaying affective warmth. They trained these over twice-weekly twenty- to thirty-minute sessions for fifteen weeks. Each training session opened with the therapist discussing the rationale for attending to that day's skill behavior. Then the therapist gave illustrations of the behavior and modeled its proper use. During the rest of each session, the youngster generated examples of the targeted skill's use, discussed it with the therapist, and rehearsed the behavior.

After the training, the boy was introduced to a conversational partner who was unknown to him. As the therapist left the room, videorecording equipment was turned on, which taped the boy and his partner as they talked to each other for about ten minutes. Usually, each clinic visit included two training sessions and two practice conversations.

The therapist emphasized the youngster's developing general conversational strategies. Thus, for example, when the sessions focused on asking questions, the therapist encouraged the boy to "find out about the other person's interests" instead of asking specified questions listed in advance. In like manner, he was prompted to discern and develop themes in conversations rather than ask a series of unrelated questions. Homework assignments were given so that the boy would practice his newly learned skills with others. The therapist provided social reinforcement (praise) for reports of skill usage and of increased interaction with peers.

Treatment led to marked improvement in all the targeted skill areas. Follow-up after three-and-a-half months found that treatment gains had been maintained. Ratings by peers confirmed that the boy had improved considerably in his conversational skill. Adults who knew him well also confirmed his gains in all areas: academic performance, social adjustment, ease in peer interaction, extracurricular activity participation, ability to carry on a conversation, and ability to make friends. Sixteen months post-treatment, telephone follow-up with the youngster and his parents revealed that his social relationships continued to improve.

COMMENTARY: The authors successfully used learning theory principles in the treatment of extreme social isolation. Note that the conversational goals were specific and that specific training and practice occurred. Training for generalization was facilitated by building in realistic simulations of social interactions and making use of novel partners. The medium of the peer group for social skills training may be effective for latency-age youngsters and adolescents. Also, the feasibility of using video-taped peer modeling may merit attention for shortening the duration of treatment and/or for enabling home learning to be enhanced.

SOURCE: Franco, D. P., Christoff, K. A., Crimmins, D. B., and Kelly, J. A. "Social Skills Training for an Extremely Shy Young Adolescent: An Empirical Case Study." *Behavior Therapy*, 1983, *14*, 568-575.

Increasing Verbal Behavior
Through Positive Reinforcement

AUTHORS: Charles Morin, Robert Ladouceur, and Renaud Cloutier

PRECIS: Treating a young boy's reluctant speech by training his teacher to apply positive reinforcement contingently to his verbalizations.

INTRODUCTION: Children with reluctant speech display occasional verbal behaviors in social situations outside the home. Reluctant speech is distinguished from elective mutism, which is characterized by a complete absence of speech in some social situations, such as the classroom. The authors report that while behavioral treatments have been effective in reinstating speech for electively mute children, the treatment of reluctant speech has received very little attention. In this case, the authors used operant conditioning techniques with the teacher serving as the behavioral change agent to treat the reluctant speech of a six-year-old child.

    Eric had been in kindergarten for five months. During that time, he generally refused to speak to his teacher or to other children in school. Often, he took home craft materials and assembled projects there rather than doing them in class. Eric was the next-to-youngest of six children in a family that was of middle to low socioeconomic status and that lived in a relatively isolated rural area. Eric's parents reported that, in dramatic contrast to the behaviors seen in school, Eric spoke fluently to members of his family when he was at home.

TREATMENT: Eric's teacher was trained to employ tangible and social reinforcers to help him. Each time Eric answered a question asked by the teacher, he received "$1.00" in "school money." When he had earned a certain sum, which was increased gradually during the course of treatment, he could exchange it for arts and crafts materials he had previously selected. The teacher asked Eric an average of ten questions each class session, and she purposely asked an equivalent number of questions under various conditions: (1) when he was alone, away from other children, (2) when he was near others (for example, engaged in pottery or drawing activities), and (3) when he was with the whole group. Concurrently, the teacher provided praise, attention, and physical contact to Eric each time he offered a verbal response.

After eight sessions in which the reinforcement procedure was in effect continuously (actually two phases of four sessions each separated by a four-session return-to-base during which the teacher deliberately avoided giving any feedback when Eric spoke), Eric was told that he could earn money on certain school days but not on others. This move to an intermittent variable ratio schedule increased the delay between exchange of school money and receipt of tangible reinforcers for Eric. A marked increase in Eric's response rate was recorded— from 20 percent during the period just prior to introduction of the treatment intervention to over 70 percent during the intermittent positive reinforcement phase. A year after treatment ended, follow-up measurements showed that Eric spoke appropriately each time he was called upon to respond.

COMMENTARY: The authors have made a worthwhile contribution to the extremely sparse literature on treating reluctant speech. While others have reported success using contingency management procedures in the treatment of reluctant speech, Morin and associates' single-case experimental design breaks new ground, as previously only case studies had been reported. Another important contribution is the authors' ability to demonstrate that the therapeutic gains were maintained after a year. Previously, no follow-ups were carried out beyond six months. This method may easily be used by parents or older siblings to reinforce appropriate speech and other social skills.

SOURCE: Morin, C., Ladouceur, R., and Cloutier, R. "Reinforcement Procedure in the Treatment of Reluctant Speech." *Journal of Behavior Therapy and Experimental Psychiatry,* 1982, *13,* 145-147.

Psychoanalytic Treatment of a Mentally Retarded Withdrawn Child

AUTHOR: Charlotte Schwartz

PRECIS: Describes the successful application of psychoanalytic psychotherapy with a mildly retarded seven-year-old boy.

INTRODUCTION: The psychoanalytic literature has generally viewed as futile the use of an analytic treatment approach with mentally retarded people. Schwartz challenges the majority position, drawing upon case records of retarded children treated with psychoanalytic therapy. One of the cases she presents is that of Rodney, a boy in a school program for children with retarded mental development. He appeared extremely shy and fearful of adult and peer contact. Also, he acted submissively with his younger sister. Rodney clung to his mother and distanced himself from his father.

TREATMENT: Initially, Rodney refused to engage with the male therapist. He was allowed to play quietly with the toys until the session ended, then he replaced them neatly on their shelves. Rodney did not speak at all during therapy at first; later, he spoke only sparsely. The therapist's silent physical presence in the playroom is seen by Schwartz as a vital ingredient in the therapeutic process, as it allowed Rodney to express his fantasies through play in an atmosphere of total acceptance.

From time to time, the therapist asked Rodney what was happening as he watched the boy play repeatedly with toy soldiers, lining them up and knocking them down. He allowed Rodney to reply, "Nothing." When the session ended, the therapist and Rodney put the toys away together. After three months, Rodney asked, "Can we play ball?" This marked the breakthrough of the boy's transference wish to act aggressively toward his father. Following this, a great deal of verbally aggressive and aggressive play behavior surfaced during treatment sessions. These were accompanied by Rodney's first attempts to communicate with his father and to separate from his mother. The boy's school performance improved as his repressive defenses were let down and allowed the direct gratification of aggressive drives.

COMMENTARY: The potential for psychoanalytically oriented therapy to help with emotional problems experienced by individuals of borderline to moderately retarded intelligence has been largely unrealized for reasons having more to do with speculation than evidence. The case of Rodney illustrates how increased independence of retarded children can be fostered through psychoanalytically based treatment. Working through the transference via the medium of play enables pathological structures and defenses to be modified as the child's identification with the therapist proceeds from "I want what you have" or "I want you" to "I want to be like you." Psychoanalytic treatment techniques appear applicable to problems encountered by children functioning in the upper ranges of mental retardation.

SOURCE: Schwartz, C. "The Application of Psychoanalytic Theory to the Treatment of the Mentally Retarded Child." *The Psychoanalytic Review*, 1979, *66* (1), 132-141.

Additional Readings

Csapo, M. "Cost Efficacy of Two Social Learning Training Procedures with Withdrawn/Isolate Children." *Psychology in the Schools*, 1983, *20*, 67-73.

The author reports a study in which twelve socially withdrawn third-grade children received social learning training, social learning plus reinforcement, or both. The social learning training was carried out in dyads with a randomly selected peer over four weeks in daily forty-minute sessions. The target skills —asking questions, giving directions, and offering praise and encouragement—were taught by means of verbal instructions, rehearsal, and self-evaluation. During the reinforcement phase, tokens were awarded whenever the child displayed more of the targeted behavior during free play time than he or she had displayed in the previous free play period. The child was able to trade in tokens earned to play one of three class games selected by peers at the end of the school day. The social learning approach was effective in reducing the children's withdrawn, isolated behavior to levels equivalent to an average peer. The social learning approach paired with reinforcement produced more rapid improvement in social skills.

Kelly, J. A. "Using Puppets for Behavior Rehearsal in Social Skills Training Sessions with Young Children." *Child Behavior Therapy*, 1981, *3*, 61-64.

Kelly states that in-session behavior rehearsal between a young child and an adult therapist often fails to maintain the child's interest. To help shy, young children develop social skills, a role play behavioral rehearsal technique using puppets is used. It consists of the following steps: (1) First, the therapist, through detailed behaviorally specific interviews with key adults in the child's life, establishes what the situations are in which the child's social skills are deficient. (2) Hand puppets then are employed for behavior rehearsal in realistic approximations of the problematic situations. (3) Finally, the teacher and parents arrange *in vivo* practice opportunities for the child. The author observes that learning principles such as modeling, feedback, and reinforcement are employed to maximize gains derived from practicing with puppets.

Kratchowill, T. R., and French, D. C. "Social Skills Training for Withdrawn Children." *School Psychology Review,* 1984, *13,* 331–338.

Kratchowill and French review the literature on social skills training for withdrawn or isolated children. Interest in treating social withdrawal is relatively recent. Childhood difficulty with peer relationships is now seen as often predictive of serious adolescent and adult disorders. The authors outline approaches to treatment, including reinforcement procedures, modeling treatments, coaching interventions, programs that teach general cognitive and social problem-solving skills, and packages that combine many of the aforementioned treatment components.

Lopez, T., and Kliman, G. W. "The Cornerstone Treatment of a Preschool Boy from an Extremely Improvished Environment." *Psychoanalytic Study of the Child,* 1980, *35,* 341–375.

Lopez and Kliman present a detailed discussion of two years of analytically oriented treatment of a young, extremely withdrawn inner-city boy. In the Cornerstone Method they employed, the therapist treated the child individually for three or more twenty- to twenty-five-minute sessions per week in the classroom during class time. Simultaneously, two teachers conducted a therapeutic nursery program. The therapist and the teachers also provided parental guidance. Play activities, dramatization, physical contact, and interpretation served as key therapeutic tools. The integration of the child analytic techniques and the therapeutic education resulted in continual improvement.

Matson, J. L., Esveldt-Dawson, K., Andrasik, F., Ollendick, T. H., Petti, T., and Hersen, M. "Direct, Observational, and Generalization Effects of Social Skills Training with Emotionally Disturbed Children." *Behavior Therapy,* 1980, *11,* 522–531.

The authors present a case in which four emotionally disturbed/learning disabled children, nine to eleven years old, received social skills training for withdrawn and antisocial behavior. The children were trained in a group that made use of natural role play situations. Two of the children observed while the other two were trained; then the treatment conditions were reversed. The authors found that direct social skills training was effective for teaching the targeted social skills, while observational learning was of minimal benefit in enhancing verbal responsiveness, affect, eye contact, and body posture. The gains achieved from direct social skills training generalized to the natural environment, and they were maintained over several months.

Mehl, L. E., and Peterson, G. H. "Spontaneous Peer Psychotherapy in a Day-Care Setting: A Case Report." *American Journal of Orthopsychiatry,* 1981, *51,* 346–350.

The authors report the successful socialization of a withdrawn, shy, and quiet preschool boy, in which the therapeutic effects were achieved in large part by a younger girl's persistent efforts to engage her peer and draw him into interactions with other children. Also contributing to the boy's improvement was the presence of a day-care staff that was emotionally available, loving, and supportive. The authors feel that children's freedom to express themselves spontaneously in free play may allow conflicts to surface and psychotherapeutic benefits to ensue.

Santostefano, S. "Cognitive Control Therapy with Children: Rationale and Technique." *Psychotherapy,* 1984, *21,* 76–91.

In this article, Santostefano discusses the underlying concepts and methods of cognitive control therapy, an approach for treating children whose cognitive development is insufficient for them to benefit from verbally oriented psychotherapy.

The central therapeutic goal is to restructure cognitive-affective balancing. The technique is illustrated with several cases, including that of a withdrawn, friendless, eleven-year-old girl. The girl participated in play activities with the therapist, which served to develop her cognitive competence while also integrating her fantasies and feelings with external information.

Sherick, I. "The Significance of Pets for Children." *The Psychoanalytic Study of the Child,* 1981, *36,* 193–215.

Sherick presents a detailed discussion of clinical and theoretical information regarding the significance of pets in child psychoanalysis. The case described concerns a very shy and fearful latency-age girl. In the course of her three-year analysis, the girl's use of fantasied and real pets helped both improve her communication and reduce her resistance to uncovering her internalized conflicts. The pets assumed the role of symbolic substitutes for the youngster's ideal self. Since animal fantasies are characteristic of the latency period, Sherick believes that the significance of pets can inform much therapeutic work with children of this age group.

Tarplay, B. S., and Sandargas, R. A. "An Intervention for a Withdrawn Child Based on Teacher Recorded Levels of Social Interaction." *School Psychology Review,* 1981, *10,* 409–412.

The authors describe a treatment package that was successful in treating an extremely isolated and withdrawn preschool-age boy. The teacher was the focal point of the intervention. She succeeded in improving the child's level of interaction with his peers by modeling participation with other children, holding class discussions about how it feels to be in the group, commenting enthusiastically during activities about the satisfaction and rewards of playing with and being with other children, praising the boy when he joined a group of children, and ignoring him when he removed himself from his peers. The authors feel that when a withdrawn child interacts more frequently with adults than with other children, then an adult should be the person around whom the intervention strategy should be designed.

White, J., and Poteat, G. M. "Improving Kindergarten Students' Social Skills Through Consultation and Teacher Directed Activities." *School Psychology Review*, 1983, *12*, 476–480.

The authors describe a study in which three withdrawn kindergarten students were trained in social skills. The four social skill strategies they were taught were: participating in a game or activity; cooperating, taking turns, and sharing; communication—talking to and listening to others; and validating or supporting. Twice-weekly training sessions of thirty- to forty-five minutes' duration each were conducted for the entire kindergarten class. The school psychologist conducted the first two sessions while the teacher observed. These sessions were preceded by three consultation sessions in which the psychologist enhanced the teacher's understandings relative to social skills. For the third training session, the psychologist and teacher reversed roles. Then, the teacher conducted the remaining five sessions alone. The training sessions consisted of instruction and discussion about the four social skills strategies and games that allowed the class to practice the targeted skill strategies. The intervention produced improvement in two of the students' social skills. The authors note that while their work contained methodological weaknesses, the method employed in this study appears to be a practical and cost-effective way to build children's social skills.

School Phobia

School phobia is an exaggerated, often illogical fear of attending school. Fear of separation from home and/or some situation in school may be operating. School phobia should be differentiated from nonattendance due to other causes, such as truancy, boredom, or fear of academic failure. Somatic symptoms of nausea, stomachaches, and dizziness are typical. They disappear once school has been avoided. Children prone to school phobia are often overly dependent and resentful toward parents, and their ambivalence and anxiety may be displaced toward school. Staying home may be inadvertently reinforced by mother, and going to school may represent loss of mother. In acute school phobia, the child should be returned to school immediately, and the parents should receive counseling. More intensive intervention—usually a combination of individual and family therapy—is required for a chronic phobia. Systematic desensitization, counterconditioning, modeling, and insight therapy have been successful. Schools have effectively used attendance contracts with specific rewards and punishments.

Desensitization Methods for
School Panic Attack

AUTHORS: Timothy J. O'Farrell, Mark A. Hedlund, and Henry S. G. Cutter

PRECIS: Treating a severe school phobia using self-monitoring, relaxation, thought stopping, imaginal desensitization, and *in vivo* exposure.

INTRODUCTION: This case involved a fourteen-year-old boy who experienced a severe anxiety attack in school after his first use of marijuana. Richard became flushed, feverish, dizzy, and nauseous, and he feared that he was dying. Because his peers who had tried the drug showed none of these symptoms, doctors concluded that Richard's reactions were not physically determined. After a five-day suspension from school, Richard feared that returning to his classes would precipitate recurrence of the panic. When he did reenter school, Richard experienced discomfort in the back of his head, and he became distraught. Repeated efforts to have him remain in school met with failure. Punitive consequences did not succeed in having Richard stay in school without becoming afraid and running off. The youngster's fears spread such that stores and other public places evoked severe phobic reactions. Treatment began after Richard had not attended school for more than five months.

TREATMENT: The boy was seen with his parents for the initial session and then alone for eight therapy sessions; these sessions were followed by another session at which both Richard and his parents were present.

Session 1. After hearing Richard and his parents recite the history of the problem, the therapist explained how the process of stimulus generalization had caused him to become fearful of anything associated with his marijuana-precipitated anxiety attack and how relearning was possible. The parties agreed that four weeks would be invested in teaching Richard coping skills for his fears at home before school-related fears would be addressed. Richard agreed to keep a daily diary, rating upsetting experiences according to the relative degree of upset they provoked. His parents expressed their support for this gradual approach toward desensitization.

Session 2. The therapist reviewed the boy's diary and questioned him in detail to ascertain his personal fear hierarchy. He instructed the boy to continue his self-monitoring. The two discussed the boy's specific behavioral manifestations of tension and anxiety and his antecedent thoughts. Then, with the help of an illustrated booklet, the therapist showed Richard how to tense and relax various muscle groups. The boy practiced this and did "homework" assigned by the therapist: continued self-monitoring and daily practice in the relaxation method.

Session 3. Richard's anxiety monitoring was reviewed. The therapist reinforced verbally his discernible reductions in anxiety, particularly those that seemed to stem from his confronting anxiety-producing situations. The boy practiced tensing and relaxing upper-body muscle groups, together with slow deep breathing. Homework again was assigned, with the deep-breathing component figuring in his coping repertoire for confronting fearful situations.

Session 4. In this session, during the self-monitoring review, the boy's thoughts when he felt most anxious were considered (for example, "My mouth is dry. Is it happening all over again?"). The therapist demonstrated the technique of thought stopping to control such upsetting thoughts and added thought stopping to the week's homework. The overall purpose of therapy was reviewed during this session—namely, to enable Richard to tolerate anxiety and to bring his experience of anxiety down from the excessive level it had reached.

Session 5. The therapist took time during this session to outline how through systematic desensitization and *in vivo* exposure to anxiety-provoking situations, Richard would become able to return to school. The week's homework exposed the youngster to these situations: walking along the sidewalk outside the school grounds when he was nearly alone and then when a lot of people were present, walking on the school grounds under these two circumstances successively, and, lastly, walking near the school's entrance.

Session 6. The boy and the therapist completed additional

hierarchy scenes for homework practice of the techniques learned to date. The scenes included: people gazing at Richard on the school bus, meeting people from school whom he knew, nearing the school building, peering in at the school, looking in at the classroom site of his panic attack.

Session 7. Review and discussion continued. Then Richard spent time on imaginal desensitization of several hierarchy scenes. These consisted of the following images: walking just inside the school entrance and walking progressively nearer to and finally into the classroom in which he suffered the severe anxiety episode. The therapist assigned *in vivo* practice of the steps covered in imagination for homework.

Session 8. During this session, imaginal desensitization covered: arriving at summer school on the first day of class; wondering halfway through the day, "Will I make it?"; self-questioning in similar fashion at day's end while feeling a bit flushed; preparing to recite aloud after being called on by the teacher. Richard's homework was to attend school, use thought stopping and relaxation as needed, and report to his therapist how he did at the end of that day.

Session 9. Richard and the therapist reviewed the week. Homework consisted of continuing to go to school and using thought stopping and relaxation as needed.

Session 10. The therapist reviewed with Richard and his parents his progress and the goals of treatment. Plans were made for a subsequent "booster session" if the need arose during upcoming stressful periods.

The treatment succeeded in increasing Richard's school attendance from 35 percent to 96 percent. A year after the desensitization treatment, he showed sizable improvement on psychological tests and sustained treatment gains behaviorally.

COMMENTARY: While the case study reported by O'Farrell, Hedlund, and Cutter pertained to a young adolescent, the authors' methods also apply to severe phobic reactions of younger individuals. The techniques used here are significant in two important respects. First, they proved to be a successful therapeutic initiative with an older youngster; therapy for older children's phobias is often not successful. Also, this case report suggests that severe panic reaction may require the sequential introduction of passive association techniques and more active treatment methods. This is because premature introduction of active participation methods can worsen a child's avoidant behavior and intensify panic. The combining of several methods and the real-life practice are in keeping with the eclectic, practical spirit of this book.

SOURCE: O'Farrell, T. J., Hedlund, M. A., and Cutter, H.S.G. "Desensitization for a Severe Phobia of a Fourteen-Year-Old Male." *Child Behavior Therapy*, 1981, *3* (2/3), 67–77.

Hypnotherapy with Young School Phobic Children

AUTHOR: Evelyn D. Lawlor

PRECIS: Use of hypnosis and environmental manipulation to treat children's separation anxieties and fears.

INTRODUCTION: Lawlor notes that, in most cases, school phobic children do not fear school per se. Rather, they fear leaving home because of the destructive fantasies they harbor. Many instances of school phobia are actually power struggles between child and parent. The child's symptoms mask unconscious conflicts and fears he or she is unable to bring to consciousness and talk about. The author uses two case presentations to illustrate how hypnosis may aid in uncovering perceptions and restoring children to a school environment faster than more traditional methods.

CASE STUDY 1: John, five years old, was the eldest of three brothers. His siblings were one and three years of age. The first day of kindergarten, John refused to participate in any class activities. On subsequent days, he became tearful, dawdled, and complained of being ill in the morning. His mother's response was to yell at him and threaten to spank him and send him to school with neighbors. She had to take him home from school several times, however, after John first projectile vomited, splattering children near him, and the next day soiled his pants. After a few days at home, his mother took him back to school, but the problems persisted, and the school advised that John remain home until his entrance into the first grade.

Hypnosis was utilized during the initial interview with John, which took place in his home in order to minimize the boy's anxiety and discomfort. By having John fixate his eyes on the beam of a pencil flashlight, the therapist was able to quickly induce a hypnotic trance. Under trance, John was questioned regarding his feelings about going to school. He shared fears that while he was at school, his mother and brothers would be hit by a car and he would not see his mother again, his wish to be an only child, and oedipal fantasies about assuming his father's role.

Lawlor's recommendations to John's parents included: (1) giving John duties to help his mother in the home, (2) entering him in a nearby nursery school for half-day sessions, (3) arranging time each afternoon (while the younger children were napping) for John and his mother to spend together reading books, (4) making arrangements with neighbors to look after John if he should return home while his mother was out of the house, (5) encouraging John's father to plan play time with John every weekend. Lawlor reported that John's parents followed through with these suggestions.

In subsequent sessions, John was able to express his rage at his siblings for supplanting him and toward his parents for bringing them home. As he became able to verbalize, to put his fears outside of himself, John's anxiety due to his guilt diminished. Rapid change in his adjustment followed. John entered a school nearer his home the following September, and there was no recurrence of the "phobic" symptoms.

CASE STUDY 2: Andrea was the four-and-a-half-year-old only child of very unstable young parents. Three weeks after she started kindergarten in a parochial school, Andrea witnessed her mother committing suicide by jumping out of a window. Prior to her mother's death, Andrea's teacher described the little girl as unable to sit in her seat, hyperactive, disruptive, destructive, and requiring an inordinate amount of attention. After the tragedy, Andrea began to soil her clothes, and she appeared extremely withdrawn, sitting in her seat with her eyes closed, rocking vigorously back and forth with her thumb in her mouth. Her father's response, when he was called to school to take her home, was to slap and embarrass his daughter in front of the teacher and her classmates. Before long, the principal discharged Andrea from the school.

Lawlor induced a hypnotic trance during Andrea's first therapy session. She was able to elicit the girl's fantasy that because she was bad, her mother had gone away and left her and the terror Andrea felt about going to school. She believed that the nuns were witches who would put her away all by herself. When Lawlor related this to Andrea's father, he gained insight into how he had failed to comfort his daughter. He decided to allow Andrea to live with his sister and her family. After the move, Andrea entered a nursery school, where she was less withdrawn and adjusted satisfactorily.

Andrea's symptoms recurred when she reentered the same parochial school at age five-and-a-half. Whenever a nun approached, Andrea became terrified and had to be removed from class. Lawlor induced another hypnotic trance, during which Andrea verbalized her fears of never seeing her mother again, of being abandoned, and of the "witches" dressed in black. She was able to vividly recall attending her mother's funeral, where black-garbed relatives told her that her mother would never return. She recalled hysterical outbursts by family members and feelings of sadness and self-blame as reactions to her maltreatment by her father and his girlfriend.

Conferences with Andrea's aunt and uncle helped them understand their niece's fears and allay her anxieties and foster

her adjustment in her new environment. Andrea later attended a
public school with her cousin, where she adjusted well, and was
adopted by her aunt and uncle. There was no recurrence of phobic symptoms.

COMMENTARY: Hypnosis appears to be a useful therapeutic
tool for modifying inappropriate behavior. In addition to the
situations considered here, hypnosis can help in other situations
in which child and parent are engaged in a power struggle that is
expressed in terms of nonperformance or lack of cooperation
by the child. Other potential uses may include dealing with
feigned illness around attending camp, refusal to participate on
sports teams or scouting groups, or friction around performing
household chores.

SOURCE: Lawlor, E. D. "Hypnotic Intervention with 'School
    Phobic' Children." *International Journal of Clinical and Ex-
    perimental Hypnosis, 1976, 24 (2), 74–86.*

Using Music to
Relieve a Child's Fears

AUTHORS: C. Peter Bankart and Brenda B. Bankart

PRECIS: Case study: helping a nine-year-old boy combat school-
related fears by employing popular song lyrics as prompts for a
self-control strategy.

INTRODUCTION: A fourth-grade student who had no prior
history of school problems displayed multiple signs of extreme
anxiety after his first day at a new school. His symptoms included intense feelings of fear and dread, uncontrollable crying,
nausea, disturbed bowel movements, headache, fever, and im-
somnia. These recurred daily for several days, causing him to be

sent home from school a number of times. Treatment was aimed at having the boy resume school attendance and gain control over the negative feelings he associated with school.

TREATMENT: Two stages were involved in treatment. In stage one, the boy learned to recognize a cue that accompanied a strong anxiety response. He focused on school-related and non-related images and discovered that the former always induced crying. In stage two, the child developed a cognitive coping response that was incompatible with the fear response.

A popular rock song, "Hot Blooded," was used during the second stage of treatment. The song's lyrics reinforce themes of courage, strength, and self-confidence. The boy was told to focus on school-related images and then to sing the lyrics aloud to fight off the anxiety summoned up by these images. He was instructed to label the negative (school-related) images as "special" and the competing response (coping strategy) as "being hot blooded." The boy was instructed to practice alternately evoking and blocking the negative feelings. He was told to sing the song as he travelled to school each day and whenever he felt himself becoming anxious during the day. He recorded the times and places he sang the song and how many times he sang it.

The intervention allowed the boy to attend school for a full day the first time it was applied. That day, there was only one brief crying episode and the boy finished all his assigned work. He reported that he had sung the song lyrics en route to school and at his locker before the opening bell rang, plus about nine or ten other times before lunch recess. At a booster session that evening, the boy was instructed to alternately focus on school-related images and sing the song for a half-hour before bedtime.

On the second day, the boy recorded five uses of the blocking strategy; on day three, one use; thereafter, none. There was no further evidence of the problem symptoms for at least two years.

COMMENTARY: The Bankarts' article describes how popular

song lyrics can be useful in helping a child cope with phobic reactions to school. There appears to be great promise for using
the sensation and cognitive aspects (that is, lyrics) of music to
build children's self-control. Other distressing symptomatology
might be combatted in similar fashion to that described here.
Social isolation, lack of self-confidence in athletic competi-
tions, and fear of the dentist's chair are three examples. The
particular songs and lyrics would have to be carefully chosen,
as many popular songs tend to reinforce themes of dependence,
aggression, and low self-esteem. Also, the type of therapeutic
intervention described might achieve its best effect with children such as the boy here, whose fear reactions are of relatively
recent onset and apparently are uncomplicated by a history of
poor adjustment.

SOURCE: Bankart, C. P., and Bankart, B. B. "The Use of Song
    Lyrics to Alleviate a Child's Fears." *Child and Family Behav-
    ior Therapy*, 1983, *5* (4), 81–83.

Eliminating School Phobia
via Behavioral Consultation

AUTHORS: Frank M. Gresham and Richard J. Nagle

PRECIS: Time-out and differential reinforcement of other behaviors (DRO) to help a child overcome fear of the school situation.

INTRODUCTION: The "rapid treatment procedure" described
by W. A. Kennedy is among the most effective and time-efficient ways to eliminate school phobia. (See Kennedy, W.A.
"School Phobia: Rapid Treatment of Fifty Cases." *Journal of
Abnormal Psychology*, 1965, *70*, 285–289.) However, this technique fails to make use of resident or consulting school psychol-

ogists as qualified behavioral consultants to school professionals and parents; nor does it deal with the classroom teacher's role as a behavioral change agent for inappropriate behaviors the child may display in the classroom setting. In this case study, Gresham and Nagle show how a modified and expanded rapid treatment procedure eliminated a girl's school phobia.

CASE STUDY: When her father took her to her elementary school classroom, Sally cried, screamed, whined, and ran out of the room. When Sally behaved in this way, the teacher held Sally on her lap, comforted her, and tried to find out what was bothering her. Five-day baseline data indicated that she cried and whined an average of eighteen minutes each day.

TREATMENT: Treatment at school consisted of applying two procedures to reduce Sally's inappropriate behavior: time-out and DRO.

   1. *Time-out*. This behavior change technique may involve removing a child from his or her environment or removing the child's opportunity to earn reinforcement for particular behaviors. Here, a mild time-out procedure was used, which was a form of a contingent observation technique. Sally remained in the classroom, but she was placed in the corner of the room whenever she cried or whined. She was allowed to remove herself from time-out when she stopped the offending behaviors.

   2. *DRO*. DRO entails reduction of an unwanted behavior by establishing a time interval for nonoccurrence of the behavior and administering reinforcement if the time interval passes without the target behavior occurring. In Sally's case, once she returned to the class group, praise, attention, and access to classroom activities she enjoyed were given as reinforcements for refraining from crying and whining.

   During the intervention period, Sally's teacher recorded the duration of her crying and whining episodes, and her parents gave their support to the school initiatives while they ignored Sally's morning protests about having to attend school. Her father took her to the classroom door every day and then left immediately, regardless of how she was acting. The school

100

Advances in Therapies for Children

principal agreed to forbid Sally from coming to see him during class time, and he returned her to class when she challenged this rule.

RESULTS: From eighteen minutes per day on average during the baseline phase, the duration of Sally's unwanted behaviors decreased to an average of three minutes and nine seconds during the ten days the intervention was in effect. By the sixth day of the intervention phase, Sally's crying and whining were entirely eliminated. The time-out and DRO procedures maintained their impact on her crying and whining; follow-up measures taken two weeks after the last intervention day showed five consecutive days without a single incidence of these behaviors.

COMMENTARY: Gresham and Nagle's approach to the problem of school phobia is most significant in that it makes effective and efficient use of the expertise and availability of a resident mental health professional in the school. Guidance counselors, school social workers, and special educators may assume roles similar to that played by a school psychologist here. This case also is noteworthy for the important roles Sally's teacher, her parents, and the school principal played in carrying out the plan of treatment. It suggests how therapists can function as consultants, instructing and mobilizing a network of adults who are important in the life of a child in the service of the child's therapy. The same methods may be used by parents for fears at home.

SOURCE: Gresham, F. M., and Nagle, R. J. "Treating School Phobia Using Behavioral Consultation: A Case Study." *School Psychology Review,* 1982, *10,* 104-107.

Additional Readings

Berney, T., Kolvin, I., Bhate, S. R., Garside, R. F., Jeans, J.,
Kay, B., and Scarth, L. "School Phobia: A Therapeutic
Trial with Clomipramine and Short-Term Outcome."
British Journal of Psychiatry, 1981, *138*, 110–118.
    The authors conducted a double-blind study (imipramine
and placebo) with forty-six school phobic children, ages nine to
fourteen. Individual psychotherapy and parent counseling were
used concurrently. Drug dosages ranged from 40 to 75 mg. per
day. The trial lasted twelve weeks. The article reports the results
of psychiatrists' ratings. Imipramine was ineffective for school
refusal syndrome. The authors discuss possible explanations for
the outcome. They consider it unlikely that insufficient dose
level, noncompliance with the drug regimen, or selective drop-
out from the study accounts for the failure to demonstrate any
significant improvement. In their view, school refusal may be
more intractable than has been thought previously.

Cretekos, C.J.G. "Some Techniques in Rehabilitating the
School Phobic Adolescent." *Adolescence*, 1977, *46*, 237–
246.
    Cretekos reviews the literature on school phobia and gives
a detailed description of the management of two school phobic
boys, ages twelve and thirteen. An attendance contract technique was instrumental in managing one boy's anxiety and facilitating his return to school. In the other boy's case, a class
meeting in his home proved crucial for his subsequent development. Cretekos highlights the importance of the school remaining active and concerned in relation to the school phobic youngster. An early return to school requires collaboration of educators
and mental health care givers.

Hsia, H. "Structural and Strategic Approach to School Phobia/
School Refusal." *Psychology in the Schools*, 1984, *21*,
360–367.
    The author reviews alternative theoretical approaches to
school phobia/school refusal. Hsia advocates intensive treatment
of the problem from the perspective of a family system model,

which emphasizes strategies to correct the family hierarchical order by putting the parent once again in charge of the child. He describes the treatment of a twelve-year-old school phobic girl, which produced lasting gains in school attendance plus improvement in the child's appearance and social skills. Treatment was conducted over nine weeks. Initially, the therapist saw the girl three times a week, then twice weekly, then once a week during the final two weeks of therapy. Components of the therapeutic program included: (1) quick therapist response to the referral, (2) frequent availability of the therapist to the family through personal appointments and on the telephone, (3) building therapeutic alliances with medical and nursing personnel to counter parental tendencies to cave in to the child's somatic complaints, (4) obtaining cooperation from school personnel to keep the complaining child in school, (5) rewarding the child for resumed school attendance and withholding privileges for school nonattendance, (6) emphasizing minimal interference with school attendance, and (7) striving to achieve a rapid return to school and full-day school attendance.

Matson, J. L., and Kazdin, A. E. "Treatment of Phobias in a Hospitalized Child." *Journal of Behaviour Therapy and Experimental Psychiatry,* 1982, *13,* 77–83.

A twelve-year-old girl who exhibited refusal to attend school and other extreme fears was helped to return to school and remain in attendance by the use of behavioral principles. Five anxiety-provoking school situations and five other situations that were fearful for the girl were role played, and her inappropriate (avoidance) and appropriate (prosocial) behaviors were noted. Then, for each scene the therapist modeled appropriate behaviors in the situation. In the next phase of treatment, the child acted out each scene and received instructions, performance feedback, and social reinforcement as she went along. Rapid improvement resulted from training.

Rangaswami, K. "School Phobia Treated by Desensitization: A Case Report." *Indian Journal of Clinical Psychology,* 1983, *10,* 47–49.

The author presents a case study describing the treatment

of an eight-year-old boy who suddenly developed a morbid fear of attending school. Treatment consisted of desensitization sessions with the therapist supported by parent and teacher administration of rewards for school attendance. The boy overcame his fear and was able to attend school without any difficulty three weeks after treatment began. He continued to attend school with no sign of relapse at follow-up seven months later.

Want, J. H. "School-Based Intervention Strategies for School Phobia: A Ten-Step 'Common Sense' Approach." *Pointer,* 1983, *27,* 27-32.

Want identifies five personality features that are characteristic of children who are school phobic. The features are: anxiety, willfulness toward the parent, dependency on the parent, depression, and unrealistic self-image. A ten-step intervention plan is recommended. The plan requires collaboration among professionals and parents and systematic planning efforts. Its components include: organization of a school team, parent involvement, prompt return of the student to school, provision of counseling that is reality based, and limiting the child's complaints.

Childhood Fears

Fear is an unpleasant feeling caused by the anticipation of danger; an exaggerated, irrational, and persistent fear is called a phobia. *Fears are most common between ages two and six. Phobias are more prevalent in girls than in boys. Feared situations are carefully avoided. Some fears, such as fear of snakes, can be avoided fairly easily. Other fears (such as fears of injury, noise, animals) can interfere with a child's daily activities. Dreams frequently reflect fears. Schaefer and Millman* (How to Help Children with Common Problems. *New York: New American Library, 1982) state that at least half of all children have the common fears of dogs, dark, thunder, and ghosts. Approximately 20 percent of children fear testing and do poorly due to those fears. Much success has been reported using the "stress inoculation" approach to help children cope with any fear. Many methods are used to combat fear, including insight therapy, implosive therapy, modeling, desensitization, counterconditioning, rehearsal, positive imagery, rewarding bravery, self-talk, relaxation, and meditation.*

Rapid Elimination of a Child's Fear
of Toileting by Relaxation Training

AUTHOR: C. Eugene Walker

PRECIS: The fear of toileting of a young boy was successfully treated through muscle relaxation, fantasy games, and imagination.

INTRODUCTION: Relaxation training is defined as a variety of techniques and procedures by which patients are taught to consciously relax the muscles of the body on demand. This type of intervention has been widely utilized with adults and its utility has been demonstrated with an array of disorders of children. It may augment other therapy approaches or serve as the sole therapy in some circumstances, such as the case reported here.

TREATMENT: The four-year-old boy treated by Walker had never defecated in the toilet, and he had repeated episodes of soiling his clothing throughout the day. His parents had spanked him many times in their unsuccessful attempts to toilet train him. They believed he was willfully resisting becoming trained. By the time he commenced treatment, the child was extremely resistant to entering the bathroom, and he was very tense whenever he was placed on the toilet.

Baseline measurements of the child's sphincter tension were taken using an instrument that consisted of a mercury manometer with a balloon fixed at one end of a rubber tube. An air pressure bulb gently inflated the balloon, which was inserted in the child's rectum. Baseline readings on the manometer averaged 80 millimeters. Six one-hour training sessions were then carried out. These made use of audiotapes to teach the child muscle relaxation exercises, fantasy games, and imagination. By the final session, the mean manometer reading dropped to 55 millimeters, which was virtually the same as the reading obtained outside the rectum with no pressure being exerted on the tube. By the second session, the boy had made a small bowel movement in the toilet. By session four, he had defecated five times in the toilet and had soiled accidentally only once over the previous four-day period. In the two weeks prior to the final session, only a single accident occurred, and no soiling accidents were reported during the seven months between the last training session and follow-up. At the time of follow-up, the boy was spontaneously producing consistent bowel movements and his parents observed general improvement in his overall behavior.

COMMENTARY: Relaxation training (RT) is an inexpensive alternative to biofeedback therapy. The latter may require equipment and trained personnel which RT does not necessitate. A particularly appealing aspect of RT is the ease of home practice. Any audiocassette player can serve to facilitate rehearsal of the techniques at home. In addition to RT's use in the present case, the method can be applied whenever a child experiences debilitating performance anxiety—in relation to academic demands, social or athletic situations, and so on. With older children, peer coaching and group applications of relaxation training may be very beneficial.

SOURCE: Walker, C. E. "Treatment of Children's Disorders by Relaxation Training: The Poor Man's Biofeedback." *Journal of Clinical Child Psychology*, 1979, *8*, 22–25.

Stress Inoculation
for Dental Phobic Children

AUTHOR: W. M. Nelson III

PRECIS: Teaching an eleven-year-old girl specific coping skills for handling the fear, anxiety, and pain of dental procedures.

INTRODUCTION: Fear of undergoing dental procedures is widespread. Nelson notes that modern methods of dental treatment effectively eliminate much of the actual pain resulting from dental work. Thus, fear reactions stem mostly from patients' subjective reactions to acute stress and anxiety. Behavioral techniques may not be the most effective way to help children who fear the dentist's chair, since the anxious behavior is not usually related to proximal environmental conditions. An alternative method trains dental phobic children to instruct themselves verbally in order to minimize their fear associated with visiting the dentist.

CASE STUDY: Eleven-year-old AP became so panic-stricken at her first of several scheduled visits for restorative dental work that no actual dental care could be carried out. The following cognitive-behavioral assessment and treatment procedures were used to help AP:

Imagery Assessment. First, AP was told to close her eyes and visualize herself experiencing the recent unsuccessful visit to the dentist. The therapist analyzed the girl's internal dialogue—that is, what she said to herself or did not say to herself before, during, and after specific critical periods in the session with the dentist. The therapist used this information to devise an individualized treatment regimen to counteract the patient's maladaptive responses by teaching alternative self-statements.

Stress Inoculation. During two sixty-minute stress inoculation treatment sessions which preceded AP's next appointment with the dentist, she was trained in and rehearsed specific coping techniques. Then a fifteen-minute booster session was held before each of her two subsequent sessions with the dentist.

The stress inoculation instruction followed the following sequence: First, the therapist modeled the coping self-verbalizations by role playing their appropriate strategic use. AP was shown what she could say: (1) as she was preparing for the dreaded visit to the dentist ("Worrying won't help anything"; "The dentist is really your friend"), (2) as she faced a stressor and/or pain ("Remember what the dentist says and it will be over a lot quicker"; "You're in control"), and (3) when she felt overwhelmed by stress and/or pain ("Just cool it and relax"; "It will be over soon"; "Take a slow, deep breath, relax your muscles"; "Distract yourself by counting to twenty quickly"). The therapist then guided AP as she rehearsed the same self-statements aloud. Following this step, she practiced saying the coping statements by herself. Lastly, AP engaged in covert self-instruction, role playing the fear-inducing scenes and rehearsing her anxiety-reducing self-statements silently.

Self-Reinforcement. The therapist taught AP to reinforce herself after she successfully applied the stress inoculation strategy. She did this by complimenting herself with such comments as, "I did it" and "Seeing the dentist was a snap!"

Relaxation Training. AP was taught to take slow, deep breaths when she noted her breathing becoming shallow and rapid in the dentist's chair.

Attention Diversion. The girl was instructed to distract herself when she began to feel extremely anxious or fearful. She was to do this by counting silently to twenty while she formed a visual image of the numerals.

The use of the stress inoculation program achieved a tremendous decrease in dentists' ratings of AP's "in-chair" disruptive behavior. On a scale ranging from "0" to "4," with high ratings corresponding to greater maladaptive behavior, AP was given an average rating below "1" for her last four visits, where she was rated nearly "4" just before the stress inoculation treatment package training started. These gains were maintained for a period of nearly six months.

COMMENTARY: The procedures Nelson devised were tailored specifically to reduce the fear and anxiety associated with dentistry. By applying elements of the treatment package "as is" with appropriate variations, therapists can help children cope with other situations that induce fearful reactions (for example, tests in school, stage performance, medical treatments, and so on). We strongly advise therapists to consider the stress inoculation method (or part of it) when treating fearful children.

SOURCE: Nelson, W. M., III. "A Cognitive Behavioral Treatment for Disproportionate Dental Anxiety and Pain: A Case Study." *Journal of Clinical Child Psychology,* 1981, *10,* 79–82.

Psychoanalysis of a Five-Year-Old Boy with a Dog Phobia

AUTHOR: Robert L. Tyson

PRECIS: Analytic treatment over a two-year period of a child's persistent fear of dogs.

INTRODUCTION: Tyson presents an extensive discussion of issues that arise in a child phobic's psychoanalysis. He emphasizes that the same surface symptom—here, a young boy's fear of dogs—can maintain its outward form while underlying psychic structures evolve and the conflicts, drive derivations, and related anxieties change in the course of development. The author also considers variations over time in the way this child's fear of dogs was expressed and how these provided critical clues to understanding the boy's developmental difficulties and conflicts and his problems in object relationships.

CASE STUDY: Larry was treated from the time he was five-and-a-half years old until he was nearly seven. Tyson discusses three phases of the boy's analysis; the first phase covered the initial three months; the second phase encompassed the next year; and the third treatment phase extended from the fifteenth month until termination.

In the first phase of Larry's treatment, the analyst watched unintrusively as the boy played with toys, then assisted Larry when he was invited to play with him. Play activities and Larry's mother's discussions with the therapist provided most of the leads to the phallic and oedipal themes the analyst interpreted during this treatment phase.

The second treatment phase was characterized by greater verbal interaction and interpretation as a result of Larry's enhanced communicative skills and his more mature cognitive level of development. During this phase, role play assumed importance as a mode of expression about his fears, including his fear of dogs. Also, Larry's mother became instrumental in providing him with appropriate explanations at home.

During the last year of treatment, analysis continued to assist the boy's maturation and enabled him to tolerate dogs without evidencing any overt signs of anxiety. This absence of panic continued for at least four years after analysis ended, indicating that Larry now had a more effective defensive system as a result of his treatment.

COMMENTARY: The way a symptom may assume a different meaning and function over time and the need to modify treatment methods as a youngster matures are important points in this article. Psychoanalysis assisted Larry in coping with his fear of dogs, and it contributed to his moving forward in his development, generally. There continues to be much discussion of the effectiveness of psychoanalysis relative to other methods, especially those based on learning theory. Those interested in psychoanalysis would benefit from the theoretical discussion and case details presented by Tyson. Many therapists would desensitize the phobia and assist the patient's development using a directive approach.

SOURCE: Tyson, R. L. "Notes on the Analysis of a Prelatency Boy with a Dog Phobia." *Psychoanalytic Study of the Child,* 1978, *33,* 427–457.

Covert Conditioning in Treating Children's Fears

AUTHOR: Joseph R. Cautela

PRECIS: Eliminating children's extreme fearfulness by having them first imagine performing the behaviors targeted for change and then imagine consequences to increase the probability of that behavior.

INTRODUCTION: In covert conditioning, thoughts, images, and feelings are manipulated. The approach has been used successfully to treat a variety of adult disorders. Cautela describes how the method of covert conditioning can ameliorate children's extreme fears.

PROCEDURES: In covert conditioning, a behavioral analysis precedes attempts to modify behavior. The problem behavior is operationally defined and behavioral antecedents and consequences are identified. For example, the therapist seeks to specify what a child means when he or she says he or she has "bad thoughts" and what overt or covert behaviors precede and follow them. Covert reinforcement, covert modeling, and covert extinction procedures are used. First in the therapist's office and then at home, the child practices covert conditioning scenes.

After teaching the child relaxation skills, Cautela tells him or her that pretend games the therapist will teach will be fun as well as helpful in overcoming the child's fears. The therapist describes a detailed scene, such as licking an ice-cream cone or feeling a bug crawling on his arm. He asks the child to pretend the scene is actually happening. After this, the therapist talks with the child about an interesting topic, or the child and therapist play a game, or they engage in some other pleasurable activity, such as taking photographs. Food or token reinforcers may be used to acknowledge the child's cooperation. For homework, the child practices what is taught during the therapy session, using audiotapes for fifteen to twenty minutes before going to bed. The tapes contain directions for the child to follow. The child's parents are asked to reinforce compliance with the homework assignment.

CASE STUDY: Eleven-year-old Brenda had an extreme fear of being alone in her room. This caused her to spend part of each night in her parents' bed. Her fear was spreading so that the girl was becoming afraid to be in any room by herself. Behavioral analysis achieved only limited success with Brenda, eliciting that she believed that something or someone was looking at her through the windows at night unless the window shades were pulled down.

The therapist did the following: (1) He had the girl draw a diagram of her house and fill out the Children's Reinforcement Survey Schedule (Cautela, J. R., and Brion-Meisels, L. "A Children's Reinforcement Survey Schedule." *Psychological Reports*, 1979, *44*, 327–338). (2) He taught her progressive relaxation combined with imagery. (3) He instructed Brenda in covert reinforcement. (4) He had the girl imagine herself in the least fearful room in her house with her family members present. While she held onto this image, she was instructed to switch to a reinforcing scene in imagination. She proceeded to alternate between progressively more fearful scenes and reinforcing ones. (5) Finally, Brenda was taught the self-control triad, consisting of thought stopping, relaxation, and imagining a pleasant scene. She was told to apply this whenever she woke up from her sleep and wanted to go to her parents' room. Also, she was given an audiotape of pleasant scenes to use at such times.

Treatment lasted four months, and it successfully eliminated Brenda's fearfulness. There was no sign of relapse at follow-up twelve months later.

COMMENTARY: Cautela presents a type of therapy in which the child is helped to employ imagination and operant conditioning principles to combat extreme fears. This type of treatment requires that the child be able to follow instructions and be motivated to cooperate with the procedures. Also, parent support is needed, as when the parents must refrain from succumbing to the child's wishes to sleep in their bed. The introduction of recordings of pleasant scenes is a good idea for two reasons: First, it provides variation, which can serve to keep the child's motivation at a high level. Also, it enables the child who may experience occasional difficulty summoning up an image to benefit from the therapeutic strategy. The self-control triad of thought stopping, relaxation, and pleasant imagery has wide applicability to fears, anxiety, depression, and obsessions. Other feasible applications of covert conditioning include its use with children who fear injections, with school phobic youngsters, and for performance-related fears.

SOURCE: Cautela, J. R. "Covert Conditioning with Children." *Journal of Behavior Therapy and Experimental Psychiatry,* 1982, *13,* 209–214.

Play Procedures and Young Children's Separation Fears

AUTHORS: Mary Ellen Milos and Steven Reiss

PRECIS: Thematic play to help children overcome their separation anxiety.

INTRODUCTION: The authors' study evaluates the effects of various types of thematic play (free play, directed play, and modeling) on children whose teachers had rated them high on a measure of anxiety about separation from parents. Thirty-two children of each sex ranging from two-and-a-half to five-and-a-half years old were studied. Prior debate over the assumption that play can reduce anxiety associated with children's psychological problems necessitated an experimental investigation of the therapeutic value of thematic play.

TREATMENT: The children were provided play experiences relevant to separation themes with a nursery school dollhouse. The activity in the *free play* group resembled nondirective play therapy in that the separation-relevant play proceeded however the children desired. The *directed play* group, in which the activity was analogous to structured play therapy, received instructions to focus their attention on separation-relevant play: They were told that a mother doll had brought her child doll to school and that they were to play with any of the dolls any way they liked. The children in the *modeling* group had an opportunity to observe an adult playing out separation themes in a way similar to the way modeling procedures are used in play therapies. "Make-believe" separation themes were portrayed in which children's feelings of fear and anger were highlighted and the child doll adjusted well to separation from the parent doll.

Each child engaged in three individual ten-minute play sessions in one of the thematic play conditions or in a nonthematic group which played with blocks, crayons, coloring books, and other typical nursery school toys. The play sessions were held two to three days apart.

The authors found that all three thematic play conditions resulted in lowered levels of separation anxiety for these children. Verbatim transcripts of the children's speech were analyzed to determine speech disturbance scores, which were taken as the post-test measure of anxiety. No differences were discovered among the free, directed, or modeling play variations. The nonthematic play did not reduce anxiety.

COMMENTARY: Even though the play procedures used here were only analogs of play therapy and the separation anxiety treated was a subclinical problem occurring in very young children, Milos and Reiss's findings lend support to the use of play therapy to help children overcome fears of separating from their parents. Modeling has been very effective in treating children under age eight. An important implication of their work is that for play to ameliorate problems of separation, there must be some thematic link between the play materials and story and the anxiety source. In addition to the usefulness of play situations in the context of therapy, psychologists and other mental health consultants can introduce thematic play into school and camp situations during the initial periods when separation anxiety is most common. This might serve a valuable preventive function, minimizing disruptions that could arise from the behavior of highly anxious children in the group.

SOURCE: Milos, M. E., and Reiss, S. "Effects of Three Play

Conditions on Separation Anxiety in Young Children." *Journal of Counseling and Clinical Psychology*, 1982, *50* (3), 389-395.

Brief Cognitively Based Preparation to Reduce Children's Fear of Needles

AUTHOR: David Fassler

PPRECIS: Reduction of hospitalized children's needle fears via a single-session intervention program entailing information giving, emotional support, desensitization, modeling, projective techniques, and correcting the child's misconceptions.

INTRODUCTION: Hypodermic needles have been found to be extremely fear-provoking stimuli for hospitalized children and adults. Fassler notes that previous attempts to reduce fear of needles have utilized mostly behavior modification procedures. A problem with these has been that substitute symptoms have sometimes appeared; also, phobic responses occasionally have reemerged after treatment ended. This study was the first controlled investigation to appear in the literature which was designed to examine the efficacy of ways of cognitively preparing hospitalized children to receive injections. Thirty children ranging in age from six to nine, patients in the orthopedic service of an urban hospital, participated in the study. They were randomly assigned to treatment and nontreatment groups such that each category was composed of children of similar age and sex.

TREATMENT: The therapist saw each child in the treatment group for approximately forty-five minutes. He or she was read the story *Tommy Goes to the Doctor* by Gunilla Wolde (Boston: Houghton Mifflin, 1972). This book tells the story of a child who receives an injection from a doctor and then reenacts this episode in play with his teddy bear at home. After reading the story, the therapist discussed the medical procedure with the child, clarifying any misconceptions the youngster might have had. He then asked the child to produce drawings of "a needle" and "getting shot." Child and therapist discussed the child's fears and fantasies relative to these. Following this, a narrative poem was read which related the story of a child who imagined himself giving the doctor a shot but discovered that the doctor feared needles. Lastly, the child pretended he or she was a doctor; using a doll, water-filled syringes, and other toys, the child play acted administering an injection.

Before and after the treatment, measures were taken of each child's pulse rate, perceived pain, and behavior. Behavioral categories rated on a seven-item, ten-point scale included: fear, cooperation, anxiety, verbal protest, physical protest, verbal expression of pain, and physical expression of pain. A hand-pressure method was used as the index of the youngster's perception of pain. The child was asked to squeeze a rubber bulb that was attached to a 300-millimeter mercury-column sphygmomanometer by a three-foot-long flexible rubber hose. A hand pressure pain index (HPPI) was derived from determining the child's scores when he or she squeezed as hard as he or she could (I), as hard as the needle hurt (II), and as hard as possible again (III). The formula used to determine the HPPI was as follows: $2(II)/(I)+(III)$.

The group that received the intervention showed considerable reduction in its fear of hypodermic needles. On all measures except verbal expression of pain, the experimental group exhibited marked improvement; no similar gains were seen for the children who did not take part in the intervention program.

COMMENTARY: This study shows that children can be helped to cope more calmly with painful medical procedures. Once again, we see an interesting combination of methods, such as information giving, desensitization, modeling, and the correcting of misconceptions (cognitive restructuring). Those who work with children undergoing other routine and emergency medical and dental treatments can adapt Fassler's methods to provide the sort of supportive context he has shown to help young patients. It may be that not all youngsters profit from brief intervention. Prior pain experience, age, intellectual level, and other variables may serve to differentiate children who respond to this form of brief treatment from those who may require more extended forms of intervention in order to tolerate painful experiences with equanimity.

SOURCE: Fassler, D. "The Fear of Needles in Children." *American Journal of Orthopsychiatry*, 1985, *55* (3), 371–377.

Additional Readings

Chudy, J. F., Jones, G. E., and Dickson, A. L. "Modified Desensitization Approach for the Treatment of Phobic Behavior in Children: A Quasi-Experimental Case Study." *Journal of Clinical Child Psychology*, 1983, *12*, 198–201.

A seven-year-old boy became a "prisoner in his home" after twice being scratched by dogs. A combination of emotive imagery, play, covert and overt modeling, and behavioral rehearsal were employed to treat the child's dog phobic behavior. The boy participated in eight treatment sessions. The procedure resulted in an increase in the number of times per day the boy left his house and fenced yard from 0.1 to 1.76 and a significant diminution in his fearful responsiveness around dogs.

Graziano, A. M., and Mooney, K. C. "Family Self-Control Instruction for Children's Nighttime Fear Reduction." *Journal of Consulting and Clinical Psychology*, 1980, *48*, 206–213.

Thirty-three six- to twelve-year-old children with severe nighttime fears were randomly assigned to a family self-control treatment group or a waiting list control group. Over three weeks, the experimental group children were instructed in, practiced, and self-monitored nightly self-control exercises. During the same period, their parents participated in a training program that enabled them to supervise, monitor, and reinforce their children's home exercises. The exercises consisted of muscle relaxation, imagining a pleasant scene, and reciting "brave" self-statements. Training time for parents amounted to about five hours and for children about three hours. Home practice required less than five minutes nightly. The family intervention package resulted in significant and sustained reduction in the children's nighttime fears.

Jackson, H. J., and King, N. J. "The Emotive Imagery Treatment of a Child's Trauma-Induced Phobia." *Journal of Behaviour Therapy and Experimental Psychiatry*, 1984, *15*, 325–328.

A five-and-a-half-year-old boy's fears of the dark, noise, and shadows were eliminated in four sessions through the use of emotive imagery and a response induction aid (a battery-operated household flashlight). A nineteen-item desensitization hierarchy was contructed, which incorporated the child's extreme fear of the dark and associated fears. Therapy involved the youngster actively in imagining himself confronting each step in the fear hierarchy in the role of "special agent," serving alongside his hero, the comic strip character Batman. The flashlight served as a means of providing protective conditions to enhance the effects of treatment. It enabled the boy to develop positive coping skills, as it was placed alongside his bed and he was allowed to turn it on for a brief time when he became afraid. Treatment gains were maintained for at least eighteen months. The authors suggest that emotive imagery represents an important alternative to systematic desensitization, which young children may find too difficult because of their limited ability to follow instructions.

Mansdorf, I. J. "Eliminating Somatic Complaints in Separation Anxiety Through Contingency Management." *Journal of Behaviour Therapy and Experimental Psychiatry*, 1981, *12*, 73–75.

The author reports the use of a contingency management procedure employed by the mother of an eight-year-old girl, which resulted in the rapid elimination of the child's separation-related somatic complaints. For a week, the mother noted the time and place of every one of the girl's somatic complaints. She also logged what was done immediately after the episode. Then the contingency management procedure was implemented. It entailed two stages: (1) extinction: the mother withheld all attention from her daughter whenever one of the characteristic complaints occurred; and (2) reinforcement: maternal attention for behaviors that were incompatible with complaining of pain. The contingency management treatment reduced the number of somatic complaints from ten during the week of log taking to three during the first treatment week and one during the next week. During the third week and thereafter, no such episodes were recorded.

Rosensteil, A. K., and Scott, D. S. "Four Considerations in Using Imagery Techniques with Children." *Journal of Behavior Therapy and Experimental Psychiatry,* 1977, *8,* 287–290.

The authors propose guidelines for therapists intending to employ imagery techniques with children. They recommend: (1) tailoring imagery scenes to fit the age of the child; (2) incorporating children's existing fantasies and cognitions, (3) using nonverbal cues to supply important information about the treatment process, and (4) utilizing the child's verbal reports of images in treatment.

Sheslow, D. V., Bondy, A. S., and Nelson, R. O. "A Comparison of Graduated Exposure, Verbal Coping Skills and Their Combination in the Treatment of Children's Fear of the Dark." *Child and Family Therapy,* 1982, *4,* 33–45.

The authors conclude that modifying children's fear of the dark is accomplished by exposing them gradually to darkness. The subjects of the study were thirty-two four- and five-year-old children who had a strong fear of the dark. Children who were taught verbal coping skills to increase their darkness tolerance did not improve significantly. Children who were gradually exposed to a nine-step hierarchy of decreasing illumination developed the greatest tolerance for darkness. Children trained in verbal coping procedures combined with direct exposure to the dark also showed significant improvement.

Twardosz, S., Weddle, K., Borden, L., and Stevens, E. "A Comparison of Three Methods of Preparing Children for Surgery." *Behavior Therapy*, 1986, *17*, 14-25.

Sixty children scheduled for ear, nose, or throat surgery that required overnight hospitalization received one of three preoperative treatments. Twenty of the three- to twelve-year-olds participated in a preoperative class given by a nurse who explained pre- and postsurgical procedures. An equal number of children viewed a videotape of a preoperative class conducted by the same nurse. The remaining children received no special preparation prior to their surgery. The preoperative class was found to be most effective in reducing the children's fear reactions relative to the impending surgical procedures.

Wallick, M. M. "Desensitization Therapy with a Fearful Two-Year-Old." *American Journal of Psychiatry*, 1979, *136*, 1325-1326.

A two-year-old girl developed excessive doctor- and hospital-related fear reactions after she underwent chest surgery. She also became frightened of strangers and of noises and faces on television. These fears were diminished through desensitization therapy of five months' duration. Treatment consisted of dramatic play with blocks and dolls and *in vivo* desensitization, during which she visited a dental school, explored the pedodontics floor, met a doctor, and allowed him to examine her. There was no return of the child's fears when she was followed up six months, one year, and two years after therapy was terminated.

Warren, R., Deffenbacher, J. L., and Brading, P. "Rational-Emotive Therapy and the Reduction of Test Anxiety in Elementary School Students." *Rational Living*, 1976, *11*, 26-29.

Thirty-six test anxious boys and girls in fifth and sixth grades were randomly assigned to a rational-emotive therapy (RET) group or a no-treatment control group. The group treated by RET met seven times over a five-week period for thirty minutes each time. The sessions covered basic RET concepts and their application to taking tests. While both groups showed significant reductions in self-reported test anxiety from pre- to post-testing, the group trained in RET showed much more test anxiety reduction. The two groups did not differ in their performance on a test of arithmetic given after the treatment period, and no evidence of treatment generalization to other anxieties was seen.

Reactions to Trauma

A trauma is an emotional or physical shock or a bodily injury, which often has some lasting psychological effect. Children are often not prepared to cope with the traumatic event, and they feel helpless, anxious, and fearful. The American Psychiatric Association's Diagnostic and Statistical Manual of Mental Disorders *(3rd ed.)* (Washington, D.C.: American Psychiatric Association, 1980) *discusses a post-traumatic stress disorder: Frequent reactions following a trauma are recurrent dreams and recollections of the traumatic event, diminished interest in activities, feelings of detachment, and constricted affect. The following symptoms may be seen: hyperalertness or an exaggerated startle response, sleep disturbance, survival guilt, poor concentration and/or memory, avoiding activities that arouse memory of the event, and intensified symptoms when exposed to events symbolizing or resembling the traumatic event.*

Psychoanalytically Oriented Play Therapy with Abused Preschool Children

AUTHOR: Arthur H. Green

PRECIS: Dynamically oriented techniques, including play, interpreting behaviors and feelings, parent counseling, and school consultation to treat physically abused children.

INTRODUCTION: Children who have been physically abused typically display personality and behavior disorders that include: basic suspicion and mistrust of adults; low frustration tolerance and impulsivity; inability to delay gratification; a need to exploit, manipulate, and control objects; preference for motoric rather than verbal expression; and use of symbols. Often, these youngsters are preoccupied with violent fantasies depicting scenes of physical attack, spankings, and retaliation. Developmental lags, particularly in the speech and language areas, and bed wetting are common. So, too, is a gross unevenness of functioning, such that precocious ability in some areas (such as unusual motor skill) coexists with the child's defective abilities. Beneath a facade of pseudoindependence and omnipotence, these children feel helpless, depressed, angry, and ambivalent about contact with others. They blame themselves for the maltreatment they have suffered, and they are convinced that they are "bad." The psychotherapeutic procedures applied are designed to modify the abused child's pathological inner world. Treatment interrupts the vicious cycle in which the child recreates the original sadomasochistic relationship derived from interaction with parents. Simultaneously with the individual therapy of the child, the family engages in multidisciplinary treatment.

TREATMENT: The goals of treatment are to alleviate the major psychopathological sequelae of child abuse and to safeguard the child's future development. The strategies used to help Josephine were based on psychoanalytic theory and emphasized ego integration, reality testing, containing drives and impulses, and strengthening higher-level defenses.

Relieving Acute Traumatic Reactions. Acute phobic anxiety related to being beaten often occurs with abused children. The initial sessions of therapy are devoted to allowing the child to master the trauma through repetition and symbolic reenactment using play, dolls, puppets, and drawings. Simultaneously the parents are counseled to curb their assaultive behavior.

Repairing Ego Functioning. The therapist encourages the child to verbalize and to refrain from acting impulsively. Structured latency games are employed in the service of strengthening the child's reality testing and promoting sublimation. Consolidating the therapist-child relationship provides support for the child and allows him or her to gratify dependency strivings. The bond between the child and the therapist is viewed as critical for the child's developing more adaptive ego defenses, such as repression, sublimation, and reaction formation, in lieu of the overuse of denial, projection, and splitting.

Improving Object Relations. The therapist assumes an active and supportive posture—for example, pointing out that the child's tendencies to act provocatively stem from the child's frustration at the disparity between his or her enormous dependency needs and the therapist's limited availability as a real object. The child's need to feel important and powerful is interpreted as compensation for conscious feelings of weakness and inadequacy. Also interpreted is the youngster's resultant sense of being bad and his or her fear of punishment, as well as the sadomasochistic nature of the child's relationship with his or her parents, which has led the child to elicit punishment from the therapist. It is pointed out that the child's attempt to recreate the original "bad parent bad child" relationship with the therapist represents the youngster's way to try to master the original parent-child relationship. The stable therapeutic alliance between the child and therapist is seen as the vehicle allowing the child to develop better reality ties, to use primitive defenses less often, and to form an identification with the therapist's values and attitudes.

Improving Impulse Controls. The child's direct expression of aggression is limited. The therapist encourages the child to verbally express anger or to express it symbolically through play, instead of hitting and breaking toys and playroom materials. Limits are adhered to regarding entering and leaving the playroom, taking toys and materials, and the length of sessions. Activities such as stories and art work and typical latency games serve to rechannel and neutralize aggression.

Improving Self-Esteem. The climate of warmth and acceptance established by the therapist fosters improvement in the child's self-image. Self-esteem is also facilitated by the child's achieving greater mastery in daily activities and improvement in his or her interpersonal relationships. The therapist sometimes confronts the child to disabuse thoughts that he or she may have brought on the beatings because of an intrinsic "badness."

Building the Child's Capacity to Tolerate Separation. The therapist strives to keep treatment interruptions to a minimum. Matters such as vacations, cancelled appointments, and changes of therapists are explained very clearly and worked through. Reassurance is actively given to communicate interest in the child in the absence of contact. To promote the internalization of the therapist's mental representation during separations, the child may be allowed to take home symbols of the therapist, such as drawings, candy, and pencils.

Improving School Performance. The therapist maintains contact with the child's teacher and serves as liaison between the child's parents and school personnel. The parents are counseled about the nonvolitional origins of the child's school behaviors, such as hyperactivity, inadequate span of attention, and impaired cognition. This information-giving function of the therapist is vital in moving toward interrupting the vicious cycle of academic failure, physical abuse, and disruptive school behavior.

COMMENTARY: Green highlights the need to approach abused children's needs in a comprehensive way. Direct psychotherapeutic and psychoeducational interventions plus family treatment must combine in order to effect changes in the child's pathological inner and outer worlds. Green reports success with this approach, based on clinical impressions involving many

abused inner-city children. The reader should note that many of
the methods described are typically employed by therapists with
very different theoretical orientations. Also, therapists should
make sure that "hyperactivity, poor attention, and impaired
cognition" are adequately evaluated. When constitutionally
based learning disabilities are identified, appropriate education
and treatment must follow.

SOURCE: Green, A. H. "Psychiatric Treatment of Abused Children." *Journal of the American Academy of Child Psychiatry*, 1978, *17*, 356–371.

Paraverbal Therapy with Traumatically
Injured and Chronically Ill Children

AUTHOR: Laura McDonnell

PRECIS: Short-term use of a multisensory expressive media
technique with hospital patients to reduce their emotional disturbance secondary to illness or trauma.

INTRODUCTION: Entering the hospital is a stressful event for
a child. Paraverbal therapy creates a pleasurable, stimulating,
and reciprocal interaction between the hospitalized child and a
nonmedical, nonthreatening adult in order to reduce the stresses
of being in the hospital. McDonnell presents several case vig-
nettes in which paraverbal therapy significantly assisted the children's hospital adjustment and adaptations. In one case, Sam, a
four-year-old boy who had been severely burned, was helped to
deal with his anxieties and concerns through the use of musical
and dramatic techniques plus discussion.

TREATMENT: The goal of paraverbal therapy is to reduce
stresses by providing an experience of human closeness and

shared pleasure, with opportunities for motor release. With Sam, the therapist improvised a song on an autoharp at the boy's bedside, and she allowed him to use the instrument and others he asked her for, such as wrist bells and bongos. During ten paraverbal therapy sessions, Sam was given many choices as to instruments and song lyrics. The therapist encouraged expression of the boy's thoughts and feelings about painful hospital procedures, such as needles, IVs, the drawing of blood, his accident, and homesickness. The boy's spontaneous comments and his responses to questions about a song's content led to discussions with the therapist that enabled him to relive the specific trauma of the accident and to tolerate the fears, pain, and loneliness attendant to being in the hospital.

COMMENTARY: McDonnell demonstrates how paraverbal therapy can supplement medical care to provide attention to hospitalized children's psychological needs. As a tool for lessening emotional distress, this technique can quickly focus on central areas of anxiety and concern for the patients. Paraverbal therapy can allow the appropriate discharge of tensions as well as communication of painful feelings. Group supervision is an excellent format for training paraprofessionals and ensuring quality treatment.

SOURCE: McDonnell, L. "Paraverbal Therapy in Pediatric Cases with Emotional Complications." *American Journal of Orthopsychiatry*, 1979, *19* (1), 44-52.

Reattachment Therapy
with Young Abuse Victims

AUTHORS: Donald Frazier and Elaine LeVine

PRECIS: Improving symptoms in very young victims of physical abuse and curbing the continuation of the abuse cycle by creating a corrective bonding relationship, prompting attachment behaviors in the child, and teaching the child how to actively induce attachment from the primary caretaker.

INTRODUCTION: Treatment approaches aimed at eradicating child abuse have focused almost exclusively on the abusers. There has been little systematic psychotherapeutic programming for children ages zero to four years, despite the facts that children of this age range are the most frequent victims of abuse, both immediate and long-term deleterious consequences result from maltreatment during this period, and the behaviors of young abuse victims often are instrumental in provoking and maintaining aggressive parental responses. Reattachment therapy (RT) reflects the assumption that therapy will be more effective if direct intervention with the child victim occurs concurrently with therapy for the adult abuser. It emphasizes the importance of bonding between young abuse victims and their parents.

Good candidates for RT are children who have suffered physical abuse during the first four to six years of life, the formative period for personality structures; youngsters whose various inhibitory, bizarre, or antisocial behaviors serve to agitate further aggression from their primary caretaker; and those whose offending parents are willing and able to undergo collateral psychotherapy.

Through the primary medium of play sessions, treatment is aimed at ameliorating the developmental disturbances associated with early abuse in young children. Another treatment goal is to enhance the victim's ability to reestablish a more healthy bond with the primary caretaker.

PROCEDURES: There are two overlapping phases of therapeutic intervention. While these are aimed at somewhat different goals, their techniques and outcomes do overlap.

Attachment Substitution Phase. The therapist does the following: (1) creates a benign, permissive, warm atmosphere by exercising patience and unconditionally accepting the child's behaviors. He or she systematically uses conditioning principles to actively countercondition the child's acquired tendency to associate adults with painful and aversive stimuli as well as to shape and model increased social interaction; (2) stimulates attachment bonding from the child by actively gratifying various infant needs, such as feeding, treating cuts and scratches, facilitating sleep, changing soiled clothes, and so on.

Parental Attachment Inducement Phase. This phase is characterized by more directive, operant, and independence-building activities as compared to the relatively passive, fully accepting and trust-building quality of the initial phase. The therapist's actions are geared toward helping the child behave so as to elicit attachment behavior from others, particularly his or her original caretaker. The guiding parameters for affecting attachment inducement are: (1) The therapist focuses on improving the child's physical appearance by attending to dimensions of physical appearance that are modifiable, such as bizarre body movements and personal hygiene. (2) The therapist reinforces aggression-inhibiting behaviors of the child, such as making eye contact, smiling, laughing, cooing, reaching, and so on. Elicitation of such responses is incompatible with aggression and facilitates positive experiences between the child and caretaker that will serve to strengthen their own attachment bond. (3) The therapist focuses on decreasing clinging behavior by encouraging the child to try novel activities and by noticing and praising the youngster's autonomous behaviors. (4) The therapist focuses on eliminating behaviors in the child that in the past frequently preceded the abusing parent's attacks by actively rewarding the child for intervals of time in which the target behavior was not displayed ("omission training") and responding nonpunitively and by withholding the reward and talking with the child about how he felt about the inappropriate behavior when it did occur. (5) The therapist terminates treatment when the child has become reattached to his or her caretaker and normal developmental processes have been restored, taking care to accomplish termination very gradually at a pace the child can tolerate and to coordinate termination of treatment with the resolution of the parents' treatment issues.

CASE STUDY: Four-year-old Linda was the victim of continual physical abuse during her entire life. She was brought to the therapist by her mother, who complained of the girl's "irritating behavior." The child's extensive body bruises were immediately apparent; her mother was referred to the local mental health center for treatment, while Linda began eight months of biweekly therapy sessions.

TREATMENT:
    Establishing a Consistently Nonpunitive Climate. At the initial session, the youngster screamed uncontrollably when her mother left the playroom. Then she fell to the floor, assuming a fetal position for the entire hour, alternately rocking her body and gnawing on her hands. For six sessions, she neither spoke to the therapist nor acknowledged his presence. Acute emotional outbursts ensued whenever attempts to comfort and soothe her were tried. Mostly, the therapist just sat as close to Linda as the child would tolerate, remained quiet or hummed children's songs, or reflected aloud to the girl in ways that signaled to her that she was being monitored.
    The therapist's verbal and nonverbal behaviors remained benign whenever the child displayed signs of distrust. Occasionally, the therapist verbally paired the child's name with his in order to facilitate an association between the two of them and offered support in an alter-ego manner (for example, "Linda seems sad and Don would like to know what to do that would help, but Linda doesn't seem to want to talk now, so maybe I'll just ask again later"). Whenever Linda interrupted her sobbing or glanced at the therapist, these behaviors were reinforced by a smile that was accompanied by verbal reflection about what

she had done, as well as by occasional presentation of novel stimuli. The therapist also systematically desensitized the child to his nearness to her by edging progressively closer each session in a benign way. By the tenth session, the two were side by side, and Linda reciprocated physical contact by grasping the therapist's thumb and allowing him to slip her hand into his.

Linda's outbursts became shorter and less intense with each session. She began to explore the toys and other objects in the playroom. Soon the crying fits disappeared entirely; they were replaced by a stated good-bye.

Stimulating Attachment Behaviors. Methods that figured prominently here were shaping gradual approach and modeling social overtures. The therapist attempted to have Linda recognize and respond to him as a real object by acknowledging all of the girl's vocalizations and trying to understand her communicative attempts, trying to make frequent eye contact with her and making available music boxes, velvet paintings to touch, clay, fur animals, and finger paints as the child overcame her initial aversion to treatment. In later sessions, responsiveness was stimulated by sitting beside Linda for the entire session, increasing the frequency of touch in a gradual fashion, and giving Linda a strong reward for her self-initiated contacts. Whenever Linda reached for the therapist, he quickly responded by placing her on his lap.

To help the child approach an adult when she wanted physical or psychological nurturance, the therapist ministered to her basic needs, thereby showing her that adults can be counted on to help children in this manner. For example, during one session the therapist observed Linda grabbing a toy baby bottle from a shelf and hiding under a table while sucking on it as if nursing. The therapist placed a sweet water solution in the bottle and lifted Linda onto his lap while gently rocking and stroking her arms and hair. For more than twenty minutes, the child continued to nurse, and her eyes met the therapist's the entire time.

Improving the Child's Physical Appearance. The therapist referred Linda for appropriate speech and ophthalmological treatment, and he reinforced discernible progress in these areas.

Further, he washed her face and combed her hair when she came to sessions unkempt; eventually Linda's mother attended to having her neat and clean when she came to treatment. Self-biting was extinguished within two months by using the response elimination technique of omission training in combination with nonpunitive confrontation when the target behavior was observed (for example, "It makes me feel sad when I see someone that I care about hurting herself. It doesn't make my hand hurt, like you're biting it, but I just don't like to see people who are special to me being hurt. Would you please stop?").

Reinforcing Aggression-Neutralizing Behaviors. When responses that are incompatible with caretaker aggression were evidenced, these were actively rewarded. Systematic reinforcement of such behaviors as smiling and eye contact caused Linda to increase them, and positive transfer to the child's interactions was noted.

Decreasing Clinging Behavior. The therapist encouraged Linda to attempt novel activities, and he pointed out and praised her autonomous behaviors. For example, once he said to her, "Today I'm sitting farther away from you, and you are doing just fine." When the child attempted a new puzzle, he remarked, "Look how fast you have figured out that new puzzle —and you'd never even seen it before. It was new, and you weren't even afraid of it!"

Eliminating Provocative Behaviors. Linda's decreased stuttering and the removal of her self-mutilating behavior contributed to lessening the tension Linda's mother felt around her daughter. Also, Linda's daytime enuresis was decreased via the omission training procedure, combined with nonpunitive ministration of the situation when "mistakes" occasionally happened in treatment.

Fading Treatment Intensity and Frequency. This was accomplished very gradually. Linda was encouraged to talk about her upcoming separation from the therapist, and her temporary regressions (recurrence of bed wetting, stuttering, clinging to the therapist) were accepted nonpunitively by the therapist, who merely reflected them, allowed Linda to play them out, or ignored them. At the same time, the therapist communicated to the child assurances that he would remain available to her by offering extended sessions and promises of occasional phone calls or visits. Also, he communicated with Linda's mother's clinician in order to enlist the mother's support for allowing Linda to continue treatment until the girl had fully resolved her separation crisis.

By the end of treatment, Linda's mother had stopped abusing her; the girl's stuttering, inaudible voice and limited vocabulary had evolved into well-articulated sentences; Linda was attending kindergarten, and she had acquired basic academic skills; her health, dress, general appearance, and physical agility had all improved notably; she could separate from her mother without exhibiting any emotional outbursts; many of her behaviors that had provoked and maintained parental aggression were no longer evident.

COMMENTARY: The authors illustrate the importance to the therapeutic process of repairing disruption of parent-infant attachment. The chances of breaking the cycle of intergenerational child abuse would seem to be best when normal growth processes are restored as early as possible in the young abuse victim's life. Most striking is teaching the child to smile, laugh, reach, maintain eye contact, and so on, which are behaviors that decrease parental aggression. While Frazier and Levine note that reattachment therapy is not appropriate for long-term older abuse victims, the rebonding may prove to be greatest when supportive psychotherapy is administered over an extended period of time.

SOURCE: Frazier, D., and LeVine, E. "Reattachment Therapy: Intervention with the Very Young Physically Abused Child." *Psychotherapy*, 1983, *20*, 90–100.

A Behavioral Package Treatment for
Children Undergoing Painful
Medical Procedures

AUTHORS: Charles H. Elliott and Roberta A. Olson

PRECIS: A stress management program for reducing the behavioral distress of children undergoing highly painful burn-injury treatments.

INTRODUCTION: Severely painful medical procedures are extremely distressful for children. Examples of such procedures are hydrotherapy, debridement, and dressing changes, which are all part of treatment for severe burns. Many burned children require these medical treatments as often as twice daily for months.

The authors report the use of a variety of stress management and coping strategies for ameliorating the distress of eight five- to twelve-year-old boys undergoing treatment for burn injuries. These children suffered second- or third-degree burns over 5 to 68 percent of their total body surfaces.

TREATMENT: The treatment package made use of a variety of strategies for reducing pain:

Attention Distraction. The therapist explained that paying attention to stimuli besides those having to do with the painful medical procedure—searching the room for hidden objects or performing mental mathematics work—could assist in lessening the experience of pain.

Relaxation Breathing. The child was taught to "pump himself up"—pretend he was an inflated tire and slowly emit air while making a hissing sound and instructing himself to remain calm and relaxed.

Emotive Imagery and/or Reinterpreting the Context of the Pain. With the therapist's help, the child imagined two scenes: one that was heroic and the other relaxing. For example, a boy developed the image of himself injured in a boating accident, and despite his injury he swam to save friends with him who were drowning. One patient's relaxing image involved envisioning himself floating in the ocean while hydrotherapy was being administered. These scenes were used during the burn treatment sessions. The heroic image was summoned up from the beginning of the treatment session through the first couple of minutes the child was in the water tank. During the remainder of the hydrotherapy treatment phase, the relaxing image was utilized.

Reinforcement. For using the coping procedures, the younger children received "happy faces" and toys, and the older children were praised by the therapist, physicians, physical therapists, and nurses. The latter patients also received model toys that they could assemble, as well as the privilege of playing electronic and other games.

The four types of pain and stress management strategies were taught and reviewed during a single forty-five-minute session conducted by the therapist with each child. Then the therapist intermittently coached each patient while he made use of the techniques during sessions of hydrotherapy. At burn treatment sessions that the therapist did not attend, the child was expected to utilize these strategies on his own.

Level of distress was measured by calculating scores over one coping behavior—hissing while expelling air (taught as part of a coping behavior)—and eight distress behaviors. These were: number of groans and screams, expressions of verbal fear, verbal pain expressions, requests for emotional support, muscular rigidity, verbal resistance, physical resistance, and flailing. Measurements were taken over three phases of treatment: while bandages were being unwrapped, during the fifteen-minute period while medication was being washed off and dead skin removed, and during physical therapy and rewrapping of the burned areas. Ten-second observation periods alternated with ten-second recording periods on a continual basis.

Examination of the data trends for the children revealed that the stress management and coping methods substantially reduced their behavioral distress associated with the burn treatment procedures. The presence of the coach (therapist) was essential, as the patients' distress levels did not show any reduction on noncoaching days.

COMMENTARY: Treatments to calm children's distress generally have focused on helping children cope with the dentist's chair and impending surgery. Elliott and Olson have demonstrated that a package treatment can produce improved behavioral adjustment when children undergo severely painful procedures on a recurring basis. It is apparently not the case that treatment benefits relate to the child's age or the severity of the burns. While Elliott and Olson found that the package treatment was ineffective when the therapist was not actually present to serve as "coach," it would be interesting to see whether filmed and/or paraprofessional coaches could be employed during the weeks and months when daily coaching is needed. Generalization training should be part of the program. Children could imagine themselves doing well without the therapist, be rewarded, and then have brief periods in which the therapist leaves during burn treatment.

SOURCE: Elliott, C. H., and Olson, R. A. "The Management of Children's Distress in Response to Painful Medical Treatment for Burn Injuries." *Behaviour Research and Therapy*, 1983, *21* (6), 675-683.

Handling Reactions
to a Teacher's Sudden Death

AUTHORS: Barbara Brooks, Gary Silverman, and R. Glen Hass

PRECIS: Case study helping a class of latency-age children cope with their feelings following the untimely death of their teacher.

INTRODUCTION: During the latency years of childhood, adults other than parents assume increased significance in a child's life. According to psychoanalytic theory, during this period sexual and aggressive drives of the child are transferred from the parent to the teacher. Therefore, the death of the teacher during this time is viewed as especially significant. Guided by their belief that the healthy development of children whose teacher dies would be more likely if they could express and experience the profound emotions and conflicts associated with the loss of the teacher, the authors devised a series of initiatives to help a third-grade class of seven- and eight-year-olds to cope with this very stressful event.

TREATMENT: The authors carried out a four-phase consultation and crisis intervention plan to support the bereaved youngsters after their young teacher died suddenly following the complications of a cold.

Attendance at the Teacher's Funeral. The class was invited to attend the funeral as a group. Their parents were encouraged to participate as well, if they wished. When some of the children explored the hearse before the funeral began, their behavior was not curbed. The authors interpreted this as the children's attempt to gain some degree of mastery over the fearful unknown through greater cognitive understanding.

Class Discussion. Upon returning to school after the funeral, the school's principal and two of the authors led a class discussion. This forum enabled the students who did not attend the funeral to hear it described by their classmates who had been there. Also, it allowed the children to progress from describing the funeral events to airing their feelings about their teacher's death. Feelings of fear, guilt, anger, and regret surfaced, often expressed in the context of remembered dreams. At the conclusion of the discussion, the children came up with the idea that they wished to contribute to a gift in memory of their teacher.

Parent Group. Two weeks after the death of the teacher, parents of children in the class met with the principal, the consultants, the school psychologist, and the new teacher. The parents were helped to provide emotional support to their children as children's typical grief responses were explained. Of particular value was the group's consideration of the impact of the teacher's death upon siblings of children in the target class.

Some of the brothers and sisters had shown a rejection of their own teachers, resistance to attending school, and a great deal of protectiveness toward their parents in the interim since the teacher had died. The replacement teacher brought up the children's difficulties in forming a new bond with her. The meeting enabled the significant figures in the children's lives to develop greater understanding and to incorporate more appropriate expectations of the children during the post-traumatic grief period.

Interviews. Six weeks after the funeral, individual interviews with nine of the children in the class took place. These helped elucidate the kind and power of the defense mechanisms employed by bereaved latency-age children. The children continued to use repression, projection, and denial as their primary defensive maneuvers. Through dreams, daydreams, and group "pretends," the children maintained emotional connectedness to their deceased teacher. They still sought emotional support from one another and, to a lesser degree, from their parents.

COMMENTARY: Brooks, Silverman, and Hass indicate that mental health professionals can serve vital roles as crisis resource managers. Children spend more time at school than anywhere else except the home as they grow up. As the authors illustrate, schools can mobilize their resident and community mental health resources to deal with the predictable emotional reverberations when there is a sudden loss of a member of the school community. Class discussions provide the ideal environment for children to learn that all emotional reactions are normal and acceptable. Other organizations, such as camps, and other recreational facilities can benefit from staff training in dealing with crises so as to facilitate the healthy expression of the grief, confusion, and anxiety that children feel.

SOURCE: Brooks, B., Silverman, G., and Hass, R. G. "When a Teacher Dies: A School-Based Intervention with Latency Children." *American Journal of Orthopsychiatry,* 1985, *55* (3), 405–410.

Additional Readings

Adams-Greenly, M., and Moynihan, R. T. "Helping the Children of Fatally Ill Parents." *American Journal of Orthopsychiatry*, 1983, *53*, 219-229.

Adams-Greenly and Moynihan discuss a sequence of anticipatory measures for children during the course of a parent's fatal illness and after the parent dies. These are designed to prepare the youngster to cope with the parental death and to foster their long-term adaptation. The interventions include enlisting parents as partners in offering support to the children, providing the children with factual diagnostic information, arranging visits to the hospital, and interpreting the medical status. When the parent expires, the child is informed quickly thereafter by the surviving parent. Also, the child is included in rituals, such as wakes and funerals, and follow-up contact with the child and the surviving parent is scheduled.

Lystad, M. "Innovative Mental Health Services for Child Disaster Victims." *Children Today*, 1985, *12*, 13-17.

The author describes immediate and delayed reactions of children following natural and man-made disasters and presents some basic principles of treating child disaster victims. Age-specific interventions for children in disasters are organized according to three developmental levels: interventions for preschoolers; those geared to elementary school-age children; and strategies for preadolescents and adolescents. The author emphasizes primary and secondary prevention and describes materials that can be used by families and schools.

Pedro-Carroll, J. L., and Cowen, E. L. "The Children of Divorce Intervention Program: An Investigation of the Efficacy of a School-Based Prevention Program." *Journal of Consulting and Clinical Psychology*, 1985, *53*, 603-611.

More than one million children a year experience the trauma of parental divorce. Pedro-Carroll and Cowen report a study of a preventively oriented, school-based, ten-week program in which forty fourth- to sixth-grade children of divorce were compared to thirty demographically matched controls.

Goals of the program included sharing common experiences and feelings, clarifying common misperceptions, learning a process for overcoming interpersonal problems, and developing skills in the areas of communication and anger control. On the basis of ratings by teachers, parents, trained group leaders, and the participating children, the intervention was seen as producing a supportive atmosphere for the participants and an increase in their competencies, such as the ability to solve personal problems.

Pruett, K. D. "Home Treatment for Two Infants Who Witnessed Their Mother's Murder." *Journal of the American Academy of Child Psychiatry,* 1979, *18,* 647–657.

Siblings, two and three-and-a-half years old, respectively, saw the shotgun murder of their mother by their father and his subsequent suicide attempt. A psychodynamically oriented approach to psychotherapy helped the sister and brother to cope following the massive trauma. Treatment was conducted twice weekly for three months in the home of the children's maternal grandparents. In addition, the therapist frequently spoke on the telephone with the children and with the grandparents between visits.

Schoettle, U. C. "Child Exploitation—A Study of Child Pornography." *Journal of the American Academy of Child Psychiatry,* 1980, *19,* 289–299.

Over a three-and-a-half-year period, a twelve-year-old girl was involved in child pornography. Schoettle's article is the first to address issues in psychotherapeutic treatment of a child victimized by pornographic sexual exploitation. Psychoanalytically oriented techniques were successful in eliciting dynamics and intrapsychic conflicts and in working through issues of resistance and transference.

Stoddard, F. J. "Coping with Pain: A Developmental Approach to Treatment of Burned Children." *American Journal of Psychiatry,* 1982, *139,* 736–740.

Stoddard describes basic therapeutic interventions for children who are experiencing physical pain from an acute burn and the emotional pain of disfigurement. The choice of treatment is influenced by the child's level of development. Pain-relief techniques include psychological preparation for the procedures, encouraging consistent substitute "holding" relationships, tolerating regression, medication, hypnotic or distraction techniques, and encouraging adaptive fantasy.

Swanson, L., and Biaggio, M. K. "Therapeutic Perspectives on Father-Daughter Incest." *American Journal of Psychiatry,* 1985, *142,* 667-674.

The authors describe a familial treatment approach for father-daughter incest that emphasizes enhancing self-awareness and self-concept in the family members by examining feelings and encouraging responsibility. The model consists of immediate therapeutic intervention, with individual counseling provided to the daughter, father, and mother. Then mother-daughter joint counseling is conducted. This is followed by counseling the mother together with all her children. The next step is marriage counseling for the mother and father. Finally, counseling is conducted with the family as a whole. In addition, peer support groups of victims, mothers, or fathers are used.

2

Habit Disorders

A habit can be defined as: (1) "a constant, often unconscious inclination to perform some act, acquired through its frequent repetition (and) (2) an established trend of the mind or character" (*American Heritage Dictionary*, 1969). This chapter concerns habits that are maladaptive, dysfunctional, or viewed in a negative manner by the child and/or adults in the child's life.

Long-established habits tend to be overlearned and become rather isolated or "walled off" within the psyche. They develop an automatic or semiconscious life of their own below the conscious awareness or control of the individual. Clients usually report that they begin the act without awareness and "catch themselves doing it." Some investigators have noted that when parents or professionals have actively tried to break

143

the habit, it has become worse and more deeply entrenched.
(See Thom, D. A., *Everyday Problems of the Everyday Child.*
East Norwalk, Conn.: Appleton-Century-Crofts, 1970.)

For these reasons, nervous habits have proven remarkably resistant to therapeutic treatment—particularly traditional
psychotherapeutic methods (psychoanalytic and nondirective
therapy). They represent a challenge of the highest order for the
practicing therapist. At the very least, it takes a great deal of patience, persistence, and flexibility to treat habit disorders of
long standing. The greatest success to date has occurred with behavioral methods, especially conditioning techniques. Accordingly, a number of the more promising behavioral techniques
are presented in this chapter.

Learning theorists view maladaptive habits as learned responses that can occur in normal as well as disturbed children;
they state that these separate clinical entities can best be unlearned by behavioral principles. Psychodynamic therapists, in
contrast, consider these habits to be manifestations of underlying personality conflicts. And family therapists view such disorders as indices of dysfunctional family interaction patterns.
The latter two approaches expect symptom substitution to occur unless the underlying conflict is resolved. The symptom substitution hypothesis states that underlying anxiety or conflict
continues to be experienced after symptom relief and shortly
emerges again in the form of a new symptom—that is, as behavior judged to be socially or personally maladjustive. After re-
viewing the literature on symptom substitution, Montgomery
and Crowder note that a general conclusion is not possible; that
is, the occurrence of substitute symptoms depends on the kind
of treatment and/or kind of initial symptom (Montgomery,
G. T., and Crowder, J. E., "The Symptom Substitution Hypotheses and the Evidence." *Psychotherapy: Theory, Research
and Practice,* 1972, *9,* 98-102). For certain maladaptive habits,
such as enuresis and encopresis, the weight of evidence to date
strongly supports the behavioral position that no symptom substitution occurs.

With such habits as enuresis and encopresis, then, the
learning theorists point to three major justifications for treat-

ing symptoms rather than the "cause" of the disorder: (1) Symptom substitution does not usually occur with these symptoms. (2) The symptom may create more psychological difficulties than the problem that caused the symptom. (3) A symptom can persist after the psychogenic forces that produced it have abated.

Other theorists, on the contrary, point out that enuretic or encopretic children typically exhibit other emotional problems, such as immaturity, and that the intensity of parental reactions to these symptoms, such as disgust and revulsion, tends to create long-lasting "distancing" effects on the parent-child relationship that need to be resolved through family counseling. It would seem, then, that clinical judgment is still needed to decide whether to treat the overt symptom or to treat a postulated underlying cause. All theorists agree on the need for long-term follow-up data to investigate the possibility of symptom substitution.

The reader will note that in treating certain "psychosomatic" disorders such as enuresis and encopresis, some of the authors utilize techniques based both on psychological and on physiological knowledge. The most effective treatment for psychosomatic disorders may often involve an integration of organic, psychological, and social principles and techniques. Indeed, most psychological disorders seem to have multiple determinants, and a disorder that originated from psychological causes can, under persistent stress, develop an organic basis.

Tics

A tic can be described briefly as follows: "(1) An intermittent but recurring muscle spasm limited to a single muscle group; (2) tends to occur whenever the patient feels anxious or tense; (3) patient may be unaware when the tic occurs; (4) etiology—most tics are of psychological origin, although local muscle and neurological pathology must be ruled out; (and) (5) more common in children than adults" (Storrow, H. A. Outline of Clinical Psychiatry. *East Norwalk, Conn.: Appleton-Century-Crofts, 1969). The following five methods are representative of the current treatment approaches to tics that traditionally have proved refractory to most forms of clinical intervention.*

Treating Tics
with Contingent Negative Practice

AUTHOR: Freddie Levine

PRECIS: Combining motor practice with a mild punishment to treat ticing behavior.

INTRODUCTION: Levine views a tic as an involuntary motor response that an individual can learn to control voluntarily; thus, he proposes that individuals can be taught to view their tic as a motor skill. This, therefore, enables the tic to be treated in the same manner as any other motor skill—that is, as a skill that can be practiced and mastered. Levine's approach combines motor practice with a mild punishment, which is contingent upon negative practice of the tic.

TREATMENT: Eight cases—four clinical and four research cases —provide the data for this study. All subjects were between the ages of seven and eleven and were demonstrating at least one nervous tic. The four clinical cases were treated with the same procedures as the research cases but did not formally participate in systematic data collection (keeping baseline records and frequency counts of tics).

The treatment for all subjects consisted of contingent negative practice. The child was instructed that he or she must practice the particular tic for fifteen repetitions (with each repetition lasting thirty seconds) each time the child realized that he or she exhibited a tic or each time the child's parents observed a tic. The subjects were seen at the clinic for three or four sessions each. Treatment was terminated when the tic was either decreased or eliminated. Upon termination, the parents were instructed to ignore all instances of tics and to occasionally praise the child for the absence of tics.

RESULTS: Upon termination, each subject demonstrated a reduction in tics of at least 80 to 90 percent. A six-month follow-up revealed that generalization of treatment effects enabled the subjects to maintain their treatment gains.

COMMENTARY: The utilization of contingent negative practice has been demonstrated to be effective in either eliminating or reducing tic behavior. Levine has replicated this finding. In doing so, the author feels that there is support of the conceptualization of a tic as a motor response that one can learn to control by practicing, just as any motor response is practiced and then mastered. Although there is not conclusive evidence for Levine's hypothesis, there is significant evidence that negative practice is an effective treatment for tics.

SOURCE: Levine, F. "Contingent Negative Practice as a Treatment of Tics." Unpublished paper, Department of Psychology, State University of New York at Stony Brook, 1979.

Habit Reversal Treatment for Tics

AUTHORS: Jack W. Finney, Michael A. Rapoff, Christine L. Hall, and Edward R. Christophersen

PRECIS: The utilization of habit reversal procedures to decrease simple and multiple tics.

INTRODUCTION: Habit reversal procedures are described by the authors as consisting of awareness training, social reinforcement procedures, and a competing response practice which is a form of overcorrection. These procedures have been found to be effective with simple tics and more effective than negative practice when treating multiple tics.

The subjects of the current study were two boys—Hugh, eleven years old, and Nick, twelve years old. Hugh exhibited multiple tics and Nick demonstrated a simple tic. Neither youngster had had any other effective treatment.

TREATMENT: Videotaped observations were recorded in each

youngster's home in order to obtain a baseline. Both Hugh and Nick demonstrated facial tics. Two observers, working independently, recorded the boys' tic behavior in order to obtain inter-observer agreement. Home observations were independent of, and prior to, any explanation of the treatment.

After the baselines were obtained, the clinic treatment, which consisted of three visits, was introduced. The habit reversal procedures employed several components, which were taught during the clinic visits. Initially, awareness training began, which aimed to teach the youngsters to be aware of their tics. This was accomplished through response description—by teaching the child to describe aloud the muscle movements occurring in his face as he looked in a mirror. In addition, during the first week, the children utilized self-monitoring by recording the occurrence of each tic. The therapist then worked with each child to devise a "situations and habit inconvenience review." This was a list of situations in which the child felt either inconvenienced or embarrassed by the tics. The boys also listed their reasons for wanting treatment. The list was reviewed daily for two weeks by both child and parents.

Relaxation was introduced as each boy was taught simple breathing and muscle relaxation. The boys were instructed to use these when they felt tense or when they were experiencing a high rate of tics. The boys also learned a competing response exercise for each tic. These were to be practiced fifteen minutes each day for two weeks, five minutes each day for the next month, and three minutes each time they experienced a tic. Examples of competing responses are: (1) for eye blinking: opening the eyes wider than usual, blinking deliberately every five seconds, and shifting eye gaze every ten seconds; (2) for head shaking: slowly tightening neck muscles isometrically until the shaking stops, with eyes and head facing forward.

The parents provided social support by praising any decreases in tics and prompting practice of the competing response exercises. The therapist kept in phone contact with the boys during the week and encouraged them to participate in activities (such as playing ball) that had been difficult in the past because of the tics.

Finally, social validation of the effectiveness of treatment was measured, since unusual appearance and social embarrassment are frequently mentioned as reasons for seeking treatment of tics. Social validation measures were achieved by comparing observers' ratings of how distracting the boys were on videotape segments taken either from baseline or during treatment.

RESULTS: Habit reversal was found to be an effective procedure for reducing the occurrence of tics in both Nick and Hugh. The decrease in tics was evident in natural settings (outside of the clinic), and a one-year follow-up demonstrated that effects were lasting. Furthermore, the habit reversal procedure proved effective both for a simple tic and for multiple tic behavior. However, suppression of multiple tics required that specific procedures be applied to each tic.

Social validation procedures demonstrated that competing responses were less distracting to observers than were the presenting tics. This indicates that the treatment enabled both Hugh and Nick to have a more acceptable social appearance.

COMMENTARY: The current study confirms previous findings demonstrating that both simple and multiple tics could be successfully treated through habit reversal procedures. However, the need to apply specific procedures to each tic comprising a multiple tic suggests that there may be a need to treat multiple tics as a series of simple tics in certain instances. However, one cannot overlook the importance of the treatment's success in enabling youngsters with tics to become more socially acceptable in appearance.

SOURCE: Finney, J. W., Rapoff, M. A., Hall, C. L., and Christophersen, E. R. "Replication and Social Validation of Habit Reversal Treatment for Tics." *Behavior Therapy*, 1983, *14*, 116–126.

Treating the Gilles De La Tourette Syndrome with a Behavioral Approach

AUTHORS: Daniel M. Doleys and Paul S. Kurtz

PRECIS: The utilization of reinforcing incompatible behaviors to reduce the frequency of ticing behaviors in a youngster diagnosed as having Gilles De La Tourette Syndrome.

INTRODUCTION: Roger, a fourteen-year-old, was referred to a university clinic for treatment of disruptive behavior and poor social skills. At the time of the referral, Roger had a five-year history of tics, which included coprolalia, guttural sounds, jerking of the upper extremities, and tongue extrusions. In addition, Roger demonstrated poor eye contact and a general lack of social and interpersonal skills. It was observed that Roger's inappropriate behaviors lessened in frequency when he was involved in certain activities in the clinic, such as solving puzzles or arithmetic problems.

The authors designed a behavioral program to reinforce those behaviors that were incompatible with the undesired behaviors. Initially, the treatment was conducted in the structured clinic setting. As the undesirable behaviors decreased, the treatment was conducted in more natural settings to maximize the generalization of the incompatible behaviors from the clinic to the natural environment.

TREATMENT: Baselines were initially obtained for four of the undesirable behaviors: jerking, guttural sounds, coprolalia, and eye contact. Initial treatment consisted of placing Roger in a small room with a special education teacher. Roger was given a switch, which he could press to elicit eye contact from the teacher, headphones, twenty small wooden blocks, and a box. Each time Roger heard music on the headphones, he was required to place a block in the box; each time he heard white noise, he was required to remove a block. When all twenty blocks were in the box, Roger had a choice of rewards. The music was played each time Roger maintained eye contact for at least ten seconds, each time Roger engaged in conversation, and each time fifteen seconds of non-ticing behavior occurred. White noise was played each time Roger engaged in jerking, guttural sounds, or coprolalia.

After four weeks, Roger's program was extended to include a more natural setting. Roger was taken to a restaurant for a soda after placing the twenty blocks in the box. Play dimes were used as token reinforcers when Roger was outside the clinic, and a snap of the teacher's fingers (or a small clicker) signified that Roger would lose a token. Tokens could be exchanged for different material reinforcers. The treatment then extended to incorporate social skills. Roger could earn tokens for engaging in appropriate social behaviors, such as greeting people, talking with people, and holding doors. Personal hygiene was brought into the program in the same manner, as Roger's parents would give him a token for washing or brushing his teeth.

Finally, other individuals in the outside environment were brought into Roger's program. At first, a waitress in the restaurant where Roger would go for his soda gave Roger contingent reinforcement by complimenting him for appropriate behaviors and walking away from the table if he engaged in an undesirable behavior. After the fourteenth week of the program, Roger was taken to the Student Union Center at the university, where a small group of students gave Roger attention contingent upon his appropriate behaviors. Treatment was terminated after five months.

RESULTS: Cumulative frequencies of guttural sounds, coprolalia, eye contact, appropriate social exchanges, and personal hygiene all revealed significant changes in the desired directions. This suggests that the reinforcement of incompatible behavior was effective in reducing Roger's tics and inappropriate social behaviors.

The investigators found that there was a correlation between successes in obtaining appropriate behavior in the natural environment and prior exposure to the contingencies in the clinic (as opposed to simply attempting to control inappropriate behaviors directly in the natural environment).

COMMENTARY: Doleys and Kurtz utilized a well-proven behavioral method, reinforcing competing responses, to decrease the frequency of undesirable social and ticing behavior in a youngster. The ability to gain success with this technique tends to lie in the change agent's ability to be consistent and persistent. The technique can and has been used with a variety of other types of undesired behaviors. However, when considering tics, which are sometimes believed to be of a neurological rather than a psychological etiology, one must be cautious, as the technique may not always obtain the desired results.

SOURCE: Doleys, D. M., and Kurtz, P. S. "A Behavioral Treatment Program for the Gilles De La Tourette Syndrome." *Psychological Reports*, 1974, *35*, 43-48.

Utilizing Self-Monitoring and
Competing Response Practice
in the Treatment of Facial Tics

AUTHOR: Thomas H. Ollendick

PRECIS: Self-monitoring and the use of competing response practice was used to enhance the effectiveness of a habit reversal treatment of facial tics.

INTRODUCTION: Habit reversal procedures, which are based on the principles of Azrin and Nunn's overcorrection technique, have been found to be quite successful in reducing nervous tics. Ollendick demonstrates the contribution of adding two components—self-monitoring and competing response practice—to the already successful treatment.

The subjects of Ollendick's study were two boys, Marty, nine years old, and David, an eleven-year-old, who exhibited facial tics. The author also addressed a secondary issue: the reliability of self-monitoring in children.

TREATMENT: The treatment of Marty and David was carried out in two different settings: home and school. Both boys presented a history of several years of excessive eye blinking.

Prior to the commencement of the baseline conditions, the teachers and mothers of both boys were trained to accurately record ticing behavior. Twenty-minute sampling periods were utilized twice a day. A study period each day in school and the twenty minutes following dinner were used as data-collecting periods. The boys were unaware that their behavior was being recorded.

The baseline data collection lasted five days. The boys were then seen by a therapist over the weekend. During the initial session, the therapist instructed the boys in how to self-monitor their tics in school and told them that this was essential if the therapist was to know when the tics began to decrease. He gave each boy a wrist counter and told him to count each tic and to record/tally it on an index card. During the next weekend session, the therapist taught David competing response practice, which consisted of extensive practice in tensing muscles antagonistic to the tic. Following mastery of self-monitoring and competing response practice in school, David was instructed to begin self-monitoring at home. Marty never required competing response practice, as his tics decreased to a near-zero frequency once be began self-monitoring in school. However, the decrease did not generalize to the home setting, so he was instructed to begin self-monitoring at home.

David was seen for eight sessions and three follow-up sessions, and Marty was seen for four sessions and three follow-up sessions. Reliability for each child in each setting was obtained by comparing the child's self-report to the teacher's report in school and to the mother's report at home.

RESULTS: Both boys proved to be highly reliable in regard to self-monitoring, as the correlations with their mothers' and teachers' observations were at least .88. In regard to the frequency of eye twitching, David's tic was reduced by 50 percent following the implementation of self-monitoring in school. With the introduction of self-administered overcorrection (or competing response practice), David's tic decreased to a near-zero frequency in five days. The frequency of Marty's tic was reduced to a near-zero level with just the implementation of self-monitoring. Therefore, it was not necessary to teach Marty overcorrection procedures. Neither boy exhibited any generalization across settings. This necessitated treatment procedures specific to each setting. However, the boys proved to be proficient in self-monitoring their behaviors and highly motivated to change.

COMMENTARY: The use of self-monitoring behaviors has proved to be a very effective technique that successfully brings about a therapeutic change with a variety of problematic behaviors. It is not surprising, then, that the youngsters' ticing behaviors showed a dramatic decrease once they became acutely sensitive to each occurrence. Giving the child an opportunity to then be in control of inhibiting his undesirable response by using a competing response proved to be highly successful. As Ollendick himself points out, the lack of generalizing across settings is disappointing and needs to be addressed in future studies.

SOURCE: Ollendick, T. H. "Self-Monitoring and Self-Administered Overcorrection—The Modification of Nervous Tics in Children." *Behavior Modification*, 1981, *5* (1), 75-84.

A Psychodynamic Approach Utilizing Parents as Effective Change Agents with Children

AUTHOR: Joseph Zacker

PRECIS: A psychodynamic intervention is utilized whereby parents become the change agents when their child is manifesting tics.

INTRODUCTION: Zacker describes a method of psychodynamic treatment that utilizes parents as the primary therapeutic change agents when their child is the identified patient. The treatment begins with a diagnostic phase, which consists of an assessment of the family's dynamics. This phase is followed by a prescriptive phase, which focuses on the parents' and clinician's efforts in instituting change in the child's maladaptive behaviors. In the prescriptive phase, the clinician actually takes on the role of a consultant. In order to achieve success with this method, Zacker states that the following should exist: (1) parents should be cooperative, careful observers and able to modify their own behavior, and (2) the problems of the child should be able to be modified by changing environmental contingencies that are under the parents' control.

The author illustrates effectiveness of this approach through three case studies. The following is a summary of one case involving the modification of a youngster's tics.

CASE STUDY: Dan, an eight-year-old, was referred by his parents because of two unusual behaviors: head shaking and a facial grimace involving a mannerism in which he opened his mouth. At the time of referral, Dan had been exhibiting the behaviors for one year.

During the initial session, the therapist saw only the parents. The session focused on the parents' description of Dan's symptoms and on gathering background information. The second session took place at the home, where the therapist had dinner with the entire family. The purpose of this was to allow the therapist to observe the family in its natural environment. With the exception of one other home visit, all additional sessions with the parents (twenty in all) took place in the therapist's office.

Sessions three through eight focused primarily on gathering more diagnostic information. It became apparent that neither parent tended to verbalize his or her feelings and that this dynamic was underlying Dan's physical expression of feelings (his tics). Therefore, the parents were instructed to record events that precipitated or correlated with the appearance of the tics. In addition, they were encouraged to begin verbalizing for Dan what some of his feelings might be.

During sessions nine through twenty, the focus remained on increasing effective communication between Dan and his father. The father modeled self-disclosure to Dan and nonjudgmentally reflected what he believed to be Dan's feelings. During these sessions, it became apparent that Dan had a great deal of repressed feelings toward his older sister, who had attempted to strangle him in his crib during Dan's infancy, and who, for years, teased and criticized Dan. As the father gained understanding of Dan's feelings, he began to interpret these to Dan.

RESULTS: Once the father was able to reflect and interpret Dan's feelings, Dan's tics began to decrease. In addition, Dan became generally less inhibited and was able to be more open and outgoing. Another positive effect of utilizing the parents as the primary change agents was the increased communication and increased insight the parents gained in relation to Dan's behavior.

At follow-up five months after the last session, the family had maintained its gains. Dan's grimacing had not returned, and his head shaking had returned only briefly during a time of stress. (Dan had volunteered to read a religious passage in front of the extended family and then had begun to exhibit the head shaking for a brief period. However, shortly after the reading, Dan joined a Little League team and did exceptionally well. This coincided with the extinction of the head-shaking behavior.)

COMMENTARY: The use of parents as change agents for their

children dates back to Freud's case of Little Hans, in which the father participated in Hans's treatment in a fashion similar to Dan's father. With proper direction, parents can be effective change agents. However, certain prerequisites, such as cooperation, desire, motivation, and persistence must be present in order for this technique to work.

As Zacker points out, the psychodynamic model is not as conducive to experimental design as are some of the other treatment approaches. Therefore, it often becomes difficult not only to measure the effectiveness of a psychodynamic approach but to replicate it. However, clinicians who feel comfortable utilizing psychodynamic approaches should be encouraged by Zacker's success.

SOURCE: Zacker, J. "Parents as Change Agents: A Psychodynamic Model." *American Journal of Psychotherapy*, 1978, *32* (4), 572–582.

Eating Difficulty

Eating difficulty in children has been found to be a very common disorder. Estimates vary, but there is some consensus that about one child in three experiences some form of eating difficulty, such as over- or undereating, finicky eating, or tantrums while eating. This section discusses a wide range of eating disorders, including adolescent obesity, food refusal, slow eating habits, and food stealing.

Modifying Activity Patterns
and Increasing Energy Expenditure
in the Treatment of Obese Girls

AUTHORS: Leonard H. Epstein, Karen Woodall, Anthony J. Goreczny, Rena R. Wing, and Robert J. Robertson

PRECIS: Obese girls between the ages of five and eight were reinforced for increased activity during free play in order to increase caloric expenditure.

INTRODUCTION: The authors studied the effects of increasing activity levels of obese girls during a free play situation. Studies on nondieting subjects of average weight have previously shown that an increase in activity level (exercise) not only increases energy expenditure during the exercise period but also increases the metabolic rate after the exercise period. The authors experimentally compared a group of obese girls whose activity levels were increased to a control group of obese girls whose activity levels were not manipulated.

TREATMENT: Nineteen overweight females between the ages of five and eight participated in a study. All of the girls were enrolled in a childhood obesity program by their parents. The parents had heard of the program through pediatricians, school nurses, media announcements, and a waiting list for a child weight control program at the University of Pittsburgh School of Medicine. All of the girls were more than 20 percent but less than 80 percent overweight for their age. The girls were randomly assigned to either the treatment group or the control group, and mothers were required to attend and participate in all meetings.

All of the girls attended a two-day-a-week morning day camp for five weeks. The camp day was from 8:00 A.M. until noon and consisted of classroom activities, free play, a structured play period, lunch, and a special privilege play period. The free play period was the focus of the study.

On days one through four, no attempt to alter the girls' play was made; however, on day three the privilege play period was introduced. This play period had to be earned and was contingent upon receiving a sticker for not eating inappropriate foods at lunchtime. Although lunch was brought from home, each girl was dieting and earned the sticker each day. On day five, the experimental group members began earning a sticker during free play if they were engaging in certain targeted behaviors at the random sounding of a whistle. The whistle was sounded with intervals varying from 2.5 to 7.5 minutes. On days seven and eight, a reversal phase was introduced. Day nine was a treatment day, and day ten was a reversal day. On reversal days, the whistle was still sounded and girls were reinforced for sharing behaviors regardless of activity.

Prior to beginning treatment, the subjects' fitness and metabolic measures were taken. A standard physical work capacity test was given, which involved pedaling a stationary bicycle.

On days three through six, exercentry total heartbeat counters were attached to the girls upon arrival at camp. Readings were taken prior to and following the free play period. During each free play period (these took place in a school gymnasium), the girls' activity was observed on a fifteen-second time-sampling basis and was rated on a scale corresponding to increasing caloric expenditure.

RESULTS: The activity level of the control group remained stable throughout the summer camp program. The activity level of the experimental group increased significantly during treatment phases of the study. As expected, on days on which activity was being reinforced, activity increased, whereas activity decreased on days on which sharing was reinforced.

The caloric expenditure data collected on days three through six revealed that the girls in the experimental group showed significant increases in their metabolic rates in comparison with the control group. In addition, the rate of change in expenditure from free play to postplay was also highly significant.

COMMENTARY: The results of the present study confirm that activity-induced enhancement of metabolic rate of obese, dieting girls is consistent with that of nondieting adults. Increased activity results in higher caloric expenditure not only during exercise but following exercise as well. Epstein and associates have demonstrated an effective method of successfully encouraging exercise in children's weight control programs. Further studies aimed at replicating the current findings should prove valuable.

SOURCE: Epstein, L. H., Woodall, K., Goreczny, A. J., Wing, R. R., and Robertson, R. J. "Brief Report: The Modification of Activity Patterns and Energy Expenditure in Obese Young Girls." *Behavior Therapy*, 1984, *15*, 101–108.

The Use of Time Limits in Treating Prolonged Eating Behavior

AUTHORS: Richard L. Sanok and Frank R. Ascione

PRECIS: A gradually reduced time limit was imposed upon a child in order to reduce her prolonged eating behavior.

INTRODUCTION: Sanok and Ascione used reduction in time limit to treat a five-year-old girl of normal intelligence who required one to one-and-a-half hours to finish eating a given meal. The targeted behavior was the time required to eat a meal. Prior to treatment, it was determined that the girl possessed all the necessary skills, such as holding a fork and chewing, to complete a meal in a timely manner.

TREATMENT: During an initial baseline period, mealtime duration was measured and defined as the time elapsed between the placement of food in front of the child and her consumption of all of it. Meal size was standardized and defined as one-third of an adult-sized portion. Treatment was carried out by the parents; the therapist made initial spot checks to ensure that the parents were being consistent and accurate in their observations of meal duration. After the first month, during which the therapist made two spot checks, the parents acted as spot checkers for one another. Treatment involved three meals per day. During baseline, the parents recorded mealtime duration. In all other phases of the treatment, meals began with the parents informing the child of an allotment of time for meal completion. There was first a thirty-minute, then a twenty-five-minute, and finally a twenty-minute treatment phase.

Prior to beginning a meal, the parents told the child, "Today you have _____ minutes to complete your meal"; they then reminded the girl that finishing before the time limit would result in her receiving a token. A timer was always placed in the child's view so that she could watch the time. She could trade tokens for privileges, prizes, and activities (each of which cost between one and ten tokens). Upon earning a token, the child was given verbal praise ("I like the way you are eating") simultaneously with the token. If the child did not finish her meal within the time limit, she was given a total of sixty minutes before the meal was removed.

Phases of treatment (further reduction of the time limit) was contingent upon three consecutive days of completing a meal within the prescribed time limit. Once the criteria of the twenty-minute phase was reached, the use of tokens was eliminated. However, a phase was introduced in which a star was placed on a chart each time the meal was successfully completed in order to reward the child and to remind the parents to continue to verbally praise the child. These procedures were carried out both in the home and in settings outside the home for a total of 105 days.

RESULTS: The introduction of a standardized meal size resulted in an immediate decrease in the child's mealtime duration. During the three initial treatment phases, the child was able to meet the criteria of each phase 100 percent of the time. Once the tokens were eliminated, the child met the criteria 91 percent of the time. Once the phase that included the placement of a star on a chart was introduced, the criteria were met 95 percent of the time. Meals eaten outside the home, either in a relative's home or in a restaurant, were more resistant to change; the child only met the criteria in these environments 43 percent of the time. One- and two-month follow-ups revealed that the criteria were still being met successfully.

COMMENTARY: The use of a standardized meal size in conjunction with announced time limits, tangible rewards, and praise proved effective in reducing a girl's maladaptive meal duration. This confirms that temporal limits can be used effectively to modify the amount of time a child needs to complete a meal or a desired task. Future research in modifying meal duration outside of the home would be valuable. In addition, using this method to modify time spent on other tasks, such as homework, would be useful to parents acting as change agents for their child's maladaptive behaviors.

SOURCE: Sanok, R. L., and Ascione, F. R. "The Effects of Reduced Time Limits on Prolonged Eating Behavior." *Journal of Behavioral Therapy and Experimental Psychiatry*, 1978, *9*, 177-179.

Treating a Child's Severe Feeding Problem Through Parents' Self-Monitoring

AUTHOR: Clarissa S. Holmes

PRECIS: A multiply handicapped boy with a severe food refusal problem was treated by parental self-monitoring of behavior and reactions during feeding.

INTRODUCTION: Holmes reports a case of a five-and-a-half-year-old multiply handicapped youngster who was demonstrating a life-threatening food refusal problem. During a three-week baseline period before any treatment began, the youngster's parents began to see both a subjective and objective improvement in the child's eating. The hypothesis is that while collecting data the parents became more aware of their own feeding expectations and of their behavior during feeding times. As the parents self-monitored their behavior and became more aware of their role in the feeding difficulties, they were able to understand the parent-child interaction and as a result began to spontaneously change the interaction.

CASE STUDY: Chad, a five-and-a-half-year-old boy classified as severely-profoundly retarded with a history of seizures, cerebral palsy, and other medical complications, was demonstrating food refusal. Chad would clench his teeth or turn his head when his parents attempted to feed him. In addition, when food was placed in his mouth, Chad would spit it out. As Chad was also hypoglycemic, his food refusal had resulted in a hospitalization in which he had become comatose and had almost died. During his hospitalization, Chad had been force fed or fed intravenously.

Upon Chad's discharge and return to his home, the parents had become extremely fearful of a recurrence, and mealtime reportedly had become more time consuming and more difficult. Chad's mother began to experience stress that dissipated only after the evening meal had been successfully completed.

After an interdisciplinary evaluation of Chad's food refusal, the parents agreed to take part in a behavioral program aimed at modifying Chad's feeding patterns. Initially, the parents participated in a three-week baseline period, during which data were collected. During this period, both parents participated in mealtime and recorded on provided charts how many teaspoons of each type of food were offered to Chad and how many of these he actually consumed. In addition, information in regard to behavioral events, such as the telephone ringing or the doorbell ringing, were recorded for each meal. At the end of each feeding, the parents agreed on a rating of between 1 (a struggle-free feeding) and 5 (an unacceptably disruptive feeding).

At the end of the three-week baseline period, Chad's parents had come to several surprising realizations. Chad was, according to the objective data, consuming much more food than the parents had subjectively assessed. In addition, Chad's disruptive, struggle-filled meals coincided with Chad's apparent degree of hunger: When Chad did not seem hungry and did not initially show an interest in eating, he was significantly more disruptive than usual and the parents' attempts to feed him were futile. In addition, the parents became aware that interruptions in Chad's feeding were upsetting to him and precipitated difficulties. Once the parents became aware of Chad's patterns and their reactions to them, and once they could objectively see that despite Chad's "food refusal" he was consuming adequate amounts of food per day, the parents relaxed and became more flexible. Chad was then permitted to refuse a meal if he had already eaten an adequate meal in a given day.

At the conclusion of the baseline period, Chad showed considerable improvement in eating. Although it was no longer necessary to implement the intended behavioral program, some specific recommendations were made to the parents in order to maintain the improvements. It was suggested that a pleasurable stimulus, such as music, be paired with mealtime and small amounts of liquids, which Chad preferred, be alternated with food.

RESULTS: By the end of the baseline period, Chad was not demonstrating any unacceptably problematic mealtimes. This was achieved by a reactive effect that the parents demonstrated while recording mealtime behavior. The parents were able to react to Chad's cues and to correlate difficult feedings to disruptive environmental effects.

The introduction of the specific recommendations that followed this phase did not result in any significant changes in Chad's behavior. Chad's body weight increased 9 percent during the baseline period.

At a one-year follow-up, Chad's mealtimes were still generally acceptable; he exhibited only occasional problems, which the parents felt that they could manage. The parents continued to use the charts, as it reassured them that Chad was consuming adequate amounts of food, and this greatly reduced their level of anxiety.

COMMENTARY: Self-recording or self-monitoring of undesirable behaviors has been demonstrated to be an effective intervention for both children and adults. For example, by self-recording what one eats when attempting to diet, one typically decreases caloric intake. The present study indicates that reactive effects of self-monitoring may also extend to parent-child interactions. By increasing their awareness of behavior in an interaction, Chad's parents became much better at understanding and consequently altering their own maladaptive behavior patterns. This study provides very valuable information, and future replication of this study will be beneficial. However, the feeding improvements cannot be solely attributed to the self-monitoring, as not only were treatment suggestions made by the therapist but these particular parents appeared to be highly insight oriented and receptive to change.

SOURCE: Holmes, C. S. "Self-Monitoring Reactivity and a Severe Feeding Problem." *Journal of Clinical Child Psychology*, 1982, *11* (1), 66-71.

Assessing Mothers' Roles in the Treatment of Obese Adolescents

AUTHORS: Kelly D. Brownell, Jane H. Kelman, and Albert J. Stunkard

PRECIS: Mothers' involvement in a treatment program for obese adolescent girls was assessed by measuring the adolescents' changes in weight and blood pressure.

INTRODUCTION: The authors report that although parents are

believed to play an important part in treating obesity in their children, the existing evidence in the literature is only correlational. Therefore, Brownell, Kelman, and Stunkard designed a study to test the effects of three different methods of parent involvement in the treatment of adolescents. The program consisted of behavior modification, social support, nutrition education, and exercise.

TREATMENT: Subjects were forty-two obese adolescents: thirty-three girls and nine boys between the ages of twelve and sixteen. All weighed at least 20 percent more than the average body weight for their size and all subjects entered treatment with their mothers, who were required to attend all sessions.

Children and mothers initially attended an orientation, at which time a $15 deposit was made. Upon completion of the program, $10 was refunded if the child and mother had attended each session. At the follow-up session, the remaining $5 was returned if both mother and child attended. In addition to the deposit, mothers were required to pay a $3 fee at each meeting, and children each deposited $8 at the beginning of each month and earned $2 back for each week that he or she lost at least one pound. At the orientation, the program was explained and participants were informed that all of them would experience the same treatment, with the exception being that some children and mothers would attend sessions together and some would not.

The program ran sixteen weeks, and each session was forty-five to sixty minutes in duration. Children and mothers weighed in together before each meeting. Meetings contained a group of five to eight subjects. During each session, didactic material was discussed, as well as feelings, family matters, and food preparation. After the sixteen-week program, follow-up sessions were conducted once every two months for one year.

The program consisted of behavior modification, nutrition education, exercise, and social support. A 100-page treatment manual was given to the subjects in sections at each weekly meeting. The behavioral section of the manual consisted of instructions on self-monitoring, food intake, physical activity, stimulus control and cue elimination, behavior chains and preplanning, attitude restructuring, cognitive control, and using alternatives to overeating. Nutrition education included sections on information about the basic food groups; information on maintaining a balanced diet that is low in sugar, salt, and fat; methods for buying, storing, preparing, and serving food; and misconceptions about diet and nutrition. Increasing physical activity was encouraged, and the manual discussed topics such as exercise, aerobic conditioning, and methods for increasing energy expenditure. Finally, a section of the manual discussed social support and how to use family and friends as a support system.

Children were ranked into stratified blocks dependent on percentage of overweight; they were then randomly assigned from the blocks to one of three treatment groups. The groups were: mother-child separately, in which mothers and children met simultaneously but in separate group meetings; mother-child together, in which the mothers and children attended all sessions together; and child alone, in which the children met in groups but the mothers did not take part in the formal treatment.

RESULTS: Several measures were utilized to assess the effectiveness of the program, including body weight, the percentage above average weight, and body mass (weight changes as compared to developmental growth).

At the conclusion of the sixteen-week program, the mother-child separately group had a significantly greater decrease in percentage overweight and in body weight than the other two groups. In addition, the mother-child separately group demonstrated significantly greater reductions in both body mass and weight changes as compared to developmental growth changes. At the conclusion of the one-year follow-up, the differences between the mother-child separately group and the mother-child together and child alone groups remained significantly different in the desired directions. Furthermore, whereas the children in the mother-child separately group maintained their weight losses, the children in the other groups had returned to above baseline weights.

Blood pressures of all subjects were monitored, and since

the experimental manipulation—that is, parental involvement—
was not expected to influence this measure, the data for the
three conditions of the treatment were combined. It was found
that the children who were the greatest percentage overweight
had the highest initial blood pressures. As expected, as the children lost weight, their blood pressures decreased. Maintenance
of weight loss correlated with maintenance of blood pressure
reduction.

COMMENTARY: The nature of parent involvement was found
to be significant in the utilization of this behavior-cognitive approach to treating obese adolescents. The findings support
psychological and developmental theories that adolescents are
striving for independence and need to have some distance from
their parents. This was optimized in the mother-child separately group, in which the adolescents still had parental support
(that was not available in the child alone group) but had privacy
and distance (not available in the mother-child together group).
The outlined program combines many techniques that have
been found to be successful in modifying adults' eating patterns. The use of this treatment with adolescents is promising,
as many programs have not proved to be as successful with this
age population.

SOURCE: Brownell, K. D., Kelman, J. H., and Stunkard, A. J.
    "Treatment of Obese Children With and Without Their Moth-
    ers: Changes in Weight and Blood Pressure." *Pediatrics*, 1983,
    71 (4), 515-523.

Treating Food Stealing
in Prader-Willi Children

AUTHORS: Terry J. Page, Jack W. Finney, John M. Parrish, and Brian A. Iwata

PRECIS: The utilization of differential reinforcement of other behaviors—consisting of rewarding nonstealing behavior at the end of progressively lengthening time periods—in the treatment of food-stealing behavior in Prader-Willi children.

INTRODUCTION: Prader-Willi syndrome is characterized in infancy by failure to thrive, hypotonia, poor sucking reflex, and a weak cry. Characteristics in childhood include hyperphagia, obesity, short stature, small hands and feet, dipmorphic facial features, and mental retardation. Food-related behavior problems are common in these children, especially stealing and consuming large quantities of food. In addition, Prader-Willi children typically ingest unappetizing items, such as dog food and garbage. In general, the children do not distinguish between appropriate and inappropriate foods and have been known to eat such things as sticks of butter, frozen foods, and dangerous items, including medication. It is often difficult to detect food stealing and consumption, as Prader-Willi children become quite adept at obtaining the prohibited items. However, the behaviors are often assumed when the children begin to gain weight at a very fast rate.

The authors developed an assessment technique for food stealing and then utilized an approach to reduce food stealing that consisted of differential reinforcement of other behaviors. They also assessed generalizability and maintenance of the desired behavior.

TREATMENT: Two Prader-Willi children, Alice, eight years old with an IQ of 75, and Paul, eleven years old with an IQ of 46, were treated. Both children frequently obtained and consumed food inappropriately despite parental attempts to curb their food consumption. Both youngsters were admitted for a short-

term hospitalization in order to establish weight control maintenance programs.

Treatment was conducted in the hospital in three settings: a training room, an individual playroom, and a group
playroom. All three settings were equipped with one-way observation windows. Each setting provided tabletop activities and
had a table of specific food items: M&M's, salted peanuts, pota-
to chips, Snickers bars cut into pieces, and two ounces of a
carbonated beverage.

Food stealing was operationally defined as any instance
in which a piece of food comes into contact with the child's
mouth. Observers seated behind one-way windows recorded the
frequency of stealing behaviors during ten-second intervals.

During baseline, the child(ren) was (were) taken into one
of the rooms and prompted to play. The trainer then left the
room, stating that he would be back, and cautioned the child(ren)
not to eat any food, as it was not snack time. Instances of food
stealing were then recorded for a fifteen-minute period. The
three settings included one Prader-Willi child alone in the training room, one Prader-Willi child in the playroom while other
children and staff were present, and the two Prader-Willi children together in a playroom while others were present.

During the differential reinforcement of other behavior
(DRO) phase, tokens were used as reinforcers each time the
child did not steal food during a specified time interval. During
baseline, the trainer entered the playroom each time a child met
the criteria and gave the child a token while using verbal praise.
If stealing had occurred, the trainer returned at the end of the
time interval and informed Alice and/or Paul that no token
would be given because food had been stolen. At the end of the
session, the child could trade ten tokens for either a low-calorie
food or a toy. Low-calorie foods consisted of sugarless gum and
lollipops, Tab, and apples. The initial time interval was ten seconds. It was doubled each time criteria were met on three consecutive intervals. This resulted in treatment sessions that were
as long as forty minutes.

Daily treatment sessions were terminated when the children were discharged from the hospital. During follow-up ses-

sions, the children's mothers conducted sessions under a trainer's supervision.

RESULTS: Upon implementation of treatment, Alice's food stealing was extinguished in the training room in four sessions. Generalization to the other two playrooms did not occur, but DRO procedures in those rooms did serve to eliminate the undesirable behavior. During a one-to-four-week follow-up, Alice did not engage in any instances of food stealing. Paul's food stealing was eliminated by the second treatment session, making analysis of generalization inappropriate. Follow-up revealed that Paul continued to maintain the changed behavior for at least nine weeks after discharge. Pre- and post-weighing, as well as weighing during treatment, revealed that both children exhibited weight gains prior to treatment and after treatment. During treatment both youngsters lost weight.

COMMENTARY: As the authors point out, the assessment method utilized to measure food stealing is quite valuable but is best suited to institutions in which one-way mirrors can be utilized easily. However, the use of DRO in successfully eliminating food stealing demonstrates that Prader-Willi children can be taught not to steal food and can subsequently lose weight. The follow-up data suggest that Alice and Paul had resumed food stealing at home, as they were both gaining weight. Therefore, in order to maintain desired behavior, a thinner DRO schedule in the home may have proved necessary upon the termination of treatment. The current techniques may be quite useful with individuals diagnosed as bulimic, as they, too, steal food.

SOURCE: Page, T. J., Finney, J. W., Parrish, J. M., and Iwata, B. A. "Assessment and Reduction of Food Stealing in Prader-Willi Children." *Applied Research in Mental Retardation,* 1983, *4,* 219–228.

Enuresis

Nocturnal enuresis is usually defined as urinary incontinence during sleep in children three years of age or older who show no signs of congenital or acquired physical defects or of disease of the nervous or urogenital systems. As opposed to primary enuresis, *the term* secondary enuresis *refers to the fact that the child established and maintained control of his or her bladder for at least one year before relapsing. About 19 percent of the normal five- and six-year-old population wet the bed at night.*

As enuresis or bed wetting has a high spontaneous cure rate, claims of successful treatment must be viewed with caution. Studies have revealed that the annual spontaneous cure rate in children between the ages of five and nine is 14 percent; between ten and twenty years, the rate is 16 percent. Accordingly, treatment procedures must considerably improve on these rates if they are to be regarded as effective. About 3 percent of children with this problem will still be wetting at age twenty.

Treating Enuresis in a Single Session
with Hypnotherapeutic Intervention

AUTHOR: Harry E. Stanton

PRECIS: Utilizing hypnotherapeutic techniques of relaxation, suggestion, and visualization to treat enuresis.

INTRODUCTION: The author has developed a technique that enables a child to utilize his or her own inner resources to overcome enuresis in a single session. This technique, which the author calls "changing a child's personal history," involves three steps. The first step is for the child to identify a desire to change—that is, to stop wetting the bed. The next step is for him or her to "anchor" the unpleasant feelings associated with the undesired response and to "anchor" an inner resource that would enable the desired response. Anchoring is achieved by having the child close his or her eyes and experience the unpleasant feelings associated with the unwanted situation. By monitoring breathing patterns, facial expressions, and skin color or tone, the therapist can observe the changes associated with the unpleasant feelings. The therapist then anchors the feeling by a touch to a particular limb, which is then repeatedly used to recreate the experience. Next, the inner resource is anchored, by a touch to a different limb. To anchor the resource, the child is told to recreate the undesired situation but to use a resource from his or her experience to change the outcome. The resource can be, for example, more maturity, more relaxation, more confidence, and so on. As the child begins to visualize the positive outcome and body language and responses are again observed, the resource is anchored. Finally, the child is instructed to attach the utilization of the resource to the undesired situation by visualizing or recreating the situation in his or her mind with a positive, desired outcome. By doing this, the child changes his or her personal history by creating new ways to deal with particular situations.

TREATMENT: Eighteen enuretic children were treated during

a single session with the hypotherapeutic techniques of relaxation, suggestion, and visualization. The case of twelve-year-old Pauline is reported to demonstrate the techniques.

Initially, Pauline identified her desired behavioral goal of achieving a dry bed every morning. The therapist used ego-supporting statements to impress upon Pauline that she could achieve her goal. For example, he told Pauline "You have the resources within you, Pauline, to have a dry bed every morning, starting tomorrow morning." In addition, he told Pauline several stories about other children who had overcome enuresis. He placed emphasis on the children's role and competency in achieving their goal by telling Pauline that the child said, "I'm a different person now—and I did it all myself."

The next step involved the relaxation techniques. The therapist told Pauline that her eyes would close when she became comfortable and peaceful. Once relaxed, Pauline visualized the undesired situation and labeled the feeling. As she labeled the unpleasant feeling, it was anchored. Next Pauline utilized inner resources, which in her case meant visualizing how her cousin would overcome the problem. Once she exhibited a more positive state and labeled it, this state was anchored. Finally, the two states were put together as Pauline was repeatedly touched on the pleasant anchor while visualizing the undesired situation, until the unpleasant feelings disappeared and Pauline could visualize mastery of the situation. The entire session lasted less than fifty minutes.

RESULTS: Of the eighteen children treated with this one-session hypnotherapeutic technique, fourteen succeeded in achieving dry beds. Upon follow-up, all fourteen had been enuresis-free for at least twelve months. In regard to the other four cases, two of the children remained enuretic, and other interventions also failed to alleviate the symptom. The remaining two cases responded to alternate interventions.

COMMENTARY: Hypnotherapeutic techniques have proved to be successful interventions for many undesired behaviors. However, previous reports have not usually found one session sufficient to bring about a total behavioral change. The author's report of success with fourteen out of eighteen cases with the utilization of only one session indicates that the validity of this particular hypnotherapeutic intervention needs to be closely studied. If other clinicians are able to replicate the technique and results, the intervention could prove to be extremely valuable.

SOURCE: Stanton, H. E. "Changing the Personal History of the Bedwetting Child." *Australian Journal of Clinical and Experimental Hypnosis,* 1982, *10* (2), 103-107.

Hypnotherapy as a Treatment for Enuresis

AUTHOR: Stephen D. Edwards

PRECIS: The use of hypnotherapy as a treatment for nocturnal enuretic boys.

INTRODUCTION: Edwards experimentally tested the effectiveness of three forms of hypnotherapy with boys experiencing nocturnal enuresis. The three forms of hypnotherapy were: (1) a hypnotic induction in which suggestions were made to facilitate decreasing nocturnal enuresis and maladjustment; (2) during the waking state, giving "task-motivational" instructions that would facilitate increasing expectancies, attitudes, and motivations, followed by a hypnotic induction in which suggestions to facilitate decreasing enuresis and maladjustment were made; and (3) a hypnotic induction in which no suggestions were made. Both primary and secondary enuretics participated. Boys were all between eight and thirteen years of age.

TREATMENT: Forty-eight boys, half of whom were classified as primary enuretics and half of whom were secondary enuretics, participated. Pre- and post-treatment psychological testing for parents and children included the Junior Eysenck Personality Inventory, the Children's Personality Questionnaire, and "Child Scale A," which is a questionnaire that parents complete regarding the child's behavior. After initial testing, each boy participated in six weekly, standardized one-hour sessions. During this time, communications with parents adhered to a standardized format involving only standardized instructions. Hypnosis tests were administered during the first two sessions. These included the Barber Suggestibility Scale, the Children's Hypnotic Susceptibility Scale, and diagnostic ratings of hypnotizability.

During each session, suggestions made during the hypnotic state were played on a tape recorder, which ensured standardization of the treatment. Contact with families in order to monitor progress was made by telephone and mail during the treatment.

RESULTS: Hypnotherapy proved to be effective in decreasing nocturnal enuresis. The treatment that utilized motivational instructions followed by hypnosis demonstrated the most significant results in decreasing both enuresis and maladjustment as measured by the pre- versus post-testing.

It should be noted that this study found secondary enuretic boys to be more maladjusted than primary enuretics. In addition, secondary enuretics exhibited a significantly higher relapse rate.

COMMENTARY: Edwards's study represents a valuable source of information, as it experimentally demonstrates the effectiveness of utilizing hypnotherapy as a treatment for nocturnal enuresis. Furthermore, it demonstrates that secondary enuretics, who are consistently found to be more maladjusted than primary enuretics, may require a more comprehensive intervention than just hypnotherapy. Therefore, hypnotherapy may be viewed as a valuable intervention when treating primary enuretics.

SOURCE: Edwards, S. D. "Hypnotherapy with Nocturnal Boys." Unpublished manuscript, 1984.

A Comprehensive, Low-Cost Behavioral
Treatment for Primary Enuretics

AUTHORS: Arthur C. Houts, Robert M. Liebert, and Wendy Padawer

PRECIS: The utilization of a complete home treatment package requiring children and parents to attend only one training session.

INTRODUCTION: The authors developed a comprehensive, low-cost, home treatment program for primary enuretics. Primary enuretics were defined as children who had never experienced at least a two-month period without bed wetting. The program was specifically designed to address the most common obstacles in treating enuresis: (1) problems in parent cooperation, (2) relapse of bed wetting, and (3) the high cost of treating the problem.

TREATMENT: Sixty children, forty-eight boys and twelve girls ranging in age from four years and six months to twelve years and ten months, participated in the treatment program. The program included: (1) self-control attention and retention training, (2) cleanliness training, (3) bell-and-pad training, and (4) overlearning. The home treatment package included all of the necessary equipment to implement the program. A commercially available bell-and-pad device, a family support agreement, a parent guide describing steps to a dry bed, a wall chart, markers, a pencil for filling in the wall chart, tacks to mount the wall chart, and a night light were provided. In addition, each family was presented with a behavioral contract. The cost of all the materials was $45.00 for each family.

A one-hour training session was conducted on a weekend. Ten families (parents and the enuretic children) attended the training session. In addition, children were separated by age so that groups consisted of youngsters either under ten years of age or ten years and older. During the training session, the child filled in the family support agreement, which required placing a name next to each of sixteen items that would show a family member's responsibility for a certain step in the treatment program. Following this, the therapists taught the families self-control attention and retention training. This required that one parent be present each day as the child practiced delaying urination. The delay was increased by three-minute intervals each day. The reward for a successful delay was a predetermined sum of money. Next, therapists and families discussed cleanliness training. The parents were required to keep clean sheets in a predetermined place so that the child could change the linens when an accident occurred. In addition, the child was required to place soiled bed clothes and sheets in a predetermined place. Next, one of the trainers sounded the alarm on the bell-and-pad device and modeled the behavior to follow. Finally, overlearning was discussed: the child would be required to drink sixteen ounces of water one hour before bedtime after reaching a criterion of fourteen consecutive dry nights. At the end of the session, parents were told to report back to the clinic in fifty-six days to report on the outcome of the program. A $65.00 fee was collected, which included a $15.00 refundable deposit. The deposit was to be returned at a follow-up interview, at which time the parents were to hand in the wall chart.

RESULTS: The results of the home treatment program revealed an initial success rate of 81 percent and a 66 percent success rate at a one-year follow-up. The treatment proved to be equally successful for boys and girls and across ages. Of the eleven children who failed to stop bed wetting, nine terminated the program prior to the fifty-six-day minimum. Furthermore, the relapse rate was 24 percent, which is lower than rates reported in most other treatments.

COMMENTARY: According to the obtained results. Houts, Liebert, and Padawer utilized a low-cost behavioral program to successfully treat enuresis that compares favorably, in regard to outcome, to other treatment programs requiring more professional input. For certain families, this may be the treatment of choice. However, the clinician needs to be cautious, since certain families may need more direction and one-to-one contact with the professional.

SOURCE: Houts, A. C., Liebert, R. M., and Padawer, W. "A Delivery System for the Treatment of Primary Enuresis." *Journal of Abnormal Child Psychology*, 1983, *11* (4), 513-520.

Additional Readings

Barnett, D. A. "Modified Dry Bed Training: A Review, Critique and Case Study." *Journal of Clinical Child Psychology*, 1983, *12*, 187-191.

The author presents a brief review and critique of treatments for nocturnal enuresis followed by a case study of a four-year-old girl. The case presented highlights the effectiveness of a modification of Azrin's Dry Bed Training (DBT) treatment. The DBT includes: (1) training in inhibiting urination, (2) training in increasing functional bladder capacity, (3) self-correcting accidents—that is, changing bed sheets and clothing, (4) self-recording of successes and failures, (5) utilization of concrete rewards and social reinforcers, and (6) training in rapid awakening upon recognizing bladder sensations and then rapidly arising from bed to urinate in the bathroom. Although Azrin states that the inclusion of a bell and pad is optional, the equipment was used with the girl presented.

The procedure utilized included an intensive training day on which the child ate salty snacks and was encouraged to drink as much as possible in order to enable practice of the techniques. The day after the intensive training, the child continued to practice what she was taught, but without the snacks and excessive drinking. Major emphasis was placed on learning to hold back urine once a sensation was felt and on getting up quickly from bed to urinate in the bathroom. By following the DBT program, the girl achieved 100 percent dryness within four weeks, at which point phasing-out procedures began. A relapse after two months was resolved within two weeks by reimplementing the program.

The modified Dry Bed Training utilizes a multimodal approach and incorporates many behavioral and behavioral-cognitive techniques that have been demonstrated to be successful in eliminating enuresis. The modified program appears to be less stressful than the original approach designed by Azrin and seems to be a viable intervention.

Diamond, J. M., and Stein, J. M. "Enuresis: A New Look at Stimulant Therapy." *Canadian Journal of Psychiatry*, 1983, *28*, 395-397.

The authors report the case study of Ashley, a seven-year-old enuretic girl. Ashley, classified as a secondary enuretic, had achieved continence at the age of three. At age five, consequent to a trauma in which Ashley was sexually assaulted, hyperactivity and enuresis developed. To treat Ashley's attention deficit disorder, 5 mg. of methylphenidate twice a day was prescribed. Within one day of beginning the medication, Ashley's enuresis terminated. Her hyperactivity responded to 10 mg. of methylphenidate twice a day. On two separate days, Ashley accidentally went without the medication. On both occasions, Ashley wet the bed on the night she missed her medicine and regained continence when she went back on the medication. Diamond and Stein's report indicates that stimulant therapy can be effective in treating enuresis and that imipramine may not be the only drug to be considered.

Haque, M., Ellerstein, N. S., Gundy, J. H., Shelov, S. P., Weiss, J. C., McIntire, M. S., Olness, K. N., Jones, D. J., Heagarty, M. C., and Starfield, B. H. "Parental Perceptions of Enuresis." *American Journal of the Disabled Child*, 1981, *135*, 809-811.

Nine medical centers from across the country participated in collecting surveys from 1,435 parents of children aged four years or older. The survey contained twenty questions, which addressed four areas in regard to parental perceptions of enuresis: (1) anticipated age of dryness, (2) degree to which enuresis was a problem, (3) cause of enuresis, and (4) management of enuresis. A comparison of responses was made for parents of enuretics versus parents of children not exhibiting bed wetting. Findings revealed that parents of boys and girls did not have different perceptions about expected age of dryness. However, there was a significant difference between parents of bed wetters, who expected dryness by a mean age of 3.18 years, and parents of non-bed wetters, who expected dryness by a mean age of 2.61. Both groups of parents viewed bed wetting as a problem, and parents with less education tended to worry more about the problem. In regard to cause, one-third of both groups of parents believed that enuresis has an emotional base. One-third of the parents of enuretics reported that they had had bed wetting problems as children, compared with only 10 percent of the parents of non-bed wetters. In addition, heavy sleeping was viewed as the primary cause of enuresis by parents of bed wetters.

Management attempts for enuresis had been employed by 95 percent of the parents, the majority of whom reported having tried several different strategies; waking the child had been attempted by 84 percent. Educational level of parents was related to three methods of treatment: Parents with only grade school education utilized punishment and medical help more frequently than did parents with higher education, who reported more attempts at medication.

The data collected in this survey are quite useful for those who deal with enuretic children and their parents. As the authors point out, though, the subjects were all patients of pediatric clinics and therefore the findings are most appropriately generalizable to a clinic population. A survey of parents who are private patients would add valuable information to the obtained data.

Mahony, D. T., Laferti, R. O., and Blais, D. J. "Evidence of a Mild Form of Compensated Detrusor Hyperreflexia in Enuretic Children." *Journal of Urology*, 1981, *126*, 520–523.

The authors conducted a study that utilized assessment techniques to evaluate the presence of detrusor hyperreflexia.

Forty-one boys and girls demonstrating varying degrees of urinary incontinence participated in the study. All of the children were evaluated with the common technique of supine cystometry, followed by a cystometrogram in the standing position. (The standing position reportedly is more sensitive to detrusor hyperreflexia.) In addition, thirty children were assessed with a micturition stop test (that is, the child was commanded to stop the flow of urine during voiding). The study revealed that some children with no apparent detrusor hyperreflexia on a supine cystometry do exhibit mild difficulty in the standing position. Furthermore, some enuretic children demonstrate only a mild detrusor instability when subjected to the micturition stop test. This study opens a new avenue of research, as standing cystometrograms and micturition stop tests can now be considered as techniques to define the presence of detrusor hyperreflexia or instability in enuretic children.

Meadow, R., and Berg, I. "Controlled Trial of Imipramine in Diurnal Enuresis." *Archives of Disease in Childhood,* 1982, *57,* 714–716.

Twenty-seven children participated in a controlled, double-blind study to assess the effectiveness of imipramine as a treatment for daytime wetting. All participants were kept free from infection during the course of the study. During the first visit to the clinic, an initial assessment included an estimate of the child's maximum functional bladder capacity. During the second clinic visit, those children found to have a troublesome day wetting problem were assigned to either the imipramine or the placebo group: Two doses of Tofranil syrup were utilized with the experimental group—a smaller dose for the first four weeks and a larger dose for an additional four weeks; a placebo syrup was used with the control group. Two ratings were used: (1) number of dry days and (2) a wetness score that reflected the degree of wetness.

The study revealed no significant differences between the drug and control groups. There was no change in maximum bladder capacities, nor was there any change in frequency or degree of day wetting. This study suggests that although imipramine has been found to be effective with nocturnal enuretics, it does not seem to be an appropriate intervention for diurnal enuresis. In view of this finding, imipramine needs to be studied much more closely before any attempts to utilize it as a treatment for day wetting are pursued.

Sacks, S., and DeLeon, G. "Conditioning Functional Enuresis: Follow-up After Retraining." *Behaviour Research and Therapy,* 1983, *21* (6), 693–694.

In this study, the authors found retraining to be an effective intervention in modifying relapse in some functional enuretics who had undergone bell-and-pad training. Fifty-two enuretics were initially treated with bell-and-pad procedures. Success, which was defined as thirteen consecutive nights without bed wetting, was initially achieved by 84.6 percent of the participants. However, 60 percent of the initially successful cases relapsed (that is, they had bed-wetting episodes once a week for at least four weeks within the first year after completing treatment). These relapsed clients were then retrained. The authors found that retraining resulted in a shorter training time needed to achieve success.

In addition, one-half of the retrained clients remained dry for the duration of the follow-up, which was one year from the time the success criteria were met during retraining. Although half of the clients did relapse a second time, the efficacy of retraining needs to be further studied as an alternative for modifying relapse in functional enuretics.

Trombini, G., Rossi, N., Umilta, C., and Bacarane, C. P. "Experimental Stress and Cystomanometric Recordings of Patients with Primary Enuresis. A Preliminary Report." *Perceptual and Motor Skills,* 1982, *54,* 771–777.

Twenty children demonstrating nocturnal enuresis participated in an experiment to assess the role of stress on the motility of the bladder. All children were hospitalized for urological diagnostic evaluation. During the routine cystomanometry, an examination that yields information about the tone and mobility of the detrusor and the capacity of the bladder, the subjects were given a jigsaw puzzle task designed to induce emotional tenseness. Recording of the physiological responses revealed that those children with a psychogenic etiology to their enuresis had contractions of the detrusor that correlated with the level of emotional tenseness. Children with known organic lesions that are the cause of their enuresis did not demonstrate the contractions. These findings provide data to support the notion of stress-induced or psychogenic enuresis. Further investigation is warranted and would be valuable.

Wagner, W., Johnson, S. M., Walker, D., Carter, R., and Wittner, J. "A Controlled Comparison of Two Treatments for Nocturnal Enuresis." *The Journal of Pediatrics,* 1982, *101,* 302–306.

In a controlled study, the authors compared the two most commonly used treatments for noctornal enuresis: behavioral conditioning with a urine alarm and pharmacotherapy with imipramine. Subjects were between the ages of six and sixteen, had IQ's of at least 70, did not exhibit daytime wetting or physical or neurological disorders, and had not undergone treatment for enuresis for at least one year prior to the study. Four male subjects and nine female subjects were randomly assigned to either the conditioning, medication, or waiting list (control) group. Youngsters in the conditioning group were seen once per week for fourteen weeks, whereas youngsters in the medication group were seen only at week eight and week fourteen.

The authors found that either treatment was more effective than no treatment and that conditioning was superior to pharmacotherapy. Compared to the control group, the youngsters on imipramine exhibited less wetting during only three of fourteen treatment weeks, whereas the conditioning group youngsters exhibited less wetting during thirteen of fourteen treatment weeks. Relapse (three wet nights in a fourteen-consecutive-day period) was a problem for both treatment groups. However, more of the youngsters from the medication group relapsed and their relapse occurred sooner (after an average of 17 days) than did that of the youngsters in the conditioning group (an average relapse time of 37.8 days). No changes in emotional or behavioral adjustment were evidenced by any of the youngsters on pre- versus post-test psychological assessment measures. Finally, the authors report that two measures—the Personality Problems of the Behavior Problem Checklist and the Enuresis Tolerance Scale—were significantly related to treatment outcome. Children whose parents viewed them as less withdrawn and more socially adequate had a higher success rate in achieving continence. Furthermore, parental intolerance for enuresis was significantly related to premature withdrawal from conditioning treatment but not from medication treatment.

As the authors themselves mention, the confounding variable of the different frequency of therapist-child contacts in the conditioning versus medication groups needs to be further explored in order to determine its influence on the treatment.

Encopresis

Encopresis has been defined as any voluntary or involuntary defecation that results in soiled clothes. The incidence of encopresis is higher in boys than in girls by a ratio of more than three to one. Children with primary encopresis have never developed bowel control, whereas children who established bowel control for a period of time but later regressed to fecal soiling are considered to have secondary encopresis. Secondary encopresis has a better prognosis and is usually the result of a child's response to stress. In America, the child is considered capable of exercising voluntary control at age two, although therapeutic treatment is usually deferred until age five. The overall incidence of encopresis in the general population in Western civilization is reported to be 1.5 percent.

Treating Encopresis
with a Systems Approach

AUTHORS: Robert Margolies and Kenneth W. Gilstein

PRECIS: Utilizing a family systems approach to treat chronic encopresis.

INTRODUCTION: Margolies and Gilstein describe a multimodal approach to treating chronic, functional encopresis, which includes engaging the entire family in therapy sessions. They discuss the importance of exploring possible etiologies of encopresis and suggest that the following sources be considered: (1) The encopresis may be the result of a neurological impairment that results in developmental immaturities and a lack of physical readiness to control the bowel. (2) The symptom may be the result of harsh punishment for failing to master toilet training that was initiated before the child was physically ready. (3) The disorder may be the result of a family structure in which the father is emotionally absent or distant and the mother is critical and domineering, which results in the child developing passive-aggressive or antisocial personality disorders. (4) The encopresis may represent an expression of the child's anger in a passive-dependent, negativistic way toward the conflicts and frustrations in the family.

The authors focus on the last two factors as they discuss the case of a fourteen-year-old encopretic boy. They suggest that the encopresis resulted from a disturbance in the boy's relationship system—particularly the family system. The symptom is viewed as maintaining homeostasis in a maladaptive family system in which the child has become the identified patient and scapegoat for the family's conflicts.

CASE STUDY: The authors describe, in detail, the case of a fourteen-year-old boy who was treated with a multimodal approach. This included admittance into a therapeutic day treatment program which afforded him both individual and group therapy. In addition, major emphasis was placed on the treatment of the entire family during weekly therapy sessions.

Family sessions were attended by the immediate family: the boy's natural father, his stepmother, and his natural sister and three stepsisters; the sessions were conducted by two cotherapists, one male and one female. During the initial session, the cotherapists observed that the family was imbalanced, as the father was distant and passive while the mother was hostile and overcontrolling. In addition, the stepsisters were judged to behave seductively and provocatively toward the boy.

The cotherapists' initial goal was to point out to the family that they not only were affected by the boy's soiling but were also affecting the soiling. Therefore, a contract was devised that required the participation of all family members.

The therapists used several strategies to shift imbalances in the family system. During sessions, seating positions were changed, relaxation techniques were used, paradoxical demands were made, assigned behavior tasks were employed, and reframing was used. In order to change the parents' roles in the family and their relationship with each other, seating changes placed the father in the leadership position during sessions. In addition, the father was given the assignment of being in control while the mother was given the assignment of relaxing. Reframing was utilized as the mother's intrusive, obsessive control was reframed into a sense of caring and concern. Between sessions, the girls were given the assigned task of bickering in a paradoxical attempt to prevent the parents from fighting. In addition, the cotherapists made a home visit and found that there was not enough privacy for all family members. This resulted in changes in the family's living arrangements.

Finally, a contract that required charting of the boy's soiling was devised, and all family members participated. The contract called for the following: (1) The family was to make an inventory of the boy's underwear each week to ensure that no underwear was missing. (2) A chart was to be kept of daily successes and mishaps in regard to toileting. (Five points were awarded for each success and fifteen points were awarded for a day without any soiling. The father checked the chart each night and signed it.) (3) Each week the boy obtained over two hundred points, he received a special reward arranged by the father (such as bowling together). (4) The mother's role (while the father monitored the plan) was to refrain from commenting on the boy's progress. (5) The boy was to clean up all of his mishaps. (6) Upon achieving three consecutive days without soiling, the boy was to achieve a reward which was decided upon at the signing of the contract.

In addition to the family therapy sessions, the boy simultaneously received individual and group therapy that focused on pointing out instances of using good body control. For example, the boy's individual therapist taught him how to juggle and used this to reinforce the boy's ability to be in control of his body.

RESULTS: Family therapy sessions lasted three-and-a-half months. Although during the first month several incidents of sabotaging occurred, during the last two months of treatment the boy made a good deal of progress, with only two soiling episodes. An eight-month follow-up revealed that the boy had been completely soil-free since ending treatment. The authors report that, following therapy, the family system did shift and was functioning as a more balanced, cohesive family with better and more frequent communication.

COMMENTARY: In keeping with a current trend of utilizing a multimodal approach to treatment, the authors successfully intervened in a boy's chronic, functional encopresis. The authors emphasize the importance of the shift in the family system as a result of the treatment. However, one must not overlook the fact that interventions can be more powerful when several modalities are simultaneously employed. In this case, it appears that a combination of several techniques, including individual and group therapy for the boy as well as the family systems approach, contributed to the elimination of the boy's encopresis.

SOURCE: Margolies, R., and Gilstein, K. W. "A Systems Approach to the Treatment of Chronic Encopresis." *International Journal of Psychiatry in Medicine*, 1983–1984, *13* (2), 141–152.

*Short- and Long-Term Effects
of Treating Encopresis and
Chronic Constipation at Home*

AUTHOR: Elaine A. Blechman

PRECIS: The utilization of a home-based treatment program for chronic encopretic youngsters who also suffer from constipation.

INTRODUCTION: Blechman points out that encopresis is often the result of chronic constipation or fecal impaction. Therefore, she discusses the treatment of children with chronic constipation. Blechman's purpose was to produce successful toileting behavior in children. This focus is in contrast to emphasizing the elimination of soiling, which is commonly utilized with encopretic children.

The treatment has two specific goals. The first is to treat the child in his or her own home utilizing positive rather than aversive antecedents and consequences. This means that laxatives, nagging, and punishment are to be avoided. The second goal is to focus the treatment on both constipation and encopresis. The rationale for this focus is that children can learn to retain stools in order to prevent soiling. However, they may not learn to control elimination, and this may then lead to constipation or impaction.

TREATMENT: The author treated five children between the ages of six and eight who exhibited chronic constipation and encopresis. The treatment was conducted at home utilizing several techniques, including preparatory instructions and rewards for appropriate bowel movement (in the toilet). In addition, once successful toileting was achieved, the families of all five children were taught to fade treatment contingencies.

Sessions with parents (both parents when possible) were conducted weekly in the therapist's office; however, all treatment was carried out by the parents in the home. Therefore, the parents kept daily charts in order to record appropriate bowel movements. Charts with spaces for daily entries were given to each mother at the initial visit. The charts included columns for checking the child's pants at three times during the day (before and after school and after dinner) and for recording an appropriate bowel movement (in the toilet). The charts also had a column for recording the child's receipt of a reward. Therapists made telephone calls mid-week to collect data.

The therapist gave preparatory instructions to the families during the initial interview. These included information about encopresis along with information about positive antecedents to toileting. She told parents about unpleasant toileting conditions that may occur, such as a toilet seat opening that is too large, a cold toilet, and so on. The therapist then gave them instructions as to how the child would be required to clean up after soiling by washing his or her body and clothing. In addition, mothers were encouraged to use mineral oil when constipation became unbearable for the child.

Parents were then instructed to give a reward for clean pants. The reward was predetermined and individually selected by parents for their child. The reward was given each day if the child's pants were clean at his or her most vulnerable times of the day. In addition, a predetermined reward was given each time the child had a bowel movement in the toilet. Fading contingencies began after the constipation and soiling were under control for several weeks.

RESULTS: The author found the inclusion of the reward for appropriate bowel movements to be a factor in the successful long-term elimination of soiling. Treatment consisting of preparatory instruction, rewarding clean pants, and then fading contingencies proved effective for short-term success. However, the component which adds a reward for the appropriate behavior of using the toilet for bowel movements was of significance in both short- and long-term success.

COMMENTARY: This treatment, which can be used by parents in the home setting, seems to be a very useful approach. The introduction of the reward for appropriate toileting behavior proved to be a crucial aspect of treatment. The emphasis on chronic constipation as a precursor to soiling is also noteworthy.

SOURCE: Blechman, E. A. "Short- and Long-Term Results of Positive Home-Based Treatment of Childhood Chronic Constipation and Encopresis." *Child Behavior Therapy*, 1979, *1* (3), 237–247.

A Variable Ratio Schedule of Reinforcement to Treat Encopresis

AUTHORS: Philip H. Bornstein, Bernard J. Balleweg, Robert W. McLellern, Gregory L. Wilson, Cynthia A. Sturm, John C. Andre, and Richard A. Van Den Pol

PRECIS: Treating chronic encopresis with a variable ratio schedule of reinforcement called the "bathroom game."

INTRODUCTION: The authors treated a ten-year-old encopretic male by reinforcing occurrences of nonsoiling as well as appropriate bowel movements. The reinforcement schedule was a variable ratio one instead of a continuous schedule of reinforcement. Furthermore, the reinforcement schedule was presented as the "bathroom game" and was "played" with the therapist.

TREATMENT: The subject, a ten-year-old male, had been soiling since five years of age, which coincided with the birth of his only sibling. Several treatments had been attempted, but none had had long-range success. The "bathroom game" was proposed as a means by which appropriate toileting behaviors could be established.

During an initial interview, recording sheets were given to the parents. On these they recorded daily incidents of soiling and of appropriate bowel movements. Soiling included full bowel movements, as well as small fecal stains. Appropriate bowel movements were those that occurred when the child was seated on the toilet. The therapist collected these records on a weekly basis.

The first phase of therapy, bathroom game 1, lasted for three weeks. The child was told that he and the therapist were going to be playing a game that would help the child gain control over his toileting. The game used two identical cards, each of which had three columns: (1) Day, (2) Soiling, (3) B.M. The therapist had one card, and the child had the other. The child was told that his parents would complete his card each day. They would place a "yes" in the soiling column each day the child soiled and a "no" each day there was no soiling. The same procedure applied to the B.M. column. The child was also told that the therapist's card would have a series of stars placed on it. On those days that the therapist's card had a star, the child would have an opportunity to earn financial rewards. For each starred "no" in the soiling column, the child would earn 50¢ and for each starred "yes" in the B.M. column, the child would earn 25¢. In addition, a great deal of verbal praise was utilized by the therapist. The starred days were randomly determined, and stars appeared on a variable ratio schedule of one star every two days for both the soiling and B.M. columns.

The next phase of the treatment, baseline 2, lasted only two weeks. This phase was a return to baseline without any experimental operations.

The final phase of treatment, bathroom game 2, lasted twenty weeks. Initially, the conditions were the same as for bathroom game 1; however, after two weeks a fading scheme began which systematically faded the reinforcement by leaving out the variable ratio schedule. During the last ten weeks of treatment, the cards were no longer utilized. Instead, verbal praise was the sole reinforcement. During the last eight weeks of treatment, the frequency of sessions was decreased, although data were still collected weekly.

RESULTS: The "bathroom game" was effective in controlling

the toileting behavior of the ten-year-old male subject. As would be expected, during baseline 2 there was a recurrence of the encopresis that had been modified during bathroom game 1. The child responded very positively to the treatment, and at the one-year follow-up the parents reported no incidents of soiling, along with appropriate bowel movements.

COMMENTARY: The authors' techniques of charting behavior and reinforcing both nonsoiling and appropriate bowel movements have been utilized successfully with encopretic youngsters. However, the introduction of a variable ratio schedule of reinforcement appears to offer additional advantages. Research supports the conclusion that variable ratio schedules are more resistant to extinction than are continuous schedules. This proved to be quite beneficial in treating the encopretic subject, as relapse or recurrence was less likely. In addition, the use of the variable ratio tends to make the reinforcement more game-like and possibly more fun for the child. Finally, the procedure offers the advantage of being easy to fade by leaving out rewards.

SOURCE: Bornstein, P. H., Balleweg, B. J., McLellern, R. W., Wilson, G. L., Sturm, C. A., Andre, J. C., and Van Den Pol, R. A. "The 'Bathroom Game': A Systematic Program for the Elimination of Encopretic Behavior." *Journal of Behavior Therapy and Experimental Psychiatry*, 1983, *14* (1), 61–67.

Additional Readings

Bornstein, P. H., Sturm, C. A., Retzlaff, P. D., Kirby, K. L., and Chong, H. "Paradoxical Instruction in the Treatment of Encopresis and Chronic Constipation: An Experimental Analysis." *Journal of Behavior Therapy and Experimental Psychiatry*, 1981, *12* (2), 167–170.

The authors successfully utilized paradoxical instruction to treat a nine-year-old male with chronic constipation and encopresis who demonstrated considerable anxiety during toileting and related activities. They used an ABAB reversal design with a one-year follow-up. Following a three-week baseline, the child was told that he was going to practice having bowel movements without really having any so he could learn to relax and "overcome these kinds of problems." The child was instructed to go to the bathroom every hour, pull down his trousers, sit on the toilet for five minutes, and act as if he had to have a bowel movement, but he was not to allow the bowel movement to occur. After three weeks of paradoxical instruction and no soiling, there was a return to baseline procedures for two weeks. Soiling occurred, and the authors returned to paradoxical instruction for eight weeks with fading—that is, a systematic decrease in the frequency of trips to the bathroom. Throughout the treatment, the two dependent measures were parental records of soiling and of appropriate bowel movements. The success of the paradoxical instruction for the treatment of encopresis indicates the need for further studies to validate and confirm the positive findings.

Christophersen, E. R., and Berman, R. "Encopresis Treatment." *Issues in Comprehensive Pediatric Nursing*, 1978, *3* (4), 51–66.

The authors present a brief review of different treatment approaches, including psychodynamic, medical, and behavioral approaches and the medical-behavioral approach, which is a multimodal intervention. In addition, they review diet, symptom substitution, expense, and length of treatment. The authors conclude that there is general agreement in the literature that treatment of encopresis is most cost-effective when medical or medical-behavioral approaches are utilized. The authors state that all encopretics should undergo a complete physical examination and medical history to rule out fecal impaction or chronic constipation. Although the medical aspect of encopresis should not be overlooked, recent studies reveal that when underlying dynamics and/or learned behavior patterns are also addressed, long-term success in appropriate bowel movements is greatest.

Kirsch, E. A., and Pfeffer, C. R. "Functional Encopresis: Psychiatric Inpatient Treatment." *American Journal of Psychotherapy*, 1984, *38* (2), 264-271.

The authors report on the successful inpatient psychiatric treatment of a multiproblem child demonstrating primary encopresis. Toby, a twelve-year-old male who had always been encopretic, became increasingly depressed, withdrawn, and suicidal after his parents' divorce. Upon admittance to a child inpatient psychiatric unit, an integrated multidisciplinary approach was used to foster age-appropriate autonomous functioning. Toby was seen in individual, group, and family therapy sessions. In addition, the therapeutic milieu provided art, occupational, and recreational therapy. A behavior modification program, which involved assigning a male staff member to sit with Toby in the bathroom, view his stool, and then praise him for appropriate bowel movements, was also implemented. Toby was then taught to respond to physical cues indicating his need to move his bowels. Finally, Toby's eating was monitored, as he tended to avoid eating to prevent bowel movements. The close supervision and the multimodal approach proved very successful in the elimination of Toby's encopresis. In addition, the authors note that he exhibited less withdrawal and the cessation of suicidal ideation. This suggests that the psychiatric unit may be utilized quite effectively for the multiproblem child who demonstrates encopresis.

Ringdahl, I. C. "Hospital Treatment of the Encopretic Child." *Psychosomatics*, 1980, *21* (1), 65-71.

The author briefly reviews differential diagnosis and management approaches to encopresis. Ringdahl then reviews the findings of a study of thirteen encopretic children hospitalized on an inpatient psychiatric unit during a six-year period. The study revealed that all the children (twelve boys and one girl) came from families displaying varying degrees of psychopathology and that all the parents were either divorced or living together with marital discord.

All of the children had at least average-range intelligence, and in 75 percent of the cases the mothers were perceived as being either hostile or depressed. The authors present the case of a six-year-old boy to illustrate a multimodal approach. This case included family therapy sessions once each week as well as individual and group sessions. In addition, occupational and recreational therapy were used in conjunction with a behavior modification program for the child, which used opportunities to participate in desired activities as positive reinforcers for soil-free periods. If soiling occurred, the child would spend his free time washing the soiled clothing. This multimodal treatment approach was effective in the twelve cases in which parental participation in family therapy occurred. This led not only to the cessation of the encopresis but also to improved family functioning, which indicates that relieving the family's stress is important in eliminating the child's encopretic symptom.

Glue Sniffing

Glue sniffing can be defined as the deliberate inhaling of glue vapors for the purpose of getting "high." In recent years, its incidence has increased among children and adolescents. The following article and the additional readings present diverse positions as to the seriousness of glue sniffing and its effective treatment.

Treatment Approaches for Preadolescent
and Adolescent Glue Sniffers

AUTHOR: Larry James Stybel

PRECIS: The use of psychotherapeutic intervention dependent upon the severity of glue-sniffing behavior.

INTRODUCTION: Stybel presents data that reveal glue sniffing to be most problematic in lower-socioeconomic environments and more common among males than females. Based on work with glue sniffers, Stybel determines the severity of the problem by assessing the frequency, duration, and social context of the glue sniffing. He discusses treatment approaches for three levels of severity: social sniffing, moderate sniffing, and chronic sniffing.

LEVELS OF SEVERITY: Most preadolescents and adolescents that engage in glue sniffing fall into the category of "social sniffers." These youngsters sniff glue in a social context, with friends. Social sniffers tend to engage in the behavior three or fewer times per month; the sniffing usually terminates in less than a year, as older youths view the behavior as childish. Stybel concludes that glue sniffing is a substitution in younger children for the intoxication that older youths achieve through the use of alcohol or marijuana. He views the behavior as resulting from the paucity of recreational activities that are available in lower-socioeconomic communities. Providing youngsters with social activities is proposed as a solution to the problem of social sniffing.

    Moderate sniffing is the category used to classify those youngsters who sniff not only with friends but also alone. Moderate sniffers engage in the behavior between four and nineteen times a month and have been doing so for over two years. More often than not, psychological evaluation of moderate glue sniffers reveals underlying situational or psychiatric problems. Moderate sniffers are viewed as youngsters who can either terminate the behavior or become chronic sniffers. Therefore, treatment tends to be most effective with this group. Stybel does not advocate any one type of therapeutic intervention for this group but states that therapy can be conducted utilizing the individual therapist's orientation and preferred intervention skills.

The chronic glue sniffer is a youngster who tends to sniff alone, as he or she does not have many friends. Sniffing occurs twenty or more times per month and has occurred for more than two-and-a-half years. Chronic sniffers tend to be isolates who rarely go to school or to work. As a result of their limited interpersonal relationships, chronic sniffers are frequently not brought to the attention of the authorities who could offer assistance. Loss of appetite due to inhalation results in an emaciated physical appearance. Chronic sniffers are believed to have an underlying psychotic component and require treatment on an inpatient ward, as they typically do not have enough ego strength to terminate the behavior in a less restrictive setting.

COMMENTARY: Stybel presents a useful categorization of glue sniffers and offers reasonable interventions dependent upon the youngster's classification. He cautions that his work is still in the developing stage. His suggestions should be considered by clinicians who treat glue-sniffing behavior.

SOURCE: Stybel, L. J. "Psychotherapeutic Options in the Treatment of Child and Adolescent Hydrocarbon Inhalers." *American Journal of Psychotherapy,* 1977, *31* (4), 525-532.

Additional Readings

Blanchard, E. B., Libert, J. M., and Young, L. D. "Apneic Aversion and Covert Sensitization in the Treatment of a Hydrocarbon Inhalation Addiction: A Case Study." *Journal of Behavior Therapy and Experimental Psychiatry,* 1973, *4,* 383–387.

The authors report the case of a nineteen-year-old male with a seven-year history of inhaling spray paint vapor. Successful treatment of the behavior utilized a combination of covert sensitization and apneic aversion, which was produced by injections of the anesthetic Anectine. Treatment sessions consisted of twelve days of covert sensitization procedures, in which the subject paired his sniffing behavior with noxious scenes of feces and vomit in his mouth while people laughed at him. This was followed by ten days of an apneic aversion technique, in which the subject sprayed paint into a bag and, as he lifted it to his face to inhale it, he was injected with Anectine. This induced paralysis and apnea for thirty seconds, at which point the subject was artificially respirated. A six-day phase followed in which covert sensitization was reinstated. This time, scenes involving the apnea were included. Follow-up at four and twelve months after treatment revealed that the youth had not resumed the sniffing behavior.

Bowers, A. J., and Sage, L. R. "Solvent Abuse in Adolescents: The Who? What? and Why?" *Child: Care, Health and Development,* 1983, *9,* 169–178.

Bowers and Sage review the characteristics of solvent abusers as well as intervention approaches used to modify glue-sniffing behaviors. The authors conclude that glue sniffing has not been found to be physiologically addictive and that the behavior appears to be, for the most part, a passing phase of adolescence. They state that although glue sniffing gives the same effects as alcohol or marijuana, it appears to upset adults more than drinking or smoking. Bowers and Sage briefly review interventions that were found to be successful in eliminating glue sniffing; however, they advocate the development of programs that aim at teaching adolescents to assert themselves and to consider their safety when confronted with peer temptations and pressures.

Clements, J. E., and Simpson, R. "Environmental and Behavioral Aspects of Glue Sniffing in a Population of Emotionally Disturbed Adolescents." *The International Journal of the Addictions,* 1978, *13* (1), 129–134.

Forty-seven adolescents who were inpatients in a mental health facility and who had a history of glue sniffing responded to an eight-question survey. The results of the survey indicated that peer pressure is the predominant motivation behind engaging in glue sniffing. The authors conclude that engaging in the behavior is symptomatic of emotional maladjustment. It is noteworthy that the youngsters surveyed reported a trend toward unpleasant experiences with continual use of glue sniffing.

Daubert, M., and MacAdam, C. "Gasoline Inhalation: A Community Challenge." *Canadian Nurse,* 1980, *76* (10), 24–25.

The authors report on the establishment of a drop-in center in a community with the goal of decreasing youngsters' gasoline inhalation. Gasoline inhalation was utilized in the community by youngsters as a form of recreation; therefore, the center's objective was to provide recreational facilities and activities for children and families, as well as counseling on developing healthier life-styles.

Epstein, M. H., and Wieland, W. F. "Prevalence Survey of Inhalant Abuse." *International Journal of the Addictions,* 1978, *13* (2), 271–284.

A survey of a housing project in Atlanta, Georgia, revealed that 4 percent of the youngsters residing there had engaged in inhalant abuse. The authors report that the typical sniffer was a fifteen-year-old male. Many of the youngsters persisted at glue sniffing into their twenties. In addition, glue sniffers used other drugs and alcohol at higher rates than youngsters not engaging in glue sniffing. Parents of the identified youngsters reported acknowledgment of drug-related problems in their children but seldom sought help for the children or the family.

Watson, J. M. "Glue-Sniffing in Profile." *The Practitioner*, 1977, *218*, 255-259.

Watson briefly reviews aspects of glue sniffing. She reports that the behavior is found predominantly in boys between the ages of eight and seventeen and that, in general, glue sniffing is a group activity. Truancy and poor school performance have been found to correlate with glue sniffing. The progressive development of symptoms during an episode of glue sniffing is compared, in table form, to the stages of anesthesia in order to provide an understanding of the effects. Watson also discusses tolerance, habituation, and physical dependence, as well as sources of referral.

Sleep Disturbance

As with eating disorders, children show a very high incidence of sleep problems. About half of all sleep disturbances can be classified as being minor in nature—for example, restlessness, mumbling, talking, teeth grinding, early or frequent waking, and difficulty in falling asleep. According to the literature, the more serious sleep disorders include nocturnal enuresis, whose incidence accounts for about a quarter of all sleep problems; nightmares (7 percent incidence); night terrors (2 percent); and sleepwalking (1 percent). The reader is referred to another section of this book for a discussion of enuresis. This section presents various techniques for treating some of the other disorders of sleep, especially insomnia and nightmares.

Treating Insomnia by Relaxation and Reductions in Parental Attention

AUTHOR: David R. Anderson

PRECIS: The utilization of relaxation training and a behavioral program to reduce mother's attention to insomnia.

INTRODUCTION: Anderson reports that current research supports using behavior therapies in place of medication as a successful treatment in eliminating insomnia. While implementing a relaxation technique in the treatment of a thirteen-year-old male with a four-month history of insomnia, Anderson utilized a simple behavioral program to reduce the attention that the boy's mother was giving to the symptom. Anderson proposed that the mother's attention was playing a role in maintaining the boy's sleep disturbance.

CASE HISTORY: At the time of referral, the boy was experiencing almost nightly occurrences of insomnia. The difficulty began at dinnertime, when the boy would become so upset that he would pace and sometimes cry. The youngster's parents were assessed to be warm, supportive, and very concerned about the boy. The mother would sit with the boy in his bedroom for hours until he fell asleep. In addition, when the boy experienced difficulty falling back to sleep during the night, his mother would sit up with him in the living room until he returned to his bedroom.

Anderson initiated a treatment program that involved two components. The first component was teaching the boy Jacobson's *Progressive Relaxation* (Chicago: University of Chicago Press, 1938)—a progressive muscle relaxation technique. This aimed at dealing with the boy's tension, and it was accomplished in three one-hour sessions. The therapist instructed the boy to practice the technique once a day and to do the exercises each night before going to bed. In addition, he was to do the exercises if he woke up during the night.

The other component of the program was aimed at reducing the secondary gain achieved from the symptom, which was the mother's attention. The mother was instructed to go to bed at her regular bedtime, regardless of whether the boy was able to go to sleep. She was permitted during the first week to sit with the boy in the living room for a short time if he came into her bedroom because of his inability to sleep. During the next week, however, the mother was not to interact with the boy if he came to her bedroom but was to go into the bathroom. Finally, during the third week and thereafter, the mother was required to stay in her bed and to tell the boy to go to his own room and do his relaxation exercises.

RESULTS: Initially, the mother was somewhat reluctant to follow the attention-reducing component of treatment. However, because of her own exhaustion, she agreed. Upon implementation of the program, a dramatic improvement in the boy's sleep was demonstrated. During the first week of treatment, only two instances of insomnia occurred. During the next eight weeks, the frequency of insomnia dropped to approximately once per week. Thereafter the boy experienced so few instances of insomnia that the symptom was no longer considered problematic. The boy reported that he consistently utilized the relaxation technique at bedtime and upon awakening during the night.

COMMENTARY: The two component treatment approaches utilized demonstrated that a severe case of childhood insomnia could be successfully eliminated through behavioral intervention. In this case, the mother's cooperation in reducing her attention to the boy's symptom appears to have contributed to the success of the treatment. As the author points out, clinicians treating children with insomnia should be sensitive to the parents' reactions and possible unintentional reinforcement of the symptom.

SOURCE: Anderson, D. R. "Treatment of Insomnia in a 13-Year-Old Boy by Relaxation Training and Reduction of Parental Attention." *Journal of Behavior Therapy and Experimental Psychiatry*, 1979, *10*, 263-265.

Eliminating Night Waking

AUTHOR: Marc Weissbluth

PRECIS: Successful treatment of an infant's night awakenings by modification of the sleep schedule.

INTRODUCTION: Night waking is reportedly experienced by about 25 percent of all babies. This sleep disturbance is defined as waking or crying between midnight and 5:00 A.M. on at least four nights a week for four or more consecutive weeks in babies between six and twelve months of age. The pathophysiology is not understood, therefore requiring treatment to be aimed at such external factors as parental responses and routines. Weissbluth presents the case of a seven-month-old girl with a severe sleep disturbance.

CASE STUDY: AB was referred for difficulty going to sleep and for night wakings that occurred up to ten times per night. At the time of referral, the parents had to hold and rock AB for two to two-and-a-half hours before she would go to sleep. The baby usually did not fall asleep until 10:00 P.M., and she would awaken at least three or four times during the night. Once awake, AB usually would be up for over an hour. Medications (diphenhydramine, promethazine, and dicyclomine) had been tried but were not effective in reducing the awakenings. With the exception of infantile colic that had developed within the first few weeks of life, the baby was physically normal. She was the product of an uncomplicated pregnancy.

TREATMENT: Initially, treatment focused on giving the parents instructions for reducing stimulation prior to bedtime. In addition, they were told to make AB's sleep schedule consistent and to handle her consistently before putting her to sleep. This did not affect the baby's sleeping pattern, and by nine months of age AB was going to sleep at midnight, waking frequently during the night, and then sleeping until 9:00 or 10:00 A.M. the next morning. The parents were then instructed to change the baby's sleep schedule by awakening her every morning at 7:00

A.M. and not allowing any naps past 11:00 A.M. In addition, they were instructed to put AB to sleep at night whenever she appeared to be tired.

RESULTS: Upon modification of AB's sleep schedule, the parents reported an immediate change in AB's sleep patterns. She began to fall asleep in five minutes or less and she had fewer night wakings. Within a few weeks, the night wakings stopped, and at a ten-month follow-up they had not reoccurred. The schedule change resulted in an earlier bedtime.

COMMENTARY: Changing the baby's sleep schedule was an effective treatment in eliminating night wakings and in producing a reasonable bedtime. Although Weissbluth points out that the exact mechanisms by which the sleep pattern changed are not clear, it does appear that the parental cooperation and consistency played a major role in the effectiveness of the treatment. The current study suggests that changes in sleep schedules may be an important tool in dealing with sleep disturbances.

SOURCE: Weissbluth, M. "Modification of Sleep Schedule with Reduction of Night Waking: A Case Report." *Sleep,* 1982, 5 (3), 262-266.

Reducing Nightmares by Systematic Desensitization

AUTHORS: A. J. Cellucci and P. S. Lawrence

PRECIS: Anxiety reduction through systematic desensitization as a treatment for nightmares.

INTRODUCTION: Cellucci and Lawrence briefly review current single-case findings utilizing behavioral techniques to reduce anxiety associated with nightmares. Systematic desensitization in which subjects construct a hierarchy of the anxiety-producing nightmare elements and then use self-talk to reduce the anxiety has reportedly been successful in eliminating nightmares. In this study, the authors treated undergraduate students having an average of two or more nightmares per week with a systematic desensitization procedure.

TREATMENT: The subjects participated in five weekly individual sessions of forty-five to sixty minutes in duration. For the purposes of the treatment, nightmares were defined as subjectively distressing or anxiety-producing dreams that usually woke the subjects from sleep. Systematic desensitization involved teaching the subjects the standard procedure developed by Wolpe (*The Practice of Behavior Therapy*. Elmsford, N.Y.: Pergamon Press, 1969). Initially, subjects were taught the theory behind the technique. The hierarchies for each subject used disturbing scenes that progressively increased his or her anxiety level. Actual portions of his or her nightmares were incorporated into each subject's hierarchy. The presenting nightmares included the major themes of threat of physical harm to self, injury or death of others, injury or death of self, interpersonal conflicts, fears of animals, fears of natural disasters, illness, social embarrassment, and religious fears.

During each session, the subject imagined a scene twice. Initially, the duration was ten to fifteen seconds, and during the next trial the scene was imagined for twenty-five to thirty seconds. Each session began with a review of the last scene imagined the week before. An element of self-control was utilized as the subjects were instructed to relax their muscles and imagine themselves coping in each situation by saying, "It's only a dream" each time they experienced anxiety during the imagined scene. If the anxiety did not dissipate in a minute or less, the scene was terminated and the preceding, less anxiety-provoking one was repeated.

The subjects were informed that once they could learn an

incompatible response to the anxiety of the nightmare not only would the anxiety decrease but the nightmares would also terminate.

RESULTS: In order to assess the effectiveness of the systematic desensitization procedure, a nightmare discussion placebo group and a control group whose members merely recorded the frequency of their nightmares were used for comparison. The systematic desensitization subjects revealed a significant decrease in the frequency of their nightmares over the five-week treatment period. The placebo discussion group revealed decreases in nightmares that were significantly greater than those of the control group. The subjects treated with the systematic desensitization not only experienced the greatest decrease in frequency of nightmares but also reported the greatest decrease in the intensity of their anxieties in regard to the fears elicited by the nightmares.

The authors also discuss other factors, such as daytime fears and time needed to fall asleep, as they reportedly improved significantly for the subjects in the systematic desensitization group.

COMMENTARY: The procedure of using systematic desensitization was found to be effective in producing desired changes not only in the frequency of nightmares but also in their intensity. This procedure has proved to be effective in eliminating various fears and anxieties in subjects, so its use with nightmares seems to be a logical extension. Further research, possibly using the procedure with younger subjects, should be considered.

SOURCE: Cellucci, A. J., and Lawrence, P. S. "The Efficacy of Systematic Desensitization in Reducing Nightmares." *Journal of Behavior Therapy and Experimental Psychiatry*, 1978, *9*, 109-114.

Additional Readings

Anders, T. F. "Neurophysiological Studies of Sleep in Infants and Children." *Journal of Child Psychology and Psychiatry,* 1982, *23* (1), 75-83.

Anders presents a summary of the normal and pathological sleep pattern development of infants, children, and adolescents. He reports that in spite of a great deal of current research in sleep laboratories, there remain many unanswered questions as to the causes of or reasons for various sleep disturbances. In addition, he points out that research is presently focusing on the interactions of daytime functioning and nighttime sleep. These correlations should provide more relevant data for clinicians working with children.

Carey, W. B. "Night Waking and Temperament in Infancy." *The Journal of Pediatrics,* 1974, *84* (5), 756-758.

Carey presents evidence to support the hypothesis that night wakings in infants between the ages of six and twelve months may be attributable to a temperamental predisposition. Carey does not believe that child illness or faulty management by parents is the sole cause of night wakings. A survey of sixty infants was conducted using a questionnaire to assess temperament, and the findings suggest that babies who experience night wakings have a low sensory threshold. The author recommends the use of medication, such as a chloral hydrate, barbiturate, or diphenhydramine, if habit training does not eliminate the sleep disturbance.

Cellucci, A. J., and Lawrence, P. S. "Individual Differences in Self-Reported Sleep: Variable Correlations Among Nightmare Sufferers." *Clinical Psychology,* 1981, *48,* 287-294.

Self-reported anxiety ratings and sleep observations were obtained from students participating in a treatment program for nightmares. Findings indicate that there is a significant correlation between anxiety, sleep disturbance, and the occurrence of nightmares. In light of this correlation, the authors recommend anxiety-reducing interventions, such as systematic desensitization, as a treatment approach.

Dollinger, S. J. "On the Varieties of Childhood Sleep Distur-
    bance." *Journal of Clinical Child Psychology*, 1982, *11*
    (2), 107–115.
    Dollinger presents four cluster types of childhood sleep
disturbances: moderate, immature, severe, and few or no sleep
problems. The children in the moderate cluster appear to be
afraid of sleeping, as they exhibit restless sleep, sleeptalking,
and refusal to go to bed or refusal to sleep without a night
light. Children in the immature cluster tend to rely on magical
attempts to protect themselves against anxiety associated with
sleeping. These youngsters demonstrate a need to take an object to bed with them; they engage in ritualistic behavior at bedtime and desire to sleep in their parents' bed. These children
tend to have trouble falling asleep and usually talk during their
sleep. In addition, the children in the immature cluster engage
in manipulativeness in regard to bedtime issues. Youngsters in
the severe cluster appear to suffer from severe anxiety that is
not well controlled during sleep. Many of these youngsters experience nightmares, night terrors, and sleepwalking. In general,
they engage in sleeptalking and restless sleep, and they cry out
while asleep. Dollinger concludes that sleep disturbances reflect
underlying conflicts that the child is experiencing.

Guillemenault, C., Eldridge, F. L., Simmons, F. B., and Dement,
    W. C. "Sleep Apnea in Eight Children." *Pediatrics*, 1976,
    58 (1), 23–30.
    The authors discuss clinical symptomatology of eight
children (ages between five and fourteen years) diagnosed with
a sleep apnea syndrome. Symptoms include: excessive daytime
sleepiness, poor school performance, abnormal daytime behavior, enuresis of recent onset, morning headaches, abnormal
weight, and development of hypertension in conjunction with
loud snoring that is interrupted by pauses during sleep. The authors discuss the diagnostic technique of all-night polygraphic
recordings, as well as surgery as a treatment for the disorder.
They present several cases to illustrate diagnostic problems.

Hauri, P., and Olmstead, E. "Childhood-Onset Insomnia."
    Sleep, 1980, *3* (1), 59–65.

The authors discuss a study comparing twenty insomniac patients who had suffered since childhood and thirty-nine patients with adult onset insomnia. No differences were found in the personality inventories of the two groups, but the childhood onset group revealed greater evidence of soft signs of possible neurological impairment. Differences in the groups were found in that the childhood onset group took longer to fall asleep, slept less, and revealed excessive amounts of REM sleep without eye movements. Adult onset insomniacs exhibited more restless sleep. The authors conclude that there is some evidence to support the notion that insomnia beginning in childhood may be more attributable to a neurological basis than to a psychological one.

Rapoff, M. A., Christophersen, E. R., and Rapoff, R. E. "The Management of Common Childhood Bedtime Problems by Pediatric Nurse Practitioners." *Journal of Pediatric Psychology,* 1982, 7 (2), 179-196.

The authors present a treatment of childhood bedtime crying in which pediatric nurses advised parents on management techniques. The treatment was conducted by the nurses in a single session during a clinic visit. The nurses advised parents in regard to managing their children's crying and getting out of bed. They taught the parents to ignore crying and to either give the child a swat for leaving the bed while returning the child to bed or just returning the child to bed. All procedures were to be conducted without parents engaging in any talking to the child. Written guidelines stating the procedure were given out. Success was achieved with three out of six children in eliminating bedtime crying. The authors point out that the parents that did not achieve success were found to be inconsistent in their implementation of the procedures.

Reid, W. H., Ahmed, I. and Levie, C. A. "Treatment of Sleepwalking: A Controlled Study." *American Journal of Psychotherapy,* 1981, *35* (1), 27-37.

The authors describe hypnotherapy treatment of adults experiencing severe somnambulism. Treatment consisted of six sessions in which subjects were hypnotized without their feet touching the floor. Subjects were given an arousal cue of placing their feet on the floor, which was paired with their awakening. Subjects were told during the sessions that once their feet touched the floor they could no longer remain asleep. The treatment was found to be effective in decreasing the sleepwalking symptoms.

Obscene Language

This section discusses the compulsive use of "dirty words," strong words, or swear words by children. The use of dirty words by children seems to serve a variety of purposes: the discharge of aggressive tension, the expression of infantile sexual pleasure, the expression of nonconformity by opposing a taboo of society, and the creation of a sense of power. In regard to the last item, children tend to use words in a very concrete, magical, and primitive way. In some primitive societies, for example, it is felt that making the sounds of an object results in one becoming the object and thereby obtaining power over it. Since coprolalia or compulsive cursing is a common symptom of Tourette's syndrome, the reader is referred to the section in this book dealing with tics for a further discussion of this disturbance.

217

Eliminating Obscene Language

AUTHORS: Michael H. Epstein, Alan C. Repp, and Douglas Cullinan

PRECIS: Differential reinforcement of low rates of swearing as a treatment for a group of behaviorally disordered children.

INTRODUCTION: In response to recent legal and ethical questions in regard to punishment procedures in schools for treating inappropriate behaviors, the authors devised an approach to modify undesirable classroom behaviors using a positive strategy. Six youngsters labeled as behaviorally disordered in a self-contained special education class were demonstrating a high frequency of the use of obscene language. The following treatment was implemented.

TREATMENT: Obscene language was defined as verbal references to body parts used for sexual activity or waste elimination, sexual or elimination behavior or the products of these behaviors, and/or negative references to another's parentage. The classroom teacher carried out the treatment of employing differential reinforcement (DRL) for low rates of swearing.

The teacher initially informed the class that each child who verbalized no more than a specific number of obscenities during a day would receive twenty tokens. Tokens could be exchanged for toys and/or preferred activities. Each curse was recorded on a chart in the classroom that was displayed on a bulletin board. The teacher recorded curses without making any comments to the children. Initially, the number of allowable daily curses was three. The DRL limit was reduced to two, one, and then zero. Each reduction was dependent upon the success of all students in meeting the previous limit.

RESULTS: The students responded positively to the DRL intervention. This was demonstrated by a significant decrease in their swearing behavior upon the program's implementation. The DRL limit of three was imposed for twelve days, the limit of two lasted five days, eight days were utilized for a limit of one, and fifteen days were used for a limit of zero. By the last five days of the treatment, all of the students had eliminated obscene language usage in the classroom. The study ended on the last day of the school year, so no follow-up data were obtained.

COMMENTARY: The authors demonstrated that a nonaversive, positive DRL strategy was effective in eliminating obscene language usage by a group of special education students labeled as behaviorally disordered. Epstein, Repp, and Cullinan point out that the individual students responded differently to the treatment: Some responded quickly, while others persisted at cursing for longer periods. No adjustments were made for individuals, as this treatment was devised to be a group approach. DRL as a nonpunitive intervention is applicable to other undesirable behaviors and can be utilized with individuals as well as with groups.

SOURCE: Epstein, M. H., Repp, A. C., and Cullinan, D. "Decreasing 'Obscene' Language of Behaviorally Disordered Children Through the Use of a DRL Schedule." *Psychology in the Schools,* 1978, *15* (3), 419-423.

Treatment of Swearing Behavior

AUTHORS: Joel Fischer and Robert Nehs

PRECIS: Reducing swearing in an eleven-year-old boy by imposing a chore as the consequence.

INTRODUCTION: The authors point out that mild, aversive stimuli can be utilized as effective treatments for maladaptive behaviors that are not severe. They present the case of an eleven-year-old boy to illustrate the use of such an aversive stimulus: the requirement of doing a disliked chore as a consequence for each incidence of an undesirable behavior (swearing).

CASE STUDY: Mark, an eleven-year-old who attended a Salvation Army facility for children, demonstrated profuse swearing at the dinner table. This behavior was extremely upsetting to the cottage parents, who had little success in persuading Mark to stop swearing. As Mark spent the weekends at home, the treatment procedures were only employed on the five days per week that Mark was at the facility.

The cottage parents informed the youngster that each time he swore he would be required to wash the windows for a ten-minute period. (The window washing was ordinarily done by a housekeeping staff.) In addition, a punishment hierarchy was devised, and Mark was told that he would lose privileges if he did not complete the window-washing requirement.

RESULTS: After initial testing of the procedure on the first day of its implementation, Mark's swearing decreased significantly. By the fifth week of the treatment (which utilized a reversal to baseline during weeks three and four), Mark's cursing behavior had terminated. Follow-up revealed that Mark engaged in little swearing for the rest of the year following the treatment.

COMMENTARY: Fischer and Nehs demonstrated that imposing a disliked chore as a consequence for an undesirable behavior (swearing) was effective in eliminating the behavior. The effectiveness of the treatment appeared to be attributable to the fact that the youngster did experience the window-washing chore as an aversive stimulus. However, an analysis of the two treatment components—engaging in a disliked chore and the threat of loss of privileges—would be valuable in ascertaining the strength of each component. The authors caution that when using this technique, a chore that the child would normally be required to do should not be assigned as a consequence, as it would likely produce negative reactions toward everyday chores that need to be done.

SOURCE: Fischer, J., and Nehs, R. "Use of a Commonly Available Chore to Reduce a Boy's Rate of Swearing." *Journal of Behavior Therapy and Experimental Psychiatry,* 1978, *9,* 81-83.

Self-Injurious Behavior

Incidents of severe self-injurious behaviors, such as head banging, hair pulling, and scratching, tend to produce a spellbinding effect on professionals and nonprofessionals alike. The extremely primitive nature of these acts usually produces strong emotional reactions in adults—typically disgust and/or pity. The following studies describe diverse techniques that have been employed to systematically eliminate self-destructive behaviors in children.

Treating Nocturnal Head Banging

AUTHORS: Barbara A. Balaschak and David I. Mostofsky

PRECIS: Behavioral contracting as a successful treatment for nocturnal head banging in a sixteen-year-old boy.

INTRODUCTION: A sixteen-year-old male, JF, was referred by his mother for treatment of nightly compulsive head banging that had been ongoing since age three-and-a-half. Head-banging behavior occurred while JF was asleep, and although it did not awaken him, it did awaken his parents.

JF reported that head banging only occurred when he was lying on his stomach, and he would strike his head on both the pillow and the headboard. The youngster also reported that at age nine he had banged his head before going to sleep because he had been scared and had thought that the banging would keep ghosts away from him. In all other respects—school performance, peer relationships, and so on—JF's functioning was not problematic.

TREATMENT: Initial interviews with JF and his mother revealed that his mother was an overbearing, controlling woman. Therefore, the therapist worked at modifying her behavior during treatment by giving her specific directions, praising her when JF showed improvements, and acting as an intermediary between JF and his mother.

During the baseline period, JF's mother recorded bedtimes and times of head banging. In addition, during this phase of treatment, the mother awakened JF only if the behavior lasted for more than fifteen minutes.

After four-and-a-half weeks, different therapists held separate interviews with the mother and JF. The mother and her therapist went over the baseline data, while JF came up with several self-control procedures. He was going to try to sleep on his back and would facilitate this by placing pillows along the sides of his body so that he would not turn over. In addition, JF was going to place a bell on his headboard so that he would awaken once the behavior began. The plan was described to the mother, and a contingency reward contract was devised. JF's mother would give JF one dollar for each night that she was not awakened by his head banging. At week six of treatment, an adjustment was made in the contract so that JF would earn five dollars for each six out of seven nights a week that he did not interrupt his mother's sleep.

RESULTS: Treatment was implemented for thirty weeks. Of those thirty weeks, the mother did not administer the reinforcement during two weeks. Those two weeks resulted in increases in JF's head banging. However, while the contract was adhered to, JF's head banging decreased significantly. Only six direct contact sessions were employed. Follow-up a year after treatment ended found JF to be demonstrating only occasional instances of head banging.

COMMENTARY: In addition to the behavioral contract that was set up, several factors seemed to contribute to the effectiveness of this treatment. Since JF was an adolescent, providing him with his own therapist and sessions separate from his mother may have played an important part in his behavior change. In addition, fostering self-control strategies by having JF come up with ideas to solve his problem must also be considered. Finally, redirecting the mother's interactions with JF seemed to be beneficial, as it resulted in a more positive way of relating.

SOURCE: Balaschak, B. A., and Mostofsky, D. I. "Treatment of Nocturnal Head-Banging by Behavioral Contracting." *Journal of Behavioral Therapy and Experiential Psychiatry*, 1980, *11*, 117–120.

Eliminating Eyebrow Hair Pulling

AUTHOR: Michael S. Rosenbaum

PRECIS: Treating eyebrow hair pulling with a modified habit reversal technique.

INTRODUCTION: Rosenbaum states that although Azrin and Nunn's ("Habit-Reversal: A Method of Eliminating Nervous Habits and Tics." *Behavior Research Therapy*, 1973, *11*, 619-628) habit reversal technique is an effective method of reducing or eliminating self-injurious behavior resulting from nervous habits, the procedures tend to be too time consuming for use in pediatric office settings. Therefore, Rosenbaum modified the procedure, resulting in shortening the therapist-patient direct contact time and thus making the technique more realistic for use in pediatric offices. The case of a seven-year-old treated with the modified procedure is reported.

CASE STUDY: The boy was referred for treatment of excessive eyebrow hair pulling that occurred at home but rarely at school. At the time of referral, the boy's eyebrows were extremely thin, and there were several bald spots in each brow. Prior to treatment, the therapist spoke to the mother on the telephone and instructed her to record all hair pulling events for a two-week period.

The modified habit reversal procedure utilized only three of the components of the procedure developed by Azrin and Nunn. In the original procedure, the following components are used: response description, early warning, situation awareness training, habit inconvenience review, competing response practice, and symbolic rehearsal. Rosenbaum utilized only the response description, early warning, and competing practice components.

The child was initially required to verbally describe the behavior of pulling hair from his eyebrows while demonstrating it to the therapist. The therapist then taught him to detect the behavior by bringing his hand toward and then placing it on his eyebrow. Finally, the child was taught a competing response involving an isometric exercise. This consisted of placing his hands either in his lap or to the sides of his body and practicing clenching his fists. This exercise was prescribed for one minute following any urge to pull hair, any instance of hair pulling, or any instance in which the child detected his hand going toward his eyebrow. The therapist instructed the mother to prompt the boy to begin the competing response any time he failed to initiate it on his own. In addition, she was instructed to praise the boy for engaging in the competing response when not prompted. The entire session of direct therapist-patient contact was approximately twenty minutes in duration.

RESULTS: Follow-up was conducted by telephone. Following the treatment session, hair pulling decreased from five occurrences per day to five instances during the first two weeks. At three-, twelve-, and eighteen-month follow-ups, no instances of hair pulling were reported, and the boy's eyebrows no longer revealed thinning or bald spots.

COMMENTARY: Rosenbaum's findings demonstrate that a modified habit reversal technique was effective in eliminating eyebrow hair pulling in a seven-year-old youngster. The technique offers a promising, cost- and time-effective approach to eliminating self-injurious behavior. However, replications of this modified technique need to be conducted in order to provide more data.

SOURCE: Rosenbaum, M. S. "Treating Hair Pulling in a 7-Year-Old Male: Modified Habit Reversal for Use in Pediatric Settings." *Developmental and Behavioral Pediatrics,* 1982, 3 (4), 241-243.

Treating Self-Injurious Scratching

AUTHORS: Edward G. Carr and Jack. J. McDowell

PRECIS: Treating severe self-injurious scratching in a ten-year-old boy using time-out procedures and tangible reinforcements for not scratching.

INTRODUCTION: Jim was referred for treatment of self-injurious scratching that had a three-year history. The scratching was precipitated by a medical condition diagnosed as contact dermatitis that was the result of poison oak. However, after the skin condition cleared, Jim continued scratching. His behavior resulted in lesions, and at the time of referral Jim had both open lesions and many scars on his skin.

Carr and McDowell propose that many medical conditions are influenced or exacerbated by social reinforcement. Therefore, an intervention aimed at removing the social reinforcement for Jim's scratching was implemented.

TREATMENT: The intervention for Jim's self-injurious scratching consisted of three phases. Initially, Jim's scratching was assessed in order to identify situations that seemed to elicit the behavior. The second phase involved the manipulation of social attention for scratching. The final phase involved a time-out procedure for scratching and positive reinforcement for reductions in the numbers of body sores.

The first two phases of the treatment resulted in the following analysis: Jim's scratching occurred most frequently during play, while watching television, and during a talk time when the family got together to discuss the day. In addition, it was found that Jim's scratching behavior resulted in either verbal or physical attention from his parents, as they either told Jim to stop the behavior or made attempts to restrain his hands.

Treatment consisted of sending Jim to a time-out room for twenty minutes each time he was observed scratching. In addition, at the beginning of each week Jim chose a reinforcer, such as a trip to a museum or going roller-skating. He could obtain the reinforcer if he had a reduction of at least two sores on his body by the end of the week. If Jim did not succeed in earning the reinforcer, he could work at it until he did so.

RESULTS: Treatment was implemented for two months, during which there was a significant decrease in scratching. During the next two-and-a-half months, the parents were unable to continue the treatment contingencies, and scratching increased. It was then reinstated for four-and-a-half months, at which point time-out procedures and tangible reinforcers were eliminated. At follow-up one-and-a-half years after treatment had begun, Jim had only two sores on his body.

COMMENTARY: The findings demonstrate two important factors. One is that self-injurious behavior can initially occur as a result of an organic etiology. However, its maintenance can become the result of secondary gains, such as social attention and reinforcement. The other important factor is that the behavior, even when long standing, can be modified by manipulating social reinforcers. In this instance, removing the child from all attention upon scratching and rewarding nonscratching behavior (that is, a reduction in the number of sores) proved to be highly effective. The procedures also are applicable to other self-injurious behaviors.

SOURCE: Carr, E. G., and McDowell, J. J. "Social Control of Self-Injurious Behavior of Organic Etiology." *Behavior Therapy,* 1980, *11,* 402–409.

Response Prevention as a
Treatment for Hair Pulling

AUTHORS: Stefan R. Massong, R. P. Edwards, Lillian Range Sitton, and B. Jo Hailey

PRECIS: A three-year-old boy was successfully treated for chronic hair pulling with a response prevention procedure.

INTRODUCTION: The authors report a case in which hair shortening served as a response prevention procedure for hair pulling in a preschooler. They point out that professionals may often overlook the simple and least-restrictive intervention while employing more complicated treatment.

CASE STUDY: E was referred for treatment of scalp hair pulling that had persisted for one month. A year earlier, E had engaged in similar behavior, but it had stopped without any intervention. E's mother reported that E was engaging in consistent hair pulling throughout the day and slept with his hand tightly wrapped in his hair. E's hair was collar length, and the mother's attempts to eliminate the behavior included spanking, isolation, verbal reprimands, and physical forcing of E's hand from his hair.

Initially, treatment was based on a program described by Forehand and King ("Pre-school Children's Non-Compliance: Effects of Short-Term Behavior Therapy." *Journal of Community Psychology*, 1974, *2*, 42–44) called attention reflection. The program involved a five-minute period each day during which the mother verbalized a description of all E's appropriate behaviors during an activity with E while ignoring all hair-pulling behavior. After ten days, E was not engaging in hair pulling, and after seventeen days the mother terminated the treatment without consulting the therapist. By day twenty-four, hair pulling had returned to its original frequency. E's mother did not want to resume the attention reflection procedure, so a simple response prevention—cutting E's hair so it would be above his collar and allow his ears to be exposed—was tried. The procedure eliminated hair pulling.

At follow-up six months after the response prevention (the haircut), E's hair was back at its original length, but E exhibited only rare, stress-induced instances of hair pulling.

COMMENTARY: In this particular case, E's hair pulling appeared to be a self-stimulating behavior that was easily prevented by eliminating the stimulus (long hair). Once E could no longer wrap his hand in his hair, he no longer engaged in the hair pulling.

As the authors point out, professionals may sometimes overlook simple, obvious solutions to undesirable behaviors. This case reminds clinicians to consider minimally intrusive procedures before implementing more complex ones.

SOURCE: Massong, S. R., Edwards, R. P., Sitton, L. R., and Hailey, B. J. "A Case of Trichotillomania in a Three-Year-Old Treated by Response Prevention." *Journal of Behavior Therapy and Experimental Psychiatry,* 1980, *11,* 223–225.

===

Treating Assaultive Hair-Pulling Behavior

AUTHOR: Wayne Adams

PRECIS: The use of an ammonia inhalation procedure in the treatment of hair-pulling behavior in a nine-year-old, moderately retarded, visually impaired boy.

INTRODUCTION: Adams reports a case of a nine-year-old boy, Eddie, who was moderately retarded, legally blind, and engaging in frequent assaultive hair-pulling behavior. Eddie was not pulling his own hair but was demonstrating aggressive outbursts that consisted of pulling the hair of others. He demonstrated this behavior at home and at school. No precipitating event could be identified, and the school staff was unsuccessful in modifying the behavior with reprimands, time-outs, or loss of privileges. The author was contacted by the school to treat Eddie's uncontrollable hair pulling.

Several well-known behavioral techniques, such as differential reinforcement of other behaviors, time-out, overcorrection, and shaping, failed to modify Eddie's assaultive hair pulling. In addition, a school transfer, medication, and respite care in a residential home had no effect on Eddie's behavior. However, the administration of ammonia salts contingent on hair pulling proved to be very effective.

TREATMENT: A hair-pulling attempt was defined as any movement toward another person's hair that involved a grasping hand posture. Prior to the implementation of the treatment, the program was explained to Eddie using a dummy with a wig. In addition, a demonstration of the consequence for hair-pulling attempts was given.

Following each hair-pulling attempt, a capsule of ammonia salts was broken directly under Eddie's nose. It was held there until Eddie withdrew from the attempt. This withdrawal took only about two to four seconds. School staff members were trained in the technique and understood the importance of the immediacy of implementing the consequence. Throughout the treatment, medical consultation was utilized in order to monitor any possible side effects.

RESULTS: On the first day of treatment, Eddie made only one hair-pulling attempt. Subsequently, only two hair-pulling attempts occurred in the classroom and four outside of the classroom. On follow-up, Eddie had not engaged in any hair-pulling attempts for thirty-eight days.

COMMENTARY: As Adams points out, the use of ammonia salts, which is an aversive procedure, should be used only as a last resort when nonaversive techniques have failed to modify harmful behavior. In addition, medical consultation must be obtained in order to monitor side effects and to keep the therapist alert to precautions.

The current findings not only point out the effectiveness of the technique but also demonstrate that in treating a youngster many techniques may fail before one is found that will successfully modify the targeted behavior. Although in Eddie's case the hair pulling was not a self-injurious behavior but was aimed at others, the technique of using ammonia salts should be considered in the treatment of severe self-injurious behavior that has not responded to less aversive techniques.

SOURCE: Adams, W. "Treatment of Assaultive Hair Pulling in a Multihandicapped Youth." *Journal of Autism and Developmental Disorders*, 1980, *10* (3), 335-342.

A Comparison of Treatments for Hair Pulling

AUTHORS: N. H. Azrin, R. G. Nunn, and S. E. Frantz

PRECIS: Habit reversal procedures and the negative practice method are compared as treatments for trichotillomania.

INTRODUCTION: The authors have utilized habit reversal procedures as an effective treatment for a variety of nervous habit disorders and self-injurious behaviors. However, most applications of the technique are reported on the basis of a small number of subjects. The authors compared their habit reversal method to a negative practice procedure in thirty-four subjects demonstrating trichotillomania.

TREATMENT: The thirty-four subjects were randomly assigned to one of the two treatments. Hair pulling involved pulling hair from the scalp, eyebrows, eyelashes, and/or beard. All subjects carried a recording chart with them and recorded hair pulling on a daily basis.

HABIT REVERSAL TRAINING: One two-hour session was held with each subject. The following are the components of the procedure that each subject was taught by a counselor using behavior rehearsal:

1. Competing Reaction Training. The subject is taught to inconspicuously clench his or her hands for three minutes whenever hair pulling is about to occur or occurs.
2. Awareness Training. By observing themselves in a mirror, subjects are taught to become aware of the movements they engage in while hair pulling.
3. Identifying Habit-Prone Situations. Situations that lead to hair pulling, such as watching television, are identified.
4. Identifying Response Precursors. The subject learns which responses lead to hair pulling, such as touching the face, and so on.
5. Relaxation Training. Deep, regular breathing and postural adjustment are taught in order to reduce nervousness.
6. Prevention Training. The competing response is practiced whenever a response precursor or habit-prone situation exists.
7. Habit Interruption. The competing response is used to interrupt the hair-pulling act.
8. Positive Attention (overcorrection). The subject practices positive hair care, such as brushing the hair or repairing eye makeup.
9. Daily Practice of Competing Reaction. Positive attention and the competing response are practiced each day in front of a mirror.
10. Self-Recording. Each instance of hair pulling is recorded.
11. Display of Improvement. Situations that were avoided because of hair pulling are sought in order to enable the subject to see and reinforce improvement.
12. Social Support. A significant other is included in the end of the training session in order to learn how to give the subject appropriate encouragement for eliminating the hair pulling.
13. Annoyance Review. A list is comprised at the begin-

ning of the training session that identifies problems caused by hair pulling. This list is later referred to as a motivation and as a source of reinforcement for eliminating the behavior.

NEGATIVE PRACTICE PROGRAM: Subjects receiving this treatment also met with a counselor for one two-hour session. Each subject received three pages of instructions on the implementation of negative practice procedures. The instructions stated that the subject was to stand in front of a mirror for thirty seconds each hour and act out hair pulling without actually pulling out any hair. The practice was to continue for four days following the breaking of the habit, at which time it could gradually be eliminated. The subjects practiced in front of a mirror during the session, and the counselor stressed the importance of practicing on a regular and consistent basis.

RESULTS: Daily reports of hair pulling were made to the counselors via telephone for the first week of treatment, then weekly for the first month, and then monthly for four months. The habit reversal subjects demonstrated a 99 percent reduction of hair pulling the first day after training. At the end of the fourth month, the reduction remained above 90 percent. The negative practice subjects revealed a 58 percent reduction in hair pulling the first day after training, and their reduction remained at between 52 to 68 percent. The comparison demonstrates that the habit reversal procedures were more effective in treating hair pulling than was the negative practice technique.

COMMENTARY: Azrin, Nunn, and Frantz found support for habit reversal procedures in comparison with negative practice techniques. Habit reversal has been shown to be effective in eliminating and/or reducing habit disorders. Based on the current findings, it appears to be a valuable procedure for treating hair-pulling behavior.

SOURCE: Azrin, N. H., Nunn, R. G., and Frantz, S. E. "Treatment of Hairpulling (Trichotillomania): A Comparative Study of Habit Reversal and Negative Practice Training."

Journal of Behavior Therapy and Experimental Psychiatry,
1980, *11,* 13-20.

Treating Nighttime Self-Injurious Behavior

AUTHORS: Thomas R. Linscheid, Anne P. Copeland, Diane M.
Jacobstein, and Jean L. Smith

PRECIS: Treating nighttime head banging and head rocking
with overcorrection procedures.

INTRODUCTION: The authors report two cases of normal children who had a long history of nighttime self-injurious behavior. Fran, four years of age, had demonstrated nighttime head
rocking since fourteen months of age, and Chuck, thirteen years
old, had engaged in head banging since eighteen months of age.
Treatment involved positive practice overcorrection procedures,
which consisted of excessive practice of responses incompatible
with targeted behaviors.

CASE STUDIES: Both Fran and Chuck were hospitalized during the treatment and were required to overpractice prescribed
responses upon their initiation of self-injurious behavior.
    Fran's head rocking was defined as her lying on her back
and moving her head from side to side more than once in succession. During treatment, Fran slept in the hospital and was
observed on a closed-circuit television. She was permitted to go
home during the day. During treatment, prior to Fran's going to
bed, she was informed that she would have to do exercises in
order to help her stop rocking. Each time Fran began to head
rock, she was told, "You're starting to rock"; then she was to
roll onto her stomach and lie still for fifteen seconds. The task,
turning onto her stomach and remaining still, was repeated fifteen times each time Fran initiated head rocking. Fran's mother

observed the procedure for three nights and then conducted the treatment under supervision on the fourth night. The next day, Fran was discharged from the hospital. The mother was to continue to utilize the technique at home. In addition, head rocking was resulting in severe tangles in Fran's hair, which her mother had been combing out each morning. Upon the initiation of treatment, Fran was required to untangle her own hair each morning.

A similar approach was utilized with Chuck, who also slept in the hospital for the initiation of treatment. He left during the day to go to school. Chuck was also told that each time he banged his head he would be required to do a series of exercises to help him stop the behavior. Chuck's exercises were cued with the statement, "Chuck, you're banging your head." He then was to practice turning from his stomach onto his back. Once turned, Chuck was to stretch out and hold still for fifteen seconds. This procedure was practiced fifteen times for each head-banging occurrence. Chuck was discharged after three nights, and Chuck's father continued the procedure at home.

RESULTS: Upon discharge from the hospital, Fran's head rocking had been eliminated. At a one-year follow-up, the mother reported that there had been only one instance of rocking, which occurred three months after treatment. However, no head rocking had occurred since that time.

Chuck's head banging was significantly reduced during the first two weeks after discharge. Instances of head banging were treated by the father. At a one-year follow-up, Chuck's head banging had decreased from an initial three or four times per night to approximately one time per month.

COMMENTARY: Overcorrection procedures are a common technique utilized to modify undesirable behaviors. In the two reported cases, the effectiveness of using this as a treatment for nighttime self-injurious behaviors is demonstrated. A very important aspect of the presented treatment is the parental cooperation and participation.

SOURCE: Linscheid, T. R., Copeland, A. P., Jacobstein, D. M., and Smith, J. L. "Overcorrection Treatment for Nighttime Self-Injurious Behavior in Two Normal Children." *Journal of Pediatric Psychology,* 1981, *6* (1), 29–35.

Additional Readings

Altman, K., and Christophersen, E. R. "Elimination of a Retarded Blind Child's Self-Hitting by Response-Contingent Brief Restraint." *Education and Treatment of Children,* 1980, *3* (3), 231–237.

The authors report the case of a seven-year-old child, John, who was both blind and retarded and who was engaging in self-injurious behaviors. John had at least a one-year history of biting and scratching his arms and hands, in addition to hitting himself in the head. Treatment was conducted in John's classroom by his teacher. Each self-injurious behavior resulted in a thirty-second contingent restraint procedure. The procedure involved the teacher's placing John in a chair and holding both of his hands behind his back for thirty seconds. He was required to remain sitting unrestrained for an additional ten to twenty seconds. If no self-injurious behavior occurred, John could return to his activity. The procedure proved effective in eliminating the targeted behaviors.

Altman, K., Haavik, S., and Cook, J. W. "Punishment of Self-Injurious Behavior in Natural Settings Using Contingent Aromatic Ammonia." *Behavior Research and Therapy,* 1978, *16,* 85–96.

Contingent aromatic ammonia was successfully utilized as a treatment for self-injurious behavior in two retarded children. Kim, a severely retarded four-year-old, had a one-year history of hair pulling, and Bob, a moderately retarded three-and-a-half-year-old, had a year-long history of biting the index fingers of both hands. Both children were treated in natural settings (home and school) by parents and teachers. Treatment consisted of administration of aromatic ammonia contingent upon the child's engaging in the targeted behavior. The adult would break open a capsule of ammonia and place it under the child's nose in conjunction with differential reinforcement of other behaviors. The authors discuss the durations of ammonia and programmed maintenance procedures.

Barrett, R. P., and Shapiro, E. S. "Treatment of Sterotyped Hair-Pulling with Overcorrection: A Case Study with Long-Term Follow-Up." *Journal of Behavioral and Experimental Psychiatry*, 1980, *11*, 317-320.

The authors successfully utilized positive practice overcorrection procedures as a treatment for hair pulling in a seven-and-a-half-year-old mentally retarded girl. The girl's hair pulling was conducted in a sterotyped manner, as she removed individual hairs from her scalp and ingested them. The treatment occurred in school and consisted of a verbal cue to the child, upon hair pulling, which stated that she must go to the classroom bathroom to brush her hair for a two-minute period. If the child did not cooperate, she was guided through the positive practice by a classroom aide. Termination of the positive practice was contingent upon the two-minute time period, as well as nondisruptive behavior. Within twelve days, the child's hair-pulling behavior was eliminated. Treatment effects were maintained at a twelve-month follow-up.

Carr, E. G. "The Motivation of Self-Injurious Behavior: A Review of Some Hypotheses." *Psychological Bulletin*, 1977, *84* (4), 800-816.

Carr reviews the literature on the five major hypotheses used to explain the etiology of self-injurious behavior: (1) the positive reinforcement hypothesis, which states that the behavior is learned and maintained by positive reinforcement, (2) the negative reinforcement hypothesis, which states that self-injurious behavior is learned and maintained by the termination of an aversive stimulus, (3) the self-stimulation hypothesis, which proposes that self-injurious behaviors are self-stimulatory,

(4) the organic hypothesis, which views the behavior as being of a physiological etiology, and (5) the psychodynamic hypothesis, which states that the behavior is an attempt either to alleviate guilt or to establish ego boundaries. Treatments are evaluated as they relate to the different hypotheses and motivations for self-injurious behavior. Finally, Carr discusses animal analogue experiments that may aid in the understanding of the motivation of self-injurious behavior.

Gray, J. J. "Positive Reinforcement and Punishment in the Treatment of Childhood Trichotillomania." *Journal of Behavior Therapy and Experimental Psychiatry*, 1979, *10*, 125-129.

A five-year-old girl with a four-year history of hair pulling was treated via her mother. The author devised a behavioral treatment package that was implemented by the mother, who attended thirteen behaviorally oriented counseling sessions. The mother was trained to provide positive reinforcement for the absence of hair pulling and punishment for the presence of hair pulling. Reinforcement consisted of the mother giving the child a marble after a specified time interval during which no hair pulling occurred. Marbles then could be exchanged for preferred reinforcers. Punishment was four hard slaps on the hand for each instance of hair pulling. The author also presents ethical implications of the use of punishment.

Hobbs, S. A., and Goswick, R. A. "Behavioral Treatment of Self-Stimulation: An Examination of Alternatives to Physical Punishment." *Journal of Clinical Child Psychology*, 1977, *42*, 20-23.

The authors present a review of behavioral treatment procedures for self-stimulatory behaviors of retarded and autistic individuals. Hobbs and Goswick conclude that there is significant evidence that positive reinforcement for appropriate responses used in conjunction with deceleration techniques, such as extinction or overcorrection, can be effective as treatment without employing physical punishment procedures. It should be noted that Hobbs and Goswick are discussing self-stimulatory behaviors that are noninjurious. Although the findings may be applicable to some self-injurious behaviors, more aversive techniques may be warranted when self-stimulatory behaviors become more injurious in nature.

Kinsbourne, K. "Do Repetitive Movement Patterns in Children and Animals Serve a Dearousing Function?" *Developmental and Behavioral Pediatrics*, 1980, *1* (1), 39–41.

Kinsbourne points out similarities between purposeless, repetitive behaviors of animals and self-stimulating behaviors of autistic, blind, and mentally retarded children. The author suggests that animals' purposeless behavior often serves to decrease arousal when it is excessive. A parallel is made to children, suggesting that repetitive, self-stimulatory actions may serve to dearouse the children. The author discusses implications for treatment based on this hypothesis.

Krishnan, R.R.R., Davidson, J., and Guajardo, C. "Trichotillomania: A Review."

The authors present a critical review of the incidence, psychopathology, diagnosis, and management of trichotillomania. They state that the incidence of chronic hair pulling appears to be greater than it was once believed to be. In addition, trichotillomania occurs not only in isolation but also in association with other diagnoses. Behavior therapy or hypnosis is felt to be a valuable treatment for isolated hair pulling. However, treatment that is directed at the principal diagnosis is recommended when the hair pulling is associated with other pathology. The authors point out that prognosis is poor when trichotillomania appears after early childhood. Two case studies are discussed.

Litt, C. J. "Trichotillomania in Childhood: A Case of Successful Short-Term Treatment." *Journal of Pediatric Psychology*, 1980, *5* (1), 37–42.

Litt discusses trichotillomania within the context of a psychodynamic conceptualization. She states that chronic hair pulling can be a symptom resulting from an inconsistent, depriving relationship between mother and child in which the child tends to use the hair as a transitional object.

The author reports the case of a five-year-old retarded boy who began to hair pull following his grandfather's surgery. The threatened loss of the child's grandfather, who was the male with whom the child identified, was viewed as the precipitating event. Therefore treatment was carried out through the mother, who clarified the traumatic events for the child, as well as the child's anxious, confused, and angry feelings. Litt discusses the importance of attaining a complete psychosocial history prior to the implementation of treatment for trichotillomania.

Mayhew, G., and Harris, F. "Decreasing Self-Injurious Behavior: Punishment with Citric Acid and Reinforcement of Alternative Behavior." *Behavior Modification,* 1979, *3* (3), 322–336.

The authors provide evidence that administration of a relatively mild aversive stimulus, such as citric acid, may serve as an effective treatment for modifying self-injurious behavior. They present the case of a nineteen-year-old profoundly retarded boy who exhibited self-injurious behavior, pushing himself in the face and hitting his head against objects while engaging in loud, tantrum screaming. After other, less aversive treatments failed to eliminate the targeted behaviors, the authors implemented a procedure in which citric acid (lemon juice) was applied to the subject's mouth contingent upon self-injurious behavior and tantrum screaming. The method proved to be successful in eliminating both behaviors when it was combined with a reinforcement technique: placing M&M's in the mouth for proximity to the therapist while not demonstrating the targeted behaviors.

Nelson, W. M. "Behavioral Treatment of Childhood Trichotillomania: A Case Study." *Journal of Clinical Child Psychology,* 1982, *11* (3), 227–230.

A seven-year-old boy with a two-year history of hair pulling was treated simultaneously in his home and school settings by mother and teacher. For each instance of hair pulling, the adult combed the boy's hair for two minutes. This was aversive to the child, as he did not like to have his hair combed. In addi-

tion, the child was required to engage in positive practice: raising his hand to his scalp and stating, "No, I'm not supposed to
twiddle!" for two minutes following a hair pull. Hair pulling
was eliminated within eight days. Maintenance of treatment effects was evident at an eleven-month follow-up.

Prytula, R. E., Joyner, K. B., and Schnelle, J. F. "Utilizing the
    School to Control Head-Banging Behavior of a Child at
    Home." *Psychological Reports,* 1981, *48,* 887–894.

The authors report the case study of a three-and-a-half-
year-old boy who engaged in head-banging behavior at home.
Since a limited number of reinforcers were available to the child
at home, a treatment was devised that linked reinforcement in
school to behavior at home. At school, the child was permitted
to participate in a preferred activity contingent upon the child's
daily report card, which the mother used to record the presence
or absence of head banging. The absence of the targeted behavior
earned the youngster his reinforcement.

Rosenbaum, M. S., and Ayllon, T. "The Habit-Reversal Tech-
    nique in Treating Trichotillomania." *Behavior Therapy,*
    1981, *12,* 473–481.

The authors report on four cases of trichotillomania that
were treated with Azrin and Nunn's habit reversal technique
("Habit Reversal: A Method of Eliminating Nervous Habits and
Tics." *Behavior Research and Therapy,* 1973, *11,* 619-628). A
single treatment session was utilized to train the subjects, and
hair pulling was significantly reduced in each case within three
weeks. The authors report complete elimination of the symptom that was maintained at six- and twelve-month follow-ups.
The data give support to the effectiveness of habit reversal procedures as a treatment for chronic hair pulling.

Sanchez, V. "Behavioral Treatment of Chronic Hair Pulling in a
    Two-Year-Old." *Journal of Behavior Therapy and Ex-
    perimental Psychiatry,* 1979, *10,* 241–245.

The authors present the case of M, a twenty-seven-month-
old boy exhibiting chronic hair pulling. The treatment consisted
of teaching the parents to utilize differential reinforcement in
conjunction with a response-chain interruption procedure. M

was placed in a time-out room (the parents' bedroom) for five minutes after each hair pull, while he was reinforced by his parents for engaging in appropriate behaviors, such as playing. Reinforcers were both social and food. The mother also commented favorably about M's siblings' hair, combed their hair in front of M, and combed M's hair each day. Finally, the parents intervened in breaking M's chain of behaviors that led to hair pulling by taping his fingers together for ten minutes each time he began his sequence. Hair pulling was eliminated completely at the end of fourteen weeks of treatment, and no recurrence of the behavior was reported at a twelve-month follow-up.

Thumbsucking

About 46 percent of the child population from birth to sixteen years of age are reported to be thumbsuckers. The desirability of eliminating this habit is indicated by its apparent social inappropriateness and its association with dental malocclusion. In the home, diverse management procedures have been tried, including sucking pacifiers, prolonged sucking from the breast or bottle, wearing special mittens or restraints, applying bittertasting chemicals to the thumb, ignoring the sucking, verbal and physical punishment, and making parental attention contingent on not sucking. The following articles explore the systematic application of some of these techniques.

Treating Thumbsucking with Glove Wearing

AUTHORS: Maureen K. Lassen and Norman R. Fluet

PRECIS: Elimination of thumbsucking by the use of glove wearing while sleeping.

INTRODUCTION: Lassen and Fluet report a case of a ten-year-old girl, Ann, who sucked her thumb while sleeping for at least six years. Frequent reminders prior to Ann's bedtime did not decrease her thumbsucking. The authors attempted to eliminate the child's habit by having her wear a glove on her hand while sleeping.

TREATMENT: During a one-week baseline, Ann's mother checked on her each night at 11:30 P.M. and each morning at 6:45 A.M. to obtain a frequency of thumbsucking. During the fourteen times sampled, Ann had her right thumb in her mouth on ten occasions. When a commercial substance was applied to Ann's thumb at bedtime, the frequency of thumbsucking remained the same for the next two-week period.

During the third week, Ann wore a glove on her right hand while she slept. The glove wearing resulted in a dramatic reduction in thumbsucking. Within three weeks, Ann's thumbsucking was completely eliminated.

RESULTS: After three weeks of no thumbsucking, Ann was permitted to sleep without the glove. Follow-up at six and twelve months revealed that Ann had not resumed thumbsucking at all.

COMMENTARY: In this case study, dramatic results were quickly obtained in the utilization of glove wearing to eliminate nighttime thumbsucking. Since the youngster studied had engaged in this habit for at least six years, it would be interesting to have data about any symptom substitutions that might have occurred. Further research and replication of this seemingly effective technique would be very valuable.

SOURCE: Lassen, M. K., and Fluet, N. R. "Elimination of Nocturnal Thumbsucking by Glove Wearing." *Journal of Behavior Therapy and Experimental Psychiatry,* 1978, *9,* 85.

The Use of Differential Reinforcement in the Treatment of Thumbsucking

AUTHORS: Glenn H. Lowitz and Michael R. Suib

PRECIS: Treating thumbsucking by reinforcing intervals of thumbsucking-free behavior with pennies.

INTRODUCTION: Lowitz and Suib devised a treatment for reducing thumbsucking behavior in an eight-year-old girl, L, that involved differential reinforcement of other behaviors (DRO). DRO is a reinforcement that occurs for not responding; that is, the subject is reinforced when the target behavior does not occur for a specified time interval. Here the authors used escalated DRO: consistently and systematically increasing the length of the interval prior to reinforcement.

TREATMENT: L, an eight-year-old girl, had been sucking her thumb since infancy. At the time that treatment began, L's most frequent thumbsucking occurred at home when she was watching television, listening to bedtime stories, going to bed, or was upset or bored. Treatment initially took place in a university psychology clinic that was set up with a television, a lounge recliner, a desk, and a glass bowl that held pennies.

A therapist conducted the first set of treatment sessions, which were scheduled two to three times per week. During all sessions, L was seated in the recliner watching the television programs that she usually would watch at home. During the first set of sessions, the therapist sat in the room and watched television with L while recording her thumbsucking. Recording was done once for every one-minute interval. Thumbsucking was operationally defined as the enclosure of any digit or part of the hand by the lips or contact of the tongue with any digit or part of the hand.

When L arrived at the initial treatment session, the therapist gave her a penny and told her that she could keep it because she did not have her thumb in her mouth. The therapist then brought a bowl of pennies into the room and gave L a penny each time she removed her thumb from her mouth during a one-minute interval. Four additional sessions occurred in this set; these were identical except for an increase in the reinforcement interval of one additional minute at each session.

The next phase of the treatment consisted of three reversal sessions, at which no pennies were given for thumbsucking-free intervals. Finally, L's mother and five-year-old brother accompanied L into the treatment room. L's mother had viewed all previous sessions from behind a one-way mirror. At this point, the mother conducted the sessions as the therapist had done.

To ensure generalization, treatment was then conducted in the home by the mother. Plastic tokens, which could be exchanged for pennies at the clinic, were utilized, and a DRO schedule was used. In addition, once the home sessions ended, a DRO variation was implemented to eliminate the thumbsucking that still occurred. Mother would spot check L ten times during the day, before L's bedtime, and in the morning before L would awake. At the end of each day without thumbsucking, L received a star on a wall chart. The reward that L was working toward was to have her ears pierced once she obtained sixty stars.

RESULTS: During baseline, L's thumbsucking rate was 100 percent. Once the therapist utilized the DRO treatment, thumbsucking decreased to 1.7 percent. When a reversal to baseline conditions occurred, L's thumbsucking rate returned to approximately 90 percent. However, once mother began treatment sessions in the clinic, L's thumbsucking once again decreased to 1.7 percent.

Treatment at home proved very effective, as L's thumb-sucking decreased to 0.0 within three months and remained at this rate through a one-year follow-up. Bedtime thumbsucking was more resistant to extinction than was occasional thumbsucking during the day. However, the utilization of spot checks was effective in eliminating both of these residual behaviors.

COMMENTARY: The use of differential reinforcement for other, or competing, behaviors proved to be an effective treatment for thumbsucking. Reinforcing a competing response is a technique that can effectively decrease a number of undesired behaviors. The maintenance of L's thumbsucking-free behavior was obtained with a spot check technique. Therefore investigation into the spot check approach without the DRO would be valuable.

SOURCE: Lowitz, G. H., and Suib, M. R. "Generalized Control of Persistent Thumbsucking by Differential Reinforcement of Other Behaviors." *Journal of Behavior Therapy and Experimental Psychiatry*, 1978, *9*, 343–346.

Treating Thumbsucking with a Nonaversive Approach

AUTHORS: Kenneth Lichstein and George Kachmarik

PRECIS: Treating thumbsucking with DRO across three settings.

INTRODUCTION: Lichstein and Kachmarik favor a nonaversive form of treating thumbsucking, which utilizes DRO. The authors find this approach more positive than some of the aversive treatments commonly used, such as oral devices and overcorrection. In an attempt to adequately evaluate the effectiveness of DRO, Lichstein and Kachmarik employed DRO in a multiple baseline design with two school-age children and then conducted a three-month follow-up.

TREATMENT: Two subjects—Amanda, an eight-year-old girl, and Jeremy, a six-year-old boy—both from upper-middle-class families, participated in the treatment. Both children had a history of thumbsucking since infancy. Amanda was reported to be quiet and cooperative by both her parents and the school, whereas Jeremy was reported to be a discipline problem. He tended to be active and talkative.

The three settings that were utilized for each child were periods when thumbsucking was highly probable. Setting 1 was a thirty-minute period prior to dinner, setting 2 was a thirty-minute period prior to bedtime, and setting 3 was a thirty-minute period in school after lunch that was supposed to be a "quiet time."

The children's mothers and teachers served as the observers and therapists (the one exception being that a research assistant provided the treatment in school for Jeremy). Teachers and mothers learned the aspects of treatment through role playing. During baseline, instructions included not mentioning thumbsucking and avoiding interaction with the child while or just after the child engaged in thumbsucking. Thirty minutes of training in observation and in DRO proved sufficient for the teachers and mothers. Thumbsucking was defined as the insertion of any portion of the thumb past the threshold of the oral cavity.

After baselines were obtained in each of the three settings, the DRO 1 phase was implemented. This phase utilized a chart that was set up in each child's home with animal stickers that could be obtained and then exchanged for rewards. Initially, the child was told that one sticker would be earned for each five minutes that he or she did not suck his or her thumb. The interval was increased by five minutes each day until it reached the full thirty minutes of the interval being measured. In addition, mothers and teachers were directed to use verbal affection and hugging for nonthumbsucking behavior. DRO 2 followed, which was a phase that employed thinning the DRO schedule to encompass the entire day. The day was divided into three intervals: school, at home prior to dinner, and after dinner until bedtime. One sticker could be earned for each successful interval. DRO 3 was then utilized, which was similar to DRO 2 but which included only two intervals: school and home. Only Amanda received the DRO 3 phase. A three-month follow-up observation was conducted in all three settings.

RESULTS: Both youngsters demonstrated a very significant decrease in thumbsucking behavior with the introduction of DRO. Comparison of baseline to DRO 3 found that Amanda's thumbsucking had been reduced by approximately 90 percent for the entire day. Jeremy also made a very significant reduction in thumbsucking. However, other undesirable behaviors increased, such as temper tantrums, bowel accidents at home, and increased oppositional behavior at school. These undesirable behaviors decreased when treatment for thumbsucking was discontinued. At the three-month follow-up, both Amanda and Jeremy were found to demonstrate complete recovery of their thumbsucking behavior with the same frequencies that were observed prior to treatment.

COMMENTARY: As previous research has shown, DRO is found to be an effective approach for reducing undesirable behaviors. In the present study, DRO was highly effective in decreasing thumbsucking behavior. However, once the reinforcement was terminated, no long-term effects were demonstrated. Therefore, consideration needs to be given to complement DRO procedures with other approaches designed to increase long-term effects, such as a highly thinned reinforcement schedule using one token for each day of no thumbsucking. Furthermore, research focusing on symptom substitution, such as Jeremy experienced, would also be valuable.

SOURCE: Lichstein, K., and Kachmarik, G. "A Nonaversive Intervention for Thumbsucking: Analysis Across Settings and Time in the Natural Environment." *Journal of Pediatric Psychology*, 1980, *5* (4), 405–413.

Treating Thumbsucking
with Habit Reversal Procedures

AUTHORS: N. H. Azrin, R. G. Nunn, and S. Frantz-Renshaw

PRECIS: Treating thumbsucking with habit reversal procedures, including competing response training, parental support, and stimulus identification.

INTRODUCTION: Azrin, Nunn, and Frantz-Renshaw evaluated the effectiveness of treating thumbsucking behavior with habit reversal procedures. The method consists of teaching youngsters competing responses, identifying the common situations in which thumbsucking occurs, arranging social support by the family, providing a period of contingent competing reactions, and identifying precipitating factors. In addition, the authors compared this treatment to the more common treatment of painting the thumb and hand with a bitter-tasting substance.

TREATMENT: Thirty children between the ages of two-and-a-half and fourteen years participated in the study. Eighteen children were randomly assigned to the habit reversal method, and twelve children were randomly assigned to the control group. All subjects were respondents to a newspaper advertisement.

At the initial session, parents provided an estimate of the child's daily frequency of thumbsucking. Parents were then given recording sheets to use for daily records of frequency of thumbsucking. Follow-up calls, to check on frequencies of thumbsucking, were conducted every ten days during the first month of the study, every two weeks during the next ten months, and then once per month for the next ten months.

Counseling of the child and his or her parents on the treatment approach was completed in one session, which lasted between one and two hours. First, the child was taught the habit reversal procedures. Then the child taught the method to the parents with the therapist's help.

Initially, the child listed all of the problems caused by the thumbsucking. Next, the child acted out the usual response sequence, using the precipitating factors in order to identify the stimulus antecedents of the behavior. The child was then taught competing responses, such as making a fist. The child rehearsed the competing response. Each response was to last for one to three minutes. The duration of the response was timed by the child as he or she counted aloud to 100 (or, with younger children, counting to ten several times was used).

Social support was achieved through the parents' use of verbal praise in conjunction with the termination of a pleasurable activity when thumbsucking occured. For example, if thumbsucking occurred while the child was watching television, the television was turned off. In addition, other significant adults, such as neighbors or relatives, were selected as individuals that the child called to give progress reports.

The children in the control group were to have a commercially available bitter-tasting substance painted on their hands every morning and evening. All of the contacts between controls and therapist were conducted by phone.

RESULTS: The children in the habit reversal group experienced a mean reduction of 88 percent in thumbsucking on the first day of treatment. At the two-month follow-up, the reduction had been maintained at 89 percent. The children in the control group had reduced their thumbsucking by only 34 to 44 percent during the three months of follow-up.

COMMENTARY: Habit reversal procedures proved to be significantly more effective in treating thumbsucking behavior than was the application of a bitter-tasting substance to the hand. However, the present results are confounded by the fact that the control group was not seen face-to-face by a therapist. This type of future comparison would be valuable in shedding light on the role of face-to-face contact versus the role of the habit reversal approach itself.

SOURCE: Azrin, N. H., Nunn, R. G., and Frantz-Renshaw, S. "Habit Reversal Treatment of Thumbsucking." *Behavioral Research and Therapy*, 1980, *18*, 395-399.

Disturbed Sexual Behavior

This section discusses disturbed sexual behavior in children and adolescents. Cross-gender identity—a child's identification with the opposite sex that leads to cross-sex stereotyped behavior and a desire to be of the opposite sex—is thought to be an early indication of later homosexuality in some instances. In addition, cross-gender identification leads to peer ridicule, as well as great parental concern. Therefore, a major focus of this section is on the treatment of cross-gender identity and transvestism. Effeminate behavior and public masturbation are also discussed.

Art Therapy with a Transsexual Boy

AUTHOR: Felice W. Cohen

PRECIS: A six-year-old boy demonstrating transsexual behavior
was treated with art psychotherapy.

INTRODUCTION: Cohen, a female art therapist, discusses the
treatment of a six-year-old boy demonstrating transsexual behavior. In working with transsexual children, Cohen adheres to
five objectives. The first involves providing a trusting and affec-
tionate relationship between the child and therapist. Although
most literature states that a male therapist is necessary for treatment of transsexuals, Cohen states that a female therapist can
facilitate the child's appropriate working through of his symbiosis with his mother. The second objective is to heighten parental concern and to elicit parental disapproval of the child's
feminine interests and behaviors. The third objective is to promote the father's involvement in the child's life, as this typically
is almost nonexistent. The fourth objective involves sensitizing
the parents to the family dynamics—that is, the mother's overdependency on the son and the father's emotional distance. Finally, the fifth objective is to help the mother separate from the
son in a healthy manner.

CASE STUDY: Don, a six-year-old male, was referred to a clinic
after teachers, friends, and relatives put pressure on the parents
to attend to his feminine behavior. The boy's cross-gender identity was reported, by him, to be established by the age of three.
Upon interview, Don's mother revealed both emotional and
physical distance between Don and his father. In contrast, she
described her relationship with Don as being quite involved.
Don was unwanted by the father but filled the mother's life.
She reported that her life had been empty prior to his birth.

TREATMENT: Don was seen in individual art psychotherapy
sessions, as well as in several joint sessions with his mother. The
mother was seen individually twice a month, and the father had

seen the therapist on two occasions. During individual sessions, Don utilized drawings as well as work on collages. Early drawings depicted Don as a female. Collages clearly illustrated his conflict in that he depicted men in women's clothing. During joint sessions with the mother, it became clear that Don received covert messages of approval for his behavior. In addition, it became apparent that Don and his mother shared a special secret, as they verbalized very little during joint sessions but worked very well together on art projects.

RESULTS: No results are reported, as this case was ongoing at the time of the write-up. After one year of therapy, Don was using the art sessions as a safe place to express his fantasy world and his conflict of feeling that he was a girl trapped in a boy's body. In addition, Don was beginning to use the sessions to explore the events in his life that resulted from his cross-gender identification.

COMMENTARY: As has been seen in other recent studies, female therapists are having success in treating transsexual boys. Cohen utilizes art therapy as an intervention. In this case, Don was given an opportunity to explore his conflicts in an accepting, nonthreatening environment. No apparent changes in Don's gender identity are reported. Ethical considerations should be given as to whether or not the goal of treatment should be to encourage gender identification reversal.

SOURCE: Cohen, F. W. "Art Psychotherapy: The Treatment of Choice for a Six-Year-Old Boy with a Transsexual Syndrome." *Art Psychotherapy*, 1976, *3*, 55–67.

Treating Adolescent Sex Problems
with a Social Learning Approach

AUTHOR: P. M. Bentler

PRECIS: Adolescent homosexuals and transvestites are treated with social learning therapy, which focuses on increasing the amount of heterosexually oriented social behavior.

INTRODUCTION: Social learning theory is used as the basis for Bentler's understanding of homosexuality and transvestism. Cross-dressing and homosexual preferences are proposed to be the result of a series of learned responses that are maintained by a variety of reinforcers. Bentler further contends that homosexual or transvestic behaviors, which may have started out as curiosity-related experimental behaviors, become maintained when the behavior is reinforced. In other words, socially inappropriate behavior is developed because it is reinforced. For example, a deviant fantasy is followed by gratifying masturbation, making the deviant fantasy a behavior that will be repeated because it was reinforced.

The author chose to treat these learned behaviors with an approach that would make reinforcements contingent upon socially appropriate behavior. Treatment consisted of two components: The first was a traditional social learning behavior therapy interview and the second was an approach that reinforced operants dealing with heterosexual encounters.

TREATMENT: Three homosexual boys and three transvestite boys were treated. The social learning behavior therapy interview, which parallels face-to-face therapy, was utilized in the sessions. In treating the homosexuals, the therapist focused on heterosexual encounters and provided contingent social reinforcement by giving verbal praise to the boys' plans to approach girls. Sexual behaviors were encouraged during the sessions, and behavior rehearsals of heterosexual interactions were carried out. As a result, social reinforcement was given for the customary sequence of dating. In addition, operants dealing with heterosexual encounters were reinforced. The operants would have to occur naturally outside of the therapy sessions in the environment. It was hypothesized that heterosexual encounters such as focusing on sexual features of a female's body, social interactions, and petting would provide heterosexual fantasy material that would lead to masturbation and as a result reinforce appropriate sexual fantasies instead of the deviant ones.

A similar treatment approach was utilized for the transvestites, with the difference being reinforcement of sex-typed behavior as well as reinforcement of masturbation without feminine clothing. In addition, an increase in the frequency in masturbation was reinforced, as these boys did not masturbate at an expected level of frequency.

RESULTS: Success in modifying the targeted behaviors in the desired directions are reported for all six adolescents. The homosexual boys began to engage in heterosexual fantasies and/or interactions. The transvestites began to masturbate more frequently while having heterosexual fantasies, and they increased their social interactions with girls. The goals of therapy, which included increasing masculine, sex-typed behavior and increasing appropriate sexual behaviors, were met.

COMMENTARY: Bentler reports on a nonaversive intervention for the treatment of homosexuals and transvestites. The approach taken, which expands the boys' repertoires of socially appropriate behaviors, has been used successfully in the treatment of other deviant behaviors.

SOURCE: Bentler, P. M. "A Note on the Treatment of Adolescent Sex Problems." *Journal of Child Psychology and Psychiatry,* 1968, *9,* 125-129.

Treatment of a Male Child's Transsexual Symptoms

AUTHORS: Doris C. Gilpin, Syed Raza, and Darcy Gilpin

PRECIS: A six-year-old boy exhibiting transsexual symptoms was treated by a psychoanalytically oriented female therapist.

INTRODUCTION: The authors point out that the consensus of existing literature on the treatment of transsexual behaviors is that the therapist should be of the same sex as the patient in order to facilitate appropriate identification. Gilpin, Raza, and Gilpin point out that an opposite-sex therapist may be quite effective when one examines and understands the underlying psychodynamics of transsexualism. They conceptualize the symptoms as resulting from a developmental progression that begins with a genetic foundation that then moves through psychosexual stages and is affected by social learning. The literature on transsexualism points to the inability of the mother to allow her son to separate from her. This prevents the boy from entering into the oedipal stage. As a result, the transsexual identifies with the mother.

Treatment of transsexuals has taken two distinct routes. The first is changing the individual's identification to match his anatomy, and the second is to change the anatomy to match the identity. The former is the focus of the authors.

Childhood transsexualism is reported to be responsive to psychotherapy that redirects the gender identity of the child if it is begun at an early age—before six or seven years old. By age seven, it is reported to be difficult to reverse or undo a gender identity; at prepuberty, treatment is not as effective, and by adolescence it is usually not effective. The task of therapy is to end the symbiosis of the mother and son.

CASE STUDY: A six-year-old boy with a significant history was referred to a female therapist for treatment. At the time of referral, no mention of transsexual symptoms was made. The referring problem was the child's sadistic, destructive behaviors, including temper tantrums, head banging, destruction of property, and an attempt to strangle the family dog. In addition to a hearing impairment, the child had been diagnosed at age four-and-a-half as autistic and was enrolled in a special school. Another significant historical event was the abrupt leaving of the child's nurse, who had been with him since his birth, when the boy was two years old.

Psychological evaluation at the time of referral revealed that the child had average-range intellectual functioning but was exhibiting emotional disturbances. His greatest conflict revolved around his deep hostility toward and fear of mother figures. He attempted to deal with his intense fear by identifying with the mother, whom he viewed as hostile and very powerful.

After eight sessions in which the boy tested the therapist to ascertain if she was a "bad" mother or a "good" mother, he revealed his transsexual symptoms. He stated that he believed he was female, and he apparently trusted that the therapist would not be angry. For six months, the boy took on the role of a baby in the therapy sessions and tested the therapist's ability to be a "whole" mother. Initially, the child feared that the therapist could not control him and thus she would be either weak about setting limits or extremely punitive if he destroyed something. Once he felt comfortable in regard to the therapist's ability to control these events, he relied upon her to help him with play.

By age seven, the therapist's initial goal of recreating the symbiosis and having the boy work through it to become a more whole person was progressing. At age nine, the boy announced that he wanted the therapist to help him to be a real boy.

RESULTS: After four-and-a-half years of psychoanalytically oriented therapy with a female therapist, the boy began to play with cars and seek out male friends and males with whom to identify. He became interested in male artists and was placed in a regular, mainstream school. Psychological evaluation revealed much-improved reality testing, with less destructive powers attributed to females.

It was also found that the nurse rather than the mother

was the most pathogenic maternal figure for this boy. This factor is hypothesized to have contributed to the good prognosis.

COMMENTARY: Although the literature supports same-sex therapists as the choice for treating transsexualism, the authors report on the success of a female therapist treating a boy's transsexualism. This approach opens up a new understanding and treatment approach for working with boys exhibiting cross-gender identification.

SOURCE: Gilpin, D. C., Raza, S., and Gilpin, D. "Transsexual Symptoms in a Male Child Treated by a Female Therapist." *American Journal of Psychotherapy*, 1979, *33* (3), 453-463.

===

Treating Cross-Gender Identity Behaviors with Modeling Techniques

AUTHOR: Peter W. Dowrick

PRECIS: A four-year-old boy exhibiting cross-gender identity behaviors was treated with video training of peer and self-modeling.

INTRODUCTION: Jeremy, a four-year-old male, was referred for treatment by his mother because of her concern in regard to his apparent strong identification with femininity. Jeremy expressed desires to be a girl, played with stereotypical "girl" toys, frequently desired to wear female apparel, and displayed feminine mannerisms. Jeremy's mother was concerned about his present and future social and sexual adjustment.

Upon assessment at a hospital psychiatric unit, Jeremy was found to engage in "girl" behavior (for example, playing with a toy iron and ironing dolls' underwear). This behavior entertained the other children on the unit and, as a result, elicited reinforcement for Jeremy.

The author decided to treat Jeremy using videotapes that would expose him to self- and peer modeling. As a result, this would expand Jeremy's repertoire of behavioral responses to include behaviors that were not girl stereotyped.

TREATMENT: Three successive videotapes were made. Pre- and post-viewing observations were conducted for each film, as well as observations during treatment. The observations on the unit at the hospital were made through a one-way screen while Jeremy played for fifteen minutes in a room that had the following toys: dolls, dresses, toy household items, an engineer's set, animals, a toy vehicle, and musical instruments. In addition, Jeremy's parents and teachers at his school collected data daily for a period of four months.

The first videotape made was of Jeremy and a therapist, who elicited appropriate play behaviors from Jeremy with toy animals, buildings, and vehicles. The mother and observers remained unaware of the videotape's content. Jeremy viewed the tape for three minutes before entering the playroom. The film had no effect after four sessions, so its use was discontinued. At this point, a second film was made; this one showed a peer of the same age and sex, who was of slim build with shoulder-length hair. The child was often mistaken for a girl; however, his behavior was stereotypically boyish. Jeremy and the peer played with the engineering set, animals, soldiers, Indians, and vehicles and became quite competitive. A self-modeling film was made from this session, which focused only on Jeremy's behavior. A third film, similar to the second one, also was made.

RESULTS: Four behaviors were rated: girl-type, boy-type, neutral, and not playing. There were no effects as a result of the first film, which utilized an adult coaxing behavioral responses from Jeremy. Significant effects were obtained with the use of the second film. However, they only lasted as long as Jeremy was viewing the film prior to a play session. Jeremy was then removed from treatment by his mother, who was satisfied with his progress.

Jeremy returned to treatment one month after termination, as his behavior had returned to baseline conditions. The third film was then used. This film had a significant effect, as did the second film. This time a two-month follow-up in the hospital revealed that Jeremy maintained his boy-type behaviors. A six-month follow-up observation at school demonstrated that Jeremy's play was boy-type at least 80 percent of the time. Self- and peer modeling proved to be an effective intervention for Jeremy, whereas adult-facilitated training of new behavioral responses was not.

COMMENTARY: Treating cross-gender identification has often met with minimal success. Therefore, Dowrick's treatment strategy with Jeremy provides valuable data. Further research is needed, as it is difficult to assess some of the variables. For instance, the play session with the peer may have had more of an impact than the videotapes, and perhaps structured peer play would be an effective intervention. As more data are collected, a better understanding of the success of the treatment will emerge.

SOURCE: Dowrick, P. W. "Video Training of Alternatives to Cross-Gender Identity Behaviors in a 4-Year-Old Boy." *Child and Family Behavior Therapy,* 1983, *5* (2), 59–65.

Additional Readings

Bates, J. E., Skilbeck, W. M., Smith, K.V.R., and Bentler, P. M. "Intervention with Families of Gender-Disturbed Boys." *American Journal of Orthopsychiatry,* 1975, *45* (1), 150–157.

The authors present a treatment program for gender-problem boys and their families that utilizes behavior modification techniques. In addition, the program focuses on improving the social skills of the children, as the boys were found to be experiencing difficulties with peer relationships. The goals of the treatment program were to increase the boys' repertoire of masculine behaviors, to increase the boys' social skills and peer interactions, and to improve the boys' relationships with family members, especially their fathers.

Initially, individual family intervention was provided for each boy and his family. Boys were seen in play sessions and masculine behaviors were given social reinforcement, while the parents were seen and taught behavioral techniques to change their sons' behavior. Following this phase of treatment, boys' groups and parents' groups were formed. The groups provided peer interactions for the boys while the parents continued to learn techniques to reinforce the child's gains while also learning new methods of interacting.

Green, R., and Money, J. "Effeminacy in Prepubertal Boys: Summary of Eleven Cases and Recommendations for Case Management." *Pediatrics,* 1961, *27,* 286-290.

A series of interviews was conducted with eleven effeminate prepubertal boys, their parents, and, in some instances, their siblings. All of the effeminate boys were demonstrating behaviors that would be considered stereotypically girl-type behavior. Findings reveal that these boys typically have closer relationships with their mothers than with their fathers. The authors discuss recommendations for managing the situation, such as bringing the behavior clearly into the boys' awareness and modifying family relationships.

Horton, A. M. "Behavioral Treatment of Childhood Gender-Role Confusion: A Case Study." Presented at 14th annual AABT Conference, New York, 1980.

Behavioral group therapy and contingent reinforcement were successfully utilized as a treatment for David, a six-year-old boy with gender-role confusion. The treatment was conducted in the school setting, where David was a first grader. A history of gender cross-play and avoidance of male playmates was reported.

David's mother and teacher were taught to use social reinforcement for gender-appropriate behavior and mild reprimands for inappropriate gender behavior. In addition, David

and two other boys who were selected because of their masculine behaviors were seen in weekly group play sessions for thirty
minutes for six weeks. The goals were to reinforce conversations between David and the boys and to allow David to establish friendships with male peers. A one-year follow-up revealed
that David maintained the effects of treatment.

Janzen, W. B., and Peacock, R. "Treatment of Public Masturba-
    tion by Behavioral Management." *American Journal of
    Psychotherapy*, 1982, *24*, 110–118.

The authors present the case of a nine-year-old girl who
engaged in compulsive masturbation in her classroom. At the
time of referral, the child reportedly was masturbating incessantly during the entire school day, with no masturbatory activity at home.

Treatment consisted of four phases, with increasing demands made upon the child. During phase 1, the child was told
that she could not masturbate for the first hour of the school
day. Initially, one reminder from the teacher was permitted, but
that was later disallowed. Success earned the child television
privileges for the evening plus one-half hour of television time
on Saturday morning. Failures resulted in loss of evening television time plus loss of one-half hour of television time on Saturday. This phase lasted two school weeks, and then phase 2
was implemented. During this phase, reinforcement was given
for the child's refraining from masturbation for the first two
hours of the school day. Phases 2 through 4 were of five days'
duration. During phase 3, reinforcement was contingent upon
the child's refraining from masturbation from 8:00 A.M. to 12
noon, and in phase 4 inhibition of the symptom was required
during the entire school day. The treatment succeeded in inhibiting the child's masturbatory activity at school. A nine-
month follow-up revealed that the child was still maintaining
the effects of treatment.

Rebers, G. A., and Varni, J. W. "Self-Regulation of Gender-
    Role Behaviors: A Case Study." *Journal of Behavior
    Therapy and Experimental Psychiatry*, 1977, *8*, 427–432.
    A four-year-old gender-disturbed boy was treated by

teaching him to self-monitor and self-reinforce gender-typed play in clinic and school settings. In a clinic playroom, the boy, wearing a bug-in-the-ear device, was trained to self-monitor and self-reinforce his own behavior. This was accomplished by having him initially wear a bug-in-the-ear device and a wrist counter. He was prompted to press the wrist counter each time he played with a boy's toy. The bug-in-the-ear was faded out, and the boy was instructed that he could help himself to available candy at the end of each session in which he had points on his wrist counter. These procedures were then carried out in the school setting, without the bug-in-the-ear, in regard to dress-up play. At a twenty-four-month follow-up, the boy continued to demonstrate appropriate gender behaviors.

Rekers, G. A., and Lovaas, O. I. "Behavioral Treatment of Deviant Sex-Role Behaviors in a Male Child." *Journal of Applied Behavioral Analysis,* 1974, *7,* 173–190.
    A five-year-old boy diagnosed as manifesting cross-gender identity was demonstrating the following behaviors: cross-gender clothing preferences, verbalizations of a desire to be a girl, use of cosmetics, feminine mannerisms and voice inflection, aversion to male activities and playmates, and a preference for a female role. The mother was trained in behavioral techniques, and she served as the youngster's therapist in the clinic and in the home environment. In the clinic, the mother wore earphones to allow prompting from the therapist seated behind a one-way mirror. The mother learned to differentially reinforce the boy's appropriate gender-related behaviors with toys. Ignoring was utilized whenever the child exhibited cross-gender play. At home, a token system was utilized whereby the mother reinforced gender-appropriate behavior; the boy could trade in the tokens for preferred candies and activities. At a twenty-six-month follow-up, the boy was not exhibiting cross-gender behaviors.

Zuger, B. "Early Effeminate Behavior in Boys: Outcome and Significance for Homosexuality." *The Journal of Nervous and Mental Disease,* 1984, *172* (2), 90–97.
    Results of a long-term follow-up study reveal that male

homosexuality begins with early effeminate behaviors. Fifty-five boys between the ages of four and sixteen displaying cross-gender behaviors were initially studied. Early effeminate symptoms included feminine dressing, aversion to boys' games, desires to be female, girl playmate preferences, doll playing, feminine gestures, and wearing lipstick. Follow-up occurred over a twenty-seven-year period, so the subjects could be interviewed at different ages. At the conclusion of the study, thirty-five of the subjects were found to be homosexual, the sexual preferences of ten subjects could not be determined, three were heterosexual, and seven were lost to follow-up.

3

Antisocial Behaviors

This chapter focuses on children who show an active, antisocial pattern of aggressiveness that results in conflict with parents, peers, or social institutions. Many of these children lack the necessary ego strength to control the overt expression of aggressive impulses. In the words of Fritz Redl, these are the "children who hate" (Redl, F., and Winerman, D. *Children Who Hate.* New York: Free Press, 1951). Since the basic causes of antisocial behaviors vary widely, one cannot speak of the delinquent or antisocial child. Some delinquent acts are transient situational reactions to stress, while others reflect deep-seated personality or ego defects. Also, important differences have long been recognized between behaviors of delinquent gang members and the actions of the lone, hostile, resentful type of

267

delinquent. Studies comparing the delinquent behavior of the gang with that of the hostile loner have indicated that the former represents adaptive behavior learned from delinquent peers. Typically, the background factors of the socialized delinquent include an overcrowded home or alcoholic father. Finding little parental guidance at home, the child seeks recognition and support from his delinquent peers. Exposure to group experiences with prosocial peers can be of substantial help to these children.

In contrast, the aggressiveness of the loner tends to be a frustration response that is associated with a long-standing rejection by the child's parents. Often the parents are inconsistent in their parenting practices; they are typically quite punitive with the child, but they can also be very permissive at times. A critical, rejecting mother or stepmother is a common feature. Family therapy seems indicated with this type of child.

Some children also exhibit antisocial behaviors that seem to be primarily related to minimal brain dysfunction. Such children are the impulsive, hyperactive, and distractible children whose capacity to delay gratification is impaired. Behavior modification procedures and/or chemotherapy seem to work best with children who display this diffuse, primitive type of aggressiveness. Knowledge of the etiology of antisocial behavior can assist the clinician in selecting the most appropriate intervention strategy.

This chapter presents some methods for helping antisocial children find better ways of coping with their impulses than acting them out. The overall goal is to help the practitioner discover specific techniques for handling different manifestations of antisocial behaviors by different types of aggressive children, including a number of the more common patterns of acting-out behaviors, such as temper tantrums, destruction of property, fighting, stealing, fire setting, and running away. It is hoped that the approaches described in this chapter will help overcome some of the apathy, defeatism, and lack of imagination that have characterized clinical interventions in the past. Traditionally, clinicians have reported much greater success in treating neurotic behaviors (phobias and inhibitions) than in treating aggressively delinquent acts. Redl states that this is because aggressive children lack the minimum ego strengths, such as frustration tolerance or readiness to relate, to profit from orthodox treatment (Redl and Winerman, 1951).

Penal methods, such as state training schools, have an even worse track record with antisocial children. These usually only succeed in making a delinquent into a more hardened criminal. Consequently, criminologists keep looking to clinicians for new solutions to the problem of rehabilitating the aggressive child. In regard to criminal justice, liberal thinkers condemn conservatives for advocating cruel and inhumane punishment that overlooks the root causes of violence, while conservatives criticize liberals for using overly permissive, ineffectual approaches. Meanwhile, the incidence of violent crimes by youth keeps rising. We need to recognize how tentative our knowledge in this area is and to work diligently toward the development of innovative approaches. Recognizing the complexity of the problem, Redl maintains that the clinician must somehow give the child "ego support and ego repair" while simultaneously performing "value surgery and superego repair" (Redl and Winerman, 1951).

One of the most promising and comprehensive approaches for treating children with multiple, persistent antisocial behaviors is an intervention that combines behavioral, relationship, and cognitive approaches. Achievement Place, for example, has become a model for boys who have committed such offenses as stealing, vandalism, running away, assault, and chronic school disruption. The group residence is run by two teaching parents who seek to build self-esteem in and teach self-control skills to the boys. The program uses behavioral methods (token economy, contracts, behavioral rehearsal), relationship-building methods (lots of love, warmth, and caring in a home environment), and cognitive approaches (teaching such problem-solving skills as identifying problems, assuming responsibility for the behavior of self and others, discovering alternative behaviors, deciding on a course of action, and monitoring and evaluating progress). In brief, Achievement Place attempts to systematically apply good parenting practices in an effort to effect multimodal change in the child's thoughts, feelings, behaviors, and relationships.

Another recent trend is to consider direct intervention

with families as important as individual work with the child. Gerald Patterson and his colleagues at the Oregon Research Institute have been among the pioneers in this regard. They have attempted to treat the aggressive child, for instance, by teaching the child's parents more effective child-rearing techniques based on behavioral principles.

A variety of individual, family, and group therapy approaches for helping the antisocial child are offered in this chapter. The goals of these approaches include helping the child "talk out" rather than "act out" his or her impulses and frustrations; helping children learn to trust adults; and helping the child's family clearly spell out expectations, rules, and the positive and negative consequences of the child's behaviors.

Temper Tantrums

A temper tantrum is a violent outbreak of anger characterized by complete loss of control, screaming, and kicking. Temper tantrums by children are very distressing to parents, because such behavior makes adults appear helpless and incompetent not only in their own eyes but also in the eyes of others. Thus, tantrums tend to arouse in parents intense feelings (hostility and fearfulness) that are difficult to keep under control. For some children, tantrums are the best way they know for coping with an emotional crisis. Tantrums only become a sign of abnormality when a child uses them frequently and over a prolonged period of time. (Also see the section on Aggressiveness.*)*

Treating Tantrums That Result from the Imposition of Demands

AUTHORS: Edward G. Carr and Crighton Newsom

PRECIS: Tantrum behavior that results from the imposition of demands is treated by presenting strongly preferred reinforcers for compliance with the demand.

INTRODUCTION: The authors conducted a study and found that tantrum behavior continues because it has a payoff for the child. In some instances, a child may tantrum in order to escape from the imposition of certain demands. By tantruming, the demands or the aversive situation are removed. This, therefore, reinforces the act of engaging in a tantrum. The child's tantrum thus can be viewed as an escape response that is successful in coercing adults into withdrawing demands.

Tantrum behavior in educational settings frequently fits into this conceptualization, as teachers tend to reduce or completely withdraw their demands when a student tantrums. Three males, ages seven, eight, and eleven, who attend a school for developmentally disabled children were the subjects of two studies. The first study analyzed their tantrums in school, where it was found that these youngsters were experiencing demand-related tantrums. The second study demonstrated the effectiveness of a treatment for this behavior.

TREATMENT: Bill, age seven, and Jim, age eight, were diagnosed as autistic, and Fred, age eleven, was diagnosed as a child schizophrenic. All three boys exhibited a lack of peer interactions and toy play, as well as poor or inappropriate relationships with adults. Each boy engaged in escape-motivated tantrums that served to terminate demand situations.

Two conditions, demands and demands plus food, were utilized to assess the effectiveness of treating demand-related tantrums with strongly preferred reinforcers. In the demands condition, each child was given a series of tasks to complete (which he had already mastered in relation to his ongoing classwork). The tasks were presented by the therapist, who sat facing the child across from him at a desk. For each success, the therapist praised the child just as his teacher typically would in the classroom. For an incorrect response or no response, the therapist would look away for five seconds before presenting the next task. A task demand was made every ten seconds. During the demands plus food condition, the procedures were identical except that, in addition to verbal praise for success, food reinforcers were provided. Food reinforcers were individualized for each child to ensure that the boys were receiving foods that they viewed as strong reinforcers.

Throughout both conditions, tantrums were defined to include instances of yelling, crying, and whining. Demands were the presented tasks, and compliance was defined as any correct response made to an adult demand. Reinforced compliance was also measured, and it was defined as the presentation of praise or praise plus food as a reward for a correct response.

RESULTS: Each child demonstrated minimal compliance (an average of 11 percent) during the demands condition, with a significant increase in compliance (an average of 65 percent) in the demands plus food condition. This indicates that praise alone did not serve as a strong enough reinforcer for these children to elicit participation in an aversive task. However, the introduction of a strongly preferred reinforcer (food) tended to elicit significant levels of compliance from these autistic boys. Within the present conceptualization, the youngsters' tantrums were not a means to gain attention but an escape behavior intended to terminate an aversive stimulus (schoolwork). The presentation of reinforcers for not escaping from the situation represents a systematic approach to dealing with this inappropriate behavior.

COMMENTARY: The authors illustrate the effectiveness of treating three severely disturbed boys with strongly preferred food reinforcers for engaging in aversive tasks. The conceptualization of tantrums as a form of escape behavior maintained by negative reinforcement rather than an attention-getting device can be useful in developing treatment interventions for disruptive classroom as well as disruptive home behavior. In addition, the concept can be applied to other populations and situations. Further testing of this hypothesis should enable the formulation of alternative treatment strategies.

SOURCE: Carr, E. G., and Newsom, C. "Demand-Related Tantrums: Conceptualization and Treatment." *Behavior Modification*, 1985, *9* (4), 403–426.

The Use of Creative Characters
in the Treatment of Temper Tantrums

AUTHOR: Robert Brooks

PRECIS: The application of the creative characters technique is illustrated as an effective treatment of children's temper tantrums.

INTRODUCTION: The author has developed a technique, creative characters, which is utilized in the treatment of latency-age children. In this technique, the therapist selects the primary emotional issue confronting the child and then develops characters that face a situation reflecting the child's conflict. The characters are frequently animals, and the stories are elaborated upon over a series of treatment sessions.

A tape recorder is used in conjunction with pictures of the characters, which the therapist draws. The technique is presented to the child by the therapist's statement that he or she has made up a story for the child to hear. The story can be either pretaped or taped during the session. The child is encouraged to comment about the story, draw pictures, or act out the story with puppets or in the form of a play. The technique relies on displacement and metaphor, which has been found to make it easier for children to communicate. In using displacement, the following are built into each story: a representation of the child, a representation of the therapist, and a moderator (such as a newscaster), who can summarize the themes. In using the technique, the therapist tries to generalize the problem-solving or coping techniques from the story to the child's real life. Therefore, the therapist does point out similarities between the characters and their situations and the child.

The technique has been effective in the treatment of children demonstrating various difficulties. The author provides an illustration of its use with a child exhibiting temper tantrums.

CASE STUDY: Billy, a seven-year-old youngster, had been referred because of his explosive temper, which frequently resulted in his hitting children in a fit of anger when provoked. Billy was not able to talk about his problem in therapy sessions. However, an evaluation revealed that Billy's behavior was the result of his feeling deprived and intruded upon.

The therapist introduced the creative characters technique by making a volcano out of Play-doh. Billy added lava spilling out on the sides and named the volcano Volly. The therapist made up a story that had Volly upset whenever people stepped on him or took food from his trees and gardens. When upset, Volly would spit out lava. This behavior upset the people who lived in the surrounding town. Doctor Safety, a volcano expert, was introduced into the story as the person who empathized with Volly. In addition, Doctor Safety introduced the notion that Volly must feel lonely sometimes, as he would not let any people step or sit on him. Doctor Safety arranged for Volly to allow a limited number of people to sit on him with permission. Next, a newsperson was introduced, who reported on Volly's and the townspeople's progress.

Over a number of sessions, Billy became quite involved in the story and worked on solutions to Volly's problem. At first, Billy decided that Volly would never spit out lava again. However, Doctor Safety redirected the anger by saying that Volly could spit lava as long as it was on the side of the volcano that did not face the town. As Billy's solutions became more realistic, the therapist began to draw parallels between Volly and Billy's behavior in school.

RESULTS: Billy became comfortable talking about his temper and his resulting inappropriate behavior. A plan was established whereby Billy could go to a school counselor when he felt his temper getting out of control. Billy exhibited growth in his ability to control his anger and verbalized an understanding of his outbursts.

COMMENTARY: Structured approaches to child therapy are becoming more common as storytelling techniques, the use of board games, and self-talk approaches are being utilized. The presented technique seems quite promising, as it addresses both cognitive and affective development. The technique does seem to require, as most interventions do, that the therapist be sensitive and quite skilled in detecting the conflicts and resistances.

SOURCE: Brooks, R. "Creative Characters: A Technique in Child Therapy." *Psychotherapy: Theory, Research and Practice,* 1981, *18* (1), 131–139.

Additional Readings

Singh, N. "Aversive Control of Breath-Holding." *Journal of Behavior Therapy and Experimental Psychiatry,* 1979, *10,* 147–149.
    A fifteen-month-old boy who engaged in breath holding whenever he experienced a disciplinary conflict with his parents was treated with an aversive control technique. The child was treated by nurses under the supervision of a psychologist, a pediatrician, and a medical registrar. Whenever the child held his breath, aromatic ammonia was held under his nose while he

was reprimanded. He was then placed in a bed and ignored for three minutes. If he did not hold his breath during those three minutes, he was picked up and cuddled. Social reinforcement was also given for periods of no breath holding. At the conclusion of a fifteen-day treatment period, no breath holding was occurring. Follow-up twelve months later revealed no recurrence of breath holding.

Thelen, M. H. "Treatment of Temper Tantrum Behavior by Means of Noncontingent Positive Attention." *Journal of Clinical Child Psychology*, 1979, *8*, 140.

Joan, an eight-year-old female who was experiencing daily violent temper tantrums at home, was treated by parental noncontingent positive attention. Joan's temper tantrums appeared to be the only behavior that afforded her individual attention from her parents. A daily, structured period of at least five minutes in duration was implemented in which Joan received individual, positive attention. Soon Joan's tantrums began to decrease. By the end of a three-month period, Joan was exhibiting very few tantrums. A six-month follow-up found Joan to be engaging in little tantrum behavior.

Aggressiveness

This section discusses children's general aggressiveness toward others—that is, trying to dominate others through unprovoked verbal and physical attacks. In other sections, a more focused type of aggression will be discussed. (Since there is considerable overlap between these behaviors, the reader should also see sections on Temper Tantrums, Impulsiveness and Low Frustration Tolerance, Overt Hostility Toward Peers, *and* Sibling Rivalry.)

Structured Learning Therapy
as a Treatment for Aggressive Adolescents

AUTHORS: Arnold P. Goldstein, Mark Sherman, N. Jane Gershaw, Robert P. Sparfkin, and Barry Glick

PRECIS: Structured learning therapy, a psychoeducational approach, is utilized to teach prosocial behaviors to aggressive adolescents.

INTRODUCTION: Structured learning therapy (SLT) evolved from a behavior deficiency model based on the authors' proposal that asocial or aggressive behaviors exist when the individual does not have prosocial, acceptable behaviors in his or her repertoire. Therefore, SLT is a skill enhancement approach that aims to teach new responses. These include negotiation, self-control, relaxation, and how to respond appropriately to anger.

TREATMENT: SLT utilizes modeling, role playing, social reinforcement, and transfer training. Therapists work with adolescents in small groups, exposing them to audiotapes, videotapes, slides, or role plays of situations in which a model demonstrates the appropriate behavior or skill that the adolescent (the trainee) is expected to learn. Role playing is then utilized in an attempt to allow the adolescents to practice the skill in situations that are relevant to their lives. Social reinforcement in the form of approval and positive feedback is given as the role playing demonstrates that the trainee's behavior is becoming similar to the model's behavior.

The groups of adolescents are arranged so that all group members demonstrate the same skill deficiencies. The group is exposed to one modeling tape per session, and two trainees work with the adolescents as they then role play or practice the skill in situations that parallel the adolescents' lives. The skill is written down in a notebook, and homework is given at the end of each session; this consists of a requirement to practice the skills learned in the group.

A list of targeted behaviors addressed in SLT includes: empathy, negotiation, self-control, resistance reduction with authority figures, following instructions, assertiveness, and perspective taking. Fifty-six tapes are available to demonstrate the various skills necessary to develop the targeted behaviors.

An emphasis is placed on transfer of training or generalizability. In order to maximize the transfer, SLT uses verbal, pictorial, and written presentations of the skills being taught, as well as role-playing and real-life practice (the adolescent practices the skills for homework). In addition, performance feedback and the training of significant others in the adolescent's life are used to promote transfer of training.

RESULTS: Research on SLT reportedly finds the approach effective in teaching aggressive adolescents more appropriate ways of responding and behaving. It has been found that requiring trainees to act as group peer leaders enhances the effectiveness of the training, as the adolescent benefits from teaching others.

COMMENTARY: Structured learning therapy is reported to be an effective means of teaching aggressive adolescents socially appropriate behavioral responses. As the technique is still being tested and modified, future research on the approach should provide valuable information on the most effective method of implementation. In general, aggressive adolescents are difficult to treat; therefore careful validation of this technique will be beneficial.

SOURCE: Goldstein, A. P., Sherman, M., Gershaw, N. J., Sparfkin, R. P., and Glick, B. "Training Aggressive Adolescents in Prosocial Behavior." *Journal of Youth and Adolescence,* 1978, 7 (1), 73-92.

Treating Aggressive Behavior with a Reinforcement/Time-Out Program

AUTHORS: James K. Luiselli, Ellen Myles, and Jack Littman-Quinn

PRECIS: A multiply handicapped youngster's aggressive and destructive behaviors were eliminated with a reinforcement/time-out treatment program.

INTRODUCTION: A treatment program was developed as an intervention for the aggressive and destructive behaviors of a fifteen-year-old male who was diagnosed as having maternal rubella syndrome. Keith was both hearing and visually impaired, and at age fifteen he had a mental and social age of approximately five years. He lived in a foster home with other developmentally disabled children. However, during the school year he lived at a residential facility, where he attended class from 9:00 A.M. to 3:00 P.M. and spent the rest of his time in a cottage with six other disabled children, two house parents, and five child-care workers.

The behaviors targeted for intervention were Keith's aggressive behaviors, which included punching, slapping, scratching, and head butting adults, and his destructive behaviors, which included the ripping, crushing, and breaking of objects. These behaviors were hypothesized to be attention-getting devices, as they would increase in frequency when staff members were holding a meeting or attending to another resident.

TREATMENT: The treatment was conducted in two settings, the classroom and the cottage. Initially, treatment occurred in the classroom. A baseline period was carried out so that teachers could record the frequency of each targeted behavior on data sheets. During baseline, teachers continued to respond to Keith's aggression and destructiveness as they always had. They either reprimanded Keith, ignored him, or placed him in the hallway outside the classroom.

A reinforcement phase was then introduced whereby a

token was placed on a cardboard mat on Keith's desk each time he acted appropriately in a session. Keith could exchange five tokens for a reinforcer: a soft drink, a piece of candy, or spending two to three minutes looking at a picture book. During this phase, when Keith exhibited aggression or destructiveness, the teachers continued to respond as they had during the baseline phase.

The next phase of treatment consisted of a nine-day period during which a time-out was expanded to include destructive behaviors. The time-out procedure involved placing Keith in a small room by himself and closing the door. Keith was left in the room for three minutes. However, his leaving the room was contingent upon Keith's being nonagitated during the last one minute. If this was not achieved within the three-minute period, Keith remained in the room until the one minute of nonagitation occurred. Nonagitation was defined as the absence of screaming, banging walls, or thrashing about. (During time-out, in order to comply with legal and ethical guidelines, the following occurred: the room was properly lit and ventilated; a teacher monitored the entire time-out period through a peephole; each time-out was recorded; and parental consent had been obtained for the utilization of this procedure.)

By the seventy-eighth day of treatment, Keith was consistently inhibiting the targeted behaviors. Therefore, fading-out procedures were implemented whereby reinforcement was used during only one-half of the sessions. This lasted for one week and was followed by a week in which token reinforcement was terminated and appropriate behaviors were rewarded by teacher praise and approval.

Overlapping the treatment in the classroom was a phase of treatment in the cottage. This began on the thirtieth day of the classroom treatment. The baseline procedure was the same as in the classroom, except that Keith was placed in his bedroom when his behavior became uncontrollable. The reinforcement phase was similar to the one utilized in the classroom. However, the tokens were earned on a time-based schedule rather than a response-ratio schedule. The cottage staff set a timer for fifteen minutes and presented Keith with one of the reinforcers. If Keith did not display aggression or destructive behavior during the fifteen minutes, he earned a reinforcer.

Time-out was then introduced and carried out as it was in the school setting. Simultaneously, the duration of the reinforcement intervals was increased by fifteen minutes each time Keith succeeded three consecutive times. When Keith failed (that is, when he demonstrated one of the targeted behaviors), the interval was decreased by fifteen minutes. This procedure was carried out until the reinforcement interval reached five-and-a-half hours. At that point, no changes in the interval were made. As in the classroom, fading-out procedures began on the seventy-eighth day of treatment and continued until reinforcement consisted of praise, approval, hugs, and tickles.

RESULTS: The implementation of the reinforcement phase did not result in decreasing the targeted behaviors to acceptable levels. However, the implementation of the time-out procedure in addition to the reinforcement procedure did result in the elimination of Keith's destructive and aggressive behaviors. In regard to behavior in the time-out room, Keith was completely non-agitated during time-out for the last six weeks of treatment in the classroom and the last three weeks of treatment in the cottage.

COMMENTARY: Reinforcement and time-out procedures have been effectively utilized in the treatment of undesirable behaviors. The current program illustrates that the treatment can be effective with a multiply handicapped youngster. Areas of further investigation might include using time-out procedures without the reinforcement phase or reversing the order of implementation of the two phases to ascertain the effect.

SOURCE: Luiselli, J. K., Myles, E., and Littman-Quinn, J. "Analysis of a Reinforcement/Time-out Treatment Package to Control Severe Aggressive and Destructive Behaviors in a Multihandicapped Rubella Child." *Applied Research in Mental Retardation*, 1983, 4, 65–78.

Reducing Aggression in Children

AUTHOR: Leonard D. Eron

PRECIS: Early socialization that teaches alternative ways of solving problems is proposed as an effective means to reducing aggressive behavior.

INTRODUCTION: The author presents two longitudinal studies on children's aggression. Aggression is defined as an act that injures another person—that is, hostile, interpersonal, acting-out aggression. In the first study, the author found that at age eight aggressive children tended to have less nurturant and accepting parents than did nonaggressive children. In addition, the more a child was punished for aggressive behavior, the more aggressive the child tended to be. Finally, children who identified less with their parents were more aggressive in school, and the higher the socioeconomic class of the family, the more aggressive the child. The two most significant models of aggressive behavior proved to be punitive parents and television programs. Ten years after the original data collection, the author reinterviewed the available subjects. At age eighteen, the subjects who had been rated by their peers at age eight to be the most aggressive were still rated as aggressive and were three times more likely than their nonaggressive peers to have police records.

    The most significant indicator of how violent a subject was at age eighteen is the degree of violence watched on television at the age of eight. However, the significant correlation between television programs viewed and later violent behavior exists only for males. The author attributes this to the socialization process whereby boys are rewarded for and usually encouraged to participate in physical expressions of aggression to solve a problem and girls are not. Furthermore, this premise is supported by the finding that when girls are rewarded for imitating aggressive models, they, too, behave aggressively. Another hypothesized contribution to boys' higher correlation of aggressive behavior to watching aggression on television is the fact that there are many more aggressive male models presented on tele-

vision than female models. Since social learning theory states
that individuals tend to imitate models that are viewed as similar to the individual, this can contribute to the differences in behavior.

Other significant findings of the longitudinal study reveal
that girls who resemble boys in regard to their responses on the
Masculinity-Femininity Scale of the Minnesota Multiphasic Personality Inventory (MMPI) tend to be similar to boys in levels
of aggression.

In the author's second study, which reports data from
year two of a proposed three-year longitudinal study, he found
that differential socialization for boys and girls has an increasing effect from first to third grade. For boys, the correlation
between television violence viewed and aggression increased
whereas for girls it decreased. Furthermore, it was found that
girls tended to have less active fantasies as compared to boys,
who fantasize about aggressive acts and then display correlating
aggressive behavior.

In terms of implications for interventions, the two areas
that Eron views as requiring change are television violence and
the values imposed upon children in regard to masculinity versus femininity. Despite the effects of violence on television,
Eron proposes that differential socialization is the greatest contributing factor to perpetuating aggressive behavior. It is hypothesized that socializing all children in the way that girls are
typically socialized in our society would promote the teaching
of alternate ways of solving problems and reduce aggression in
boys.

COMMENTARY: Eron proposes that aggression is a reinforced,
learned behavior that society tends to nurture in boys. Although his premise is supported by many other studies, his suggested intervention will not be easily implemented, as it calls
for a societal change. This type of change tends to be a very
slow process.

SOURCE: Eron, L. D. "Prescription for Reduction of Aggression." *American Psychologist*, 1980, *35* (3), 244-252.

*Treating Highly Aggressive Children on an
Inpatient Ward with Social Skills Training*

AUTHORS: Mitchell Bornstein and Alan S. Bellack

PRECIS: Social skills training is utilized as a treatment approach for modifying aggressive behavior in children on an inpatient psychiatric ward.

INTRODUCTION: Bornstein and Bellack present the hypothesis that aggressive children exhibit their inappropriate behavior
as a result of a lack of appropriate social skills: Not being capable of appropriate behavior and therefore of maintaining interpersonal relationships, the youngsters resort to aggression as a
way of achieving attention. The authors discuss treatment for
aggressive behavior—teaching appropriate social skills—as it relates to four youngsters who were inpatients at a children's
psychiatric hospital.

TREATMENT: The four subjects of this study were youngsters
who demonstrated extreme levels of aggression with peers and
who appeared to be incapable of expressing dissatisfaction or of
asserting themselves in a nonhostile manner. All subjects were
between the ages of eight and twelve, and all had been diagnosed as exhibiting mixed behavior disorder of childhood. The
children exhibited violent disruptive behavior and often became
physically assaultive.

The Behavioral Assertiveness Test for Children (BAT-C)
was used as a dependent measure. This is a role-playing test that
requires interpersonal encounters. In addition, the subjects were
observed pre- and post-treatment in a group therapy session
with other children. The session was videotaped, and eye contact, hostile tone, requests for new behavior, and overall assertiveness were recorded.

Each subject received social skills training that consisted
of three fifteen-to-thirty-minute sessions for each target behavior. Initially, the therapist presented an interpersonal situation
from the BAT-C, a role model (either male or female) delivered

a prompt, and then the child had an opportunity to respond. The therapist gave feedback to the child, with emphasis on the specific behavior being targeted. Discussion of the feedback followed. Next, the role model displayed an appropriate response, after which the therapist gave specific instructions about a target behavior. Rehearsals continued until the therapist was satisfied that the target behavior had been reached. Training then focused on a new interpersonal situation and target behavior.

RESULTS: Each subject demonstrated changes in the desired direction on each target behavior as the specific behavior became the focus of the treatment. Improvements in eye contact, hostile tone, and overall assertiveness were achieved. However, requests for new behaviors in lieu of responding to a frustrating event without expressing dissatisfaction were inconsistent. In addition, generalization to the group therapy sessions was inconsistent.

The most significant finding was that each child, despite the same diagnosis and similar behavior on a behavior analysis pre-test, responded differently (that is, in varying degrees) to the treatment. Speed of change, the specific behaviors responding to treatment, the pattern of generalization, and the extent of maintenance varied among the subjects.

COMMENTARY: The current findings indicate that social skills training may be a promising treatment approach for reducing highly aggressive behavior in hospitalized children. Although the findings are not consistent across subjects, there are desired changes in each instance. Assuming that hospitalized, aggressive youngsters are deficient in social skills, a program to correct this deficit appears to be valid. However, it seems that other components should be added to social skills training for this population, which typically displays pathological behaviors that are multiply determined.

SOURCE: Bornstein, M., and Bellack, A. S. "Social Skills Training for Highly Aggressive Children in an Inpatient Psychiatric Setting." *Behavior Modification,* forthcoming.

288 Advances in Therapies for Children

Additional Readings

Campbell, M., Anderson, L. T., and Green, W. "Behavior-Disordered and Aggressive Children: New Advances in Pharmacotherapy." *Developmental and Behavioral Pediatrics,* 1983, *4* (4), 265–271.

The authors present an overview of recent psychopharmacological developments in the treatment of childhood behavioral disorders. The disorders discussed include: attention deficit disorder, Tourette's Syndrome, infantile autism, self-mutilation, aggressive behavior, tic disorders, enuresis, encopresis, sleepwalking and sleep terror disorder, anxiety, phobias, and eating disorders. The disorders are presented in categories according to the potential usefulness of psychopharmacological intervention. The authors report that although medication is not the treatment of choice when used in isolation for many of these disorders, it can be quite beneficial when used as part of a treatment strategy.

Dodge, K. A. "Social Cognition and Children's Aggressive Behavior." *Child Development,* 1980, *51,* 162–170.

Ninety boys from grades two, four, and six participated in a study focusing on integrating cues and assessing intent of aggression in social situations. The author categorized the boys as either aggressive or nonaggressive. All subjects were then exposed to a frustrating negative outcome by an unfamiliar peer who acted with a hostile intent, a benign intent, or an ambiguous intent. Both groups of subjects, aggressive and nonaggressive, responded with more aggression in the hostile condition, and there was no significant difference between the groups' responses. However, aggressive boys demonstrated a significant difference in their aggressive responses to the ambiguous situation. Aggressive boys tended to attribute the outcome to a hostile intent, whereas nonaggressive boys were more likely to attribute the negative experience to a benign intent. The findings provide valuable information to those treating aggressive children, as the author points out a cycle whereby aggressive children tend to view situations as having hostile intentions which then lead to increased aggression. This increased aggression then serves to increase the frequency of actual, elicited hostile intentions from others.

Fleishman, M. J., and Szykula, S. A. "A Community Setting Replication of a Social Learning Treatment for Aggressive Children." *Behavior Therapy*, 1981, *12*, 115–122.

The authors report on the utilization of a social learning intervention program for aggressive children that was initially used in a laboratory setting. The treatment program, which was developed at the Oregon Learning Center, was replicated in a community-based setting. Although no control group was evaluated, the program appears to be effective in this setting, as observations and parental reports found significant decreases in the treated groups' aggressive behaviors.

Hayes, S. C., Rincover, A., and Volosin, D. "Variables Influencing the Acquisition and Maintenance of Aggressive Behavior: Modeling Versus Sensory Reinforcement." *Journal of Abnormal Psychology*, 1980, *89* (2), 254–262.

Forty-eight preschool children participated in a study consisting of three conditions: watching a film of a limited-movement Bobo doll being struck, watching a film of a free-moving Bobo doll being struck, or not watching a film. The children were then given access to either a limited-movement or free-movement Bobo doll, and the frequency of their aggression was recorded. The authors found that although modeling served to initiate aggressive behavior, sensory consequences maintained aggressive behavior. The visual, tactile, auditory, and proprioceptive feedback of the aggressive act served to reinforce and encourage the behavior.

Loeber, R. "The Stability of Antisocial and Delinquent Child Behavior: A Review." *Child Development*, 1982, *53*, 1431–1446.

The author presents a review of the literature on children who display antisocial behaviors. Significant findings reveal that children who demonstrate a high rate of antisocial behavior are most likely to persist in this pattern, whereas children demonstrating a lower rate of antisocial behavior are not as high-risk for chronic delinquent behavior. In addition, the author found that youngsters who engage in overt antisocial acts, such as fighting and disobedience, tend to demonstrate a decline in such behavior between the ages of six and sixteen. Youngsters demonstrating covert social acts, such as theft and drug abuse, tend to show an increase in antisocial behavior. Loeber presents strategies for the early identification of chronic delinquents.

Madden, D. J., and Harbin, H. T. "Family Structures of Assaultive Adolescents." *Journal of Marital and Family Therapy,* 1983, *9* (3), 311-316.

The authors compare the family structures of assaultive adolescents to those of the families of nonassaultive adolescents in regard to the families' perceptions of authority hierarchies. Findings reveal that families of assaultive adolescents either tend to see the adolescent as being on the same level as one of the parents in regard to authority or perceive that the adolescent is in charge and has more authority than the parents. These results should be taken into consideration when working with families of assaultive adolescents, as the families typically do tend to convey feelings of helplessness as well as a lack of control over the teenager.

Pfeffer, C. R., Plutchik, R., and Mizruchi, M S. "Predictors of Assaultiveness in Latency-Age Children." *American Journal of Psychiatry,* 1983, *14* (1), 31-35.

A study to identify psychosocial variables that are predictors of assaultive behavior in children aged six to twelve used 103 children for data collection. The authors found that boys generally were more assaultive than girls and that boys tended to use fire setting and hitting with objects much more than girls. Children diagnosed as having conduct disorders, developmental disorders, or mental retardation proved to be more assaultive than children diagnosed as having a neurotic disorder. A child's past instances of aggression, the presence of anxiety and depression, and past parental assaultive behavior were found to be the best predictors of children's assaultive behavior.

Stewart, M. A., Adams, C. C., and Meardon, J. K. "Unsocialized Aggressive Boys: A Follow-Up Study." *Journal of Clinical Psychiatry,* 1978, *39* (11), 797-799.

The authors examined short-term prognosis for boys who had been hospitalized with a diagnosis of unsocialized aggressive reaction. At follow-up twenty-one months after discharge, they found that two-thirds of the boys had maintained improvements. While certain temperamental traits, such as impulsiveness, remained, the boys' aggressiveness and noncompliance had generally diminished. The type of treatment the boy or family received between discharge and follow-up was not taken into account in the obtained results, as the treatments varied a great deal.

Vaughn, S. R., Ridley, C. A., and Bullock, D. D. "Interpersonal Problem-Solving Skills Training with Aggressive Young Children." *Journal of Applied Developmental Psychology,* 1984, *5,* 213–223.

Twenty-five preschool children identified as aggressive participated in an interpersonal problem-solving training program. The program consisted of fifty sessions conducted for twenty minutes each, five days per week, for ten weeks. The program used puppets to model interpersonal problem-solving processes and taught children to generate solutions and to think through problems. The program was found to be effective in teaching children who were not succeeding in interpersonal situations to generate appropriate, relevant problem-solving skills. Significant improvements in interpersonal relations and a resulting decrease in aggression occurred.

Stealing

This section focuses on stealing—that is, taking the money or possessions of others without permission. Typically, stealing is done in a secret or surreptitious manner. Studies have shown that the children most frequently involved in "aggressive" stealing are diagnosed as showing "group delinquent reaction." Aggressive stealing, such as burglary, involves some degree of courage, in contrast to the furtive stealing of the sneak thief.

Treating Car-Stealing Behavior
with Covert Sensitization

AUTHOR: Joseph R. Cautela

PRECIS: Adolescents' car-stealing behavior is treated with a procedure, covert sensitization, that builds an avoidance response to the targeted stimuli.

INTRODUCTION: Cautela developed an approach to treating undesirable behaviors that is termed *covert sensitization*. Covert sensitization involves a technique in which the undesirable stimuli and the aversive stimuli are presented in fantasy (covert) and an avoidance response is built into the undesirable stimuli (sensitization). The entire procedure is conducted with the utilization of the patient's imagination. The approach has been utilized with alcoholics, obese patients, homosexuals, and juvenile delinquents. The author presents an illustration of the procedure in which juveniles' car-stealing behavior is treated.

TREATMENT: Cautela describes the treatment of boys who repeatedly steal cars. Initially, as with all of the patients treated with this approach, the boy is taught to relax in the same manner used in Wolpe's desensitization procedures (Wolpe, J. *Psychotherapy by Reciprocal Inhibition.* Stanford, Calif.: Stanford University Press, 1958). Once this is taught, the youngster is asked to raise his index finger when he is relaxed. Typically, this relaxation is learned in three to four sessions.

While relaxed, the therapist tells the boy that he is unable to stop stealing cars because it is a habit that gives him a great amount of pleasure. The boy is then told that the way to break the habit is to learn to associate the pleasurable object (the car) with an unpleasant stimulus. Next, the boy is instructed to visualize the car and to again signal the therapist by raising his index finger. Upon raising his finger, the therapist tells the boy to associate nausea and throwing up with the act of stealing. To accomplish this, the boy visualizes the sequence of behaviors leading up to stealing a car (seeing the car, approaching it, touching the car, opening the car door, and so on), and the therapist verbalizes—in very clear, descriptive terms—increasing feelings of nausea culminating with the youngster throwing up all over himself and the car. In addition, the boy is taught that the way to rid himself of the nausea is to turn around and run away from the car.

After several practice sessions in the therapist's office, the boy is instructed to practice the treatment twice a day on his own at home. The practice requires ten to twenty repetitions of the procedure.

RESULTS: Cautela reports that juvenile offenders have cooperated with the covert sensitization procedures. However, no experimental data or results are given. The controlled studies using this technique appear to have utilized alcoholics and homosexuals as the subjects. With these populations, positive and encouraging results are reported.

COMMENTARY: Covert sensitization, as presented, appears to be a good approach for treating adolescent car-stealing behavior. However, controlled studies need to be conducted, as several issues need to be addressed. For one thing, adolescent juvenile offenders may not be the most receptive to this technique requiring at-home, independent practice, as peer pressure may be a stronger influence than the desire to do the home practice. In addition, juvenile offenders may experience many secondary gains from maintaining their stealing behavior. Further research with this population would be quite beneficial.

SOURCE: Cautela, J. R. "Covert Sensitization." *Psychological Reports*, 1967, *48*, 12-24.

Paradoxical Procedures
as a Treatment for Stealing

AUTHORS: Ed Jessee and Luciano L'Abate

PRECIS: Paradoxical procedures were utilized on an inpatient unit to treat stealing behavior in children.

INTRODUCTION: The authors illustrate that utilizing paradoxical procedures on an inpatient child unit can be effective in changing the child's family system. Although hospitalizing a child seems to identify that child as the patient and as a result usually protects the family homeostasis, the family system tends to be perpetuated on the unit. Therefore, the hospital setting can replicate the child's family, allowing an intervention to produce change in maladaptive family systems.

Jessee and L'Abate discuss several paradoxical procedures, examine the appropriateness of using the techniques, and give three case illustrations of the effectiveness of paradoxical interventions. The following case of an eleven-year-old exemplifies the procedures.

CASE STUDY: Billy was admitted to the inpatient unit as a result of repeated instances of stealing. He was the youngest of three children, and both of his older siblings had a history of juvenile offenses. Billy's father worked a night shift and usually slept during the day. Therefore, Billy's mother, who was described as depressed, handled all issues regarding Billy except the instances when he was caught stealing. Following stealing, Billy's parents would discuss the problem and then the father, not the mother, would discipline Billy.

Upon being admitted to the hospital, Billy had no problem forming positive relationships with female staff members but did have difficulty relating to male staff members. Despite obvious indications that Billy wanted to develop relationships with male staff members and despite their attempts to engage Billy, his inability to relate persisted.

A paradoxical technique that paralleled the family dy-

namics was implemented. Billy was told that the staff was aware
of his desire to develop a relationship with male staff members.
However, they acknowledged that Billy had difficulty letting
staff know when he wanted to spend time with them. A prescription was made which required Billy to steal a magazine,
which would be left on a counter, each time he wanted to spend
time with a male staff member. Billy was then told that whenever he took a magazine the male staff would first have to meet
with the female staff to discuss Billy's behavior and then a male
staff member would spend time with Billy. When the intervention was being explained, Billy was congratulated for giving
male and female staff members a chance to be together. Billy
was told that staff were usually so busy that they did not have
time to get together.

RESULTS: Billy's reaction to the prescribed technique was initially confusion but quickly turned to anger. Billy did agree to
the procedures; however, he never followed through. He also
never stole anything again. The following week, Billy and his
father spent an afternoon together. This was something they
had not done in years. Billy's mother reported feeling better,
and Billy was discharged. At follow-up several months later,
Billy had not engaged in any more stealing.

COMMENTARY: Paradoxical intervention, or prescribing the
symptom, has been used effectively in the treatment of both
families and individuals. The most important issue in regard to
this approach is when it is or is not appropriate. Oppositional
individuals and defiant individuals tend to respond positively to
this approach, as they are given an opportunity to be noncompliant and to not acknowledge that they have control over a
specific behavior. The authors demonstrate that paradoxical
procedures not only can be effective on a children's inpatient
unit but also can change a family system even when only a sub-
system of the family is treated.

SOURCE: Jessee, E., and L'Abate, L. "The Use of Paradox with
  Children in an Inpatient Treatment Setting." *Family Process*,
  1980, *19*, 59-64.

Treating Adolescent Stealing
with Rational Behavior Therapy

AUTHOR: Maxie C. Maultsby, Jr.

PRECIS: Rational behavior therapy is used to treat an acting-out adolescent who engages in stealing.

INTRODUCTION: Maultsby uses rational behavior therapy (RBT) to treat acting-out adolescents. Acting-out adolescents are defined as youngsters whose major problem is persistent, neurotic conflict. These youngsters tend to try to act their way out of emotional conflict instead of thinking their way out. Therefore, the initial step in treating these youngsters is to eliminate the emotional conflict.

Five rules of RBT are taught to the adolescent in order to enable him or her to recognize rational as opposed to irrational thinking. The five rules are that thinking is rational if: (1) it is based on objective reality, (2) it causes people to protect their lives, (3) it enables people to achieve their goals most effectively, (4) it keeps people out of significant trouble with other people, and (5) it prevents significant personal emotional conflict. In addition, the adolescents are helped to see that what is rational thinking for one individual may not be rational for another and that what may be rational thinking at one time is not necessarily rational at another time. RBT teaches adolescents to make their own decisions as to the rationality of a behavior. In doing so, the youngsters are taught that no one is rational all the time and that in order for thinking to be rational it need only meet three of the five criteria.

The next step is to teach the adolescents what are known as the ABC's of rational self-analysis (RSA). In an RSA, the youngster learns to analyze him- or herself by taking a piece of paper and writing the following:

A	Da
Facts and events	Camera check of A
B	Db
Self-talk	Rational debate of B

1.	1.
2. etc.	2.
C	E
Emotional consequences of B	Emotional effects of Db

The youngster writes down an event under A and then writes thoughts about A under B. Under C, he or she writes the five rules of rational thinking. In the Da section, the adolescent must write the event(s) the way they would appear if someone had made a movie of the situation. In the Db section, he or she makes a rational debate of each sentence in B. If the sentence seems rational, the youngster writes that under Db; if the sentence seems irrational, it must be changed so that it is acceptable to the youngster while obeying at least three of the five rules of rational thinking. Finally, the adolescent fills in section E, which is the description of the new emotional feelings that the youngster would like to experience in situations similar to A. The youngster is then encouraged to consistently think and act according to the Da and Db sections.

CASE STUDY: Richard, a fifteen-year-old, was classified as an acting-out adolescent after being arrested for stripping a car with a gang of boys. Richard had no previous record and in fact had been described by parents and teachers as being a quiet, nice stable boy until only a few months preceding the arrest, when he had become involved with a gang. An intake revealed that Richard's motivation was to prove to himself that he was no longer inferior, as he had always felt. When the gang began to strip cars, Richard tried to break his ties with them. However, he was persuaded by the gang members to remain.

　　After Richard's arrest, he was mandated to psychotherapy. His first rational self-analysis examines the event of his trying to leave the gang. The analysis demonstrates how Richard was able to use the rules of RBT to understand his behavior.

RESULTS: Richard attended individual therapy sessions for three months. He completed at least two RSA's each week and began to feel less inferior. For the next three months, Richard attended group sessions instead of the individual sessions. At the end of six months of therapy, Richard was discharged. He came off probation and he had made new friends.

COMMENTARY: Rational behavior therapy has been used as an effective treatment with some individuals. Richard responded very well to this treatment, and the transcript of the behavior analysis reveals that this youngster had a good capacity for insightful thinking. With a youngster who can benefit from RBT, it seems to be a highly effective approach.

SOURCE: Maultsby, M. C., Jr. "Rational Behavior Therapy for Acting-Out Adolescents." *Social Casework*, 1975, *56*, 35-43.

Utilizing Self-Reinforcement and Family Contracting in the Treatment of Stealing

AUTHOR: Jerome S. Stumphauzer

PRECIS: Self-control techniques, self-reinforcement of alternative behaviors, and family contingency contracting are used in the treatment of a twelve-year-old girl's stealing behavior.

INTRODUCTION: A twelve-year-old girl with a five-year history of stealing behavior was referred by her school for treatment. At the time of referral, the youngster was stealing on almost a daily basis in school, at home, and in neighborhood stores. The youngster reportedly was not experiencing any other major problems besides this stealing of small objects and small amounts of money. Her schoolwork was reported to be satisfactory. An analysis of the girl's environment revealed many secondary gains for stealing, such as teacher and parental attention, with little reinforcement for prosocial or incompatible behavior.

CASE STUDY: The girl was seen for fifteen treatment sessions, which initially occurred once per week and then occurred once every four weeks. Each session combined individual therapy with family therapy. The first three sessions focused on analyzing the girl's behavior. During this time, both the mother and the teacher recorded daily incidents of stealing.

The remainder of the sessions focused on teaching the girl self-control techniques and on enforcing family contracts. The self-control techniques were role played by the therapist and the youngster. The role playing consisted of seeing desirable objects to steal and then shifting focus to an incompatible response, such as an activity that was followed by self-reinforcement. Self-monitoring and self-reinforcement were accomplished through such self-statements as, "I'm proud of myself."

Beginning with the fourth session, the girl was instructed to record her own daily incidents of stealing. This was followed by the girl's initiation of wanting to use her own self-statements instead of using the therapist's words. Family contracts were devised to shift the parents' and the school's attention toward nonstealing behavior. Praise and 20¢ were the rewards for each day of no stealing. Each week of no stealing was rewarded by special activities and meals on Sundays.

In addition, the father, an avid reader, was given a bibliography of books on behavioral techniques, which he read. As a result, the father not only was able to shift his attention but was able to get his wife to shift her attention to the child's nonstealing behaviors. Finally, the family was encouraged to allow the girl to go out into the neighborhood. This had been prohibited by the parents, who feared that the youngster would steal.

RESULTS: By the sixth week of treatment, the girl had stopped stealing. She was treated for an additional three months before being terminated. Follow-ups were conducted at six, twelve, and eighteen months and revealed no recurrence of stealing, along with improved family functioning. In addition, the girl found new ways of receiving gratification, the most obvious being her development of new friendships.

COMMENTARY: In keeping with current trends, the author utilized a multifaceted approach to treating a maladaptive behavior. Family contracting and self-monitoring have been successful techniques in the treatment of many undesirable behaviors. Combining these techniques proved effective in eliminating a long-term stealing problem. However, it is difficult to assess whether or not the family changes or the self-monitoring could have been used independently to achieve the same results. Perhaps further study of this approach will address that issue.

SOURCE: Stumphauzer, J. S. "Elimination of Stealing by Self-Reinforcement of Alternative Behavior and Family Contracting." *Journal of Behavior Therapy and Experimental Psychiatry,* 1976, 7, 265–268.

Additional Readings

Azrin, N. H., and Wesolowski, M. D. "Theft Reversal: An Overcorrection Procedure for Eliminating Stealing by Retarded Persons." *Journal of Applied Behavior Analysis,* 1974, *1,* 577–581.

An overcorrection procedure in which subjects were required to give back not only the stolen property but also an additional item identical to the stolen one was compared to a procedure in which the subject was required to simply give back the stolen item. The subjects in the study were thirty-four retarded residents of an institution that was experiencing a high rate of daily food thefts among residents. The use of overcorrection reduced the thefts by 50 percent the first day, 75 percent the second day, and 100 percent by the fourth day. This was quite significant in comparison to the simple restitution correction procedure, which had little impact on stealing behavior.

The authors attribute the overcorrection technique's effectiveness to several factors. The technique serves as a negative reinforcer when the thief must give back not only the item but also an additional item. In addition, it serves as a source of pleasure for the victim, who gains an item and is no longer annoyed. This, therefore, eliminates the thief's secondary gains. This technique seems very promising, and its applicability to children and nonretarded populations should be examined.

Moore, D. R., Chamberlain, P., and Mukai, L. H. "Children at Risk for Delinquency: A Follow-Up Comparison of Aggressive Children and Children Who Steal." *Journal of Abnormal Child Psychology*, 1979, *1* (3), 345-355.

The authors conducted a comparison study of three groups of adolescents. Forty-six of the adolescents had been treated in the past two to nine years either for aggression in the home or for stealing behavior. A third group of fourteen adolescents served as the control group. These youngsters were matched by age and family composition to the aggressive sample. (These youngsters and their families had not sought psychological help during the year prior to the study.) It was found that 77 percent of the adolescents who had experienced earlier stealing problems had become adolescents with court-recorded offenses, whereas only 13 percent of the aggressive youngsters and 21 percent of the control group had acquired court records. This suggests that young aggressive children are not at risk for developing juvenile records, whereas children who steal are at high risk. In addition, it was found that parental reports of stealing served as a reliable predictive measure for later criminal acts.

These findings give professionals working with aggressive children and children who steal information that can be extremely valuable when formulating treatment procedures. It appears that aggressive children who are treated by professionals are at lower risk for later court contact than are their matched controls who are not treated.

Sanderson, H. "Dependency on Mother in Boys Who Steal." *The British Journal of Criminology*, 1977, *17* (2), 180-184.

One hundred and fourteen boys aged six to thirteen and their mothers participated in a study to assess boys' levels of dependency on their mothers. The boys were categorized into three groups: *subjects* were youngsters who had had at least three instances of known stealing in the preceding six months, *clinic cases* were youngsters referred to the clinic for some problem other than stealing, and *normal controls* were youngsters referred for educational problems. All of the boys' mothers completed the Eysenck Personality Inventory and the Highlands Dependency Questionnaire. A psychologist estimated the boys' IQ's and reading and math levels.

Findings reveal that the boys had similar IQ's and academic levels. The mothers of the boys referred for stealing were found to be the most neurotic and introverted and to have the most marital difficulties. Therefore, these mothers had the least energy to exert in giving their children affection and attention. As would be expected, the boys referred for stealing were therefore less dependent on their mothers for affection and communication. Mothers of the clinic cases were not different from control mothers in any significant way. These findings indicate that when treating boys who steal, dependency issues as well as maternal affection and communication should be addressed.

Fire Setting

The juvenile who deliberately sets fires poses a serious threat to the well-being not only of his or her family but of the entire community as well. Because of the obvious danger, the treatment of a fire-setting syndrome must be a high priority for the therapist.

Treating Fire-Setting Behavior
with a Graphing Technique

AUTHOR: Eugene R. Bumpass, F. Diane Fagelman, and Royanna Just Brix

PRECIS: The utilization of a graphing technique that sequentially correlates events, feelings, and behavior as a treatment for fire-setting behavior.

INTRODUCTION: The authors present a brief review of treatment for fire-setting behavior and discuss prognostic indicators. Although their general treatment approach is to engage the child and family in psychodynamically oriented therapy that relates to the child's specific psychopathology, all children engaging in fire setting are initially treated with a graphing technique. The authors hypothesize that the graph, which is a concrete visualization, aids the child's ego in correlating cause-and-effect relationships between feelings and actions. Once the child becomes aware of the correlation and can engage in more adaptive behaviors, therapy focuses on underlying factors. The authors present case studies that illustrate the graphing technique.

TREATMENT: The goal of the technique is to bring fire-setting behavior under control. Initially, the child is told that behavior is the result of feelings and that once feelings are recognized, behavior can be controlled. The child is then asked to describe his or her behavior, external stimuli, and feelings in regard to the most recent fire-setting episode. The therapist constructs the graph while the child describes, in sequence, the behaviors and feelings. As parents and child are present in the session, they are all asked to make any corrections in the graph that they see fit.

The graph consists of a chronological list of the events that preceded and followed fire setting. The events are listed across the bottom of the page, and fire-setting behavior is placed in the middle of the graph. The child then describes feelings, which are graphed in regard to intensity (intensity correlates to how high the feeling will extend on the graph). Each feeling is represented by a separate line and is labelled. The graph usually reveals that a sequence of events and feelings resulted in the fire setting. The common feelings reported are sadness, loneliness, and anger. In addition, children report feelings of fear just prior to and subsequent to the act of setting the fire.

The therapist interprets the graph to the child upon its completion, and both parents and child are asked to verbalize what information the graph has revealed to them. The goal is to have the family see a sequence of a precipitating event, feelings, and the resulting behavior. Once the family members recognize the cause-and-effect relationships, they are asked to discuss ways that they can break the cycle of events. The child is told that feelings are the part of the cycle that signal the presence of a risk of fire-setting behavior. Therefore, the child is told that once the feelings are experienced, a choice of behavior should be made. Since children do not typically set fires each time they feel an urge to do so, they are helped to reflect on the alternative behaviors they use.

At the end of the graphing session, the child is told that he or she probably will not set a fire in the coming week. If the child gets the urge to set a fire, he or she is encouraged to call the therapist. If fire setting occurs, the next session is used to graph the episode. If no fire setting occurs, the treatment reverts to traditional psychodynamic therapeutic interviews.

COMMENTARY: The present approach utilizes a concrete representation of a sequence of events, feelings, and behavior to interrupt fire-setting behavior. The treatment combines a family crisis-oriented model of treatment with an innovative graphing technique. The authors point out that the child's ability to see the cause-and-effect relationship of feelings and actions is the most important aspect. The technique appears to be very promising for use with children who are not resistant or opposed to describing events and feelings.

SOURCE: Bumpass, E. R., Fagelman, F. D., and Brix, R. J. "Intervention with Children Who Set Fires." *American Journal of Psychotherapy*, 1983, *37* (3), 328-345.

Elimination of Fire-Setting Behavior

AUTHOR: David J. Kolko

PRECIS: Training the mother of a six-year-old boy to eliminate the youngster's fire-setting behavior.

INTRODUCTION: Bobby, a six-year-old boy who was developmentally disabled, was referred for treatment of a fire-setting episode in which he set his mother's bed on fire and then immediately told her about the incident. Previous evaluations found Bobby to be delayed in cognitive, visual-motor, and language development. The mother had been diagnosed as mentally retarded as a child and was illiterate. Upon initial interview, the mother revealed that Bobby often set fires and often fought with his sister. She did not report the imposition of any consequences for Bobby's fire setting.

TREATMENT: A multicomponent behavioral intervention was implemented when it became apparent that the consistent application of a reprimand and subsequent time-out procedure contingent upon fire setting had no effect on Bobby's behavior. Furthermore, no specific set of antecedent conditions or reinforcement contingencies could be consistently correlated with the boy's fire-setting episodes. The multicomponent behavioral intervention was taught to the mother during three sessions through the use of simple instructions, modeling, feedback, and social reinforcement.

The first component of the program consisted of the mother imposing upon Bobby daily sessions of negative practice with corrective consequences. This involved Bobby's setting a fire under the mother's supervision each day. The purpose was to reduce any reinforcement Bobby was obtaining from the spontaneous fire setting or the damage that the fire caused. The fire setting was standardized so that each day Bobby would obtain a pack of matches, two pieces of paper, a metal basin, a pail of water, a hose, a scrub brush, and dishwashing liquid. The mother helped Bobby light the fire in the metal basin. This was followed by corrective consequences, as Bobby was required to wash the basin. During this entire practice, the mother discussed fire safety procedures with Bobby. This component of the treatment occurred daily for four weeks and then was reduced to every other day for two weeks. The negative practice was then thinned out to once per week and was then discontinued.

The other component of the treatment was the implementation of token reinforcement. Bobby received a puzzle piece for each day that he exhibited no fire-setting behaviors. When Bobby completed a puzzle, he was permitted to keep it and also to have a reinforcer he had previously chosen. If fire-setting behavior occurred, Bobby would lose all the puzzle pieces he had already obtained. Puzzles with increasing numbers of pieces were selected in order to establish a noncontinuous schedule of reinforcement for appropriate behavior. Reinforcers were earned for twenty-two weeks before they were eliminated and replaced by social reinforcement.

RESULTS: Treatment procedures were implemented for twenty-three weeks. Upon their initiation, Bobby's fire-setting behavior terminated; there were no reported instances of fire setting during the treatment period. A follow-up fifteen months later revealed no recurrence of the targeted behavior. In addition, Bobby's nontreated aggressive behaviors (fighting with his sister) also decreased significantly.

COMMENTARY: The multicomponent behavioral program proved to be effective in eliminating Bobby's fire setting. Saturation, overcorrection, and paradoxical intention, as well as token reinforcement implemented by the mother, appeared to be beneficial interventions. In addition, value lies in the program's simplicity, as a mother diagnosed as mentally retarded and illiterate was able to carry out the procedures with her developmentally disabled son. Replications of the program and further research are certainly warranted.

SOURCE: Kolko, D. J. "Multicomponent Parental Treatment of Firesetting in a Six-Year-Old Boy." *Journal of Behavior Therapy and Experimental Psychiatry*, 1983, *14* (4), 349-353.

Treating Fire Setting
with Structured Fantasies

AUTHOR: Terry L. Stawar

PRECIS: The use of structuring fantasies in order to promote more adaptive cognitive control in a youngster demonstrating fire setting.

INTRODUCTION: Stawar suggests that the structuring of children's fantasies leads to the strengthening of adaptive fantasies, which results in children gaining cognitive control over their behavior. The case of a seven-year-old fire setter illustrates Stawar's technique.

CASE STUDY: The seven-year-old boy had a history of frequent fire-setting episodes. At the time of referral, the mother's reprimands, spankings, and lectures had all proved ineffective in controlling the boy's fire setting. A treatment was devised in which an operantly structured fantasy, in conjunction with a contingency management program, was implemented.

The structured fantasy was repeatedly told to the boy during two fifty-minute sessions. The fantasy, which was to provide an incompatible response to fire setting, involved a boy who found matches and who immediately would take the matches to an adult without striking any of them. The story was acted out several times with dolls. In the story, the boy was rewarded with candies for giving the matches to an adult. During the sessions, the boy was asked to tell the story after hearing it, and he was rewarded with candies and praise for telling it back correctly. In addition, he was reinforced each time the boy in the story was reinforced.

After the two storytelling sessions, the mother left a nonfunctional book of matches where the boy could find them and rewarded him for following the story (giving the matches to an adult).

RESULTS: After the two weeks of storytelling, no episodes of fire setting were reported. The mother was instructed to retell the story once a week and to continue to reinforce the boy for appropriate behavior, such as giving matches to an adult.

COMMENTARY: The structured fantasy technique proved to be very effective in providing this seven-year-old with an appropriate behavioral alternative to fire setting. This approach could be utilized with other undesirable behaviors, and thus research on the technique should prove valuable. The inclusion of reinforcers during the storytelling may be a crucial aspect of the treatment and therefore should not be overlooked.

SOURCE: Stawar, T. L. "Fable Mod: Operantly Structured Fantasies as an Adjunct in the Modification of Firesetting Behavior." *Behavior Therapy and Experimental Psychiatry*, 1976, 7, 285-287.

<hr>

Psychodynamics and Family Dynamics of Boys Exhibiting Fire Setting

AUTHORS: Jay C. Williams and Landrum S. Tucker

PRECIS: Exploration of the meaning of fire-setting behavior in eight boys.

INTRODUCTION: Williams and Tucker analyzed the psychodynamics and family dynamics of eight latency-age boys between the ages of six and thirteen who had been treated on a child psychiatry inpatient unit for fire-setting behavior. According to psychoanalytic theory, fire setting is a multiply determined symptom of an underlying conflict that involves a wish to burn a parent who has been a rival or who has withheld love, as well as an expression of conflict that the child fears will kill him or her.

Child Psychodynamics: Many similarities were found in the eight boys' histories and dynamics. The boys demonstrated strong oral and phallic themes in play, as well as anal preoccupations. In general, the boys' development was arrested at pre-oedipal levels, as oedipal conflicts had never been resolved. Parental loss and parental pathology were viewed as the cause of this arrested development. In all cases, the fathers were absent from the homes, and no father had lived in the home past the boy's third year. In addition, four of the eight boys were diagnosed as borderline psychotic. However, all eight of the youngsters experienced destructive fantasies.

Family Dynamics: Although the fathers were not present in the home and did not regularly visit the boys, information about the fathers was obtained from the mothers. Reportedly, the fathers had impulse control problems (that is, they experienced alcoholism and had used physical abuse). All of the mothers were severely disturbed. Seven were diagnosed as having personality disorders, and one was diagnosed as being a paranoid schizophrenic. Seven of the mothers had histories of depression, and four had attempted suicide. In all the families, the boys experienced closer relationships with their mothers than with any of their siblings. The relationship was a hostile-dependent one in which the child was sometimes favored and sometimes scapegoated by the mother. Seven of the mothers were openly hostile toward the fathers.

Summary: In summary, the boys studied revealed a hostile-dependent relationship with their mothers, which led to the children's acting out of the mothers' aggressive impulses toward the fathers. The youngsters exhibited behavior disorders or borderline psychotic functioning and remained fixated at a pre-oedipal level of development.

COMMENTARY: The authors conclude that the boys' fire-setting behavior was a multidetermined symptom. The behavior represented not only the mothers' impulses to destroy the fathers but also the boys' rage at the fathers. This formulation can be helpful in aiding clinicians who work with fire setters in focusing their treatment interventions.

SOURCE: Williams, J. C., and Tucker, L. S. "Fire Setting: A Family Affair." Unpublished manuscript, 1984.

Behavioral Treatment
of Fire-Setting Behavior

AUTHORS: Patrick McGrath, Peter G. Marshall, and Katherine Prior

PRECIS: Utilizing a comprehensive behavioral treatment program for modifying fire-setting behavior.

INTRODUCTION: Tony, an eleven-year-old resident of a group home who was placed because of fire-setting behavior, was referred for treatment. Tony was referred as a result of his having set fire to the group home. An analysis of Tony's behavior and history led to the formulation of four hypotheses regarding his fire setting. Fire setting was thought to be the result of the following: (1) difficulties in coping with stress, (2) difficulties in relating appropriately to peers, (3) the reinforcing aspect of fire setting, and (4) lack of acknowledgment of the realization of the dangers of fire setting. The authors devised an intensive treatment program that addressed these four hypotheses.

TREATMENT: To address the first two hypotheses (that is, that fire setting was the result of difficulties in coping or in peer relationships), social skills training was implemented. In fourteen one-hour sessions, Tony was trained through the use of role play modeling and rehearsal with videotaped feedback. Situations introduced during the training sessions included Tony being teased or losing in a game. As role playing occurred, Tony was videotaped. The tapes were then viewed and appropriate alternative responses were discussed, modeled by the therapists, and rehearsed by Tony each time an inappropiate behavior was observed. An example of an alternative response was covert self-talk statements.

The authors introduced overcorrection procedures to address the hypothesis that fire setting occurred because it was reinforcing. The overcorrection involved Tony's setting of a fire in a metal basin and then a thorough cleaning of the basin. In addition, Tony was required to repeat statements about the dangers of fires throughout these sessions.

Covert sensitization was utilized to increase Tony's awareness of the dangers of fire setting and to make the behavior aversive. Covert sensitization involved anxiety-inducing audiotapes that gave a description of Tony setting a fire and then getting caught in it. These tapes were followed by tapes describing Tony thinking about setting a fire but finding alternative coping methods. Finally, a fire safety component was used, in which Tony visited a fire station, viewed fire safety films, visited sites of fires he had set, and read books on fire safety.

In order to guide the treatment, collateral behaviors such as conversation, sharing, and sportsmanship were monitored on a daily basis. The treatment program was effective in eliminating fire-setting behavior and in increasing collateral behaviors.

COMMENTARY: The effectiveness of components of this approach, such as overcorrection, has been demonstrated in other cases. Adding together several components to devise a treatment proved effective, but it did not allow for the assessment of the value of each separate component. As has been found with other antisocial behaviors, social skills training that enables the expansion of appropriate social responses is beneficial in decreasing inappropriate social acts.

SOURCE: McGrath, P., Marshall, P. G., and Prior, K. "A Comprehensive Treatment Program for a Fire-Setting Child." *Journal of Behavior Therapy and Experimental Psychiatry*, 1979, *10*, 69-72.

Additional Readings

Carstens, C. "Application of a Work Penalty Threat in the Treatment of a Case of Juvenile Fire Setting." *Journal of Behavior Therapy and Experimental Psychiatry*, 1982, *13* (2), 159-161.

Carstens presents the case of a four-year-old who was engaging in fire-setting behavior. Parents were instructed to impose a work penalty on the child for each instance of his touching matches or a cigarette lighter. The work penalty involved one hour of hard labor, in which the child was required to engage in a tedious chore, such as scrubbing the spaces between the kitchen tiles with a toothbrush. Immediate suppression of the fire-setting behavior occurred, with no instances of recurrence at a six-month follow-up. The author cautions that the technique needs to be further researched and that it may be best suited for young children with a short history of fire-setting behavior.

Last, C. G., Greist, D., and Kazdin, A. E. "Physiological and Cognitive Assessment of a Fire-Setting Child." *Behavior Modification,* 1985, *9* (1), 94–102.

The authors discuss use of a multidimensional intervention approach for fire-setting behavior. Data for the development of the approach are generated through assessment of physiological and cognitive responses of a twelve-year-old fire setter during the viewing of slides of fire-setting and non-fire-setting scenes. The physiological measures obtained were heart rate and skin potential; those could be used to establish a hierarchy of the boy's responses to fire-setting activities. In addition, cognitive responses were assessed by having the boy write down comments using a thought-listing procedure for each slide. Although the boy was not treated, as he was institutionalized prior to the implementation, the multidimensional assessment reveals valuable information in regard to this boy's reactions in relation to fire setting.

Pine, S., and Louie, D. "Juvenile Fire Setters: Do the Agencies Help?" *American Journal of Psychiatry,* 1979, *136* (4A), 433–435.

The records of a local fire marshal, juvenile court, and psychiatric clinic were reviewed for sixty-nine juvenile fire setters who had been identified in the previous three-year period. The review revealed that these agencies were not effective in coordinating their efforts or in modifying the fire-setting behaviors of the identified individuals. The authors recommend removal of the child from the home for a short period of time, with placement in either a foster home or a residential treatment center as an appropriate intervention for fire setters, as maladaptive family environments seem to contribute to the behavior.

Runaway Reaction

The "runaway reaction" is a fairly new diagnostic category. It is described as follows: "Individuals with this disorder characteristically escape from threatening situations by running away from home for a day or more without permission. Typically they are immature and timid and feel rejected at home, inadequate, and friendless. They often steal furtively" (American Psychiatric Association. Diagnostic and Statistical Manual of Mental Disorders. *[3rd ed.]* Washington, D.C.: American Psychiatric Association, 1980).

Each year between 600,000 and 1,000,000 American teenagers run away from their homes. Most of these youth are from white suburbs, at least half are females, and many are no older than thirteen or fourteen. Drug abuse is similar to the runaway reaction as a high-frequency mental health issue for teenage Americans. Like drug abuse, running away has proven extremely difficult to understand and to treat.

Parental Feelings and Perceptions
in Regard to Their Runaway Children

AUTHOR: Eileen Spillane-Grieco

PRECIS: Parental viewpoints are examined in an attempt to fa- cilitate understanding of runaways.

INTRODUCTION: Although most literature pertaining to ado- lescent runaways focuses on the child's point of view, Spillane- Grieco decided to focus on the feelings and perceptions of par- ents of runaways. The author notes that teenage running away may be a result of either pathology on the youngsters' part or poor family relationships. However, the most recent data sug- gest that there are multisystems involved in children's lives and cause-effect explanations may not be as clearcut as they once appeared to be. Therefore, Spillane-Grieco focused on the par- ents and their perceptions.

Empathic understanding, defined as the ability to put oneself in the place of another and to see the world as he or she does, and positive regard, defined as the ability to give and re- ceive positive feelings, were the two concepts used. Runaways were operationally defined as youngsters between the ages of twelve and eighteen who left home with the intent of running away and who stayed away from home without parental permis- sion for more than forty-eight hours. In addition, the runaways in this study did not have records and were not considered juve- nile delinquents.

TREATMENT: Forty-three parents of thirty runaways (twenty- nine mothers and fourteen fathers) participated in the study. In all cases, the runaways had returned home and were included in the data collected. Initially, both the parents and the runaways participated in an interview that took place in their own homes. Specific questions about the child's running away were asked of both parents and teens. The parents were then asked a set of standardized questions: Why did the child run away? Did an in- cident lead up to the event? Did they want the child to return

home? Had they ever run away as children? The parents and
children then responded to the Barrett-Lennard Relationship
Inventory designed to measure empathy and positive regard.
The parents' scores on the scale were then compared with those
of a control group. The control group consisted of forty-three
parents of high school students who had never run away.

RESULTS: Parents' scores were separated into three categories
for each factor: empathy or positive regard felt by the mother
from the child, empathy or positive regard felt by the father
from the child, and empathy or positive regard felt by the parents together from the child. The last category was used only in
the thirteen instances in which the parents were living together.
In regard to empathic understanding, the runaways' parents
scored significantly lower in each category than did the non-
runaways' parents. When comparing scores of the parents of
runaways with the scores of the non-runaways' parents, the authors note that there was no significant difference in feelings of
empathy between parent and child. In regard to positive regard,
similar results were obtained, with runaways' parents feeling
much less positive regard from their children. However, the runaways' mothers reported feeling significantly less positive regard
from their children than the children reported feeling from their
mothers.

COMMENTARY: The current study adds valuable information
to the understanding of families in which youngsters use runaway behavior as a coping mechanism. Apparently, the parents
in this study experience relationships with their adolescents that
are characterized by poor communication and more negative
than positive feedback. The results obtained suggest that professionals working with runaways need to focus on the family and
not only teach more effective communication skills to parents
and children but also aid families in developing empathy and
positive regard.

SOURCE: Spillane-Grieco, E. "Feelings and Perceptions of Parents of Runaways." *Child Welfare*, 1984, *63* (2), 159–166.

The Family Structure of Runaways

AUTHOR: Thomas P. Guillotta

PRECIS: A conceptual model of the family structure of runaways is used to gain understanding of a youngster's running away.

INTRODUCTION: Guillotta examines existing information on runaways and proposes that in order to understand runaway behavior the relationships between the runaways and their parents need to be understood. Guillotta points out that not all adolescents who are considered runaways actually meet the criteria of being classified a runaway. The National Center for Health Statistics definition states that running away is "leaving or staying away on purpose, knowing you would be missed, intending to stay away from home at least for some time." The author points out that this definition leaves a group of youngsters who cannot be classified as runaways but who can be categorized as throwaways. Throwaways are defined as "young people who do not willingly choose to leave home but are for whatever reasons placed out of their homes by their parents with the intention that they not return." This situation calls attention to the need of differentiating between runaways and throwaways and understanding the different family structures that lead to each situation.

Family structures of runaways typically reveal conflicts between parent(s) and child over control issues. In addition, runaways and their parents typically demonstrate a lack of trust in each other. The youngsters usually perceive their parents as not listening to them, and the parents usually perceive the youngsters as disobedient, insensitive, and uncaring. There is generally a fear of being hurt or rejected, and communication between the child and parents is typically very weak. In spite of these characteristics, the prognosis for the runaway and his or her family is much better than that of the throwaway.

The throwaway usually comes from a family that is much more pathological. When parents ask the youngster to leave or abandon a youngster, the bonds between the child and parents tend to break. The parents of throwaways are often found to have neglected their child and to have exhibited a lack of caring for the child. Therefore, throwaways tend to be much more pathological than runaways, as they usually have a history of social and academic failure that precedes the parents' rejection. As a result, most throwaways are isolated youngsters who tend to feel useless and inadequate.

COMMENTARY: In discussing two different categories of youngsters not living with their families, throwaways and runaways, Guillotta reminds professionals to look closely at the etiology of a behavior. In treating a youngster and/or his or her family, it is always important to understand the family structure. Research on the families of both runaways and throwaways is apparently needed and would be valuable. In addition, it is important that the youngster not always be singled out as the maladaptive family member.

SOURCE: Guillotta, T. P. "Leaving Home: Family Relationships of the Runaway Child." *Social Casework: The Journal of Contemporary Social Work,* 1979, *56,* 111-114.

Additional Readings

Adams, G. R., and Munro, G. "Portrait of the North American Runaway: A Critical Review." *Journal of Youth and Adolescence,* 1979, *8* (3), 359-373.

The authors present a review of the literature on runaways. Current findings reveal that runaways cannot be classified as the pathological group they were once thought to be, as no definite relationship between personality and runaway behavior is found. Many factors are reported to precipitate running away, including parental rejection, family conflict, and school problems. In addition, runaways are found to be dissatisfied with existing values not only in their families but also in society. An alternative values model is reviewed, as is the deindividuation model. This suggests that runaways see themselves as being inadequately reinforced socially and psychologically.

Gutierres, S. E., and Reich, J. W. "A Developmental Perspective on Runaway Behavior: Its Relationship to Child Abuse." *Child Welfare*, 1981, *60*, 89–94.

In this article, the authors examine a correlation between child abuse and later runaway behavior. Data from a study of 5,392 children referred for child abuse to the Arizona Department of Child Protective Services reveal that abused children tend to be more likely to engage in withdrawal types of behavior than do nonabused children from a control group. Victims of physical abuse reportedly engage in more truancy and runaway behavior than in aggressive, violent types of juvenile delinquent acts. This escape behavior can be viewed as an appropriate coping device for a child who is repeatedly abused while remaining in a family situation. Therefore, implications for the classification and treatment of runaways need to be examined.

Margolin, M. H. "Styles of Service for Runaways." *Child Welfare*, 1976, *60* (3), 205–215.

Margolin examines available services for and groups delivering services to runaways. A flowchart is presented with accompanying critiques of a number of delivery styles and systems. The information is quite useful to individuals needing to adopt a plan of action for dealing with runaway behavior.

Mirkin, M. P., Raskin, P. A., and Antognini, F. C. "Parenting, Protecting, Preserving: Mission of the Adolescent Female Runaway." *Family Process*, 1984, *23*, 63–73.

The authors present a structural/strategic model for the treatment of families with a runaway female adolescent. In this model, the family is approached as a system that is developmentally inappropriate and therefore maintaining patterns of behavior that encourage running away. The runaway is viewed as serving three functions in the family: parenting her parents and siblings, regulating marital distance and therefore preserving the parents' marriage, and keeping the family at a preadolescent developmental stage.

Interventions are implemented to lessen the adolescent's power in the family and to enable the family to deal with the adolescent's need to separate, individuate, and become more independent. This is accomplished through uniting the parents to take control of the adolescent by redefining the child versus the adult role. This enables a hierarchy to be established or reestablished in the family whereby the teenager becomes aligned with the siblings. In addition, interventions are made in the marital relationship that redirect the focus from the marital conflict to effective parenting. This waives the runaway's role as the protector of the marriage. Finally, the family is helped to deal with the new stage of development—the transition into adolescence—which allows the teenager to separate appropriately while remaining a functioning family member.

4

Hyperkinetic
Behavior

The word *hyperkinetic* literally means abnormally increased and usually uncontrolled, purposeless movement. This chapter divides hyperkinesia into three types of behaviors. The first type, restless, hyperactive behavior, clearly fits the literal description of hyperkinesia. The second (short attention span) and third (impulsiveness and low frustration tolerance) types are related problems, but these do not necessarily include excessive movement. These three categories of behavior have been linked together under many different labels. In a nationally sponsored study to define minimal brain dysfunction, ten characteristics most cited in the literature were listed in order of frequency. Hyperactivity was first on the list, disorders of attention fifth, and impulsiveness sixth (Clements, S. D. *Minimal Brain Dys-*

function in Children—Terminology and Identification. Washington, D.C.: U.S. Department of Health, Education and Welfare, 1966). In the recent literature, children showing some combination of behaviors covered here increasingly have been called *learning disabled.*

It is striking that the most recent revision of the American Psychiatric Association's *Diagnostic and Statistical Manual of Mental Disorders* (3rd ed.) (Washington, D.C.: American Psychiatric Association, 1980) (DSM III) uses the diagnosis attention deficit disorder with or without hyperactivity; the two key symptoms are inattention and impulsivity. This new diagnosis fits perfectly with the classification we have used, which is based on factor-analytic research. Restless, hyperactive behavior is the same as DSM III's hyperactivity. Short attention span is similar to DSM III's inattention. Impulsiveness and low frustration tolerance is somewhat more inclusive than DSM III's impulsivity.

DSM III reports a usual number of symptoms for children from eight to ten years old, the peak age range for professional referral. Younger children usually have a greater number of and more severe symptoms. Older children have fewer and less severe symptoms. The onset is before seven years, and the duration is of at least six months. A child in the *inattention* category exhibits at least three of the following symptoms: He or she often fails to finish things, often does not seem to listen, is easily distracted, has difficulty concentrating on schoolwork or other tasks requiring sustained attention, and/or has difficulty sticking to a play activity. In the category of *impulsivity,* at least three of the following are true: The child often acts before thinking, shifts excessively from one activity to another, has difficulty organizing work, needs a lot of supervision, frequently calls out in class, and/or has difficulty awaiting turn in games or group situations. Symptoms of *hyperactivity* include at least two of the following: The child excessively runs about or climbs on things, has difficulty staying seated, moves about excessively during sleep, and/or is always on the go or acts as if driven by a motor.

A continuing issue has been the inferred physiological

(neurological, biochemical, and so on) cause of learning disabilities or attention deficit disorder. Many professionals believe that accepting the neurological basis of hyperkinetic behavior leads to tolerance and improves the attitudes of the children and adults around them. There is still a difference of opinion as to whether it is possible to diagnose a child's difficulty as being caused by a central processing dysfunction. The evidence points to the feasibility and desirability of fully evaluating children in order to pinpoint deficits in processing information and responding appropriately. As in the rest of this book, the articles in this chapter present problematic behaviors and alternative approaches. The techniques employed may well diminish the behaviors in question and promote more adaptive, satisfying behavior. Most therapists agree that even if the cause of the problem is physiological, treatment (cognitive behavior modification, counseling, drugs, relaxation, and so forth) still can be effective.

This chapter reports considerable success in improving hyperkinetic behaviors, using very different methods. Although stimulant drugs have been used for many years, the evidence suggests that other approaches should be tried first. In many cases, drugs are not necessary, because the behavior can be modified. There is general consensus that the teaching and maintaining of adaptive behavior and reduction of problem behavior are essential. Adaptive behavior may be defined as purposeful, calm, attentive, reflective, and tolerant. When behavior is not improved even though methods are well planned and followed through, drugs may be an invaluable asset in helping the child respond to treatment procedures. When drugs are used, psychological and educational methods should be employed at the same time.

An important study (Stableford, W., Butz, R., Hasazi, J., Leitenberg, H., and Peyser, J. "Sequential Withdrawal of Stimulant Drugs and Use of Behavior Therapy with Two Hyperactive Boys." *American Journal of Orthopsychiatry*, 1976, *46*, 302-312) found that placebos were as effective as stimulant drugs in maintaining behavior that was not hyperactive. This indicates that the drug itself did not produce appropriate, controlled behavior. Therefore, even when drugs are used to reduce extreme behavior, natural consequences soon may maintain appropriate behavior. Drugs might then be successfully discontinued in a very short time (rather than being given for many years) by substituting placebos. Careful, thorough psychotherapy might be effective in preventing psychological dependency on drugs.

We suggest that family discussions of a child's behavior and probable neurological causes often may improve the family atmosphere. More tolerant and accepting parental attitudes alone may lead to some improvement in behavior. We believe that better attitudes improve receptivity to the methods presented here. In addition, many school-based approaches are applicable to home use. Parents may employ many of the individual techniques with their child and can use the group approaches with siblings. We strongly urge that parents use methods similar to those being used by the child's school. This type of consistency and coordination leads to quicker and more enduring improvement. A simple and very effective procedure is for parents to use a powerful reinforcement at home when the child shows improved behavioral control in school.

Restless, Hyperactive Behavior

The word restless *means "without rest" or "continuously moving." Whether or not restlessness is under a child's control has long been an issue. Restlessness has been interpreted as caused by diffuse anxiety, an attempt to feel more at ease, or constitutional factors. Hyperactivity is excessive movement, going beyond a normal or acceptable limit. Excessive activity may be caused by physiological factors, learning (purposeful or inadvertent reinforcement), or reactions to psychological stress. Regardless of the cause of hyperactivity or restlessness, children can learn to slow down and be more purposeful and efficient. Estimates of hyperactivity in young children vary from 5 to 10 percent. The magnitude of the problem may be seen by the fact that approximately 40 percent of children are referred to mental health clinics for hyperactivity. Hyperactive boys outnumber girls by about seven to one. An unusually large number of different methods reportedly have been effective in reducing hyperactivity. These include relaxation, meditation, behavior modification, dietary management, psychotropic drugs, environmental manipulation (especially curriculum adjustment), modeling, verbal self-instruction, self-monitoring, and insight-oriented psychotherapy.*

Sugar Consumption and Hyperactivity in Young Children

AUTHORS: Ronald J. Prinz, William A. Roberts, and Elaine Hantman

PRECIS: Reducing hyperkinesis in four- to seven-year-old youngsters by limiting their ingestion of sucrose.

INTRODUCTION: Recently, researchers have given increasing attention to toxicological factors in the environment, such as lead and food additives, that may cause or contribute to children's hyperactive behaviors. Largely neglected, however, has been systematic research on sugar ingestion as a factor that may be responsible for nervous or restless behaviors. Prinz, Roberts, and Hantman report that sucrose consumption did significantly correlate with observed hyperactivity in a study involving twenty-eight four- to seven-year-old hyperactive boys and girls.

TREATMENT: The children were recruited primarily by means of media advertisements soliciting parents who wanted help for their offspring's problem behaviors; in addition, eight of the children were referred by mental health professionals, schools, and physicians. Participants were youngsters who had presented problem behaviors over two or more years in multiple settings. As a group, these descriptors applied: excessively active, difficult to manage, moody, frequently failing to finish tasks, restless, fidgety, exhibiting social adjustment difficulties with peers. The twenty-eight children in the treatment group and the twenty-six controls (who were paid to participate on the basis of their parents' assertion that their behavior was not excessively active) were matched on a number of demographic variables—family income, parents' occupation, education level, and family size.

Each mother meticulously recorded her child's total food and beverage consumption at and between meals for a week, not changing the child's habitual eating patterns for this time. The scorers, who did not know the behavioral characteristics of the child associated with each record, analyzed these dietary records according to four categories: (1) products containing a substantial amount of sugar, (2) refined carbohydrates (for example, white bread), which were not considered sugar, (3) nutritional foods that did not fall into either of the above-named categories (such as meats, vegetables, fresh fruits, dairy products, and whole-grain breads), and (4) unclassifiable food entries, such as sugarless gum and sauces. Quantitative computations were made daily of total food consumption, sugar-product consumption, and other combinations of the data, such as ratio of sugar products to nutritional foods score.

After gathering the dietary data, the authors made nonintrusive videotaped records of the children's play activities during two fifteen-minute observation periods. Trained observers who were ignorant as to the children's dietary information rated them on four behavioral categories: (1) *destruction,* defined as attempts to damage any objects in the playroom, (2) *hitting or kicking* (striking any objects in the playroom), (3) *throwing* any playroom objects, (4) *restlessness,* considered repetitive movements of the head or extremities. Additionally, they noted the frequency of each child's movements from one playroom quadrant to another.

RESULTS: Significant positive associations were found between sugar intake and the young hyperactive children's behavior in the playroom. Most striking was the correlation between sugar-product consumption and expression of agitated behavior. In the case of the control group, the sugar intake variable related to movement patterns (quadrant changes). The authors conclude from their data that not only does high sucrose ingestion lead to adverse effects in hyperactive children, but possibly sugar affects nonhyperactive children, too, albeit in different ways.

COMMENTARY: While causation cannot be proved from correlation and further experimental studies are needed, Prinz and his colleagues have opened the door to investigating a facet of diet not previously explored. Acknowledging the fledgling state of research on sucrose consumption and hyperactivity and the conclusions that can be drawn based on what is now known, counselors, psychotherapists, and others who work with hyperactive children and their families (and other children as well) can caution them about the possible detrimental impact of consuming large quantities of sugar. It would be interesting to see other investigations carried out that examine dietary effects on measures other than activity level and aggression, such as self-image and attributions about the determinants of outcomes.

SOURCE: Prinz, R. J., Roberts, W. A., and Hantman, E. "Dietary Correlates of Hyperactive Behavior in Children." *Journal of Consulting and Clinical Psychology*, 1980, *48*, 760–769.

Food Allergy Treatment for Hyperactivity

AUTHOR: Doris J. Rapp

PRECIS: Reducing hyperkinetic symptoms in six- to fifteen-year-olds by food therapy.

INTRODUCTION: The efficacy of dietary management of hyperactivity has been controversial for more than three-quarters of a century. The theories of Dr. Ben Feingold (Feingold, B. F. *Why Your Child Is Hyperactive.* New York: Random House, 1975) gave renewed impetus to vigorous debate on treating hyperactive children by controlling their ingestion of "problem foods." Rapp reports a study of food allergy treatment for eight hyperactive youngsters with a positive allergy history, most of them markedly so.

TREATMENT: In the study, Dr. Rapp first placed the patients on a simple one-week diet that eliminated the major foods thought to cause or be related to hyperactivity—for example, artificial food coloring, sugar, milk, corn, cocoa, wheat, eggs, preservatives, and orange juice. After following the diet for one week and showing evidence of improvement, the children were challenged on a daily basis with each of these individual foods, one per day, during the second week of the diet. Obvious cause-and-effect relationships were noted in some children in relation to specific foods. The children were then placed on individual diets that excluded the foods to which they appeared to be sensitive for three to six months; during that period of time the youngsters improved. The children were then tested for allergies by using the provocation/neutralization method of allergy testing. This means that they were skin tested in a single-blind manner with stock allergy extract for the individual foods in such a way as to reproduce their symptoms. Usually the intradermal skin-test wheal increased in size. Progressively weaker dilutions of the same food allergy extract were then administered to eliminate the symptoms that had been produced by the provocation dosage. The dilution that was found to eliminate the symptoms was called the "neutralization extract dosage."

The children were then treated with an extract that contained the treatment or neutralization dilutions for each food to which they were sensitive. Treatment was administered either once a day subcutaneously or three times a day sublingually (under the tongue). After one to three months of such treatment, the youngsters were found to be able to ingest moderate amounts of the foods to which they had previously been found to be sensitive without adverse effects.

In the final double-blind food treatment phase of this study, three bottles of extract were prepared. All of them were identical in color and taste and were labeled A, B, and C. They were coded by a local pharmacist. Two bottles contained placebos, the other contained the food allergy extract solution. During this phase of treatment, the youngsters were instructed to refrain from eating all artificially colored foods. Daily dietary records were maintained. Parents were told to give their children the randomly coded solutions, A, B, or C, in the same manner as they had given them their allergy extract in the past, for a period of five to seven days. (Two sets of parents, however, decided to test their children only on weekdays.) Five children could easily differentiate the two placebos from the active antigens. Of the three who could not, two had a recurrence of their original symptoms within two to four weeks. Only one remained well on an unrestricted diet without allergy extract therapy.

The global behavioral impressions reported by parents in their ratings on the Parent Abbott Hyperkinesis Index Sheets (a variation of the Conner's Teacher Rating Scale) indicated that prior to the diet the children's activity scores were abnormally elevated (15 to 30). After the one-week diet, the scores had decreased to a normal level (1 to 15). During the diet and the food therapy phase of therapy, the activity scores remained in the normal range. If errors were made in relation to the diet or therapy, it was obvious because the youngsters' symptoms recurred and their activity scores increased.

CASE STUDY: Rapp presents a case history of one of the youngsters participating in this study whom she considers representative of numerous patients seen in her clinical practice. A diet that eliminated artificial food coloring, cocoa, milk, wheat, sugar, corn, eggs, oranges, and preservatives usually produces discernible improvement within three to seven days. Symptoms such as headache, abdominal pain, congestion, muscle ache, irritability, depression, and so on returned shortly after the previously omitted foods were returned to the youngster's diet during the second week. The boy's baseline hyperkinesis sheet score was 22, indicating major home and school activity level problems. Dietary restriction resulted in a lowering of the Abbott score to 12 on the 1-to-30 point scale. For the five months that the child avoided foods to which he appeared to be sensitive, the average Parent Abbott rating fell to 8, reflecting few perceived activity problems. Teachers rated him similarly regarding hyperkinesis, and they reported improved behavior in schoolwork, as well. Prolonged treatment with sublingually administered food allergy extract enabled him to eat in moderation the foods that had previously caused reactions. After two months of such treatment, his activity score was 5. Marked improvement continued to be evident for more than a year after subcutaneous therapy began.

COMMENTARY: This study indicates that food allergy treatment can be an important part of the therapeutic process with certain hyperactive children. Rapp's experience with some families' noncompliance with modified diet prescriptions led her to try treatment with food extracts. The promise of this approach certainly argues for therapists, parents, and school personnel becoming familiar with clues that a child's behavior and learning problems may be allergy-related. Combining this type of treatment with appropriate talk therapy and corrective educational interventions holds promise for maximizing gains for this subset of children. Readers interested in the food allergy treatment approach may wish to consult the following books and articles suggested by Dr. Rapp.

Rapp, D. J. *Allergies and the Hyperactive Child.* New York: Cornerstone Library, 1979, pp. 89-118.

Rapp, D. J., and Bamberg, D. *The Impossible Child.* Buffalo, N.Y.: Practical Allergy Research Foundation, 1986. (P.O. Box 60, Buffalo, NY 14223-0060)

King, D. S. "Can Allergic Exposure Provoke Psychological Symptoms? A Double-Blind Test." *Biological Psychiatry,* 1981, *16,* 3-19.

O'Shea, J. A., and Porter, S. F. "Double-Blind Study of Children with Hyperkinetic Syndrome Treated with Multi-Allergen Extract Sublingually." *Journal of Learning Disabilities,* 1981, *14,* 189.

SOURCE: Rapp, D. J. "Food Allergy Treatment for Hyperkinesis." *Journal of Learning Disabilities,* 1979, *12,* 608-616.

Insight-Oriented Psychotherapy
for Hyperactive Children

AUTHORS: David F. Freeman and Thomas P. Cornwall

PRECIS: Reducing neurotic children's excessive activity levels by resolving intrapsychic conflicts and providing parent guidance.

INTRODUCTION: The authors note that the literature on hyperactive neurotic children is extremely sparse. Such children, whose high level of activity is viewed as being caused by psychogenic conflicts rather than organic or constitutional factors, may represent a majority of cases in which hyperactive symptoms are present. Freeman and Cornwall consider how hyperkinetic behavior may serve as an expression of neurotic conflicts and other emotional factors from various developmental levels rather than merely signalling secondary emotional reaction to a constitutionally based disorder. The authors present five case studies that illustrate combinations of presumed organically determined hyperactivity and psychoneurosis, hyperactivity with neurotic etiology, and a transient form of hyperactivity brought on by unstable family conditions. The two neurotic hyperactivity cases are illustrated below.

CASE STUDY 1: Four-and-a-half-year-old Henry presented aggressive, negativistic, repressive, and hyperactive behaviors. He had undergone an unpleasant medical procedure, which had precipitated a severe angry and anxious reaction. Henry had two weekly psychotherapy sessions for ten months. During this time, collateral therapy was conducted with his parents once weekly. The therapist talked with Henry about his fascination with superheroes, such as the Lone Ranger, Batman, and Superman, and his tendency to subjugate the therapist to the role of his assistant while he played the boss. The therapist interpreted Henry's behaviors to him as reflecting his need to be unusually strong in order to fight off his fears of being weak and his oedipal fears. Gradually, Henry's fantasies changed: He and the therapist became partners who collaborated against an unspecified enemy in order to achieve a common, noble goal. Later, Henry, in his fantasy, allowed himself to assume the role of competent boy and learner whose mentor was the therapist. Anecdotal evidence indicated that as therapy progressed, Henry's hyperactivity decreased in all settings and his school achievement became particularly good for the first time. At five-year follow-up, such gains were sustained.

CASE STUDY 2: Sally, age six-and-a-half, was of small stature, talkative, and imaginative. Also, she was prone to crying spells and was demanding, noncompliant, inattentive, and very distractible. She wanted to be a boy, and she refused to attend school. Psychoanalytically oriented therapy and parent meetings were conducted each week. Sally's fantasies centered on themes of tricking and controlling her parents so that she could receive absolute nurturance. These play themes emerged: the advantages of being a tomboy, curiosity and concerns about body injury, and conflicts and confusions about being strong or weak and about having babies and mothering them rivaling her mother. As she entered latency, elaborating and resolving her wishes, Sally no longer displayed the symptoms that manifested when she began treatment. Six years after finishing analysis, Sally gave signs of adjusting well to the developmental tasks of adolescence.

COMMENTARY: This article addresses a neglected area in the treatment of children presenting hyperactive behaviors. Too often, in focusing on overt behaviors only or by presuming organic etiology, therapists may fail to deal with intense sexual, aggressive, and other conflicts that may underlie—or at least figure prominently in—producing the behaviors that are seen. Insight-oriented psychotherapy and psychoanalysis in such cases can develop understanding and resolve conflicts that inhibit functioning and create anxiety; thus, they can lead to improved emotional development with age-appropriate interpersonal functioning. The therapists' work concurrently with the children's parents appeared to be important to the overall effectiveness of the approach.

SOURCE: Freeman, D. F., and Cornwall, T. P. "Hyperactivity and Neurosis." *American Journal of Orthopsychiatry*, 1980, *50* (4), 704-711.

Behavioral Methods
for Treating Hyperactive Children

AUTHORS: Everett L. Walden and Sheila A. Thompson

PRECIS: Reducing hyperactivity in school and at home by non-medical management means, including environmental manipulations, curriculum adjustments, operant procedures, parent-managed methods, biofeedback, and relaxation training.

INTRODUCTION: Walden and Thompson observe that psychotropic drugs, the most common treatment for resolving hyperactive behavior problems, cause negative side effects for some children and that the long-term consequences of their prolonged use is unclear. They assert that drug therapy should be viewed as an extreme alternative to nonmedical behavior management techniques, and they discuss available intervention methods that therapists, teachers, and parents can use with hyperkinetic children. Such children, it has been conservatively estimated, number 3 million and constitute 7 percent of all children in American elementary schools. Their behavior is characterized by restlessness, attention seeking, disruptiveness, and distractibility.

TREATMENT: Walden and Thompson describe several approaches that can be used to help the hyperactive child adjust to the demands of school and home:
Environment manipulations. These entail changing, structuring, or initiating new activities within various aspects of the child's school or home setting. In the classroom, these may involve altering aspects of the environment that contribute to ex-

cessively stimulating the child, as by removing the child to a quiet area that is devoid of distractions. Providing structure through established routines and avoiding overstimulating activities are other strategies that can assist the hyperactive child to better adjustment.

Curriculum Modifications. The quantity of work, the rate at which the child is expected to complete work, and the sequence of material presented are adjusted. Materials that are clearly defined, tangible manipulatives aid the child by sustaining his or her attention and engaging him or her actively in learning by doing. Tasks are selected that the child can complete successfully in a relatively short time, and short-term learning goals are established. The sense of accomplishment that this promotes in the child is viewed as crucial to creating long-term behavior improvements.

Behavior Management Techniques. Included here are techniques for shaping new behaviors and eliminating undesirable ones. The methods include *positive reinforcement*—tangible and social means of responding to desired behaviors to encourage their recurrence, *shaping*—reinforcing successive approximations of the behaviors ultimately desired, *modeling*—learning through observation and imitation, *contingency contracting*—establishing through prior agreement between the child and the adult who dispenses reinforcement the conditions under which the child will receive his or her rewards, and *time-out*—removing the child from a reinforcing and desirable setting to an environment that is neutral or not desired for a designated period of time.

Home Management Techniques. Parents and even siblings can dispense rewards to children for attaining behavior standards, and behavior management methods commonly used by therapists and other professionals can be applied by trained key family members.

Biofeedback. A child can be made aware of involuntary body functions and learn to control these to some degree. This can result in lowered tension levels and reduced activity levels, along with heightened self-regard and self-confidence.

Relaxation Training. Some hyperactive children are capable of reducing muscle tension by this method of alternately tensing and relaxing various muscles, and by practicing breathing control (that is, holding their breath and then releasing muscles and breath) and comparing the physiological differences between the tensed and relaxed states.

COMMENTARY: The six categories of psychotherapeutic and teaching methods are clearly spelled out, and the authors cite considerable research that supports the efficacy of these techniques with hyperactive children. Many of the methods also have applicability to various other behavior problems covered in this book. The authors advocate specific approaches to confronting the characteristic troublesome behavior of hyperkinetic children, which can be used directly by therapists or taught by consultants to other behavior change agents.

SOURCE: Walden, E. L., and Thompson, S. A. "A Review of Some Alternative Approaches to Drug Management of Hyperactivity in Children." *Journal of Learning Disabilities*, 1981, *14*, 213-217.

Training Parents
to Manage Their Hyperactive Children

AUTHORS: Susan Pollard, Eric M. Ward, and Russell A. Barkley

PRECIS: Training parents to use child behavior management in improving parent-child interactions with young hyperactive boys.

INTRODUCTION: There has been relatively little examination of the efficacy of parent-training programs for hyperactive children and/or children with attention deficit disorders. These children typically present major compliance problems for their parents. The authors looked at the effects of parent training alone and in combination with a psychostimulant (methylphenidate or Ritalin) on three hyperactive boys' compliance with parental commands. They found that instructing mothers in child behavior management was as effective as using methylphenidate in decreasing the frequency of maternal commands to their children and that no additional therapeutic gain was realized from combining treatments. Only the parent training achieved improvement in the amount of positive attention mothers demonstrated after their children complied.

TREATMENT: The boys and their mothers participated in two fifteen-minute sessions per week for at least ten weeks. At these sessions, the mothers were given preprinted instruction pages containing a list of fifteen tasks they were to have their children perform. These activities included home and school chores, such as picking up toys, working at math problems, and so on. At the end of the fifteen minutes, each mother completed a questionnaire comparing the child's playroom behavior to his or her home behavior. Following each session, the mother filled out other behavior-rating scales concerning her child. Baseline observations were gathered on all participating children during the same week.

Three boys were involved in this study. One of the boys took a daily Ritalin dose (7.5 mg. b.i.d.) following the drug-free baseline phase, as prescribed by his pediatrician. The other two boys remained off medication during this time, while their mothers took part in eight training sessions on effective child management. The training covered such topics as improving attending to play and ways to increase compliance. Two two-hour parent-training sessions were held each week for four weeks. After the final parent-training session, these two boys returned to their pretreatment methylphenidate doses (10 mg. b.i.d. and 12.5 mg. b.i.d., respectively), while the other boy remained on his medication and the mothers of all three boys practiced the skills they had been taught earlier. The authors conclude that parent training or Ritalin can successfully improve behavioral problems.

COMMENTARY: Both parent education and individual psychotherapy with children may serve as alternatives to drug therapy
for youngsters diagnosed as hyperactive or having attention
deficit disorder with hyperactivity. Although in the cases presented here little treatment-related changes in child compliance
were noted, this may have been an artifact of the experimental
design, as playroom compliance was rather high initially. In
fact, *sustained* child compliance or attention span improvements were seen, as measured by the mean duration of compliance. The findings of Pollard, Ward, and Barkley should sensi-
tize all who do therapy with hyperactive children and their
families to the fact that treatment reactions have to be carefully examined as to their effectiveness. It is very important to
take into account the type of child behavior and the context,
including others' reactions to the behavior.

SOURCE: Pollard, S., Ward, E. M., and Barkley, R. A. "The Ef-
    fects of Parent Training and Ritalin on the Parent-Child Inter-
    actions of Hyperactive Boys." *Child and Family Behavior
    Therapy,* 1983, *5,* 51–69.

Additional Readings

Abikoff, H., and Gittelman, R. "Does Behavior Therapy Nor-
    malize the Classroom Behavior of Hyperactive Children?"
    Archives of General Psychiatry, 1984, *41,* 449–454.
    Twenty-eight hyperactive children between six and
twelve years old received eight weeks of intensive behavioral
treatment in school and at home. The authors instructed their
parents and teachers in general learning theory principles for
managing their behavior. They developed behavior contracts
that specified goals, for which the children received rewards,
and violations, which were punished. Other techniques in the
behavioral program included therapist modeling and role play-

ing of appropriate behaviors and cognitive restructuring with parents to change attitudes. The behavior therapy program produced a reduction to normal levels in the children's aggression. In other aspects of classroom conduct, however, such as attentiveness, activity level, and impulsivity, the children's behaviors were not normalized.

Bhatera, V., Arnold, L. E., Lorance, T., and Gupta, D. "Muscle Relaxation Therapy in Hyperkinesis: Is It Effective?" *Journal of Learning Disabilities,* 1979, *12,* 411–415.

The authors review the literature on two forms of muscle relaxation in the treatment of hyperkinetic children from six to fifteen years old. The methods reviewed are electromyographic (EMG) biofeedback and progressive muscle relaxation. Different studies have had conflicting results, which probably reflects sample heterogeneity. Bhatara and associates believe that the available evidence is insufficient to support the clinical utility of EMG biofeedback with hyperkinetic children. They point out that progressive muscle relaxation may be at least equally effective and is certainly a more convenient and economical intervention.

Darveaux, D. X. "The Good Behavior Game Plus Merit: Controlling Disruptive Behavior and Improving Student Motivation." *School Psychology Review,* 1984, *13,* 510–514.

Two second-grade boys with a history of inattention and high activity levels participated in a group contingency intervention in a regular classroom over a four-week period. Their classroom was divided into two teams, with one of the boys on each team. The teams earned story time, free play time, or candy in one of two ways: (1) by accumulating less than five violations of posted class rules by team members in a class period or (2) by acquiring merits for completing assigned work at 75 percent or greater accuracy and participating actively in the classroom. Disruptive behavior was reduced markedly, from 72 percent during the initial baseline to 6 percent during the final treatment phase. The boys' academic performance improved from 40 percent accurately completed math assignments pretreatment to 75 percent during treatment phases.

Dunn, F. M., and Howell, R. J. "Relaxation Training and Its
Relationship to Hyperactivity in Boys." *Journal of Clinical Psychology*, 1982, *38*, 92-100.

Over twenty treatment sessions (two to three per week),
ten hyperactive six- to twelve-year-old boys were taught to relax
using relaxation tapes, EMG biofeedback, and/or a combination
of biofeedback and relaxation suggestions. All the treatment
modalities reduced muscle tension for the boys. The children
who learned relaxation methods alone responded most quickly,
but the EMG biofeedback group members made the greatest
long-term improvement in their ability to relax.

Hunsberger, P. "Uses of Instant-Print Photography in Psychotherapy." *Professional Psychology: Research and Practice*, 1984, *15*, 884-890.

Hunsberger discusses psychotherapeutic uses of conventional and instant-print photography. With hyperactive and lan-
guage-delayed children, instant-print materials can facilitate
development of basic perception and communication skills.
With one five-year-old hyperactive boy, for example, the therapist verbally labelled Polaroid snapshots the boy took of his
world and then discussed these with him. In this way, the child
was helped to communicate ideas better with language. Beyond
its contribution to therapeutic dialogue, Hunsberger considers
picture taking to have numerous therapeutic effects, including
increased mastery, self-confidence, and self-esteem, in addition
to being very playful and fun in the context of individual and
group therapy.

Lee, R. M. "Psychopharmacology and Hyperactivity: The Im-
perfect Panacea." *Journal of Clinical Child Psychology*,
1981, *10*, 90-92.

Lee examined research in pharmacotherapy for treating
hyperactive children and found that controversy reigns in definition of terms and in preferred treatment approaches. While
there is a general consensus that psychostimulants are effective
in reducing hyperactivity, long-term social and academic benefits of such treatment are unclear. The three categories of medication reviewed were: psychostimulants, phenothiazines (major
tranquilizers), and tricyclics (antidepressants).

O'Shea, J. A., and Porter, S. F. "Double-Blind Study of Children with Hyperkinetic Syndrome Treated with Multi-Allergen Extract Sublingually." *Journal of Learning Disabilities*, 1981, *14*, 189-191, 237.

Improved activity and behavior patterns were produced in eleven of fourteen hyperkinetic children by means of allergy extract therapy. The children ranged in age from five to thirteen years old. They were tested by the provocative intradermal and sublingual method. Positive tests were determined through behavioral symptom response, and a neutralizing dose was obtained by testing for an improved behavior response. The neutralizing dose was included in a multiallergen extract for sublingual treatment for a period of three weeks. A total of seventeen allergens was tested. Eleven of these were foods, three were inhalants, and three were dyes. During the period of the study, parents kept a daily food diary noting behavioral and physical symptoms. Additionally, the parents and teachers were interviewed weekly.

Short Attention Span

Attention span is the amount of time a child can concentrate. It is the length of time an activity is pursued. Attention requires focusing on relevant stimuli and ignoring irrelevant stimuli (distinguishing figure from background). Without an effective "filtering mechanism," the child cannot attend to the tasks of everyday living or academic demands. The child with a short attention span often is easily distracted, fails to finish what was started, does not listen, and has difficulty with sustaining concentration. It is important to note that even very inattentive children have periods during which they can sustain attention (to a favorite activity or television). Approximately 5 to 10 percent of children have a seriously short attention span. Although attention span increases with age, many people remain relatively inattentive throughout their lives. As will be seen in this section, the treatment approaches for this problem are extraordinarily varied (drugs, diet, conditioning, response-cost lotteries, running, and so on).

Cognitive Self-Instruction
for Increasing Attention

AUTHORS: Ronald T. Brown and Norma Alford

PRECIS: Improving learning disabled children's ability to attend and think by teaching them procedures to define a problem, consider alternative solutions, and verbalize a strategy.

INTRODUCTION: Attentional deficits accompanied by inadequate inhibitory controls are characteristic of many children with learning disorders. Usually efforts to ameliorate these deficiencies have utilized contingency management techniques or stimulant medication. A problem with the former has been that positive reinforcement may actually increase impulsivity and attract the child's attention away from the task and toward the reinforcement. A major concern with the use of psychoactive drugs has to do with the possibility of deleterious side effects associated with their use. In contrast to these means of controlling faulty attention by relying on external agents, Brown and Alford trained children with learning disorders to utilize various methods of self-control. They produced improved performance on measures of reading, attention, and inhibitory control. Moreover, improvement was sustained three months after the training ended.

TREATMENT: Twenty children diagnosed as severely learning disabled participated. All demonstrated faulty attentional processing and poor inhibitory control, as well as reading levels more than two years below their expected grade placement as measured by the Wide Range Achievement Test. The children all scored at least in the low-to-average range on IQ tests. Their average age was twelve-and-a-half years. Over a two-month period, half of the children (the treatment group) were seen individually for two one-hour sessions per week, totalling sixteen sessions, during which they were trained to process information and selectively attend to visual discrimination problems more effectively.

The materials and exercises presented to the children in the treatment condition are described as follows:

Match-To-Sample Tasks Using Arithmetic and Reading Problems. At first, the children were presented simple problems with six alternatives. They were taught to scan and to observe particular details of each problem. Increasingly more difficult problems were given as training progressed. When the children completed each match-to-sample task, they were instructed to correct each wrong choice by drawing in the corrections and verbalizing the necessary change.

Match-To-Sample Tasks Using Drawings. Ten tasks of graduated levels of difficulty were presented in similar fashion to the match-to-sample tasks using arithmetic and reading problems as described above.

Component Analysis Training Using Lists of Words. The participants were presented with a list of words. Their task was to break each word into its component parts.

Detail Analysis Training. Picture cards containing a host of essential details were presented. After the trainer informed the child of the size, shape, and shading of the pertinent detail, the participant had to identify the detailed component.

Memory Task. Here, a picture containing a number of details was presented for ten seconds. The child then had to recall the picture and its details from memory. Increasingly more numerous details were presented as training progressed.

Visual Sequence Training. The children assembled comic strips, attended to each story segment, and related the rationale of each portion of the comic to the final assembled strip. They were required to verbalize their strategy throughout the exercise. As with the previous categories of training tasks, exercises progressed in difficulty level from very easy to quite complex.

Self-Verbalization Procedures. Throughout the training, self-verbalization techniques were utilized. These emphasized: (1) stopping to define a problem and the various steps within it, (2) considering and evaluating several possible solutions before acting on any one, and (3) verbalizing the strategy throughout the training. Whenever children committed an error, they had to correct it and demonstrate to the trainer that they understood the problem and how to proceed to arrive at the correct answer.

The ten children who composed the control group were not exposed to any of the training exercises or materials presented to the treatment group. They were tested with a battery of assessment measures simultaneously with the treatment group at three points: prior to training, at the end of the two-month training period, and three months after training.

RESULTS: The cognitive training package appeared to be effective in modifying the maladaptive performance and inappropriate behaviors of the learning disabled children in that the children in the treatment group improved their performance dramatically on several measures. Reading scores improved an entire grade level, despite the fact that no attempt was made to train the children in the mechanics of reading per se. Training also had a significant effect on attention, particularly attention to letters. Large improvements were also observed on measures of inhibitory control and response efficiency. Little effect was seen in attention to logical synthesis of visual materials, and there was no significant change in spelling and arithmetic achievement. The authors believe that the training period was likely of insufficient length to produce substantive changes on these measures of academic achievement. However, the potential for a cognitive training package to increase academic performance was suggested by the reading improvement that was noted, as well as by anecdotal observations indicating that the treatment group members displayed markedly better on-task classroom behavior and generally improved conduct, particularly when they were aware of the appropriate strategies to use on the tasks they were presented.

COMMENTARY: The method used here can be applied by therapists, parents, and others to help children think through cause-and-effect sequences and logical consequences of past and contemplated actions. The helping agent may begin, for example, by having the child recount what happened at school and then

proceed to consider anticipated problematic situations for the
child. The applications may extend to the interpersonal domain,
including family and peer problems, as well as school-related situations.

SOURCE: Brown, R. T., and Alford, N. "Ameliorating Atten-
   tional Deficits and Concomitant Academic Deficiencies in
   Learning Disabled Children Through Cognitive Training."
   Journal of Learning Disabilities, 1984, *17*, 20–26.

Increasing Focused Behavior
with a Response-Cost Lottery

AUTHORS: Joseph C. Witt and Stephen N. Elliott

PRECIS: Response-cost procedure used in conjunction with
three latency-age boys resulted in improved percentage of task-
appropriate behavior and better academic performance.

INTRODUCTION: A major problem with many techniques that
could assist teachers to control and teach their classes is the im-
practicality of the procedures. Interventions that require excessive time to implement, specialized material resources, or paraprofessional personnel are unrealistic in many cases. Here Witt
and Elliott combined a response-cost technique, in which classroom violations caused the children to lose scrip they had been
given, and a lottery, which required only a small investment of
teacher time and resources and resulted in marked increases in
both appropriate behavior and academic performance. There
was no evidence of negative side effects that sometimes are associated with response-cost procedures.

TREATMENT: Three fourth-grade boys of average intelligence
in an urban public school class had engaged repeatedly in dis-

ruptive school behaviors. Categories of inappropriate behaviors that were targeted for intervention included: gross-motor, object noise, disturbing others' property, contact, verbalizing, turning around, and mouthing objects.

During the baseline phase, the boys' task-appropriate behaviors and observed incidents of inattention were recorded at ten-second intervals during four thirty-minute work periods. No specific contingencies to alter the participants' behavior were in effect at this time. The reversal phase also lasted four days.

The first treatment phase consisted of four half-hour sessions per week for two school weeks. The second treatment phase lasted one week. Prior to the first session, a three-inch by five-inch card was placed on top of each of the three boys' desks. Each card was taped down on three sides, with the fourth side remaining open so that four small slips of colored paper could be placed inside with ends protruding for easy removal. A different color was used for each child's slips. The children were told how the system would work, and classroom rules were explained. Violation of any rule would result in the removal of a slip of paper. Students could turn in slips of paper remaining at the end of a study period; these would be placed in a box for a lottery on Friday. The boy whose slip was selected could choose a reward. Rewards available to the lottery winner included activities, such as extra recess time, and prizes, such as pencils. When the response-cost procedure was carried out, the teacher was careful to explain her reason for removing a slip of paper each time she noticed a rule violation that might not have been obvious to the child committing the infraction.

RESULTS: Participants showed great increases in both on-task behavior and academic performance in the treatment conditions. Time-on-task during baseline averaged 10 percent. When the response-cost lottery was implemented the first time, average appropriate behavior improved to 68 percent. When treatment was discontinued, on-task behavior decreased to 43 percent; it rose again to 73 percent during the second treatment phase. The percentage of completed assignments also changed dramatically as a result of treatment, from 27 percent during the baseline phase to 87 percent when the response-cost lottery was put into place initially; it dropped to 38 percent in the reversal phase and rose back up to 90 percent at the second treatment phase.

The authors emphasize that inappropriate responding cost the boys access to extra privileges but did not intrude on their access to regular privileges, such as recess. This may explain why negative side effects sometimes seen when response-cost procedures are implemented were not observed in this case. At the end of treatment, the teacher acknowledged the superiority of this intervention to the verbal reprimands she had employed in the past.

COMMENTARY: The response-cost method holds great promise for application in nonacademic settings, as well. Professionals may develop a response-cost lottery for parents to use, for example. A goal might be paying attention to family conversations, doing chores in a responsible fashion, and so on.

SOURCE: Witt, J. C., and Elliott, S. N. "The Response-Cost Lottery: A Time-Efficient and Effective Classroom Intervention." *Journal of School Psychology*, 1982, *20*, 155-161.

Relaxation Training to Improve Attention

AUTHORS: David L. Redfering and Mary J. Bowman

PRECIS: Meditative relaxation used with nine eight- to eleven-year-old behaviorally disturbed children increased their focused behavior.

INTRODUCTION: Teachers have traditionally served as primary behavior change agents for children who display impulse control and attentional problems. The behavior modification programs they have administered have tended to meet with limited success. Positive effects have not endured, and many teachers have not been skillful in utilizing behavior management techniques. The need has arisen, therefore, for an internally controlled method of reducing nonattending behavior levels that children can learn and practice easily without relying on external control. Benson's relaxation response technique (Benson, H. *The Relaxation Response.* New York: William Morrow, 1975) meets these criteria. The technique is a meditative method practiced ten to twenty minutes daily, which incorporates four essential elements: (1) a quiet environment, (2) a mental device, such as a word or phrase that is repeated in a specific fashion over and over again, (3) the adoption of a passive attitude, and (4) a comfortable position. The technique was used as treatment for nine behaviorally disturbed children in the following study.

TREATMENT: Eighteen boys and girls from varied socioeconomic backgrounds were selected because parents, school personnel, and other agencies cited their consistent and persistent inability to adjust to regular school programs. They were randomly divided into two equal-sized classrooms such that eight boys and one girl constituted the treatment group and the remaining six boys and three girls made up the class that served as the control group. The children ranged from eight to eleven years old, and none was mentally retarded, psychotic, or organically impaired. All were of average or slightly above-average measured intelligence.

Prior to the treatment phase, children of each group were observed daily for five days as they engaged in their usual class activities. Nonattending behaviors and attending behaviors were recorded at the end of ten consecutive three-minute intervals, with the observation period chosen so as to be at the same time each day. Attending behavior, recorded as "A," was defined as follows: face oriented toward assigned work, carrying out tasks that had been assigned. All other behaviors were considered nonattending and were recorded as "N."

The children receiving relaxation training were given tape-recorded instructions daily over a five-day period in sessions lasting thirty minutes. While the children in the treatment condition practiced Benson's meditative relaxation exercises, the no-treatment group was simply instructed to rest. During the group sessions, the same time-sampling technique that was employed during the baseline phase was used for recording nonattending behaviors.

RESULTS: Treatment resulted in a significant decrease, nearly 60 percent, in nonattending behaviors for the children who learned Benson's relaxation response technique. This was more than triple the mean change in total number of nonattending behaviors that was observed among members of the rest group. Moreover, the children who participated in the treatment group reported that they enjoyed the calming effects that resulted from applying the procedure, as well as the time devoted to a new activity. Past studies were reviewed in which relaxation training helped children to improve levels of attention, classroom behavior, and other cognitive and academic performances.

COMMENTARY: This is an economical procedure easily administered by any professional or by a parent. This type of technique may be enhanced by having children practice relaxing by themselves, in groups with peers, or while supervised by a parent. Periodic relistening to the relaxation tape should be planned. As with any method with children, the procedure should be done in a positive context. Parents or professionals should describe the process as fun or as a game. The potential uses of relaxation practice should be discussed with the children. They should be helped to see how relaxation methods may be used before stressful situations, such as tests, important sports events, or parties, and even before serious family discussions. When a child experiences overanxiety, distractibility, or anxiety, he or she should relax and feel calmer.

SOURCE: Redfering, D. L., and Bowman, M. J. "Effects of a Meditative-Relaxation Response on Non-Attending Behaviors of Behaviorally Disturbed Children." *Journal of Clinical Child Psychology,* 1981, *14,* 126–127.

Dietary Approaches to Attention Deficits

AUTHOR: Christopher K. Varley

PRECIS: Treating developmentally inappropriate inattention via diet.

INTRODUCTION: Varley observes that there appears to be an inverse relationship between experimental rigor and the positive impact of dietary interventions for attention deficit disorder (ADD); in other words, the percentage of children scientifically demonstrated to respond favorably to such treatments is far less than clinical observations initially suggest. The author reviews the most common dietary therapeutic modalities for ADD children and describes a way for therapists to work with parents who persist in believing that dietary strategies are worthwhile.

TREATMENT: Varley covers the following strategies:

Megavitamin Approaches. First popularized by Linus Pauling in the late 1960s, these therapies hold that a general organizing and calming effect on children can result from administration of doses of Vitamin C, the fat-soluble vitamins, thiamin, and Vitamin B_6 in much larger than the recommended daily allowance.

Food Allergies. Substances implicated as behavioral pathogens by adherents of this view include orange juice, milk, eggs, and wheat products.

Feingold Hypothesis. In 1975, Dr. Ben Feingold initially suggested that foods and food additives (for example, coloring dyes) containing aspirin-like salicylates produce harmful effects. He further stated that most children diagnosed as inattentive will respond to systematically eliminating such substances from their diet.

Role of Trace Minerals. Proponents declare that behavioral disturbances can result from various combinations of high levels of some trace minerals, coupled with deficiencies in others. An example is a low zinc level plus high copper level.

Role of Sugar. Presumably, refined sucrose produces toxic effects on the behavior of children.

Varley asserts that while a good deal of confusion reigns as to the validity of these dietary approaches to ADD, it makes sense for therapists to observe several guidelines in responding to the increasing popularity of such strategies: Try to learn how the parent interprets his or her child's behavior; refrain from immediately dismissing a dietary option; always take a detailed history; establish rapport with the family before offering any prescription; review with them the research literature pertaining to dietary measures for treating ADD; if the family chooses the dietary path, offer nutritional guidance and offer to assist in monitoring so that toxic effects can be picked up.

COMMENTARY: This article effectively encapsulates several controversial approaches for helping ADD children. Varley gives thoughtful suggestions that appear particularly relevant to the clinician who must accept his or her client's determination to try an approach the therapist may not endorse. The author notes that families more often comply with interventions recommended by therapists and consultants when they feel that they are listened to and when their questions about diet are addressed directly.

SOURCE: Varley, C. K. "Diet and the Behavior of Children with Attention Deficit Disorder." *Journal of the American Academy of Child Psychiatry*, 1984, *23*, 182-185.

*Increased Attention
Through Self-Monitoring*

AUTHORS: Karen J. Rooney, Daniel P. Hallahan, and John Wills Lloyd

PRECIS: Training second graders to monitor their own attending behavior and reinforcement to increase attention to assigned work.

INTRODUCTION: The authors note that the number of children identified as learning disabled is growing rapidly and that they are increasingly being served in regular classrooms. In this context, self-monitoring—if found to be effective as a management/educational technique—holds great promise as a practical intervention for assisting children with learning and attention disorders. In particular, self-monitoring may counter the tendency of such children to remain passive and dependent, because it is designed to engender initiative and independent functioning.

TREATMENT: Over a period of four months, an entire class of urban second graders learned to self-monitor. Four of the children had been diagnosed as having severe attention problems. The authors give a detailed description of the self-monitoring intervention and of the self-recording with reinforcement:

Self-Monitoring. The children were given self-recording sheets, and they were instructed to ask themselves, "Was I paying attention?" whenever a tone sounded on a tape recorder that was placed at the side of the room. The children marked a "yes" box or a "no" box according to whether they had been attentive when they heard the tone. The teacher modeled attentive and inattentive behavior for the children and reviewed the recording system.

Self-Recording with Reinforcement. The teacher informed the class that the maximum possible number of "yes" and "no" marks would be noted and that children earning 100 percent would receive candy or cracker rewards. The accuracy of the self-recordings here and in the earlier phase was not considered.

Rules set by the teacher stayed in force during both phases of the treatment. Essentially, these prohibited conversation or other communication among the children, such as looking at one another's recording sheets. Twenty-minute observation sessions were carried out about three times weekly during academic portions of the school day.

RESULTS: The authors found that task-appropriate behaviors at least doubled in frequency for each of the ADD children. (Their nonhandicapped classmates' performances were not measured.) When they were reinforced for adhering to the system, the children did even better than they had during the purely self-monitoring phase.

COMMENTARY: The self-monitoring appears promising for other behavior disorders and for settings and tasks beyond the classroom (for instance, during athletic competition, as household chores are being done, while engaged in social conversations, while following directions by work supervisors, and so on). The technique may be applied with minimal intrusion into the activities of others in the setting if an earphone apparatus is used. Even more positive results may result from peer monitoring and administration of group and/or social reinforcements.

SOURCE: Rooney, K. J., Hallahan, D. P., and Lloyd, J. W. "Self-Recording of Attention by Learning Disabled Students in the Regular Classroom." *Journal of Learning Disabilities,* 1984, *16* (6), 360–364.

Additional Readings

Bass, C. K. "Running Can Modify Classroom Behavior." *Journal of Learning Disabilities,* 1985, *18,* 160–161.

Bass discusses the psychological and physiological benefits of running. She considers running to be viable as a treatment for children's attention span and impulse control problems. The article reports the results of six case studies involving eight- to eleven-year-old learning disabled children. Over a period of four weeks, the children ran with their classmates on alternate mornings for forty-five minutes. The running program resulted in improved attention span on classroom tasks on running days versus nonrunning days for five of the six youngsters. Running was found to be effective with impulse control in classroom behavior for three of the children. Bass calls for further study of running programs for learning disabled children.

Hallahan, D. P., and Sapona, R. "Self-Monitoring of Attention with Learning-Disabled Children: Past Research and Current Issues." *Journal of Learning Disabilities,* 1983, *16,* 616–620.

Hallahan and Sapona describe an intervention technique, self-monitoring of attention, which has produced impressive results with inattentive learning disabled children. Increases in attentional behavior and academic productivity have resulted from its implementation. The authors point out that self-monitoring requires the child to participate actively in the treatment process. They report two studies that illustrate individual and small-group instruction procedures for implementing self-monitoring.

Omizo, M. M., and Michael, W. B. "Biofeedback-Induced Relaxation Training and Impulsivity, Attention to Task and Locus of Control Among Hyperactive Boys." *Journal of Learning Disabilities,* 1982, *15,* 414–416.

The inattentive and impulsive behavior of sixteen ten- to twelve-year-old hyperactive boys was decreased by means of biofeedback-induced relaxation training. Four treatment sessions, each twenty to twenty-five minutes long, were held at two-week intervals. The boys received a demonstration of the biofeedback equipment, listened to audiotapes that taught relaxation and self-control methods, and attempted to register a pattern of low activity on the biofeedback unit. Evaluation failed to demonstrate that the intervention had any effect on the boys' perceptions of whether outcomes are controlled internally or externally. Omizo and Michael believe that the apparent lack of negative side effects makes biofeedback a particularly promising method for helping children with attention deficits.

Pfiffner, L. J., Rosen, L. A., and O'Leary, S. G. "The Efficacy of All-Positive Approach to Classroom Management." *Journal of Applied Behavior Analysis,* 1985, *18,* 257–261.

The authors report a study to assess what happened to the behavior of eight second and third graders described as inattentive and conduct disordered when various combinations and degrees of positive and negative classroom management approaches were applied. They found that academic performance and attentiveness improved when the children selected their own rewards. Such individualized reinforcers as a positive note to home, board games, helping the teacher with chores, and special lunch privileges were used in a system of frequent and exclusively positive reinforcement. An all-positive approach that relied primarily on praise was ineffective.

Rapport, M. D., Murphy, A., and Bailey, J. S. "The Effects of a Response-Cost Treatment Tactic on Hyperactive Children." *Journal of School Psychology*, 1980, *18*, 98–111.

The authors report two studies in which a response-cost procedure reduced distractible behaviors and increased academic assignment completion. In the first study, a seven-year-old hyperkinetic boy lost one minute of his thirty minutes of free time daily over a period of fourteen days each time his teacher observed him being inattentive to his schoolwork. The free time earned could be used for himself or for the entire class, as determined by the teacher. With this boy, individual consequences were more effective than group consequences. In the second experiment, with an eight-year-old hyperkinetic, nonattentive girl, Ritalin in conjunction with the response-cost program proved effective, while no increase in academic assignment completion resulted when Ritalin was used alone.

Stephens, R. S., Pelham, W. E., and Skinner, R. "State-Dependent and Main Effects of Methylphenidate and Pemoline on Paired-Associate Learning and Spelling in Hyperactive Children." *Journal of Consulting and Clinical Psychology*, *52*, 104–113.

The authors conducted an experiment with thirty-six five- to eleven-year-old children who met the criteria for diagnosis of attention deficit disorder with hyperactivity. Each child learned spelling lists and paired associations under each of three conditions: (1) placebo, (2) methylphenidate, and (3) pemoline. The drug dosage was determined by the child's body weight, in a 0.3 mg./kg. dose for methylphenidate and a 1.9 mg./kg. dose for pemoline. Retention of the items learned was tested after one week. Each drug facilitated learning and relearning to a marked extent on both tasks. There was no evidence of state-dependent learning (that is, decrement in transfer of learning between states) in any of the drug/placebo states. There was, however, a significant state-dependent interaction between pemoline and methylphenidate on spelling word retention.

Weizman, A., Weitz, R., Szekely, G. A., Tyano, S., and Belmaker, R. H. "Combination of Neuroleptic and Stimulant Treatment in Attention Deficit Disorder with Hyperactivity." *Journal of the American Academy of Child Psychiatry*, 1984, *23*, 295-298.

Children treated with stimulant medications, such as methylphenidate (Ritalin), for attention deficit disorder with hyperactivity do not always show great responsiveness. In contrast to stimulants, which release dopamine in the brain, neuroleptics block the brain's dopamine receptors. In this article, the authors present the results of a study involving fourteen six- to ten-year-old children who had a history of only partial response to stimulant treatment. While treatment with Ritalin continued, a neuroleptic medication, propericiazine, was added for two weeks at a maximum dosage of 0.2 mg./kg. The neuroleptic-stimulant combination produced marked improvements in the children's mood and behavior, most notably in levels of restlessness, fidgeting, and frustration.

Werry, J. S., Aman, M. G., and Diamond, E. "Imipramine and Methylphenidate in Hyperactive Children." *Journal of Child Psychology and Psychiatry*, 1980, *21*, 27-35.

Thirty children, ages five to twelve, who were diagnosed as moderately inattentive and hyperactive, demonstrated responses to an antidepressant (imipramine) that closely resembled their responses to methylphenidate, a stimulant medication: heart rate and blood pressure were elevated, seat movement was reduced, impulsive responses decreased, motor performance improved, and social behavior was rated by psychiatrists as improved. Dosages in this study were 0.40 mg./kg. for methylphenidate and 1.00 to 2.00 mg./kg. for imipramine. The lower imipramine doses were associated with less motor tremor and slightly superior clinical response. Compared with methylphenidate, imipramine appeared to be clinically more effective, but side effects of the antidepressant were greater.

Impulsiveness and
Low Frustration Tolerance

An impulse is an inclination to perform an unpremeditated action without considering the consequences. Frustration is a sense of dissatisfaction at being unable to attain some goal. In order to attain goals, a tolerance of frustration is often necessary, especially for intermediate or long-term goals. Immediately gratifying an impulse shows low frustration tolerance. In social situations and in school, the best solution is often not obvious and alternatives must be considered. Quick responses without deliberation have been called an impulsive cognitive tempo. Taking the time to consider alternative hypotheses is called a reflective cognitive tempo. Estimates of serious impulsivity in children range from 5 to 30 percent. Impulsivity is a key component of constitutionally based learning disabilities (a central nervous system dysfunction). Impulsive children often act without thinking, frequently shift activities, inappropriately blurt out comments, and are disorganized, poor planners, and impatient. As will be seen in this chapter, there are now a number of ways of training children to have a more reflective cognitive tempo. Increasingly popular are packaged programs (an excellent example is Kendall, P. C., and Braswell, L. Cognitive-Behavioral Therapy for Impulsive Children. *New York: Guilford Press, 1985). Even when such programs are successful, therapeutic work with parents, siblings, and teachers is often necessary to improve their understanding, tolerance, and coping methods.*

360

A Cognitive-Behavioral Program
for Building Self-Control

AUTHORS: Philip C. Kendall and Lauren Braswell

PRECIS: Use of multifaceted techniques, including self-instructions, self-rating of performance, response-cost, modeling, and reward, for teaching impulsive children to stop and think before they act.

INTRODUCTION: Characteristically, children who are considered impulsive and non-self-controlled fail to inhibit action. They "do" without thinking about the quality or consequences of their actions and without examining the available range of response alternatives. The authors demonstrate that increased self-regulation can be achieved by a child and therapist working together to overcome cognitive and behavioral difficulties associated with overactivity, impulsivity, excitability, and inattention.

TREATMENT: Self-management training consisted of exercises carried out in twelve weekly one-hour sessions. While Kendall and Braswell found this format to be effective in their research, they advise that an extended format may be suitable in many clinical situations because most youngsters present multiple symptoms needing correction. At each session, the therapist taught the child to use self-instructional procedures via modeling while working on impersonal and interpersonal problem-solving tasks. These began with simulated classwork and concluded with role plays specifically designed to address behaviors that were problematic for the individual child being treated. This progression allowed self-instruction to be practiced first with regard to simple and relatively nonstressful recurring situations so that skill with the technique could be achieved before application was attempted and practiced in emotionally charged situations. Throughout the duration of therapy, response-cost contingencies were in effect for violation of "therapy rules," such as failing to verbalize the steps of a problem-solving plan.

Social reinforcers and self-administered rewards were given upon demonstration of successful performance and appropriate behavior. The authors provided a detailed session-by-session treatment manual giving sample dialogue between therapist and child. A therapy checklist summarizing the processes and activities that occur in all sessions and a series of guidelines (do's and don't's) also appeared in the manual.

COMMENTARY: Kendall and Braswell successfully used learning and cognitive theory in the treatment of a common childhood behavior problem. They emphasize that four elements combine to optimize treatment impact: confidence in the chosen therapeutic strategy, enthusiasm for the therapist-child interaction, thorough knowledge of the treatment program, and monitoring of progress, which entails adjusting the program's implementation as needed. Child variables, such as age and level of intelligence, should be considered in planning and carrying out treatment. Also, professionals should try to enlist parents as collaborators in the treatment. For example, parents can enhance treatment by modeling appropriate task performance for their child, and they can promote generalization of the treatment effects by arranging home contingencies to reinforce reflective problem solving.

SOURCE: Kendall, P. C., and Braswell, L. *Cognitive-Behavioral Therapy for Impulsive Children.* New York: Guilford Press, 1985.

Modifying Impulsiveness in
Developmentally Disabled Children

AUTHOR: Clarissa S. Holmes

PRECIS: Self-instruction training produced relatively less impulsive behavior and reflective responding was sustained over time in mildly retarded children.

INTRODUCTION: Holmes points out that impulsive children characteristically blurt out answers without stopping to think about all available response alternatives. Compared to their peers of average intelligence, mentally retarded children have been found to demonstrate more impulsive behavior.

Previous efforts to reduce children's impulsive responding have utilized such techniques as these: operant treatment procedures, including response-cost; contingent social reinforcement; and cognitive behavior modification, including self-instruction training wherein the child observes an adult model who systematically evaluates task demands, adopts a scanning strategy, monitors his or her own behavior, and then self-reinforces for compliance and success.

Previous studies that worked with developmentally disabled populations did not investigate whether the methods used in the laboratory succeeded in affecting the child's behavior in the real-life classroom environment: That is, the question of generalization was ignored. Moreover, the durability of treatment effects—whether improvements observed immediately after intervention were sustained over time—was ignored by previous investigations. Holmes examined these factors with regard to various operant methods and self-instructional types of intervention with mildly mentally retarded children.

TREATMENT: Thirty young people whose chronological age ranged from eleven to eighteen years and whose mental age averaged about nine years (IQ = 66, range = 53 to 78) participated. The youngsters were divided into a younger group, averaging twelve-and-a-half years old, and an older group, averaging fourteen-and-a-half years old. Thirteen of the children attended special education programs in elementary schools; the rest went to junior and senior high school settings. The author conducted the training, and two undergraduate assistants did individual pre- and post-testing. These students were unaware of the retarded youths' group assignments, and the youngsters were presented for testing in a random order to further reduce the chance of obtaining biased results. Details of the instruments and the procedure are described.

Measure of Impulsive Responding. The Matching Familiar Figures Test (MFFT) was used to examine each youngster's ability to inhibit responding and the accuracy of the matching responses given. With the MFFT, the child views a stimulus picture and then indicates which among six to eight facsimiles is identical to it.

Measure of Child's Causal Attribution System. The impulsive children were read the Intellectual Achievement Responsibility Scale (IAR), which assessed whether they believed responsibility for their academic performance rested within or outside of themselves. On the basis of their responses, the children were characterized as internalizers or externalizers, respectively.

Measure of Task Generalization. The Porteus Mazes were used to assess possible task generalization. This is a paper-and-pencil test that serves as a measure of planning and general thinking ability.

Measure of Generalization of Reflective Behavior to the Classroom. Portions of the Conners Teacher Rating Scale (CTRS), consisting of items rated on a four-point scale, were used to determine whether reflective behavior was generalized to the classroom. The hyperactivity and aggressivity scales of the CTRS, specifically, were utilized for this purpose.

After pretesting, the youngsters were randomly assigned to one of four groups: (1) operant, (2) self-instruction, (3) extended self-instruction, or (4) controls. Over a two-week training period, six twenty-minute training sessions were conducted using Form B of the MFFT; these sessions took place in the school, with the students in training groups of up to five students.

The *operant group* members received attention and praise when they responded appropriately during the training sessions. They received the standard MFFT directions. Besides being told to work slowly and carefully, they were not taught any strategy for performing the matching task. The *self-instruction group* members were taught the self-instruction training procedure developed by Meichenbaum and Goodman (Meichenbaum, D. H., and Goodman, J. "Training Impulsive Children to Talk to Themselves: A Means of Developing Self-Control." *Journal of Abnormal Psychology*, 1971, 77, 115-126). Using this procedure, the children observed the college student modeling questions and answers concerning the MFFT ("What is it I have to do?") and then deciding how to proceed ("How should I do this?"). Then the children saw the model use self-guiding statements ("Go carefully"). Following this, self-reinforcement was given for corresponding motoric action ("Good, I did it!"). The children were prompted to carry out the self-instructional sequence, first aloud, then silently.

Additionally, they were taught a visual screening strategy that incorporated inhibiting overt responding and examining critical features of stimulus likeness and difference. This group received little social reinforcement; the emphasis was, instead, on encouraging them to direct and evaluate their own performance. The *extended self-instruction group* members were taught similarly to the self-instruction group children. In addition, these children were taught to use the self-instruction approach with three supplemental tasks that resembled common classroom activities. The *control group* received the standard directions for the MFFT but no training or contingent performance feedback. Some random praise was given, equal to the amount the self-instructional group's children received. Most of the twenty-minute session was spent in free drawing activity.

RESULTS: Post-testing took place within a week after training, using an alternative form of the MFFT, the Porteus Mazes, and the CTRS hyperactivity and aggressivity scales. A week later, these same tests were again administered to determine the durability of treatment effects.

Self-instructional training helped the mentally retarded children in both the self-instructional group and the extended self-instructional group to make fewer post-test errors on the MFFT, indicating that the training was effective in teaching a visual discrimination strategy. In contrast, the operant reinforcement proved to be ineffective. Interestingly, age-related performance differences were found in the self-instructional groups—namely, younger children consistently displayed more reflective behavior in the form of fewer errors, and increased latency effects were shown to remain at the time of the follow-up two weeks after the training had ended.

Personality factors were shown to interact with treatment in regard to learning task approach strategy. Internally oriented children made fewer MFFT errors in both self-instruction groups than did their externally oriented peers. This was true for the post-test that immediately followed training as well as for the delayed post-test. No differences were discovered in the operant and control conditions. In the case of latency to response, no similar interaction of personality and training condition was observed.

Generalization of treatment effects was not observed using the Porteus Maze pencil-and-paper task. All groups' hyperactivity scale ratings, curiously, increased. The author speculates that this may be attributable to the fact that pretest ratings were taken during the winter, while the post-test ratings were taken at a time in the spring when children's activity levels may naturally be higher.

COMMENTARY: This is an important extension of the literature on treating impulsivity via self-instruction training in a developmentally delayed portion of the population. It was especially impressive—beyond the statistically significant results—that the retarded children trained with self-instruction were brought to an error-performance level that matched that of children in the general population. Also, the durability of the treatment effects is impressive. Holmes's failure to obtain generalization to the classrooms should cause future investigators to think carefully about the metamemory deficits that characterize mentally retarded individuals. Perhaps future training efforts will have to more carefully tie the training to the "back-home" classroom demands. Holmes offers a good suggestion when she advises that future efforts have peers serve as models and agents of feedback, instead of an adult serving in these ways exclusively. In the future, tangible rather than social rewards may prove to be superior with mentally retarded children.

SOURCE: Holmes, C. S. "Reflective Training and Causal Attributions in Impulsive Mildly Mentally Retarded Children." *Journal of Clinical Child Psychology*, 1981, *10*, 194-199.

Building Tolerance for Anger and Anxiety Through Stress Inoculation

AUTHORS: Anthony Spirito, A. J. Finch, T. L. Smith, and W. H. Cooley

PRECIS: Reduction of a boy's extreme displays of anger and anxiety by teaching him about emotions, analyzing his maladaptive self-statements, instructing him in overt and covert adaptive alternative responses, and using videotaped role plays, social reinforcement for appropriate responsiveness, relaxation skills instruction, and *in vivo* practice in the regular classroom.

INTRODUCTION: In stress inoculation training, cognitive and behavioral coping skills are taught, and then the client is exposed to gradually increasing amounts of stress, which he or she can master. This enables the client to "become immune" to greater intensities of threat. In this study, the authors helped a ten-and-a-half-year-old boy in residential treatment who exhibited severe anger and anxiety control problems in school to develop the skills to tolerate the enormous stress brought on by "difficult" academic work.

CASE STUDY: John, ten-and-a-half years old, was in residential treatment because he set fires, lied incessantly, and presented a history of stealing, encopresis, academic underachievement, and management problems at school and at home. Testing suggested that John was extremely intelligent and that he harbored major fears of being rejected and abandoned. In a school classroom with four other boys, John verbally abused his teacher, refused to comply with the teacher's instructions, and provoked and fought with the other students. The authors observed that these disruptions were prompted by presentation of school assignments that John perceived as being too difficult for him, even though intellectual test data and academic achievement evaluations indicated otherwise.

TREATMENT: The treatment program commenced with John's teacher noting in detail the antecedents and consequences of his disruptive behaviors, the time and setting in which they occurred, and who else was involved. This recording procedure determined that before John acted disruptively, he typically progressed through a sequence of behaviors: commenting on the assigned work's difficulty, leaving it in order to do some other assignment, declaring that he was getting mad, starting to yell or curse at his teacher or peers, acting in an aggressive fashion, and then starting to cry.

The stress inoculation procedure utilized with John entailed two weekly half-hour sessions for four weeks. The initial session was devoted mostly to education; the next five sessions emphasized rehearsal; the final two sessions were devoted to application training.

Education Phase. In a direct, simple way, the therapist and John discussed the purposes served by anger, the roots of anxiety, and how these emotions gained expression in John's specific school situation. The therapist focused John's thinking on self-statements that provoked maladaptive responses. John was told that these inappropriate self-statements produced his angry and worried feelings. For example, a statement such as, "My teacher will think I'm dumb if I do badly and not like me anymore" (an anxious self-statement) was paired with, "I'm losing control; I'm going to hit something" (angry self-statement). Then, John assessed which of the presented statements (or which similar ones) he had used. Following this, a number of alternative adaptive self-instructional responses were introduced.

Rehearsal Phase. John began to practice adaptive self-statements at the end of the first therapy session. Rehearsal was facilitated by a five-minute videotape in which his therapist modeled the desired behaviors. On the tape, the therapist portrayed a student talking aloud as he worked at assigned schoolwork. At the end of the tape, John's teacher praised the model for refraining from showing signs of anger or anxiety. Following the tape presentation, John, assisted by prompts and modeling, practiced the actor's adaptive self-statement. A combination of tangible reinforcement (candy) and social reinforcement (vigorous praise) were afforded John's correct verbalizations.

Review, more rehearsal, and repeated viewing of the videotape occupied subsequent therapy sessions. Additionally, John was taught response-inhibition (study skills) self-statements (for example, "Read the directions carefully" and "Stop, wait, and think"). Also, he was instructed in relaxation skills, whereby he was told to take a deep breath and relax when he noticed physiological signs that he was becoming angry. The last two sessions of this phase of therapy involved practice and reinforcement of self-reinforcement statements, such as, "I got them right without getting angry" and "I'm doing better at this all the time." Throughout the rehearsal phase, John was assisted in moving from verbal (overt) self-instruction to silent self-talk.

Application Training. The thrust of this phase was generalizing John's newly acquired self-control skills to real-life academic demands in the classroom setting. First, John worked at an assignment generated by his teacher but administered by the therapist, who tried to provoke the boy's anger and then praised John for exhibiting restraint and discussed the range of alternative responses he could have given to the provocation. Later, actual classwork was presented, followed by discussion between the therapist and John and the administration of reward for John's successful performance.

RESULTS: Stress inoculation training succeeded in bringing John from no acceptance of classroom assignments to acceptance of nearly two-thirds of the classwork. Physical destructiveness and crying, quite common before treatment started, were virtually eliminated. The incidence of verbal abuse was reduced 350 percent. John's teacher characterized him after treatment as the best controlled of all the students in his class. Anecdotal evidence six months after therapy indicated that treatment gains had been sustained both behaviorally and academically.

COMMENTARY: This represents an exciting extension of cognitive behavioral therapy methods, which have been demonstrated to be effective with adults and teenagers, to a preadolescent with behavioral disorders. One can speculate that the efficacy of the therapy might be comparable if group treatment were undertaken. Certainly, cost and caseload considerations would argue for group treatment approaches where these could be shown to work. Also, it would be interesting to determine if peer modeling—both in the treatment groups and on videotapes that present agemates of the youngsters in treatment—facilitated therapy.

SOURCE: Spirito, A., Finch, A. J., Smith, T. L., and Cooley, W. H. "Stress Inoculation for Anger and Anxiety Control: A Case Study with an Emotionally Disturbed Boy." *Journal of Clinical Child Psychology*, 1981, *10*, 67-70.

Foul Shots, Verbal Reminders, and Hand Signals to Reduce Impulsiveness

AUTHOR: Mike Berger

PRECIS: Training in physical skills, encouragement, challenges, and conditioning hand and verbal signals to build an eight-year-old hyperkinetic boy's impulse control.

INTRODUCTION: Impulsive behavior is a major reason children are referred to mental health services. Various studies have used cognitive-behavioral interventions, such as self-instruction training procedures, to try to treat impulsivity. In this case report, training and competition in an athletic skill were combined with operant and cognitive-behavioral procedures to help an eight-year-old hyperkinetic boy reduce his impulsiveness.

TREATMENT: John, an eight-year-old hyperkinetic boy, participated in forty-six twenty- to thirty-minute sessions over eighteen weeks (three per week for forty weeks, then two weeks apiece of first two sessions and then one session). Afterward, irregularly scheduled sessions occurred once every two weeks. During these sessions, the boy and the therapist played basketball; the boy could earn M&M's for shooting foul shots and for pausing ten seconds between foul shots. The distance from the foul line and the height of the basket were reduced—to seven and nine feet, respectively—prior to the first session. In the next session, the boy took foul shots under the terms that either three baskets in a row or six out of ten attempts would earn him M&M's. After seven sessions, these contingencies were raised to five in a row or eight out of ten.

Prior to the second session, the boy received instructions on how to hold the ball, how to push off with his legs to propel the ball high enough and far enough, and how to concentrate on where he wanted the ball to go. "Think the ball through the hoop" was presented as a formula for the boy to remember. The boy reported his progress to his parents after each session.

The words, "John, think!" and a simple hand signal indicating "Stop!" were then introduced. The therapist used these whenever the boy acted impulsively (that is, shot a ball before thinking). Also, a once-per-week challenge competition between the boy and the therapist was established for purposes of variety, and the signal, "John, think!" and the hand signal were taught to the boy's teacher. She proceeded to use them in the classroom whenever he left his seat, was inattentive, or behaved inappropriately with other students.

At the end of six weeks, treatment sessions were lengthened from twenty minutes to half an hour. For the first ten

minutes, John played with building blocks. Additional basketball time was made contingent upon his constructing a tower
more than two feet high or using all the blocks. He could have
only a single block touching the floor as a base. As John played
with the blocks, the therapist coached him to think about what
each block would do to the balance. "John, think!" and the
hand signal were the therapist's responses if he acted impulsively.

RESULTS: Before the treatment program began, John left his
seat 1.5 times every five minutes in the morning and 8.0 times
every five minutes in the afternoon. The base rate level for the
afternoon became approximately 1.5, when the boy's 2:00 P.M.
Ritalin dosage doubled to 20 mg. (This was in addition to 10-
mg. doses at breakfast and at 10:00 A.M.) The boy's productive
work at times of acute hyperkinesis was below 30 percent, but
it dropped to near 0 percent when he was medicated. After
thirteen weeks of treatment, John's out-of-seat episodes were
reduced to 1.1 per five minutes, and productive work was recorded at 65 and 40 percent, respectively, in the morning and
afternoon. Ritalin dosage was halved six weeks into the program and discontinued after the fortieth session. After program
phaseout began, John's out-of-seat episodes were recorded at less
than 1.0 per five-minute period on the average, and his productive work percentage was recorded at more than 70 percent.

COMMENTARY: This study represents an innovative effort to
treat a child's classroom impulse control problems through a
gym-based remediation program. The therapist not only coached,
played with, and rewarded the boy in the gym, but he also con-
sulted with the classroom teacher. Greater self-control was accomplished, and this generalized to the classroom. The parents'
role was supportive in that they provided the candy that served
as tangible reinforcers in this program. Berger observes that it is
important to determine whether a child is capable of demonstrating the improved standard of behavior that is desired before beginning a program such as this one. Other forms of physical
challenge activities would seem to hold potential as effective

treatment approaches for children with low impulse control. We have found the following verbal signals very helpful with impulsive children: "think before acting" and "engage brain before tongue." Children can write these phrases down and think of them in appropriate situations.

SOURCE: Berger, M. "Remediating Hyperkinetic Behavior with Impulse Control Procedures." *School Psychology Review,* 1981, *10,* 405-407.

Additional Readings

Baxley, G. B., and Ullman, R. K. "Psychoactive Drug Effects in a Hyperactive Child: A Case Study Analysis of Behavior Change and Teacher Attention." *Journal of School Psychology,* 1979, *17,* 317-324.

The authors observed an impulsive, distractible nine-year-old girl during two fifteen-day periods when she received her standard dose of 40 mg. of methylphenidate per day. They also observed her during an intervening five-day period, during which she received an inert placebo tablet that was identical in size, shape, and color to the drug. When the girl was receiving methylphenidate, she was appropriately directed to academic activities to a significantly greater extent, and she displayed disruptive behavior significantly less. Also higher during the methylphenidate condition was the percentage of time that teacher interactions with the girl were instructional in quality. Teacher ratings of the girl's behavior were more favorable when she was receiving the drug than when she was receiving a placebo.

Brown, R. T., and Conrad, K. J. "Impulse Control or Selective Attention: Remedial Programs for Hyperactivity." *Psychology in the Schools,* 1982, *19,* 92-97.

In a study that involved forty-eight hyperactive boys whose average age was nine-and-a-half years old, Brown and

Advances in Therapies for Children

Conrad found that a combination of attentional and inhibitory control strategies was most efficacious in enhancing their ability to give accurate answers and to refrain from responding impulsively. Children in the group that received attention training alone committed fewer errors and achieved longer latency scores on the Matching Familiar Figures Test than did children who were taught inhibitory control solely. Attention training entailed focusing the child's attention on differences between visual stimuli. Inhibitory control training taught the child to ask himself four questions as problems were confronted: (1) What is my problem? (2) What is my plan? (3) Am I using my plan? (4) How did I do? The boys participated in ten training sessions. The authors' findings support the view that problems with impulse control and attention can occur concurrently in hyperkinetic children and that inhibitory control training alone is insufficient to produce better cognitive performance. Rather, these children need to "look and listen" as well as to "stop."

Dulcan, M. K., and Piercy, P. A. "A Model for Teaching and Evaluating Brief Psychotherapy with Children and Their Families." *Professional Psychology: Research and Practice,* 1985, *16,* 689–700.

Dulcan and Piercy describe a model of planned, time-limited therapy for children and their families that is applicable with a wide range of cases. Included among the authors' case reports are illustrations with impulsive children and children displaying developmentally inappropriate inattention. The short-term treatment model the authors present derives from a family systems perspective that emphasizes flexibility, allowing the use of behavioral and cognitive-behavioral techniques to address specific target problems. Ten to twelve weekly therapy sessions are held, plus a follow-up session a month later to evaluate progress and act as a "booster." The approach recommended by Dulcan and Piercy emphasizes having the child and family select treatment goals and specify criteria for evaluating improvement. The approach stresses ways to develop alternative strategies of behavior rather than pathology. Specific methods include education about normal development, behavioral contracts, training and practice in communication and negotiation techniques, and reinforcement.

Gettinger, M. "Improving Classroom Behaviors and Achievement of Learning Disabled Children Using Direct Instruction." *School Psychology Review*, 1982, *11*, 329–336.

The author describes a study in which systematic teaching procedures were effective in reducing impulsive and inattentive behaviors of eight learning disabled children who ranged in age from six to nine years old. Concomitant academic achievement gains were attained from the nine-day instructional intervention. The five components of the direct instruction method recommended for small-group teaching are: (1) teacher-directed, step-by-step learning, (2) group instruction and practice in round-robin and group practice formats, (3) mastery learning, (4) continuous, controlled practice, and (5) immediate, corrective feedback.

Hinshaw, S. P., Henker, B., and Whalen, C. K. "Self-Control in Hyperactive Boys in Anger-Inducing Situations: Effects of Cognitive-Behavioral Training and of Methylphenidate." *Journal of Abnormal Child Psychology*, 1984, *12*, 55–77.

This article presents the results of two studies that investigated the effects of cognitive-behavioral interventions and methylphenidate on anger control in hyperactive boys. In both studies, direct taunting and teasing from peers served as the provocation. In the first study, with twenty-one eight- to thirteen-year-old boys, groups of three boys were trained twice weekly for two hours over a three-week period in self-instructional strategies and problem-solving strategies for academic, fine-motor, and interpersonal situations. Eleven of the boys (dispersed among the triads) received the medication in doses ranging from .14 to .55 mg./kg. After coaching and rehearsal in special cognitive-behavioral strategies, the boys exhibited greater self-control in response to the provocation—that is, they inhibited angry and aggressive responses and also displayed alternative behavioral responses. Methylphenidate was associated with a calmer, more peaceful style of behavior and a reduced tendency to leave the provocation.

The second study involved twenty-four boys, ages eight to thirteen, all of whom participated in cognitive-behavioral training groups daily for two weeks. In groups of four, the boys learned specific steps for problem-solving and self-talk strategies, and they discussed their attitudes and attributions toward stimulant medication. They also learned how to apply cognitive self-instruction strategies to academic problems. Then, following verbal provocation, half the boys received training in and rehearsed stress inoculation strategies. They were taught to recognize external threats that can produce anger and internal anger warning signs; also, they learned and rehearsed alternative behavioral responses and specific self-control strategies. After two days of this training, the boys were again provoked. As was the case in the first study, half the boys received stimulant medication. Doses ranged from .15 to 1.16 mg./kg. The methylphenidate reduced the intensity or stylistic vigor and forcefulness of behavior. The boys trained in the cognitive-behavioral methods were found to use a significantly greater number of coping strategies and display better self-control than did the controls. The authors suggest that active strategy training appears to be a necessary ingredient in helping hyperactive boys achieve self-control in anger-inducing situations.

Kendall, P. C., and Zupon, B. A. "Individual Versus Group Application of Cognitive-Behavioral Self-Control Procedures with Children." *Behavior Therapy,* 1981, *12,* 344–359.

Thirty boys and girls, eight to eleven years old, who exhibited problematic lack of self-control at school, were treated with cognitive-behavioral procedures. Components of self-control training included problem definition, strategy planning, focusing of attention, answering the question, self-reinforcement for correct responding, and coping statements following performance errors. The children participated in twelve forty-five- to fifty-five-minute treatment sessions over a six-week period. Classroom analog tasks, interpersonal play situations, and personal problem areas were used. In individual and group treatment conditions, modeling, reinforcement of correct performance, and response-cost penalties for errors were employed. Both the individual and the group cognitive-behavioral conditions produced improved self-control according to blind teacher ratings. Perspective-taking skill also was improved.

Truhlicka, M. "An Investigation of the Effects of Behavior Therapy Versus Drug Therapy in the Treatment of Hyperactive Children." *Journal for Special Educators*, 1982, *18*, 35-40.

Stimulant medications have been widely used to calm impulsive and hyperactive children. Behavior therapy has also served as an adjunct or alternative intervention in the treatment of this population. Truhlicka reviews the literature, comparing the relative and combined effects of stimulant drug and behavioral management treatments. For social behavior problems of hyperkinetic children, the use of stimulants appears to be more immediately effective than behavior therapy. However, the effectiveness of the two approaches seems to be roughly equivalent. It is not clear how the two approaches compare in terms of influencing academic behaviors.

Williams, D. T., Mehl, R., Yudofsky, S., Adams, D., and Roseman, B. "The Effect of Propranolol on Uncontrolled Rage Outbursts in Children and Adolescents with Organic Brain Dysfunction." *Journal of the American Academy of Child Psychiatry*, 1982, *21*, 129-135.

Uncontrolled rage outbursts are common in most types of brain dysfunction. Some form of brain dysfunction was present in eleven children, fifteen adolescents, and four adults who all had previously undergone unsuccessful medication treatment; most had also received psychotherapy. Attention deficit disorder was diagnosed in fifteen of the participants in the use of propranolol. Dosages were individualized, starting at either 10 or 20 mg. three or four times a day and then increasing until sustained behavioral improvement or persistent side effects were seen. Potential adverse cardiovascular, neurological, or allergic effects of propranolol are rare in children. Moderate to marked improvement in control of rage outbursts and aggressive behavior was seen in more than 75 percent of the patients. There was no additive benefit in giving concurrent psychotherapy.

5

Disturbed Relationships with Children

Social ineffectiveness with agemates represents a serious obstacle to the psychological adjustment of school-aged children. Social difficulties correlate highly with emotional problems, school maladjustment, and general psychological deviance. Moreover, social problems with peers are highly predictive of emotional difficulties in adulthood. This chapter is concerned with children who clearly have a deficiency in the skills and/or motivation necessary to engage in cooperative, mutually satisfying transactions with other children. Characteristically, these deficits are manifested in either fight (hostility) or flight (withdrawal) reactions to peers and/or siblings. Prolonged use of either reaction inevitably results in social isolation or rejection. The underlying causes of maladaptive peer relations are numerous, including parental rejection or overdependency, marital

conflict, minimal brain dysfunction, reactions to trauma or
stress, and poor self-esteem. Parental modeling also seems to be
a factor, because individualism and competition are highly val-
ued behaviors in our culture. Alienation and mistrust of others
are becoming increasingly prevalent, especially in our larger
urban centers.

Specific techniques for achieving group acceptance for socially inept children are presented in this chapter. Since the
problem lies in peer interactions, the treatment of choice in recent years has been to involve peers in the treatment by means
of group or dyadic therapy. Typically, behavioral methods are
used to motivate the peers to exert pressure on a child so that
he or she will engage in more cooperative social interactions.
Often a child's parents and/or teachers are trained to administer
the behavioral contingencies in the natural environment.

The use of group methods for socialization problems reflects the fact that the peer and sibling subcultures exert a
strong influence on preadolescents to conform to group norms.
In adolescence, these group pressures become even more powerful. For instance, one study revealed that when high school students' friends encouraged or approved of drug use, 73 percent
of the students used drugs. When friends disapproved, only 27
percent reported using drugs.

A major problem in the use of groups with preadolescent
children is control—that is, the handling of aggressive behavior.
Almost immediately upon entering a group situation, children
will test its limits. The most difficult aspect of child group therapy is the management of disruptive behavior. For this reason,
therapists have turned to the following procedures: setting and
enforcing clear limits, providing physical activities to drain off
excess energy, and employing heterogeneous grouping (aggressive children mixed with shy, withdrawn children). A major advantage of the group approach is that it tends to be slightly
more efficient than individual methods in that more children
can be treated with the same resources.

It appears, then, that peer and sibling subsystems are
finally getting the attention from therapists that they deserve. It
remains to be seen whether this is a current fad or a therapeutic
breakthrough.

Social Isolation

An earlier section of this book discussed the treatment of shy, withdrawn children whose low level of social interaction was caused, in general, by a passive failure to approach others because of inexperience, lack of confidence, or a pleasurable absorption in solitary activities. This section focuses on the severely withdrawn child who not only has no friends but shows an active avoidance of peers because of intense anxiety and fearfulness. (Also see section on Shy, Withdrawn Behavior.*)*

Reinforcing Components
of Social Interactions

AUTHORS: Hill M. Walker, Charles R. Greenwood, Hyman Hops, and Nancy M. Todd

PRECIS: Socially withdrawn children were taught to initiate positive interactions, respond to invitations from others, and maintain social interactions over time.

INTRODUCTION: The authors report on three studies representing the initial stage of research that resulted in a package called PEERS (Procedures for Establishing Effective Relationship Skills); this package was designed to remediate social withdrawal in such settings as classrooms and playgrounds. The goal of the initial research was to identify topographical components of the interactional process that would increase social interactions. The authors' aim was to produce changes in withdrawn children's social interaction patterns by differentially reinforcing components of interactive behavior. The components were: 1) *Starts*—positive initiations to peers, 2) *Answers*—positive responses to peers' initiations, and 3) *Continues*—maintaining social interactions over time.

TREATMENT: In the first study, the authors selectively reinforced in sequence the topographical components *Starts, Answers,* and *Continues.* Study 2 controlled for sequence effects by reinforcing the components in a reverse order, and Study 3 simultaneously reinforced the components.

Three different groups of six withdrawn youngsters in grades one through six were treated in succession in an experimental classroom for approximately four months. Children were referred by teachers and counselors because of withdrawn behavior or social isolation. The following describes the setting and general procedures for the three studies.

The school day included three thirty-minute unstructured activity periods. Toys and games were available during these times, and social interactions were free to occur. A system of token reinforcement was in effect whereby points were earned contingent upon certain behaviors during free play time. In addition, the points were paired with teacher praise and could be exchanged daily for reinforcers. The behaviors reinforced during play time depended upon the study and particular component(s) being reinforced at the time.

In all three studies, the reinforcement of the topographical component *Continue* produced significant increases in social interactions. The reinforcement of *Starts* and *Answers* increased these behavioral components but resulted in an overall decrease in the time spent in actual interactive behavior. The authors explain this finding by noting that observation of the reinforcement of *Starts* and *Answers* seemed to be disruptive to social interactions, as it interfered with the youngsters' natural interactive styles. This resulted in mechanical and unnatural social interactions.

COMMENTARY: The authors point out the value of these studies not only in their subsequent development of a treatment package for withdrawn elementary school-aged children but also in understanding different components of an interactive process. The results indicate that reinforcing the component *Continue* serves to increase the time spent in social interactions. However, if the aim is to increase a child's response to another's initiation, then the component *Answer* would be a more appropriate target behavior to treat. This initial research provides clinicians who treat withdrawn children with information that enables a cost-effective approach to treatment. As has been found in other studies, imposing and then reinforcing peer interactions is an effective technique for treating withdrawn youngsters in school settings.

SOURCE: Walker, H. M., Greenwood, C. R., Hops, H., and Todd, N. M. "Differential Effects of Reinforcing Topographical Components of Social Interaction." *Behavior Modification*, 1979, *3*, 291–321.

Treating Socially Withdrawn Preschoolers

AUTHORS: Wyndol Furman, Donald F. Rahe, and Willard W. Hartup

PRECIS: Withdrawn preschoolers were successfully treated through socialization sessions with other children, particularly younger children.

INTRODUCTION: One-to-one social interaction between withdrawn preschoolers and younger children was found to be effective in increasing the social activity of isolate children in school. The imposition of one-to-one play sessions afforded the withdrawn children experiences that they did not have in school. The children had opportunities to be socially assertive and to receive reinforcement for this assertiveness. The authors report evidence that socially withdrawn children lack leadership skills. Socializing with younger children fosters leadership skills, as younger children eagerly follow and imitate older children. This serves as reinforcement for the isolate child and also enables the withdrawn child to direct social activity during the interaction.

TREATMENT: Observations of preschoolers in a day-care setting identified twenty-four youngsters who engaged in peer interactions less than 33 percent of the observation period. These youngsters were assigned either to a control condition or to one of two treatment conditions. In one treatment, the withdrawn youngster was assigned to a same-aged peer, and in the other, assignment was made to a younger child. Teachers were not informed as to the youngsters' classifications.

Treatment began with the isolate children engaging in ten play sessions with an assigned child. The treatment sessions were conducted over a four- to six-week period. The isolates had two different peer partners, each one for five sessions, over the course of treatment. Each play session was twenty minutes in duration and took place in a playroom with toys that were chosen to promote positive social interactions. Blocks, puppets, felt and cardboard figures, dress-up clothing, and train sets were utilized. During each of the first five sessions, new toys were introduced. The toys were reused in the remaining five sessions. During the play sessions, an observer was seated in the corner. However, interaction with the children was minimal.

RESULTS: Observations conducted subsequent to the treatment revealed that the isolate youngsters in both treatment conditions improved significantly in their peer interactions in the classroom. The youngsters who had interacted with younger children demonstrated the greatest increase in social activity in school. Prosocial activity, coordinated effort, and social reinforcement tripled in frequency in the isolates matched with younger children, while they doubled in the isolates matched with same-aged peers.

COMMENTARY: The authors' findings reveal that providing withdrawn preschoolers with one-to-one peer interactions enables reinforcement of successful socialization and therefore results in elimination of the child's isolate behavior. In addition, the current findings indicate that a leadership skill deficiency may be an underlying cause of withdrawn behavior, as the youngsters who interacted with younger children showed the most improvement in appropriate social activity. Implications for grouping preschool children with same- versus mixed-aged peers should be considered based on this study. However, further research is needed.

SOURCE: Furman, W., Rahe, D. F., and Hartup, W. W. "Rehabilitation of Socially Withdrawn Preschool Children Through Mixed-Age and Same-Age Socialization." *Child Development*, 1979, *50*, 915–922.

Additional Readings

Appoloni, T., and Cooke, T. P. "Socially Withdrawn Children: The Role of Mental Health Practitioners." *Social Behavior and Personality,* 1977, *5* (2), 337-343.

The authors present a review of the literature regarding social withdrawal in children and offer a critical analysis of behavior therapy classroom procedures. They conclude that there are presently sufficient effective behavioral techniques that enable treatment of social withdrawal in mainstream classroom settings. The authors suggest that mental health workers serve as resource personnel to teachers in order to facilitate the social development of withdrawn youngsters.

Fuller, J. S. "Duo Therapy: A Potential Treatment of Choice for Latency Children." *Journal of the American Academy of Child Psychiatry,* 1977, *16* (3), 469-477.

Duo therapy, a modality in which two unrelated latency-age children are seen together for treatment, is presented. Duo therapy aims at fostering a child's development through identification of the healthy functions of the other child and the therapist. Fuller finds this treatment approach especially appropriate for children experiencing difficulties in developing autonomy and social skills. The author discusses several treatment pairs in order to illustrate principles of the therapy.

Janes, C. L., Hesselbrock, V. M., and Schechtman, J. "Clinic Children with Poor Peer Relations: Who Refers Them and Why?" *Child Psychiatry and Human Development,* 1980, *2* (2), 113-125.

As schools are viewed as an essential link between children and mental health services, the authors studied the role of the schools in referring children because of poor peer relationships. They found that schools do not tend to refer children because of poor peer relationships per se; however, many of the children referred by schools exhibit poor peer interactions. Referrals by schools are typically initiated when the child's behavior poses a problem for the teacher in some way. Poor peer relationships do not seem to fit this criterion. It is suggested that teachers become more aware of the need for referring children for treatment of peer relationships, as they are usually children at risk for later difficulties.

Kendel, H. J., Ayllon, T., and Rosenbaum, M. S. "Flooding or Systematic Exposure in the Treatment of Extreme Social Withdrawal in Children." *Journal of Behavior Therapy and Experimental Psychiatry,* 1977, *8* (1), 75–81.

Two children, aged eight and four, respectively, were treated for extreme social withdrawal. The four-year-old was treated by flooding, and the eight-year-old was treated by systematic exposure. Both treatments occurred in the youngsters' natural environments. In both instances, several children provided social stimuli for the treatment. The authors conclude that severe social withdrawal is an anxiety-related problem that can be effectively treated through either flooding or systematic exposure techniques.

Overt Hostility Toward Peers

This section deals with overt, frequent, intense fighting (verbal and physical) between peers. Other sections in this book relate to hostility directed at parents or siblings, as well as to a more diffuse type of aggressiveness that spills over onto everybody. (Also see sections on Aggressiveness *and* Sibling Rivalry.*)*

Treating Poor Peer Interactions on a
Psychiatric Inpatient Unit

AUTHORS: Vincent B. Van Hasselt, Douglas L. Griest, Alan E. Kazdin, Karen Esveldt-Dawson, and Alan S. Unis

PRECIS: A seven-and-a-half-year-old boy was treated for poor peer interactions utilizing social skills training that consisted of didactic instructions, coaching, modeling, feedback, and reinforcement.

INTRODUCTION: Bob, a seven-and-a-half-year-old, was admitted to a psychiatric inpatient unit because of aggressive behavior, a high activity level, temper tantrums, suicidal threats and gestures, somatic complaints, and poor peer interactions. Bob had been in foster care, as his natural parents were experiencing marital difficulties. Both parents were reported to be of below-average intelligence. The mother was diagnosed as an alcoholic and had been abusive toward Bob, and the father reportedly was passive and controlled by the mother.

Upon admittance to the hospital, an evaluation of Bob resulted in the diagnoses of conduct disorder and attention deficit disorder. On the unit, Bob exhibited poor peer relations, which included both social isolation and aggressiveness. A combination of social skills training and contingency management was implemented in order to improve Bob's interpersonal functioning.

TREATMENT: The focus of the treatment was to increase appropriate social interactions. In order to achieve this goal, two behaviors were targeted: increasing time engaged in appropriate peer interactions and decreasing the time Bob spent playing alone. Treatment occurred in a variety of settings in the hospital and consisted of didactic and *in vivo* training. Following a baseline period, Bob received three weeks of social skills training. The first week, Bob's training was conducted during an afternoon free play period. During the second week, training took place during lunchtime. Social skills training involved an initial ten-minute period of didactic discussion in which a rationale was presented (to make new friends). A token reinforcement program involved checks on a card for each two-minute period of appropriate peer interactions. A predetermined number of checks earned Bob a small toy and a sticker. Four stickers earned Bob a larger item (such as a coloring book). The record sheet of checks and stickers was kept in Bob's room so that he could have constant access to his progress.

After the didactic session, Bob was taken to the natural setting, which was either the cafeteria or the unit, for *in vivo* training. The *in vivo* training consisted of modeling one of five social skills elements: approval, compliments, compliance, sharing, or affection. In addition, Bob was prompted to initiate interactions with peers using one of the five skills learned, if appropriate. Finally, Bob received feedback regarding his interpersonal interaction. After the *in vivo* session, Bob was directed to continue interacting with his peers.

A fading procedure was then implemented involving a delay in reinforcement so that Bob had to wait to trade in his stickers until the end of the day. In addition, *in vivo* prompts and checks were eliminated. Finally, the therapist's role was eliminated, and the earning of toys became contingent upon the staff's judgment of the appropriateness of Bob's social interactions with peers.

RESULTS: The goals of the training—to increase appropriate social interactions and to decrease time spent playing alone— were achieved on the unit. A twelve-month follow-up at Bob's community school revealed that the overall improvements had been maintained. However, Bob still demonstrated some adjustment problems in regard to emotional and social development. Despite Bob's difficulties, he had generalized his appropriate social behaviors to home and school.

COMMENTARY: This multifaceted social skills training program was effective in increasing appropriate social interactions in a severely emotionally and socially impaired boy. Further research into the components of the treatment program may reveal that some of them could be eliminated with the same results. The authors showed that increasing an inappropriate, aggressive child's repertoire of appropriate social skills reduces maladaptive behavior—in this instance disturbed relationships with peers.

SOURCE: Van Hasselt, V. B., Griest, D. L., Kazdin, A. E., Esveldt-Lawson, K., and Unis, A. S. "Poor Peer Interactions and Social Isolation: A Case Report of Successful In Vivo Social Skills Training on a Child Psychiatric Inpatient Unit." *Journal of Behavior Therapy and Experimental Psychiatry,* 1984, *15* (3), 271–276.

Reducing Disruptive Play Behavior in Toddlers

AUTHORS: Janet K. Porterfield, Emily Herbert-Jackson, and Todd R. Risley

PRECIS: Disruptive play behaviors in a day-care setting were reduced by having disruptive children observe peers' appropriate social behavior.

INTRODUCTION: A primary difficulty in day-care centers tends to be the frequent minor disruptions caused by the preschoolers' immature or inappropriate play behaviors. In keeping with the approach found in the literature, most teachers and parents rely on incidental teaching to foster appropriate group participation in young children. Incidental teaching typically involves telling the child what he or she is doing wrong, explaining the inappropriateness of the behavior, and then distracting the child by giving him or her a different toy or activity. Although this method has proven to be effective, the authors propose that the disruptive child or behavior is actually being reinforced, as the child is receiving adult attention and, in many instances, a toy as a result of inappropriate behavior.

A less reinforcing procedure, utilizing contingent observation, was developed by Porterfield and her colleagues. In this procedure, disruptive behavior is followed by telling the child what behavior was wrong, explaining an appropriate alternative, separating the child from the group (thereby making the child an observer), telling the child to watch the appropriate behavior of the group, and allowing the child to return to the group when he or she can describe or show an understanding of the appropriate behavior.

TREATMENT: Twenty-six children between the ages of one and three who attended the Toddler Center of the Lawrence Day-Care Program were exposed to the contingent observation procedure. Disruptive behavior was defined as:

     1. Aggression: any physical act, such as hitting, biting, or kicking another child.
     2. Crying and fussing: verbalizations accompanied by tears.
     3. Tantruming: a loud upset with or without tears.
     4. Destructive use of a toy: any use of a toy that could result in damage to the toy or to something in the Day-Care Center.
     5. Creating a dangerous situation: situations that could result in the child's hurting him- or herself or someone else, such as throwing toys or climbing on furniture.

     Prior to the implementation of the contingent observation procedure, the caregivers in the center were trained for a period of nine days. Training consisted of written as well as verbal instructions, and modeling and feedback were provided in individual and group meetings. The procedure was introduced as the "sit-and-watch" technique.
     Caregivers were instructed to respond to a child's inappropriate behavior by pointing it out to the child and explaining an appropriate alternative. They were then to move the child away from the group and instruct the child to sit and watch the behavior of the peers. For example, if a child had grabbed a toy, he or she would be told to sit and watch how the other children

asked for the toys they wanted. After the caregiver had observed the child watching the children for a period of time, usually less than one minute in duration, the caregiver was to ask the child if he or she was ready to join the group and use the appropriate behavior. This was to be accomplished through the caregiver's verbalization of the proper behavior ("Are you ready to ask for the toys you want?"). Upon the child's positive response, the child was to be permitted to return to the group. If the child responded negatively or not at all, the child was again to be instructed to sit and watch until ready to join the group. The child was to be praised or given positive attention for utilizing appropriate behavior alternatives once he or she rejoined the group.

Caregivers were instructed to comfort crying or fussy children. If a child could not be easily comforted, he or she was to be placed in a beanbag chair and told to relax until he or she was feeling better. In this instance, the child could return to the group without the caregiver's invitation. However, if a child was quite disruptive or loud during the contingent observation period and this behavior lasted more than a few minutes, the child was to be taken to a "quiet place," which was a time-out area. Once the child calmed down, he or she was to be returned to the sit-and-watch area.

RESULTS: The contingent observation procedure was experimentally compared to a redirection procedure—that is, the common incidental teaching method. The sit-and-watch procedure was found to be considerably more effective than the redirection procedures in reducing aggressive and disruptive behavior in the day-care center. During the contingent observation procedures, the children's level of disruptions was less than half of those during redirection. It is also noteworthy that it was not necessary for any child to go to the "quiet place" during the implementation of the "sit-and-watch" technique.

COMMENTARY: The reported method of decreasing mild disruptive behavior in a day-care center was found to be an effective alternative to the commonly employed method of redirect-

ing a child. The described procedure eliminates the reinforcement of the inappropriate behaviors and uses peers as models of
appropriate, expected behaviors. Removing young children
from the situation in which they are exhibiting negative behaviors is an established, effective technique. Combining this with
an observation period appears to be an easy technique to implement in a group setting. Implications for responding to toddlers'
disruptive group behaviors should be considered.

SOURCE: Porterfield, J. K., Herbert-Jackson, E., and Risley,
    T. R. "Contingent Observations: An Effective and Accep-
    table Procedure for Reducing Disruptive Behavior of Young
    Children in a Group Setting." *Journal of Applied Behavior
    Analysis*, 1976, 9, 55-64.

Modifying Aggressive Behavior
in Adolescent Psychiatric Patients

AUTHORS: John P. Elder, Barry A. Edelstein, and Marianne M.
Narick

PRECIS: Aggressive interpersonal behavior is modified by
teaching socially appropriate behavior through instructions,
modeling, and feedback.

INTRODUCTION: Four adolescents, one female and three
male, residing on an adolescent psychiatric ward were trained in
social skills so as to offer them appropriate behavioral alternatives to aggressive responses. All of the adolescents had a history
of verbally and physically aggressive interpersonal behavior. Despite a behavior modification program on the ward that utilized
a point system, no decreases in the adolescents' aggression had
been achieved.

TREATMENT: The four adolescents participated in group social skills training run by two staff members. The group met four days a week for approximately forty-five minutes a day. Through observations and interviews with the adolescents, the therapists determined targeted behaviors that were sources of interpersonal conflict and resulted in aggression: interruptions, responses to negative communication (responses to teasing, threats, and so on), and requests for behavior change.

During each group session, role playing was used to simulate instances of the targeted behaviors. One therapist acted as a confederate for each role play. Each role play lasted two minutes, and the group members rotated their participation in it. During the sessions, the therapist who did not act as the confederate provided instructions, modeling, and feedback on the role play. Generalization scenes (scenes role played without therapist intervention) occurred during each rotation. An example of a role play for the targeted behavior of "interruption" might be a scene involving a classroom situation in which the teacher is speaking and the adolescent does not understand something. A role play for "response to negative communication" might be a scene in which a peer teases the adolescent. An example for "requesting a behavior change" might be a scene involving a peer playing a radio loudly, which distracts the adolescent's concentration.

During the treatment period, token fines were the consequence for inappropriate interruptions, responses to negative behavior, and inappropriate requests for behavior changes on the ward. In addition, seclusion (time-out) was imposed on the ward as a consequence for inappropriate response to negative communication and inappropriate requests for behavior change. The targeted behaviors were rated in various settings on the ward, including the dayroom, the cafeteria, and the classroom.

RESULTS: The use of instructions, role playing, and feedback proved effective in modifying the aggressive, interpersonal behavior of the adolescents. All four benefited from the treatment, as they learned alternatives to their aggressive behaviors.

In addition, both fine rates and seclusion periods decreased as the adolescents became more effective in relating appropriately on the ward. At a three-month follow-up, three of the four adolescents had been discharged, and at a nine-month follow-up, they were still functioning in the community.

COMMENTARY: In keeping with current findings in the treatment of aggressive adolescents, the authors found the utilization of social skills training involving the introduction of an appropriate repertoire of social behaviors to be successful in modifying inappropriate interpersonal interactions. The authors found that this particular treatment was effective in obtaining stimulus generalization to various settings on the inpatient ward, such as the lunchroom and the dayroom. Elder and his associates acknowledge the fact that their findings are based on limited data. More research involving this treatment for hospitalized adolescents is warranted.

SOURCE: Elder, J. P., Edelstein, B. A., and Narick, M. M. "Adolescent Psychiatric Patients: Modifying Aggressive Behavior with Social Skills Training." *Behavior Modification*, 1979, *3* (2), 161-178.

Sibling Rivalry

Sibling rivalry tends to occur when a child's need to feel worthwhile is frustrated, whereas jealousy occurs when the need to love and be loved is frustrated (Smart, M., and Smart, R. An Introduction to Family Relationships. Philadelphia: Saunders, 1953). Feelings of jealousy are more likely to be directed toward a younger sibling and rivalrous feelings toward an older sibling. Competition and envy are also involved when a child endeavors to do as well as or better than another sibling.

The sibling relationship is an area that has been relatively neglected in the social psychology literature. We still know very little, for example, about "normal" sibling interactions at different age levels. Consequently, it is very difficult to define disturbed sibling relations in cases that fall short of actual physical injury. We also do not know why siblings in some families generally act in a positive and supportive manner toward one another while negative feelings and verbal putdowns among siblings prevail in other households.

Excessive fighting among siblings is a common complaint among parents. A most effective intervention for reducing this fighting is time-out—that is, sending all the children who are involved in the altercation to time-out areas, such as their bedrooms. No attempt is made to determine who was to blame for the fight. In this way, siblings are discouraged from baiting one another. Parents should couple this time-out technique with praise and attention when the siblings are playing cooperatively together. The following articles present alternate strategies for coping with more intense expressions of hostility among siblings. (Also see section on Overt Hostility Toward Peers.)

Parent Education as a Treatment
for Sibling Rivalry

AUTHOR: Carole E. Calladine

PRECIS: Using parent groups to educate parents on issues affecting and maintaining sibling rivalry.

INTRODUCTION: Calladine initially discusses a theoretical framework that defines sibling rivalry. This framework is utilized in parent education groups prior to teaching parents effective preventive and intervention strategies for controlling rivalry in their families.

Calladine states that all sibling rivalry is the result of children's difficulties in sharing their parents. Three types of rivalry are presented. In the first, labeled heir/heiress, the siblings believe that there is one child who is favored by the parents and therefore receives the greatest amount of parental attention. In the competitors form, siblings compete to get parental attention, as they believe that the parents favor different children at different times based on behavior. Finally, in the peers form, children feel important to each other as members of a family and feel that parents acknowledge each child as being special. Based on this formulation, peer sibling rivalry is the form that families should strive for, as sibling rivalry is a naturally occurring event in all families. Calladine discusses skills that parents can learn in order to achieve peer sibling rivalry: leadership styles, the family judicial system, contracting, and group discipline.

The author presents three leadership styles—laissez-faire, autocratic, and democratic. In the laissez-faire style, parents do not offer direction to the children. This leads to frustration, which can result in rivalries. Autocratic parents take absolute control over the children and do not allow them to make any decisions. Although these children tend to regress when parents are not around to control things, they feel secure knowing that their parents will take charge. Democratic parents involve the children in family decisions, which promotes the greatest degree of cooperation between children. As parents become aware of leadership styles and their advantages and disadvantages, they become more adept at choosing the best type of leadership style for their children in different situations. This is one step toward unifying the family and reducing sibling rivalry.

Calladine proposes that, once parents understand sibling and leadership styles, a discussion of the family judicial system should occur. To facilitate peer sibling rivalry, she recommends that parents act as mediators in sibling disputes. As mediator, the parent encourages problem solving by moderating the siblings' discussion about the problem. Problem solving is accomplished through a process whereby parent(s) clearly state the problem. Solutions are given by each child, as the parent's role is to keep the discussion focused until a decision is reached. If no decision or solution is worked out by the children, the parent may intervene by not allowing the object or issue being disputed to be utilized by anyone until discussion resolves the problem.

Calladine next presents contracting skills as an effective technique for parents to use in repetitive disputes. The contract should emphasize that decisions are the siblings' responsibility. The author offers specific rules for setting up contracts. Finally, group discipline techniques are discussed. These emphasize interactions, not individual behaviors. The author gives examples of group discipline techniques (for example, the taking away of a family privilege, such as watching television, from all siblings if a rule is broken).

A correlation can be found among parental role in the family, leadership style, and sibling rivalry form. This demonstrates that parents who act as meditators employing a democratic leadership style tend to have children who engage in the healthiest form of sibling rivalry, which is peer rivalry.

COMMENTARY: Educating parents, as Calladine suggests, to the various leadership styles, sibling rivalry styles, family judicial systems, and contracting techniques, can be an effective intervention or prevention of inappropriate sibling rivalry. Naturally, clinicians working with families must be sensitive to family dynamics, as educative techniques are not always the treatment of choice, especially with pathological families.

SOURCE: Calladine, C. E. "Sibling Rivalry: A Parent Education Perspective." *Child Welfare,* 1983, *62,* 421–427.

Additional Readings

Kendrick, C., and Dunn, J. "Sibling Quarrels and Maternal Responses." *Developmental Psychology,* 1983, *19* (1), 62–70.

A longitudinal study examined mothers' interventions in sibling quarreling when the second-born children were eight months and fourteen months of age. The age of the first-born child was found to be positively correlated with the number of quarrels in which the mother prohibited the first-born and was negatively correlated with the proportion in which maternal distraction techniques were used. Mothers of boys were more consistent in their responses to hostile behavior than were mothers of girls. In addition, first-born boys demonstrated more hostile behavior when siblings were fourteen months of age and mothers had used prohibiting six months earlier. In first-born girls, a higher frequency of quarreling was revealed when siblings were eight months and mothers had intervened six months earlier with prohibition.

Levi, A. M., Buskila, M., and Gerzi, S. "Benign Neglect: Reducing Fights Among Siblings." *Journal of Individual Psychology,* 1977, *33* (2), 240–245.

The authors tested Rudolf Dreikurs's hypothesis that parental noninterference would decrease sibling fighting. Six families were studied, with three families comprising a cognitive group and three families comprising a role-playing group. Both groups were instructed in Dreikers's techniques and principles.

The difference between the groups was only in the role playing. Results revealed that all six families experienced a significant decrease in sibling fighting, with no differences between the families in which the parents had role played situations and the families in which parents only received cognitive instructions.

6

Disturbed Relationships
with Parents

Successful intervention in disturbed relationships between child and parents has been accomplished mainly by psychodynamic and learning theory methods. There is a growing trend toward combining these approaches to reduce tension, increase satisfaction, and improve communication. Behavioral and psychodynamic therapists focus on the same problems but use different language when explaining cause and treatment. However, the behavioral methods frequently are more detailed and formalized and more consistently applied. Some of the techniques used in this chapter are unique to therapists operating within a learning theory framework.

When a family is seen together, an eclectic approach can be used to influence the behavior and attitudes of the child and the parents. Interaction patterns can be observed and destructive patterns can be pointed out and changed. More satisfying responses may occur both during therapy and at home. Focus-on and discussing each member's perceptions may lead to changes in the habitual, long-standing pattern. When family members' goals become clearer to themselves and others, their goals may become more reachable. In discussions, once individual goals (desires) are identified, specific behavioral techniques or communication exercises may be beneficially employed. For example, a therapist may see a hostile daughter and her parents, all of whom desire a more pleasant, calmer atmosphere. The angry girl feels that her parents are unfair and that her own belligerence is justified. It soon becomes clear that the parents expect cooperative and respectful behavior from the girl and that they feel disappointed.

At this point, a behavioral approach might be suggested—that all family members begin to reinforce each other positively and ignore inappropriate behavior. This intervention may change the pattern, reduce the girl's hostile behavior, and lead to more positive interaction and the perception that their wishes are being more adequately achieved. Family members may be asked to deliberately not respond with disappointment and anger, which only lead to an increase in angry responses. The girl might be taught to control her angry responses by using relaxation when aroused or by thinking about a pleasant event or key words (such as "calm down"). It can be particularly effective to arrange a situation in which the girl views her parents as being helpful by participating with her in the new control process. They might remind her, in an agreed-on manner, to employ her own self-control methods. Similarly, the girl might play a helpful role by reminding the parents when they lapse into a previously agreed-against negative mode of reacting. Some families prefer a formal discussion hour in which everyone has a turn to speak while others listen. This approach fosters a feeling of importance and respect, because each individual is taken seriously.

A growing trend is to analyze the family system, understand the interactive pattern, and directly influence the system.

This approach is especially applicable when the predominant problem is the disturbed parent-child relationship, manifested by a child's hostility or overdependency. An angry girl, for example, might be incorrigible when with the parents. Their inability to cope with her may be a result of their marital differences, which prevent them from taking a unified, effective position. A grandparent might be playing a contributing role by siding with the girl or interfering in some way. The analysis of the *system* makes for a different type of intervention than does viewing the child as a hostile individual who requires individual psychotherapy. Regardless of theoretical orientation, the therapist can then approach the identified disturbed pattern within the family system.

Overdependent Relationship with Parents

Dependency problems arise when a child becomes overly reliant on parents for support. At different ages, varying degrees of independence are expected of children. Although norms may differ widely, enough consensus exists so that adults and other children can reliably identify a child as being overly dependent on adults. The child may lack self-direction, insist on continuous care and affection, and be unable to engage in give-and-take interactions with peers.

Brief Therapy for Overly
Dependent Behavior

AUTHOR: Louis A. Chandler

PRECIS: Brief therapy, consisting of six sessions with the child's mother, resulted in improving a seven-year-old's overly dependent behavior.

INTRODUCTION: The author outlines the process of brief therapy as an intervention in four phases. First, the therapist identifies the problem by interviewing the concerned adults. He or she then formulates a precise behavioral intervention based on the information obtained. This formulation becomes the focus of the second phase of the brief treatment as the therapist presents explanations for the behavior to the parents and then sets realistic goals. Achievement of the goals is obtained by the parents' participation in changing the child's behavior. A time limit is set, which imposes an expectation as to when behavioral change on the child's part should be noticed. During the third phase of the treatment, the therapist discusses with the parents problem-solving strategies. The therapist provides educative information in the form of observations, reflections, interpretations, support, advice, and guidance. Finally, at the conclusion of the previously set time limit, the child's progress is assessed. A procedure for future follow-up also is arranged. Chandler illustrates the effectiveness of brief therapy with the case of an overly dependent youngster.

CASE STUDY: Ronny, a seven-year-old, was referred for treatment by his mother, who was concerned about her son's behavior. At times, Ronny was reportedly passive, compliant, and quiet; at other times, he became overactive, loud, and noncompliant. The mother felt that Ronny's greatest behavioral shift occurred in his grandmother's presence, at which time he became overly dependent and demanding as he regressed and frequently asked for help with tasks he was capable of doing independently.

Ronny was with his grandmother a great deal, as she

cared for him when the mother, a single parent, worked. The mother and grandmother differed in their beliefs about raising Ronny. The grandmother was permissive and encouraged regressive, dependent behaviors, whereas the mother required more independent behaviors from Ronny. At the time of referral, Ronny was doing poorly in first grade, and retention was being considered. Treatment was conducted by the school's psychologist, who worked with the mother for six weeks.

TREATMENT: Several treatment goals were formulated at the first session: change the grandmother's behavior or lessen her influence on Ronny, develop consistency in adults' expectations of Ronny with reinforcement of age-appropriate behavior, demand performance in school, and monitor Ronny's weight, as he was mildly overweight.

In order to meet the prescribed goals, the mother shifted her work schedule and hired a baby-sitter so that Ronny would spend less time with the grandmother. This led to issues between the grandmother and mother in which the mother had to assert her own independence. In addition, the mother and teacher participated in placing consistent demands on Ronny and providing reinforcement in the form of praise for age-appropriate independence and school performance. Finally, the mother was given a height/weight chart to place over the bathroom scale, where Ronny's weight was to be recorded.

RESULTS: Reportedly, the most dramatic change was Ronny's attitude in regard to his weight: He actively participated in weight reduction. Ronny's schoolwork began to improve and peer relationships developed. The grandmother and mother resolved their conflict, which resulted in greater consistency of their handling of Ronny. The mother also reported that Ronny began to act more appropriately, with less regressive behavior. As a result of Ronny's improvements, he was recommended for promotion to second grade.

COMMENTARY: The use of structured brief therapy proved highly effective in treating overly dependent behavior in a seven-year-old boy. Utilizing a time limit and seeing the mother, not the child, for treatment sessions produced significant changes in a relatively short time frame (six weeks). The treatment described is an important one for professionals, such as school psychologists, who are not afforded the time to engage in long-term interventions with cases.

SOURCE: Chandler, L. A. "Brief Therapy: Ronny G." *Psychology in the Schools*, 1983, *20*, 215-218.

Treating Dependency with Time-Out and Assertiveness Training

AUTHOR: Roger L. Patterson

PRECIS: A nine-year-old boy who was overly dependent and lacked assertiveness was treated for frequent crying with a time-out procedure and assertiveness training.

INTRODUCTION: A nine-year-old boy was referred for treatment by his teacher because of frequent crying and a lack of appropriate peer play. The child frequently ran to the teacher crying as a response to peers' aggression. Similar behavior was reported at home, where the boy would go running to his mother and as a result receive attention either in the form of consolation or scolding.

TREATMENT: Since the child was treated over summer vacation, only one setting, the home, was used. During an initial baseline period, it became apparent that adult attention was playing a major role in sustaining the boy's episodes of crying. A time-out procedure was implemented in which the mother told the child to go to an unoccupied room until he stopped crying. By the third week of treatment, it also became apparent that the boy's smaller, seven-year-old brother's aggressive acts often precipitated the crying. This seemed to be the result of the subject's inability to assert and defend himself.

The next phase of treatment was aimed at increasing the subject's assertiveness. The therapist saw the two brothers in an exercise room and told them that they were to participate in college-type wrestling games. The rules included no hitting and no hair pulling. After three rounds, in which the subject, because of his size, was easily able to pin down his younger btother, the brother refused to participate. The therapist then wrestled with the subject and allowed him to pin the therapist several times. The mother observed the wrestling sessions and was instructed to encourage assertive behavior at home. She was not to punish the boys but to allow them to engage in rowdy play at home.

RESULTS: When the time-out procedure was implemented, crying episodes began to decrease. However, after the wrestling sessions, the mother withdrew the child from treatment, as she reported that crying episodes were no longer problematic. In addition, the youngster had asserted himself at home and as a result had made the younger brother cry. As the mother seemed to understand the importance of this behavior, she socially reinforced the subject's assertiveness. Follow-ups at two weeks after school resumed and at the end of the school year revealed that the subject no longer ran to adults crying and that he was adequately asserting himself with his brother and with peers.

COMMENTARY: The time-out procedure was an effective means of extinguishing the inappropriate crying behaviors. However, the assertiveness training seemed to focus on the etiology of the dependency behaviors, thereby removing the child's need to depend on adults for protection. The effectiveness of the treatment undoubtedly was greatly enhanced by the mother's willingness to change her behavior toward the subject.

SOURCE: Patterson, R. L. "Time-Out and Assertive Training for a Dependent Child." *Behavior Therapy*, 1972, *3* (3), 466–468.

Noncompliance

Noncompliance is a child's refusal to comply with commands, directions, suggestions, or orders. These behaviors may be in response to a specific, verbalized parental or adult instruction, or they may be in response to an ongoing rule that is not directly stated but is in effect. Noncompliant children often whine, engage in aggression toward others, and destroy property. Since parental behaviors and parent-child interactions tend to perpetuate noncompliance, many of the treatment approaches train parents in effective management techniques.

411

Treating Severely Oppositional
and Aggressive Behavior

AUTHORS: Robert G. Wahler and James J. Fox

PRECIS: Treating children exhibiting severe oppositional and aggressive behaviors with solitary toy play and a time-out procedure.

INTRODUCTION: Most treatment strategies for dealing with oppositional and aggressive behaviors focus on teaching parents methods of obtaining compliance or appropriate child responses. While obtaining baselines of oppositional behavior, the authors found that children tended to have their best days when the day involved their participation in an activity that was incompatible with negativism or aggression. Since aggression is a social behavior, children experienced periods without aggression when they were involved in something that did not necessitate their interacting with others. Children tend not to be noncompliant to parental demands when they are engaged in an activity that keeps them focused on an appropriate response. Solitary play is one instance in which children are engaged in a response that is incompatible with opposition and aggression. Therefore, increasing a child's solitary play time is used as a treatment for children who exhibit severe aggressive and oppositional behavior.

TREATMENT: Wahler and Fox report the treatment of four children who were referred for behavior problems involving aggression toward other people. In each of these treatments, the therapist conducted initial home observations and parental interviews. Then each family was required to choose a time during the day for the implementation of a play contract. The play contract, as explained to parents and child, consisted of the child playing alone with any toy(s) for a specified time period (up to thirty minutes) in the presence of others. The play had to be reasonably quiet, and the child could not interact with anyone during the play. The child was instructed not to attempt to get others' attention and to ignore anyone who approached him or her during this time. If this procedure was followed, the child earned points that could be traded for rewards at the end of five consecutive days of completing the play period.

Three of the four children were also required—prior to the play contract—to engage in a cooperative *social* contract; this contract involved a social activity in which parent and child cooperated. One child was required to engage in a television-watching contract, as the child was overly dependent on adults and needed to succeed in solitary activities.

A time-out contingency was found necessary as a means of inhibiting all of the children's oppositional activities. Time-out was used all day for any violation of family rules or for non-compliance with parental demands. In addition, parents were instructed to use approval for instances of appropriate, compliant behavior.

RESULTS: The effects of increasing the children's time spent in solitary play did result in a decrease in oppositional and aggressive behaviors. The planned increase in cooperative social behavior and in television watching did not produce the desired decreases. It was only the introduction of the time-out procedure, with the increases in solitary play, that resulted in less problematic behavior.

COMMENTARY: The techniques of increasing solitary play in conjunction with time-out procedures proved effective in modifying aggressive, oppositional behaviors. However, as pointed out elsewhere in this chapter, the time-out procedure alone may have been the most important intervention, and its power and effectiveness need further investigation.

SOURCE: Wahler, R. G., and Fox, J. J. "Solitary Toy Play and Time-Out: A Family Treatment Package for Children with Aggressive and Oppositional Behavior." *Journal of Applied Behavior Analysis*, 1980, *13*, 23-39.

Brief Family Intervention for
Improving Parent-Child Interactions

AUTHOR: Barclay Martin

PRECIS: Teaching families conflict resolution and contingency management in order to improve disturbed parent-child relationships.

INTRODUCTION: Martin conceptualizes treatment of disturbed parent-child interactions in two components: one component addresses how the parent and child communicate about a problem, and the other investigates what they actually do about a problem. Both behavioral interventions and expressive therapy interventions have met with some success in treating oppositional, aggressive children who do not comply with parental demands and requests. The author combines these two approaches in order to intervene with a brief treatment. The training includes communication-building as well as conflict resolution skills and contingency management techniques.

In addition, Martin focuses on the issue of including the father in the treatment, as most programs dealing with noncompliance treat mother-child dyads and exclude the father.

TREATMENT: Forty-three families with a noncompliant child ranging in age from five to ten years participated in the treatment. The families were separated into three treatment conditions: in one the father was included in the treatment; in another, the father was not included; and the third was a waiting list control condition. All parents attended an initial interview session, in which information about the problems between the parents and child was obtained. Following the interview, mothers were required to report on problematic interactions for seven consecutive weekdays via daily telephone calls made by the therapist to the mother.

Weekly sessions constituted the next phase of treatment, either with or without father involvement. Parent(s) were taught to decrease blaming, questioning, and long lectures by participating in behavior rehearsal and by being exposed to modeling techniques. In addition, they were taught to communicate more effectively by expressing their desires, listening to the child's feelings and desires, and negotiating agreements that were acceptable to parent(s) and child. Children were also taught to express their feelings and desires in an appropriate fashion. Contingency management skills were taught to parents. These included contingent rewards, mild punishments, such as a time-out, social reinforcement, and prompting cues. All material rewards were offered as an initial step in gaining new behaviors and were later faded out. This brief intervention consisted of a maximum of ten treatment sessions.

RESULTS: Families were kept in treatment, up to ten sessions, until the problematic behaviors between parent(s) and child decreased to near zero. Families required from three to ten sessions, with the average being five sessions. The training in conflict resolution and the contingency training in conflict resolution and contingency management procedures resulted in immediate decreases in problematic mother-child interactions. These results did not differ based on the father's inclusion or exclusion from the treatment.

COMMENTARY: Martin focuses the treatment of noncompliant youngsters on the parent-child interactions. This approach is consistent with much of the literature, which finds that parents play a major role in maintaining negative, problematic child behavior. Many hypotheses could be generated in order to explain the absence of any differences in treatment effects when including or excluding the father. Perhaps more research on the father's role in dealing with problematic child behavior needs to be conducted.

SOURCE: Martin, B. "Brief Family Intervention: Effectiveness and the Importance of Including the Father." *Journal of Consulting and Clinical Psychology*, 1977, 45 (6), 1002-1010.

Time-Out as a Treatment for Noncompliance

AUTHORS: Mark W. Roberts, Linda C. Hatzenbuehler, and
Arthur W. Bean

PRECIS: Increasing preschoolers' compliant behaviors by training mothers to use a time-out contingency.

INTRODUCTION: The authors question the use of contingent
parental attention to compliance behavior as an effective treatment for noncompliance. They point out that using differential
attention procedures in isolation often has resulted in failure to
increase compliance. In addition, they point out that most
studies combine the use of differential attention with time-out
procedures and/or command training procedures. Finally, the
authors report that in some interventions for noncompliance,
compliance was not achieved until a time-out component was
introduced. Roberts and his associates found support for their
hypothesis that time-out alone could be an effective treatment
for preschoolers' noncompliance.

TREATMENT: Thirty-two preschool children and their mothers participated in the treatment. The children were all referred
for noncompliance, which included tantrum behavior, talking
back to adults, and/or fighting. Four different treatment procedures were utilized. One treatment focused on attention—mothers were taught to praise the child for each event of compliance.
The second treatment focused on a time-out procedure whereby
the mother immediately placed the child in a chair in a corner
following noncompliance. The time-out lasted a minimum of
two minutes, and the child could only leave the time-out corner
after fifteen seconds of quiet behavior. If the child left the time-
out chair without permission, he or she was spanked. The third
treatment consisted of attention plus time-out, and the fourth
treatment was a control condition in which child and mother
interacted with no interventions implemented.

All parent-child dyads attended sessions in a clinic playroom. Mothers wore a bug-in-the-ear device and received communications from the therapist, who was situated behind a one-

way mirror. The playroom was equipped with small toys (animals, cars, blocks, people), a box, a house, and a truck.

An initial baseline session was conducted in which the mother pointed to objects and issued commands. Commands all directed the child to place one of the small toys in the box, house, or truck. During the treatment sessions, the child engaged in free play and then the baseline session was repeated using either the attention, time-out, or attention plus time-out as consequences for the child's behavior.

Two behaviors were measured: compliance, which was defined as a motoric response within five seconds of the mother's command, and noncompliance, which was defined as all other behaviors that could not be rated as compliant.

RESULTS: The time-out procedure proved to be significantly more effective than the attention treatment in producing compliance. In addition, the differential attention procedure actually resulted in a decrease in compliance. Attention plus time-out produced a significant increase. However, the findings indicate that the time-out component resulted in the desired change.

COMMENTARY: The authors obtained support for their hypothesis that time-out procedures have significant effects on modifying noncompliant behaviors in preschoolers. The authors do not advocate eliminating the teaching of differential attention to parents. However, they do propose that programs that delay the teaching of time-out procedures until differential attention is mastered should caution parents not to expect changes in the child's behavior until the time-out procedures are introduced.

This is a significant study which should be replicated so that more information in regard to its implications for treating noncompliance in preschoolers and in school-aged children can be examined.

SOURCE: Roberts, M. W., Hatzenbuehler, L. C., and Bean, A. W. "The Effects of Differential Attention and Time-Out on Child Noncompliance." *Behavior Therapy*, 1981, *12*, 93–99.

Using Parents as Change Agents
for Child Noncompliance

AUTHORS: Rex Forehand, Ellie T. Sturgis, Robert J. McMahon, Dian Aguar, Kenneth Green, Karen C. Wells, and Jeri Breiner

PRECIS: Noncompliant children who were treated with a standardized behavioral program in which mothers acted as the change agents revealed positive changes in the home setting with no generalizability to the school setting.

INTRODUCTION: The authors use a standardized training program with mothers acting as change agents to treat children's noncompliant behaviors. The training program focuses primarily on parent behavior, as the authors report that parents' commanding behavior is largely responsible for children's noncompliance. As parents become less demanding of their children, an increase in compliance is manifested. The authors discuss the long-term effects of this intervention, as well as its effect on generalizing child behavior to an untreated setting—school.

TREATMENT: Two studies generated the data for the current findings. All subjects were treated with the standardized training program. In the first study, eleven mother-child dyads were treated. The children who were identified as being noncompliant ranged in age from three to eight years. Mothers were trained in a variety of behaviors, which were recorded by therapists. In addition, several child-parent behaviors were recorded. Recordings occurred in the clinic during mother-child play sessions, as well as in the home. The following constitute the parent behaviors that were recorded:

　　　1. Rewards—positive attention, either verbal or physical, that refers to the child's behavior, play, or appearance.
　　　2. Commands—either alpha commands (orders, rules, suggestions, or questions that allow for an appropriate motor response) or beta commands (commands that do not allow the child an opportunity to comply. These include vague com-

mands, commands that are interrupted by additional commands, and commands for which parents carry out the behavior for the child without giving the child a chance to comply).

3. Time-out—removing the child from the room or from the opportunity to receive any attention as a result of his or her inappropriate behavior.

The parent-child behaviors that were recorded include:

1. Child compliance—an appropriate motoric response that occurs within five seconds of a parental alpha command.

2. Child noncompliance—lack of initiation of an appropriate motoric response within five seconds of a parental alpha command.

3. Contingent attention—a reward given by the parent within five seconds of the child's compliance.

All treatment sessions took place in a clinic playroom. Treatment consisted of two phases. The first phase taught the mother to increase her frequency of positive reinforcement. The mother was trained to attend to the child's behavior while eliminating all commands, questions, and criticisms. After the mother accomplished this, she was taught to use contingent rewards. Mothers were required to practice these behaviors at home and to use appropriate rewards, such as television time or treats, for desirable behaviors.

The second phase of treatment focused on teaching the mothers to use alpha commands and the time-out procedure. Time-out included one warning that made the child aware of the time-out consequence if noncompliance continued. Time-out consisted of placing the child in a chair and not allowing the child to leave the chair until he or she exhibited two minutes of quiet behavior.

Each treatment session included an initial five-minute data collection period followed by a discussion between mother and therapist about the mother's use of the treatment techniques. The therapist would then model techniques for the mother. A role play, with the therapist acting the part of the child, followed. Wearing a bug-in-the-ear device in the playroom, the mother then practiced the techniques with therapist instruction and feedback. At the end of the session, a five-minute data collection period was again conducted. Ten of the original eleven families participated in a follow-up study at six and twelve months after treatment.

The second study employed the same treatment program but examined the generalizability of treatment effects to the child's behavior in school. Eight mother-child dyads participated in this study, with the children ranging in age from five to seven years. Eight control children were also selected in the school setting. The recorded home behaviors were the same as in the first study. In the school setting, the following behaviors were recorded by the therapists:

1. Child noncompliance—which was the same as before except that the child was now being observed with the teacher giving commands, not the mother.

2. Child inappropriate behavior—whining, crying, yelling, destruction of objects, aggression toward others, self-stimulation (thumbsucking, head banging, and so on), tantrums, negativism, and leaving an area without permission.

3. Teacher commands—a direction or suggestion made to the child that required a motoric response.

4. Teacher attention—questions asked of the child, rewards, physical contact, and general comments that were not negative.

RESULTS: Results of the first study revealed that the treatment program was effective in changing parent and child behavior in both the clinic and home settings. The six- and twelve-month follow-ups demonstrated that treatment effects were maintained, with one exception: Mothers' use of contingent attention was not sustained, and there was no difference between contingent attention from pretesting to follow-up. However, the use of social reinforcement was powerful enough to continue to elicit child compliance. Another significant finding was that mothers' use of alpha commands did not increase but their use of beta commands significantly decreased. Evidence indicates that the reduction of beta commands also served to increase the children's compliance.

The second study found similar results, with parent and child behaviors changing in the predicted directions. This resulted in an overall increase in compliance in the clinic and at home. However, no significant behavior changes were found at school.

COMMENTARY: The authors' findings indicate that this training program does not yield evidence of generalizability to school settings. However, it is quite effective in changing parent-child behaviors at home. Several factors may contribute to these findings. The positive change at home appears to be the result of training mothers to manage their children in a more positive, appropriate manner. However, the teachers did not treat the children any differently; thus their interactions probably maintained the noncompliance. Therefore, when treating noncompliant children of school age, the school environment should be considered in the treatment program.

SOURCE: Forehand, R., Sturgis, E. T., McMahon, R. J., Aguar, D., Green, K., Wells, K. C., and Breiner, J. "Parent Behavioral Training to Modify Child Noncompliance: Treatment Generalization Across Time and from Home to School." *Behavior Modification*, 1979, *3* (1), 3-25.

Long-Term Effects of Treating
Noncompliant Children

AUTHORS: Phillip S. Strain, Peggy Steele, Toni Ellis, and
Matthew A. Timm

PRECIS: Long-term follow-up revealed that utilizing mothers as
therapists in the treatment of youngsters' noncompliant behaviors had lasting effects.

INTRODUCTION: Follow-up data are reported for forty children who were treated for noncompliant behaviors. At the time
of referral, the youngsters, ages three to five, were demonstrating prolonged tantrums, opposition to adults' demands and requests, and physical aggression toward their parents. Mother
and child participated in a standardized treatment program,
which was based on Wahler's oppositional child treatment (Wahler, R. G. "Setting Generality: Some Specific and General Effects of Child Behavior Therapy." *Journal of Applied Behavior
Analysis*, 1969, 2, 239–246). Follow-up of these families was
conducted in order to ascertain the long-term effects of using
mothers as change agents for preschoolers exhibiting severe
noncompliant behaviors.

TREATMENT: Criteria for selecting the families to be included
in the follow-up study included: the child had either entered or
completed first grade, families lived within twenty miles of the
clinic, and families had participated in the program until they
fulfilled the criteria of completion. Treatment and follow-up
were conducted by the Regional Intervention Program (RIP).

The original treatment program was known as RIP's generalization training (GT) module, which used treatment rooms
that were replicas of home environments. The training, which
utilized mother-son dyads, occurred in twenty-minute sessions
that took place four to five days per week. A weekly class was
also provided in which parents who had previously been in the
program taught mothers social learning principles. In addition,
a supervising parent was assigned to each new mother.

The supervising mothers instructed the new mothers in the requirements and techniques of the program. Mothers were instructed to ask their child to play with ten different toys during the course of the twenty-minute sessions. At the end of each session, the mother was given feedback on her child's frequency of cooperation and oppositional behavior as well as on her attention to these types of behaviors. When appropriate, the supervising parents demonstrated management techniques through role play and behavior rehearsal.

The program was standardized so that each dyad was exposed to the same treatment in the same sequence. The first phase lasted three to five days and was a baseline phase in which no interventions were implemented. The second phase was "differential reinforcement I." This phase was conducted as mothers were learning social learning techniques, specifically contingent attention, through role playing, modeling, the reading of materials, and receiving feedback. The third phase of treatment, the reversal phase, required a reversal in contingent attention whereby mothers ignored cooperative behaviors and attended to noncompliant behaviors. The final phase of the treatment, "differential reinforcement II," required mothers to again use appropriate differential reinforcement as they began to fade out the frequency of attention. Children typically maintained compliant behaviors in the play sessions, with only five or fewer parent "attention events" in each session. The program provided assistance in preschool placements, and telephone contacts were conducted with parents for over a year.

At the time of follow-up, data were obtained from both home and school observations. The school observations looked at a variety of adult and child behaviors in both structured, group learning situations and unstructured situations, such as gym or recess. The behaviors observed during structured, group time included:

1. Adult command, demand, request: This referred to all noninstructional commands, such as getting out books, sitting in one's seat, and so on.

2. Repeated adult command, demand, request: This cate-

gory included all commands that needed to be repeated, as the child did not comply with the initial communication.

3. Positive social reinforcement: This referred to contingent statements or gestures of adults given to either the child or the group for compliance.

4. Negative feedback: This included adults' verbal behaviors to either the child or the group which were contingent upon noncompliance.

5. Compliance with adult command, demand, or request: This referred to the child's compliance that occurred within five seconds.

6. Noncompliance with adult command, demand, or request: This referred to the child's lack of compliance.

7. On-task behavior: This included all behaviors that demonstrated a physical and/or visual orientation to the academic work being presented.

8. Off-task behavior: This referred to behaviors, such as looking around the room, that reflected the child's lack of orientation toward schoolwork.

Behaviors observed during unstructured situations included:

1. Positive social behavior: This referred to verbal and behavioral instances of socially appropriate sharing, playing, and praising of peers.

2. Negative social behavior: This referred to behavioral and verbal instances of nonsharing or inappropriate social interactions.

3. Appropriate nonsocial behavior: This included any appropriate behavior that did not involve direct interactions with peers.

4. Inappropriate nonsocial behavior: This included all behaviors that reflected a lack of participation in ongoing activities, such as leaving the play area, throwing a ball during exercise time, and so on.

Behaviors observed in the home during follow-up consisted of all the behaviors that were considered in both structured and unstructured school situations. Naturally, the definitions applied to home-related interactions and behaviors.

RESULTS: The data from this follow-up study revealed that commands, demands, or requests made by adults were generally met with the child's compliance. The youngsters' social interactions in the home tended to be characterized by appropriate positive and nonsocial behavior. Parent behavior in the home revealed that the management skills were being utilized effectively.

The children's school behavior proved to be compliant and appropriate, as well as generally on-task during academic instructions. Teachers did not respond to or rate the targeted youngsters any differently than they did the rest of the class on the Walker Behavior Checklist.

These findings reveal that the preschoolers who were treated for noncompliance by the standardized Regional Intervention Program maintained the effects of the treatment into elementary school. In addition, the parents maintained their gains, as they continued to use the management techniques they had been taught. This finding supports the program's effectiveness in obtaining long-term changes in the behavior of children with severe behavior problems.

COMMENTARY: The use of differential reinforcement and the application of social learning techniques have been effective in modifying noncompliant behaviors. However, the maintenance of the treatment effects has not been consistent. Although the present findings are quite positive, several factors need to be considered. First, the child was not initially singled out as the only problem, since mother-child *dyads* were treated. Second, parent supervisors worked with each parent. Perhaps most important, intervention occurred while the youngsters were of preschool age. This was before their negativism could elicit a pattern of negative feedback in a school environment. These factors need to be considered in any future research that examines these variables.

SOURCE: Strain, P. S., Steele, P., Ellis, T., and Timm, M. A.

"Long-Term Effects of Oppositional Child Treatment with
Mothers as Therapists and Therapist Trainers." Unpublished
manuscript, Regional Intervention Program, Western Psychiatric Institute, 1984.

Additional Readings

Ammons, P. W., Ammons, F. M., and Wodarski, J. S. "Modeling
   as an Operant Alternative to Time Out: A Case Study."
   Behavioral Engineering, 1981, *6* (4), 153-157.
      The authors present the case of an eleven-year-old girl
who refused to comply with adults and who frequently made
inappropriate negative verbalizations to peers and adults. During
treatment, the girl resided at a children's home for predelin-
quent youths. Time-out procedures did not affect the youngster's negative behaviors; however, modeling procedures were
very effective. Modeling occurred after each inappropriate verbalization or event of noncompliance. It consisted of a house
parent explaining to the girl that her behavior was inappropriate, followed by a discussion of alternative, appropriate behaviors. The house parent and girl then role played the event with
the appropriate alternative. If the girl cooperated in the role
play, she received social reinforcement and points toward a reward. The findings of this study support the research proposing
that inappropriate, aggressive behaviors may be the result of a
limited repertoire of socially appropriate behavior.

Bean, A. W., and Roberts, M. W. "The Effect of Time-Out Release Contingencies on Changes in Child Noncompliance."
   Journal of Abnormal Child Psychology, 1981, *9* (1), 95-
   105.
      Twenty-four preschoolers who were referred because of
noncompliant behavior were treated with one of two techniques. Parent release procedures involved the child's remaining

in time-out until either behavioral or temporal release contingencies were met. Child release procedures involved the termination of the time-out when the child left the time-out chair. During the child release procedure, the child was told that he or she could leave the chair when he or she decided to do what he or she was told. During the parent release procedure, the child was spanked upon leaving the chair prematurely. Although both procedures increased compliance with maternal commands, the child release increases in compliance were not significant.

Chethik, M. "Work with Parents: Treatment of the Parent-Child Relationship." *Journal of Child Psychiatry,* 1976, *15,* 453-463.

This article presents a psychodynamically oriented treatment for parents of "identified patients" who are demonstrating noncompliance. Chethik labels this mode of treatment "treatment of the parent-child relationship." The goal of the therapy is to provide parents with ego clarification and limited insight into the unconscious meanings of the child for the parent(s). The author presents case studies that illustrate the technique and a discussion of the principles involved.

Day, D. E., and Roberts, M. W. "An Analysis of the Physical Punishment Component of a Parent Training Program." *Journal of Abnormal Child Psychology,* 1983, *11* (1), 141-152.

Day and Roberts question the necessity of spanking children who escape from time-out. This spanking procedure is often a component of parent training programs for treating noncompliance. In a study of sixteen noncompliant, clinic-referred preschoolers, the authors found that barrier procedures were equal in effectiveness to spanking in increasing a child's adherence to time-out and in overall compliance. The barrier procedure used involved placing the child who prematurely escaped from time-out in an empty, carpeted closet. The mother turned the light on and left the door open but placed a barrier—a plywood sheet—in the door slot. The mother leaned against the barrier with her back turned in order to allow the child to see her. Although research on the long-term effectiveness of this procedure needs to be conducted, it does present an alternative to physical punishment.

Drabman, R. S., and Creedon, D. L. "Marking Time-Out; A Procedure for Away From Home Disruptive Behavior." *Child Behavior Therapy*, 1979, *1* (1), 99–101.

The marking time-out procedure is a procedure for parents to utilize when they are in public or away from home with a child who is disruptive or noncompliant. The technique is used with children who are subject to time-out procedures at home. While away from home, the parent marks the child's hand with a felt pen to signify that the child will immediately go to the time-out area upon returning home. Marks are not limited in number, and the child will serve one time-out period for each mark on the hand. The authors discuss a practice and implementation procedure.

Erickson, M. F., Farber, E. A., and Egeland, B. R. "Antecedents and Concomitants of Compliance in High-Risk Preschool Children." Paper presented at 90th annual convention of the American Psychological Association, Washington, D.C., Aug. 23-27, 1982.

A sample of high-risk children and their mothers participated in a longitudinal study that assessed infant, parental, interactional, and environmental factors that contribute to developmental outcomes. At age four-and-a-half, when the children were in preschool, the compliant children clearly had had different early experiences than had the children who were assessed as noncompliant. The compliant preschoolers were from more secure home environments in which there was a supportive relationship between the caregiver and the child. In addition, the homes of the compliant children were found to be stimulating but organized learning environments. For the compliant children, these factors correlated with better ego control, less negative emotion, and more positive affect in school.

Forehand, R., Rogers, T., McMahon, R. J., Wells, K. C., and Griest, D. L. "Teaching Parents to Modify Child Behavior Problems: An Examination of Some Follow-Up Data." *Journal of Pediatric Psychology*, 1981, *6* (3), 313-322.

Eighteen mother-child dyads who had successfully completed a standardized treatment program participated in an
eight-month follow-up. The treatment program, described elsewhere in this chapter (Forehand and others, 1979), involved
two phases. In the first phase, parents learned to increase social
rewards and to decrease competing verbal behavior. The next
phase involved teaching parents to give clear commands that
allowed the child an opportunity to comply; parents also
learned to reward compliant behavior with contingent attention. At the follow-up, home observations indicated that the
child continued to be compliant even though the parents did
not maintain the same level of rewarding. In addition, the
child's behavior was more appropriate than before treatment.
Parent perceptions of change in the child's adjustment were
maintained over the eight months. Forehand and others state
that a decrease in parental trained behavior is actually built
into the program, as social rewards initially are almost continuous and they should be faded out over time.

Gilpin, D. C., and Maltz, P. "The Oppositional Personality in
     Childhood." *Child Psychiatry and Human Development,*
     1980, *11* (2), 79-86.
     The authors discuss data on thirty children who were
diagnosed as having oppositional personalities. Gilpin and Maltz
state that in general these children tend to be caught in a struggle for autonomy, as their mothers are extremely controlling
and their fathers tend to be passively aggressive. The child, who
cannot obtain gratification for autonomy, becomes withholding
and negative. Oppositional children typically exhibit temper
tantrums, aggressiveness, and negativism. In addition, they tend
to be loners and perform poorly in school. Gilpin and Maltz
state that these children tend to be unhappy and constricted.
In addition, based on the family dynamics, a risk for homosexuality is reported.

Lytton, H. "Disciplinary Encounters Between Young Boys and
     Their Mothers and Fathers: Is There a Contingency Sys-
     tem?" *Developmental Psychology,* 1979, *15* (3), 256-
     268.
     Lytton reports that parents of young boys between two

and three years old tend to employ erratic control systems for the child's behavior. Despite this, compliance will develop in a normal environment without specific training. Parental responses to their children's compliance or noncompliance tend to be most frequently ignoring or giving no response to the behavior. However, mothers tend to respond more often to compliance than do fathers, and fathers' presence tends to positively affect the mothers' interaction with the child. The major finding of Lytton's study is that parental physical control responses or action responses are not contingently determined by the child's behavior but by the parents' preference for specific actions.

Roberts, M. W. "The Effects of Warned Versus Unwarned Time-Out Procedures on Child Noncompliance." *Child and Family Behavior Therapy*, 1982, *4* (1), 37-53.

The mothers of twenty-four preschool children who were referred for noncompliant behaviors were trained to use time-out procedures. One group of mothers was instructed to warn the youngsters of the likelihood of a time-out. This was accomplished by the mother's restatement of the command to be followed and her warning the child that a time-out would occur if noncompliance continued. The other group of mothers did not warn the children but implemented the time-out as a consequence of initial noncompliance. Both procedures were found to be equally effective in increasing compliance. However, the unwarned time-out procedure resulted in a higher incidence of actual time-out. The author discusses benefits of warned time-out, such as less aversive child management.

Author Index

431

Subject Index

26; psychopharmacology for, 182, 184-185, 186-187; readings on, 181-187; retraining for, 185; stimulant therapy for, 182; and stress, 185-186

Enuresis Tolerance Scale, 187

Environment, for restless hyperactivity, 336-337

Exposure, systematic, for social isolation, 387

Extinction: for fears, 119; for hysterical behavior, 50; for nightmares, 17-21

Eysenck Personality Inventory, 303

Family structure, and aggressiveness, 290

Family therapy: for antisocial behavior, 270; for depression, 64; for encopresis, 189-191, 199; for fears, 117-118; and habit disorders, 144; for hysterical behavior, 48-49, 51, 54-55, 58; for impulsiveness, 374-375; and school phobia, 101-102

Fantasies, structured, and fire setting, 309-310

Father. *See* Parents

Fears, childhood: advances in therapies for, 104-121; of being alone, 111-112; cognitive techniques for, 115-117, 119-120; concept of, 104; covert conditioning for, 110-113; of dark, 118, 119-120; of dentistry, 106-108; desensitization for, 117, 118, 120; of dogs, 109-110, 117; emotive imagery for, 118; extinction for, 119; and imagery techniques, 119; of needles, 115-117; nighttime, 117-118; play therapy for, 109, 113-115, 120; psychoanalysis for, 109-110; rational-emotive therapy for, 120-121; readings on, 117-121; and reinforcement, 108, 112, 119; relaxation for, 105-106, 108, 112; of separation, 113-115, 118-119; stress inoculation for, 106-108; of surgery, 120; of tests, 120-121; of toileting, 105-106;

trauma-induced, 118. *See also* School phobia

Febrile illness, sleepwalking and night terrors related to, 27

Feedback, for hostility, 389-391, 394-396. *See also* Biofeedback

Fire setting: advances in therapies for, 304-315; and agencies, 315; behavioral techniques for, 307-308, 312-314; covert sensitization for, 313; graphing technique for, 305-306; multimodal approach for, 314-315; overcorrection for, 313; psychodynamic therapy for, 305-306, 310-312; readings on, 314-315; and social skills training, 312-313; and structured fantasies, 309-310; work penalty for, 314

Flooding, for social isolation, 387

Foods: and attention spans, 353-354; refusal of, 164-167; and restless hyperactivity, 328-333, 343; stealing, 171-173

Freudian analysts, decline of, 4

Frustration. *See* Impulsiveness

Functional analysis approach, for obsessive-compulsive behavior, 30-34

Gasoline inhalation, 204

Gilles De La Tourette syndrome, behavioral approach for, 151-153

Girls: aggressiveness in, 284-285, 290; attention spans of, 351-352, 358; depression in, 63-66, 73; eating difficulty in, 160-164, 167-173; encopresis in, 188, 199; enuresis in, 176, 179-182, 184, 186-187; fears in, 106-108, 111-112, 118-120; hostility in, 394-396; hysterical behavior by, 50, 57-60; impulsiveness of, 373, 376-377; nightmares by, 16-21, 26; noncompliance by, 426; obsessive-compulsive behavior by, 36-38; restless hyperactivity in, 327-330, 335; as runaways, 321-322; school phobia in, 95-96, 99-100, 102; self-injurious behavior by, 235-236, 238, 239;